S0-BRD-613

THE CHALLENGE OF LEADERSHIP
IN HIGHER EDUCATION

BROWN

EDUCATION SERIES

Edited by

Lowry W. Harding, Ph.D.
The Ohio State University
Columbus, Ohio

THE CHALLENGE OF LEADERSHIP
IN HIGHER EDUCATION

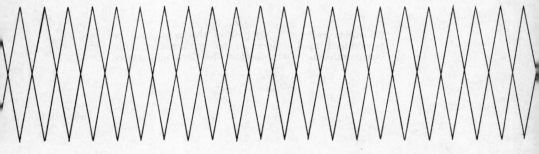

Raymond C. Gibson

Indiana University
Professor of Higher Education

WM. C. BROWN COMPANY PUBLISHERS

135 SOUTH LOCUST STREET • DUBUQUE, IOWA 52003

Copyright © 1964

by

Raymond C. Gibson

Library of Congress Catalog Number: 64-20982

All rights reserved. No part of this book may be
reproduced in any form or by any process without permission in writing from the Copyright owner.

Manufactured by WM. C. BROWN CO. INC., Dubuque, Iowa
Printed in U. S. A.

Acknowledgment

The philosophy, ideas, principles, and practices set forth in this book have emerged over a period of many years of teaching and administrative experience. I am greatly indebted to all of the individuals and groups of people who have contributed to my understanding of the relationships that can and should exist between the means and the ends of education, and the significance of administrative decisions based upon benchmarks of theory and values that transcend immediate problems or personal frustrations.

Special acknowledgments are made to the following individuals: Professors John Guy Fowlkes and Matthew Willing*, University of Wisconsin, and John M. Gaus, Harvard University, who were my mentors at Wisconsin when the foundation for my philosophy of education, and how it should be administered in a free society, was being formulated.

I was influenced most significantly by the first college president under whom I studied, Henry Hardin Cherry* at Western Kentucky State College, and by the first college president under whom I worked, Mr. William Hansen at Wisconsin State College, Stevens Point.

To the faculty at the University of Minnesota, Duluth, I am indebted for cooperation and understanding during the years 1946 to 1950. It was that faculty and its administrators working with me who

---

*Deceased.

v

demonstrated the fact that good theory and intelligent practices in administration are synonymous. Among members of the Duluth groups, I must mention Provost Raymond Darland, Professors Chester Wood, Valworth Plumb, Charles Saltus, John C. Cothrane, Ezra Pieper*, Dale Miller, and Henry Ehlers, and President John E. King, Kansas State Teachers College, Emporia.

Special appreciation must be accorded to the educational leaders and the people of Peru (particularly Dr. Antonio Pinilla, Rector, University of Lima), and of Vietnam and Thailand where many of the basic principles of this volume have been made operational through our cooperative efforts in improving existing institutions of higher learning or in building new ones.

Finally, I shall never be able to repay the debt to my doctoral students in higher education and to the officials at Indiana University for giving me the privilege of teaching administrative concepts and principles in situations where ideas are challenged, sifted, and winnowed.

I am indebted to Dr. Leo Muller for his help in the areas of public relations and development, to Dr. Philip Chamberlain for his assistance on the University Grants System of Great Britain, and to Dr. Loren Mc-Mackin for research on the Dartmouth College Case. My two daughters, Marilyn and Lucille who typed the first drafts of the manuscript, and Miss Cindy Orme, graduate assistant during the year preceding publication, deserve my highest gratitude.

Raymond C. Gibson

---

*Deceased.

Preface

Highly specialized personnel can be compared to a centrifugal force which can bring about the disintegration of any organization. Professors and research workers in higher education are required to be specialists in narrow aspects of knowledge. Both the tendency toward greater specialization and the growth in the sizes of colleges and universities make it increasingly difficult for the professor or the administrator to know anything about the whole institution in which he works.

The challenge to leaders in higher education is to work with external forces of society on the one hand and with faculties on the other in developing policies and purposes that are educational in character and to help the total faculty and students to achieve synthesis through purposes and programs that transcend departments and individual personalities. This is the work of the generalist in education.

The nature of man makes the achievement of organizational and educational synthesis practically impossible, because man is generally infinitely more concerned for the things which affect him as an individual (in an educational institution as a departmental specialist) than he is for those things which affect other people or society in general. Notwithstanding this inclination, one can find increasing evidence that man is by nature social, and hopefully increasingly so, as the world community becomes a reality.

Conflicts between private and public interests make it necessary for any organization and for society itself to become institutionalized through government, policies, executives, and the usual division of power between legislative, executive, and judicial functions. An institution of higher learning cannot escape the same conditions which give rise to orderly policies and management in other aspects of society.

The development of broad policies and purposes through democratic participation on the part of boards of control, administrators, faculties, and students is a *sine qua non* of higher education in America. Executive leadership for the implementation of such policies and purposes is equally fundamental to the functioning of higher education in the United States. This is a distinctive aspect of our system which makes it significantly different from the universities in Europe, in Latin America, and in Asia.

The principal purpose of higher education is to develop the intellectual powers of students and to give them experience in cultivating their ability to think, as the basis for active participation in a democratic community. However, the thesis of this volume is based upon the theory that it is virtually impossible to teach democratic ideas except through the university as a laboratory in which students and faculty participate in a free society.

Another fundamental principle which guided the development of this volume is the unity between philosophy and administration, between theory and practice, and between knowledge and action. Professors need to be oriented toward the total university, and college administrators must provide that orientation rather than join the professors as academic specialists without institutional direction. Otherwise, the university may be eclipsed by departments or schools or colleges which constitute only a part of the whole.

The principal responsibility of the college administrator is to bring about institutional unity among individuals with clashing intellectual ideas. No administrator can do this unless he has become infected with vibrant ideas. Therefore, the preparation of college administrators, whether in formal classroom or laboratory situations or in the quietude of their studies, must be grounded in philosophy, the humanities, the social sciences, and the sciences.

Highly compartmentalized specialization in one aspect of an academic department, even to the level of the Ph.D., is no more suitable for the development of educational statesmanship than is the accumulation of over-proliferated courses and credits on the techniques of administration. The former is an invitation for clever public relations officers to fill the leadership vacuum; the latter degenerates into means without ends.

The college administrator must be, first of all, an educated man with a fundamental understanding of the broad divisions of knowledge; and secondly, a man who has (1) certain technical skills which are indispensable if one is to avoid anarchy in the management of facilities, buildings, and budgets, and (2) great social skills necessary for providing leadership among intellectuals on the one hand and among ordinary citizens on the other.

A university is greater than any one of its parts; indeed, it is greater than the sum of its parts where imaginative and innovative leadership is present. Without such leadership, the university can never discover its potential strength. It is as a large corporation without management, government without an executive, a ship without a captain, an orchestra without a conductor.

The humanities and social sciences can contribute to the cultivation of leadership for higher education, but they are not enough. Public administration and business administration can add limited ingredients to the tools of administration, but they are not enough. Higher education is not a business enterprise. Patently, it cannot be governed by political expediency. Higher education must help to set new standards in both business and government instead of being taken over by them. The inescapable fact is that the study of higher education is rapidly developing as an appropriate discipline at the advanced graduate level. Unless this discipline is embraced and mastered by responsible administrators in higher education, catastrophe in our colleges and universities by 1975 will be inevitable, and college administrators may, within a decade or two, be required to secure a license before practicing their profession.

This volume represents a concern for the ideas, skills, courage, and integrity necessary for leadership in the efficient, economical, and educationally sound management of higher education.

R.C.G.

List of Tables

List of Figures

Contents

PART III

Design for the Support of Higher Education

Chapter

1

A Philosophical Foundation

"No aspect of American life is more indicative of man's liberation from drudgery, ignorance, and superstition than the privilege of attending college." Both the number and percent of American youth in college point to the fact that our civilization has advanced beyond the crucial concern for life's necessities which, in earlier societies, precluded the possibility of widespread formal participation in the cultural heritage.

This extensive freeing of man from manual labor to sustain life, a result of the continuous industrial revolution and renaissance in learning, is also a consequence of an increasingly rich cultural heritage which is dependent upon formal learning for its transmission. Such learning, formerly one of the greatest and most powerful privileges of small minorities, has become a possibility for increasingly large numbers, which may soon result in the balance of cultural, social, and political power (if not economic power) passing to the majority. The consequences of a universally shared cultural heritage, infinitely richer than that of any previous civilization, have the greatest possible implications for the triumph of free men in a divided world. The most profound consequence would be for all men to become free, not by force because someone or some nation has decreed that men shall be free, but because of intellectual liberation.

One of the greatest challenges to man and to organized cultural institutions such as higher education is to find a cultural substitute

1

that can absorb the enormous energy which men formerly devoted to ekeing out a subsistence. Otherwise the new freedom could lead to cultural deterioration, disintegration, and decay.

Arnold Toynbee[1] has stated that . . . "the creative use of leisure by a minority of the leisured minority in societies in process of civilization up to date has been the mainspring of all human progress beyond the primitive level."

If surplus leisure becomes as serious a problem in the United States as surplus agricultural products have already become, it will be a direct indictment of every school administrator in the nation. The production of leisure must be for a positive purpose of increasing not only the cultural heritage but also the participation of people in its benefits. Music, art, literature, and esthetics should become functional for large groups. Higher education in America has become an enterprise of kaleidoscopic magnitude not only in terms of physical facilities, budgets, personnel, number of students, and the investment of the savings of parents, but more significantly in terms of social, economic, and political consequences. The enterprise is of even greater significance because of its consequences for the survival of American society, with its emphasis upon increasing participation of free men in the great cultural heritage of the West.

If this thesis regarding the grave significance and future consequences of higher education is accepted, there should be no question concerning the necessity for careful management and support of the enterprise. Management in terms of efficiency and economy will not suffice, however, because the central problem is management of an educational effort of infinite variety, involving the fundamental integrity of freedom to teach and to learn. This latter problem in the management complex cannot be solved by considering it as being outside the scope and responsibility of administration, which is precisely what most administrators in universities and colleges seem to do.

The first and primary problem of this volume, therefore, concerns the means by which the most responsible, most highly paid, and, hopefully, the best qualified personnel in higher education can provide educational leadership. There has developed in America, to a greater extent than in any other country, a cult in university life known as central administration. It is composed of the president, vice presidents

---

[1]Edward D. Myers, *Education in the Perspective of History* (New York: Harper Bros., 1960), p. 284.

for major divisions of central administration (sometimes without any consideration of the educational enterprise), a few deans who are not affiliated with any college, and a myriad of administrative assistants and clerical personnel. In most cases, this group tends to isolate itself from the educational enterprise. Its time is consumed by problems that are only indirectly related to teaching and learning.

Oxford and Cambridge have avoided this top layer of administrators, unassociated with colleges, by invoking and following the principles of collegiate universities. This means that the college rather than the university is the center of power. When a key official of Cambridge was asked whether or not the elected Vice Chancellor would attempt to initiate or to promote a new educational idea, his reply was, "Oh, no, the Vice Chancellor respects the complete autonomy of the colleges; he would not think of proposing an educational change affecting the colleges, because in two years he will go back to his position as master of a house." The first two parts of his statement could be used to describe far too many college and university administrators in America where, in theory, we have universities rather than collegiate universities. However, the rationale for such a viewpoint in America would not be the same as in Britain.

Administrative cabinet meetings, university committees, deans' conferences, and personal interviews given by central administrators too frequently involve almost every conceivable subject except education. In colleges where several layers of administrators insulate the dean against teaching and learning, the problem is nearly as serious. The disease may reach its ultimate devastating effect when the faculty itself becomes involved in excessive hours of committee meetings only remotely related to research, teaching, and learning but eclipsing all three in time and significance. This last error takes place because many central administrators at college and university levels appoint the committees and give them status out of proportion to their accomplishments.

Where the above conditions prevail, educational leadership is left to the departments of the various schools and colleges, and a departmental university (a step closer to anarchy than Cambridge and Oxford) is the inevitable result. Moreover, departments are staffed with specialists who frequently have difficulty in communicating with one another. Therefore, there is seldom anyone who knows what goes on in a large American university. That the results are so favorable is a great tribute to the integrity and loyalty of university personnel, notwithstanding the serious problem identified above.

Two factors seem to have brought about this situation in American universities. The first cause lies with faculties. They do not want to be bothered by central administrators at any level. They resist especially bureaucratic administration which involves nearly everything except education. The second reason for the isolation of administrators from teaching, learning, and educational leadership lies with the administrators. They are either academic specialists who respect other specialists too much to interfere with them by offering leadership, or else they are specialists in administration which, by their definition, does not involve educational leadership. This type of administrator tends to belong to the managerial class. Either type can be disastrous to a university.

This volume was inspired by the notion that it is possible to prepare individuals, through formal liberal studies and experiences, for educational leadership and that there is a demand for educational generalists whose specialty is leadership based upon ability to comprehend the total situation rather than the manipulation of budgets, buildings, personnel, and public relations. It is believed that the humanities and social sciences have great potential for such preparation, but it is obvious that educational administration grounded upon educational philosophy is the basic discipline for college administrators. Otherwise, they tend to become "quacks" who learn their skills at the expense of the patient.

Administration as conceived in this volume is a process through which learning, teaching, and research are facilitated. This is an essential function of the professors and students, but it is also the objective that must provide the basis for administrative action.

The most difficult problem of implementation of such an idea arises in consequence of the administrative vacuum in the knowledge, thinking, and practices of the great majority of professors. The academic set, from Cambridge to Harvard to California, is not only unconcerned and inept in administration but views with suspicion anyone in its ranks who succumbs to positions of administrative responsiblity. Professors are generally very poor administrators, even of academic affairs for which their responsibility is inescapable. Moreover, they very appropriately question the wisdom of too much external administration of academic departments.

The inevitable result has been the development of a career group of professional managers sometimes divorced from all aspects of university life that deserve to exist. Highly paid officials—deans, vice-presidents, public relations directors, and presidents—devote time and energy to the management of great forensic programs, athletic programs, community conferences, and special endeavors which may not serve the best interests of teaching, research, and learning. While Cambridge University struggles to maintain a collegiate university which subordinates the whole to its organic and autonomous colleges, America moves too far in the direction of campus unity directed by activities and clever public relations schemes not always related to basic purposes or intellectual excellence.

University administrators, overwhelmed by increasing enrollments, have brushed aside the importance of the intimate community of scholars, permitting each department to form its own community under a loose federation known as the college. This separation of university life into cells of specialized academic life on the one hand and central administration on the other has led many administrators to the conclusion that no university can be too big. Size is of little consequence as long as academic anarchy is to be the form of government, committees are to be appointed as a substitute for academic development, and a managerial class is to control universities by manipulating means without serious concern for ends.

There probably is not a campus in America where a curricular problem or committee could draw a dean, or even a professor, from a meeting of the athletic committee. We are greatly over-committeed, but relatively few committees involving central administrators deal with teaching, learning, or academic programs. The solution to the dilemma is not simple when administrators are without general academic motivation and professors are without administrative skill or interest. Both groups must know the university as a whole or else it is not a genuine university.

Scope and Size of Universities

Sir James Duff, in a lecture on British Universities in 1961 stated:[2]

> There is an optimum size for universities and some in Britain have already reached it. If pressed further in growth, they will deteriorate. A university benefits by growth up to the point that it ceases to be comprehended as a whole by its members, senior and junior alike. When those in a department cease to know those outside of the department, it is too large.

If America has failed to come up with a satisfactory solution to the question as to how large a college or university should be, it is due,

[2]Sir James Duff, *The Scale and Scope of British Universities* Haldane Memorial Lecture, 1961.

in part, to the isolation of central administration from education. Electronic computing machines have contributed to the economical and efficient management of university budgetary problems, enrollment, records of students, and other housekeeping administrative affairs. Long rows of neat filing cabinets, adequate administrative assistants and clerical personnel have given the very largest universities the physical appearance of efficient business enterprises, all of which appeals to the businessman on the Board of Control. But these administrative functions, however effectively and economically performed, have very little to do with the education of students.

The combination of small businesses into large corporations— airlines, automobile manufacturers, steel companies, oil companies, etc.— has permeated the thinking of Boards of Control and central administrators for higher education. The result is seen most clearly where large state universities are unwilling to place any ceiling upon their enrollments, and where all planning is being based upon growth without limits. For example, in the decade following the second World War, the University of Minnesota had about 29,000 students and was making plans for doubling everything on the campus, even if it meant building a mall across the Mississippi River. At the same time, this large state university followed a carefully prepared scheme designed to inhibit the growth of all other state colleges in Minnesota, including its own branch at Duluth. Minnesota's anticipated enrollment for 1975 is 60,000. Wisconsin adopted a more liberal policy toward the University of Wisconsin, Milwaukee; and by joining the Milwaukee State College and extension resources of that University, a second great state university, coordinated with the University in Madison, is developing in Milwaukee.

 California, which is confronted with the greatest growth problem of any state, has developed a master plan for higher education, a plan which encompasses the building of new junior colleges, state colleges, and universities, and places a ceiling on their enrollments. The Master Plan for Higher Education in California, 1960-1975,[3] recommends minimum, optimum, and maximum enrollments for different types of state institutions. Full-time enrollments which it recommends are shown in Table 1. The new plan for California will admit only the top 8½ percent of high school graduates to universities and the top one-third to state colleges.

[3] *A Master Plan for Higher Education in California, 1960-1975* (Sacramento: California State Department of Education, 1960), p. 9.

TABLE 1.

PROPOSED ENROLLMENTS, CALIFORNIA COLLEGES			
Type of Institution	Minimum	Optimum	Maximum
Junior Colleges	400	3,500	6,000
State Colleges			
In densely populated centers	5,000	10,000	20,000
Outside metropolitan centers	3,000	8,000	12,000
University of California Campuses	5,000	12,000	27,500

Private universities in metropolitan centers are beginning to become state universities. This is a result of enrollment pressure for which states are making inadequate plans, and the resultant financial pressure of operating a private university whose growth in students exceeds its growth in financial resources. Wayne, Buffalo, Temple, and Houston are examples of private universities becoming state universities.

Several questions regarding size need to be answered on the basis of educational research rather than on the basis of debate or vectors of power:

1. At what point in the growth of a university would it be just as efficient and economical to establish a second university in another section of the state?
2. What are the savings to parents when students in metropolitan centers attend the university and live at home?
3. What are the educational advantages and disadvantages of living at home while attending college?
4. What is the optimum size, by educational criteria, for a single-purpose college, a multi-purpose college, a multi-purpose university?
5. What educational advantages accrue to an institution where professors, administrators, and students are able to communicate with one another?
6. What are the consequences of imposing quantitatively unlimited graduate programs upon quantitatively unlimited undergraduate programs?

The question of optimum size for educational institutions cannot be resolved through debate between administrators or by decrees from boards of control. The solution calls for educational research with at least as much weight accorded to quality as to quantity.

Only brief consideration of the scope of higher education can be given here, but it is certainly obvious that America has progressed without any criteria as to what a university should teach. Lack of communication between departments in a university as a whole, and even between departments within the same school, has resulted in expensive duplication of effort.

The principal question raised here is not the effect on the unmotivated student with limited talent when he is enrolled in the adademic program leading to a degree, but rather what the standards established to accommodate the average or below-average student have done to the most capable students. A well-known British authority has stated that America's policy for admitting students to the university is based on the assumption that there is no such thing as a bright student, and that Russia's policy is based on the assumption that there is no such thing as a stupid one.

A brief study of British and continental universities leads one to the conclusion that much of the curricula in American universities could be removed and placed in two-year community colleges to the advantage of the gifted as well as of the academically inept students. The British are willing to make and do make a decision similar to this when children are eleven years old. We never make the decision in America. To continue this cafeteria-type growth in the scope of higher education without recognizing its interference with intellectual excellence so necessary to our survival is to prepare, even within our universities, for the decline of American civilization.

Finance of Higher Education

The problem of finance is threatening the balance between private and public higher education in America. All institutions of higher learning are public institutions regardles of how they are supported, and it has become increasingly difficult to distinguish between them on the basis of source of support. For example, Princeton's Department of Aeronautical Engineering has received as much as $120,000 from the United States Government for the support of each professor in the department. Such grants tend to shape policy even in a private university according to United States Government policy and to make Princeton more public in its nature than are some state universities.

Income from endowments and gifts have increased tremendously in actual dollars during the twentieth century but have declined sharply as a percentage of the total cost of higher education. Tuition has increased so rapidly during the last twenty-five years that it constitutes an economic criterion for admission to most private colleges and even in some public ones.

Increasing costs of all public services provided by the states and the increasing percentages of total taxes being collected by the Federal Government have already created the pressure necessary to bring about large Federal grants of funds for higher education.

Unfortunately the Federal Government supports only those aspects of higher education which are necessary for the implementation of federal policy, and federal policy changes frequently. It is almost axiomatic that when any government at any level prescribes the curricula that shall be emphasized, it will be wrong in terms of sound educational policy. Officials at both Cambridge and Oxford Universities in 1962 recognized in their curricula definite "white elephants" which were instituted upon definite requests and support from the British Government. The support seemed as generous as that provided by the United States Government for Princeton's Department of Aeronautical Engineering. Cambridge officials indicated that in two government-inspired programs there were more professors than students. A detailed account of the British method of supporting higher education will be given in a later chapter.

America has not developed a long range plan for supporting the important enterprise of higher education. There is no significant agreement even among leaders in higher education as to how to accomplish this task. As long as the leaders in higher education fail to develop a plan on which they agree and which they will all support, the politicians will fill the vacuum in leadership by supporting their current whims; and we shall have our "white elephants," especially in many major universities which tend to receive the bulk of federal funds.

A tentative conclusion at this point is that programs in higher education should not be based upon support, but that support should be based upon programs that deserve to be supported. Survival of Western freedom is just as dependent upon the development of excellence in the humanities and social sciences as it is upon superiority in the sciences and technology. To agree with this statement in theory is one thing, but so long as the Federal Government and the various foundations continue to give huge grants for science and technology while ignoring impoverished programs in the humanities and social sciences, the world will know that America's policy is a materialistic response to immediate emergencies.

Graduate Education

Graduate studies very appropriately involve a major emphasis upon research by both masters and scholars. It is the continuous search for truth, new ideas and concepts, new connections between facts and phenomena, and the consequences of research that give depth, breadth, and excellence to graduate education. If these are the objectives of graduate education, then its ultimate control must be in the hands of masters and scholars with a minimum of direction from any outside source.

It may be reasoned that the president of an institution is responsible for everything. One dean stated that the president controlled the teaching of Chaucer, because it was the president who signed the necessary papers when the professor of Chaucer was appointed; but everyone knows that the professor and his students today enjoy the authority and responsibility for what is taught and learned in a given course.

Graduate research, in most areas, cannot be regulated or controlled even through budgetary allocations, because professors and good students will somehow pursue their research without financial resources. Of course, it is possible for the government to purchase any type of research it desires, but this is only one aspect of the total research program. The basic control of research in all areas of human endeavor lies within the situation being explored. This is the type of free enterprise that can be regulated from without only at the risk of destroying the integrity of research.

College administrators must recognize these fundamental characteristics of graduate education when they attempt to establish patterns of organization. The basic process of advanced research and study simply cannot be placed in the hands of administrators; but competent administrators who understand the process can facilitate, encourage, and help to finance a balanced graduate program of high quality and of great social and economic significance.

There is one compelling reason that college administrators and boards of control should provide the best possible environment for graduate education: out of the graduate programs will come the professors for higher education as well as capable scientists, engineers, and executives for business, industry, and government; also, it is possible that college administrators and leaders may come from this source. These consequences of graduate education make it even more imperative to invoke the democratic proces in its control.

The management of our colleges and universities should be a cooperative enterprise among administrators, professors, and students, whose central objectives are learning and teaching. This can be accomplished only if professors and students accept responsibility for guiding their own destinies. The means of education will thus be in the domain of those who are the results or ends; means are enhanced, dignified, and perfected by their indispensable relationship to ends, because it is in the province of administration to oil the wheels, to secure resources, and to manage those resources for the production of educated men. Management of the educational enterprise is different from that of other enterprises, because it is one with the purposing, programming, and evaluation of human effort in developing human qualities.

Universities should be relieved of all individuals who seek anything less than full intellectual development. Social activities, athletics, and other peripheral public relations trappings should be relegated to holidays or else to other institutions. The universities are places for education. We should not permit unmotivated students to succeed in college. The quantitative aspect of higher education must give way to a qualitative criterion. We must quit assuming that there are no bright or stupid students—only average.

It is not important that anyone secure any degree—bachelor's, master's or doctor's. We have confused the production of degrees (at all levels) with the achievement of excellence. Even the Ph.D. has become a public relations symbol of status rather than the achievement of intellectual competence. The Ph.D. as such is unimportant for any position in the world—it is no substitute for competence. Degrees at all levels have become status or power symbols, but this barrier can be breached by people who continue to learn and to work even though they have no degrees. Increase in human knowledge has made it imperative that every degree from the B.A. to the Ph.D. be a qualitative rather than a quantitative test of the student's power. The major emphasis must be upon the sustaining intellectual power of students rather than upon ability to recall unrelated facts.

Design for Action in Higher Education

Throughout history, men of insight and dedication to learning have periodically challenged us to view the educational landscape from the peaks, under the telescopic light of reason and perspective rather than from narrow specialization which may eclipse the broad vista necessary for educational leadership. Our great challenge is to think critically and imaginatively about the design of higher education for the future.

Policy and Purposes. Policy is concerned with the philosophical determination of direction. It is a process that can never be completed in a dynamic society, but there are some touchstones by which to guide our thinking. All citizens in America have the right and the responsibility to express themselves wherever possible on important policy for higher education. But ultimate policy for higher education should be determined, in the words of Emerson[4] in "The American Scholar," by the delegated intellect: "In the right state, he is *Man Thinking.* In the degenerate state, when the victim of society, he tends to become a mere thinker, or, still worse, the parrot of other men's thinking."

One of the bench marks to which one can return when in doubt about direction is the Ordinance of 1787 which stated: "Religion, morality, and knowledge being necessary to good government and the happiness of mankind, schools and the means of education shall be forever encouraged."[5]

Education has played a prominent part in conquering this great territory. In doing so, it has combined the practical and the ideal. In 1824, in founding an institute named for him, Steven Van Rensselaer[6] stated:

> [I wish to apply] science to the common purposes of life . . . My principal object is to qualify teachers for instructing the sons and daughters of farmers and mechanics, by lectures or otherwise, in the application of experimental chemistry, philosophy, and natural history to agriculture, domestic economy, the arts, and manufactures. . . .

The land-grant movement, for which we celebrated the one-hundredth anniversary in 1962, was another step in this direction. It opened the

---

[4]Ralph Waldo Emerson, "The American Scholar," an oration delivered before the Phi Beta Kappa Society at Cambridge, August 31, 1837, (*The Harvard Classics, Essays and English Traits,* Vol. 5, ed. Charles W. Eliot, LLD, [New York: P. F. Collier & Son, 1909]), pp. 6-7.

[5]Edward Danforth Eddy, Jr., *Colleges for Our Land and Time* (New York: Harper & Bros., 1957), p. 21.

[6]*Ibid.,* p. 10.

doors of higher educational opportunity to the sons and daughters of working men and women for the first time in the history of man. Institutions, including especially state universities and land-grant colleges, founded under the aegis of the Morrill Act of 1862, have placed the whole domain of physical and human phenomena within their scope. In the words of Van Hise, "No part of the domain of human experience, knowledge, or ideas can be set off as forbidden ground."

Dedicated men at home and abroad have different ideas for higher education. About two decades ago, the political leader of a very strong nation stated: "In front of us stands the citadel of learning. This citadel we must capture at any price. This citadel must be taken by our youth, if they wish to be the builders of a new life, if they wish, in fact, to take the place of the old guard."[7] This quotation is attributed to Joseph Stalin as he challenged the Russian youth to capture and replace Western culture as a center of learning.

In 1959, Harold Stoke, president of Queens College, stated at the National Conference on Higher Education in Chicago: "If the powers and policies of the national government cannot be exercised effectively and by dependence upon the traditional organization and operation of American higher education, then the Federal Government will have to provide for itself the educational resources its functions require."[8]

Against the error of President Stoke, we are safe as long as men of the incisive mind and practical bent of President Charles R. Van Hise[9] proclaim, and then practice, what he proclaimed at his inauguration in 1904: "The practical man of all practical men is he who, with his face toward truth, follows wherever it may lead, with no thought but to get a deeper insight into the order of the universe in which he lives." The one thing that seemed to characterize the efforts of such giants as Van Hise was the opportunity and the responsibility to prepare intellectual pioneers.

But they did not work fast enough. The men and women who have guided the destiny of higher education of modern times have not worked fast enough in the right direction. Our right to perpetuate the culture of free men is challenged today as never before.

---

[7]James B. Conant, *The Citadel of Learning* (New Haven, Conn.: The Yale University Press, 1956), p. 2.

[8]Harold W. Stoke, "National Necessity and Educational Policy," *Current Issues in Higher Education, 1959,* (Washington, D.C.: Association for Higher Education 1959), p. 14.

[9]Maurice M. Vance, *Charles Richard Van Hise,* (Madison: The State Historical Society of Wisconsin, 1960), p. 89.

Programs and Curricula. The second element of the design is a curriculum or program in harmony with policy. The ideas of two old authorities can be used to justify a new approach to curricular development. Cardinal Newman[10] stated: "The general principles of any study you may learn by books at home; but the detail, the colour, the tone, the air, the life which makes it live in us, you must catch all these from those in whom it lives already." Alfred North Whitehead stated that the purposes of the university are not in knowledge conveyed, nor in research by the faculty, both of which could be accomplished at a cheaper rate ever since the invention of the printing press. A university, according to Whitehead, preserves the connection between knowledge and the zest of life by uniting young and old in the quest of learning.[11] He believed that education is the imaginative acquisition of knowledge. He believed that a university is imaginative or it is nothing.[12]

Both of these educational giants stated that knowledge or facts can be transmitted outside of the classroom. This suggests the development of a carefully designed program of research to differentiate between what the student learns from the professor and what he learns on his own. Given the necessary skills in basic tool subjects, it is possible that at least 50 per cent of what we test for on final examinations has been learned outside of the classroom. It may be as high as 90 per cent in some cases. If this hypothesis should be validated, it could pave the way for reducing considerably the number of courses in college catalogues and then having most of the three-credit courses meet two hours per week in order to give the student a better chance to obtain his education and study for the final examinations.

The final result could be much more effective utilization of one of our most scarce resources, namely, effective professors. It is conceivable that the number of teaching personnel could be reduced or be used much more effectively. If this is curricular heresy, it is good to be associated with Cardinal Newman and Alfred North Whitehead in such heresy.

To pursue the idea a little further, we might have all faculty members evaluated by students, by one another, and by administrators. In making the reductions in personnel, we could keep the top two-

---

[10]John Henry Newman, "The Idea of a University" (*The Harvard Classics, Essays English and American,* Vol. 28, ed. Charles W. Eliot [New York: P. F. Collier & Son, 1910]), p. 33.

[11]Alfred North Whitehead, *The Aims of Education and Other Essays,* (London: Williams and Norgate, Ltd., 1950), p. 139.

[12]*Ibid.,* p. 145.

thirds on the basis of quality. If those who were asked to leave were evenly distributed throughout the faculty by salary, the reduction in force would provide substantial increases in academic salaries. If the reductions were among those at the top of the pay scale, the resultant increases could be very substantial. Such action would have to be based upon careful research, but this is clearly an area of academic concern and responsibility.

In developing purposes and curricula, educational leaders must maintain the initiative rather than surrender it to politicians. The Land-Grant Act was, in a real sense, a response to the catastrophe of the Civil War. Lincoln's predecessor, in time of peace, vetoed the first Land-Grant Act.

The Smith-Hughes Act of 1917 established the federal program for vocational education, provided for teachers' salaries, and provided for federal supervision of studies in agriculture, home economics, industry, trade, and commerce. This was a response to the first World War and the shortage of trained manpower for running American industry and for developing the implements of war, but one result of the Act was to divide the public school system of this country against itself. Teachers qualifying under the Smith-Hughes Act, in many schools, were paid substantially more than were those teachers who taught English, foreign languages, history, civics, mathematics, and science.

Ever since the end of the second World War, conferences have been held continuously advocating special consideration for gifted students and for the teaching of foreign languages. In February, 1953, the Modern Language Association of the United States advocated, for the first time in its history, the teaching of foreign languages in the elementary schools. The United States Commissioner of Education during the early 1950's was pleading with Congress to appropriate funds in order to provide for greater research and attention to the education of gifted students; but Congress chose to appropriate millions for special education of mentaly retarded children and notified the Commissioner that the "Lord had done enough for the gifted and that they could take care of themselves." Then in 1957, Russia launched the first Sputnik; and all of the Commissioner's dreams came true. The foreign language programs, special funds for the development of guidance counselors to discover and develop the gifted, comparative education, and research programs mushroomed under the encouragement of federal subsidies.

If we continue in this direction, it will not be unusual on Monday morning for college presidents to receive a communication from Washington stating, "In view of the announcement made from the Kremlin on Friday evening, it will be necessary to modify our objectives and our programs accordingly."

These illustrations are not distorted. We have recognized the fact that higher education is synonymous with our survival. Yet, our policy is a vacillating movement from one catastrophe to another, a reaction to immediate change, to local environment, and to vested-interest pressure rather than a dynamic policy which controls the environment, directs change, successfully resists pressure, and recognizes the fact that America is strong and has developed its economic and material resources primarily because our educational institutions have remained free from political domination.

Approximately sixty thousand men and women, young and old, from nations all over the world, are studying in this country. Most of them come from countries that have a ministerial system of education, which means that one cabinet officer in the federal government directs the entire enterprise of education from the primary schools through the universities. Most of these nations are underdeveloped, and it appears that there is a close relationship between the system of control of higher education and this lack of economic, social, and political development, which stems from lack of initiative and free enterprise on the part of the people.

It is not sufficient for policies and purposes to exist in the minds of presidents, boards of regents, faculties, deans, and students. We must remember that more than eighty-nine million adults in this country who are expected to help pay for higher education, have never been inside a college or university to take a single course. Our case must be told in language which is meaningful to that group. Otherwise, higher education will continue to suffer for lack of support because the people do not understand the problem.

Organization and Management. The University of Chicago's first great president, William Harper,[13] stated: "The president should never do himself what he can find someone else able and willing to do." Even if presidents follow that advice, they will still have more hard work to do than anyone else on their campuses. But as President Van Hise pointed out, you may succeed in directing forty different individuals to perform tasks, any one of which would take all the time of the president, and thereby you multiply your effectiveness by a factor of forty.

---

[13]Maurice M. Vance, *Charles Richard Van Hise* (Madison: The State Historical Society of Wisconsin, 1960), p. 86.

We probably shall have approximately the same number of senior colleges in 1970 as in 1960; but the size of the operation may have trebled in terms of operating costs, and the size of faculties will have increased significantly. Therefore, the size of the administrative task will be entirely different in each of the colleges and universities in 1970 than it was in 1961. The institutions will not add another president, but they will add a substantial number of new positions in order to help the president carry out the increased administrative responsibilities.

One of the most serious mistakes that could be made with reference to increasing administrative personnel would be failure to make long-range plans for administrative organization which would reduce to a minimum the cost of administration. The approach to this problem requires careful analysis of the responsibilities of central administration for colleges and universities, based upon the functions which must be performed.

In any institution of higher learning, regardless of its size and whether or not it is public or private, there are certain functions which must be performed by the president or by his administrative assistants. These functions have been delineated in small institutions where the president has performed all of the functions himself, as well as in large universities enrolling twenty-five thousand or more students.

The four divisions of central administration most generally found in institutions of higher learning are: business affairs, academic affairs, student personnel services, and public relations. An even more functional design which could reduce to three the number of major divisions of administration would be research, instruction, and administrative services.

Regardless of the specific pattern used, job descriptions for all positions in this area are needed for purposes of functional grouping of services, for recruitment of personnel, for determining levels and types of authority and responsibility, and for determining horizontal and vertical relationships between elements of the organization.

College administrators have been inclined to invoke the principle of infinite variety in the management of institutional problems, sometimes loosing sight of the fact that there is no virtue in inefficient and compartmentalized administrative units.

A major responsibility or administrative function of the president is fiscal management. This problem involves more than four billion dollars per year for operating expenditures. Higher education is one of the largest business enterprises in America. It demands application of the best possible business procedures if the budgets of the colleges and universities are to result in the maximum in teaching, learning, research, and service.

All information and costs should be shared. Boards of control and legislators are entitled to know all the facts. We need to arrive at decisions on the basis of what costs should be, rather than assuming that present costs should always be increased. It is impossible to find a study that deals with what costs should be in higher education. Cost studies always deal with what costs are rather than with what costs should be.

During a study of the colleges in Iowa in 1960, one responsible official was asked to give an analysis of costs by whatever unit of measurement the institution used. His reply was: "What use do you plan to make of the costs? You know costs vary in terms of the uses you plan to make of them." This type of thinking about a great public trust, whether it be in a private or in a state-supported institution will, in the end, be disastrous. It must be admitted that costs and quality are generally related, but this is not the case where highest costs are for purposes that may not be related to the educational function.

Finally, there is the problem of institutional relations. More recently the function has been referred to as planning and development. Regardless of the title used to describe these functions, this is one of the most rapidly growing areas of central administration in institutions of higher learning. The budget for this office in one large private university was over one million dollars in 1962-63.

In an enterprise as large as higher education, there should be no timidity in the development of a forthright, accurate institutional image necessary for its advancement and support. The principle is as applicable to state institutions as it is to private institutions. What is involved here is essentially accounting to the publics which support the institutions. This means the constant interpretation and evaluation of the long-range objectives and of the more immediate achievements in such a way as to provide constituents with the basic facts and understandings necessary for fundamental public decisions regarding support.

No director of public relations and his immediate staff can possibly be large enough to perform this function alone. Every member of the faculty, every employee of the institution, members of the alumni association, student body, and boards of trustees must share the responsibility for the development and interpretation of the institution's image for its various publics. The first step in the successful fulfillment of this function is for every employee of a college or university to justify his own position in relationship to the institution's objectives. This problem cannot be solved by employing directors of public relations to compensate for lack of direction and institutional greatness. The first step in the development of a successful institutional image is the building of a great educational plan. The second step is the implementation of that plan through programs and actions that are meaningful and significant to those who are asked to support the institution.

Statewide Cooperation in Higher Education

The most significant enterprise in America, measured by its consequences for the future of our nation, is higher education. Our security and freedom, our high standard of living and our help to other nations, and our intellectual, social, economic, and ethical advancements are all bound up with, and dependent upon, a vibrant, dynamic, and adequately supported system of private and public higher education.

To measure up to this challenge demands sincere cooperation not only among state institutions but among all institutions, public and private. In no other way can the necessary strength be achieved. And cooperation does not mean conformity to a common pattern based upon the dead level of mediocrity. Maximum strength will come through cooperation in diversity.

First, we need a citizenry with faith in American education. We need to recognize the high correlation between survival and universal education that develops talents of all of the people and arms them with intelligence, initiative, resourcefulness, and devotion to work. We need a citizenry willing to pay for education and intelligent enough to recognize that the cost of education wisely planned and implemented is not a cost at all but a long-range investment in the future of America. Finally, as citizens, we need to renew our faith in the possibility, expressed so cogently by Jefferson, that universal education can improve the corporate intelligence. We live in a society in which the greatest single instrument of power is the maximum development of human intelligence through the process of education. Failure of citizens in this task would mean that the democratic process had failed.

The second element for the development of cooperation in higher education is that we have legislatures or constituents that place social above personal interests and weigh social consequences instead of private gain. We need legislative and executive officials in government who, in truth, recognize government as an agency to do for the people what they cannot do for themselves. Partisan politics simply cannot be injected into the deliberations of legislative bodies concerned with the educational consequences of their actions. This high purpose for legislative actions applies to all programs, but it is unique in education.

The third element is to have on boards of trustees in all of our institutions, public and private men and women who represent all of the people —not just certain groups—and who give time and means in the support of their institutions. One of the most ingenious organizational schemes of American education is that we from the very beginning, decided to have lay boards of trustees to serve as the connecting link between institutions of higher learning (frequently inclined toward concentrated effort in theoretical pursuits rather than in practical ones) and American society. To be sure, boards of trustees are but one of the connecting links. But higher education enjoys more adequate support in America than it does on any other continent in the world, and one of the differences is that the policy-forming groups for our institutions represent the people and form a connecting link between higher education and the American people. In contrast with this system, one may observe that in Latin America and in most of the universities in the Far East, the Middle East, and Europe, policy is in the hands of the faculty and of a few part-time administrative officers almost completely divorced from the societies which they serve.

The relationship between the development of policy for higher education and the implementation of policy have been influenced rather significantly by the process by which men govern themselves in any democratic community. The division of power within our government at the local, state, and national levels has significance for the governing of institutions of higher learning. No one has stated the case for this division of power more clearly and more convincingly than Immanuel Kant in a little classic called *Perpetual Peace*. Kant's[14] thesis is simply this: Most of the perplexities, miseries, and problems of societies have arisen in consequence of the fact that legislative and executive authority, either by accident or by design, get into the hands of the same person. In brief, Kant does not believe that anyone who is charged wih administrative responsibility for implementing legislation can be objective, or that he should have final authority with respect to what legislation should be enacted.

If this is true in government—and the division of power within our government certainly indicates that farsighted, intelligent men who de-

---

[14]Immanuel Kant, *Perpetual Peace* (New York: Columbia Univesity Press), 1939.

signed our scheme of government believed it to be true—then is there anything inherent in the nature of men and women in higher education which would make them objective when given both legislative and executive responsibilities? This is the heart of the American division of responsibility between the board of regents and the president and his staff.

The fourth element of a statewide program is competent leadership in every institution involved. Needed are presidents who have the courage to perform the two greatest functions which any college president can perform: (1) to release the creative talents of a great faculty, carefully selected and adequately supported in terms of educational facilties, libraries, and salaries at least sufficient to permit creative minds to be devoted to teaching and learning rather than to the procurement of the necessities of life; (2) to posess the ideas, the philosophy, and the sense of direction gleaned from a keen insight into the policies of the board and the needs as well as the policies and mores of society, sufficient to make it possible to channel the creative talents of a great faculty toward a united purpose. An institution is greater than the sum of its parts. Working together, the different schools and departments, the deans, professors, president, and students can achieve objectives impossible for achievement by the same individuals working at cross purposes. Any president can turn the faculty loose to do as it pleases. This requires no genius. And, in a sense, this releasing of creative talents seems to be incompatible with the channeling of those talents toward a unified purpose, but it is the second objective which tests the creative talents and leadership of the executive.

Fifth, we need in each of our institutions a faculty whose professors and departments recognize that an institution is greater than the sum of its parts and that every employee of the university is responsible for its results. We cannot accept Emerson's statement that a university is but the lenghtened shadow of a great man. The concept of centralized responsiblity is obsolete in education. We must develop the concept that the student himself is ultimately responsible for what he learns. We cannot tell him what to remember or what attitudes he should form toward what we teach. We cannot design all the experiences which go to make up college life. Therefore, the faculty and the administration must recognize their own limitations in designing the curriculum. The lengthened shadow to which Emerson referred is a configuration. Ideally, it must be a configuration; and in it one sees the contributions from professors and instructors, from janitors and secretaries, from students and alumni, from legislators and citizens.

Sixth, we need alumni and alumni associations that understand that they received more than their money's worth and that athletics are not the most important business of higher education. It is reported by economists that every year spent in college adds $20,000 to the total income of an individual during his career. This makes it a good investment for taxpaying bodies and citizens, because it is reasonably safe to assume that 20 per cent of that increased earning power will be syphoned off in the form of taxes. This means that the state that appropriates $1,000 per year for the education of a college student will get a return of $4,000 in the form of taxes. Alumni, because of these obvious benefits from higher education, and because of the greater responsibility incumbent upon those who have been the recipients of its benefits, should be among the most militant, dynamic, and realistic supporters of higher education.

Seventh, we must preserve, develop and maintain in our students something of the idealism which built America. This includes the dignity of the individual, the worth of the individual, the dignity and worth of work, and a devotion to the basic as well as the emerging principles of democracy.

If the conditions and qualities mentioned characterized each of our institutions, no mandate from the legislature or from society would be needed to initiate the spirit and the practice of cooperation among our institutions. In the decades ahead, it will be essential that all institutions of higher learning cooperate and work toward the fulfillment of a joint public trust, because all of them are public institutions.

The Continuing Frontier

Selection of the title for this section, even in these critical times, is a consequence of a reasoned optimism concerning the future of higher education and Western culture. Western civilization has not reached its zenith from which the long painful descent is the inevitable despair of the future. On the basis of social, economic, political, and moral criteria, we are more likely to be at the dawn of modern civilization. In the realm of understanding the physical elements of our universe and of bringing its manifold energies within the service of man, we are only at the dawn of enlightenment. However, the national and international resolve with which social, economic, political, and moral enlightenment are brought into balance with the physical conquest of the universe will determine whether or not the decade of the sixties ushers in the dawn or the decline of civilization. This challenge is the new frontier of higher education.

The frontier has been an essential element in the development of American character. As a nation and as individuals, we have been developed rather than defeated by the rigorous toil, the adversities, the almost insurmountable physical obstacles, and the opposition of the forces of man and nature as we advanced in the conquest of wilderness and the construction of the American nation. It is appropriate to analyze the consequences of the physical frontier and to delineate a few of the specific challenges inherent in the new frontier.

Frederick Jackson Turner[15] stated that the frontier strips man of his garments of civilization and arrays him in hunting shirt and moccasins, planting Indian corn, plowing with a sharp stick, and learning to take a scalp in orthodox Indian fashion. Indeed, he defined the frontier as the outer edge of civilization, the meeting point between savagery and civilization. The frontier tends to develop coarseness of strength combined with inquisitiveness. It makes man practical, inventive, expedient, materialistic, lacking in artistic qualities, restless and energetic; it develops individualism, buoyancy, and exuberance. The frontier has always been a gate of escape from the bondage of the past.

According to historian Turner, the frontier's greatest effect was in the promotion of democracy, of individualism, of working politicians, not so logical as men in advanced societies, but men of bone and muscle. It made men intolerant of government and education. It caused them to press forward for individual liberty sometimes without social responsibility, as evidenced by laxity in business ethics and the spoils system in government. Conquering the physical frontier required skills and power so practical that anti-intellectualism was a natural consequence. This may have influenced recent trends to look upon the college degree as a status symbol rather than as an intellectual one.

Men of the frontier traditionally pay tribute to the dignity of the individual and the dignity of work. The significance of both of these has been lost by reviving the old Greek dichotomy between mind and body. This concept, based upon the slave-master relationship, has resulted in serious dichotomies between vocational and liberal education,

---

[15]Frederick Jackson Turner, "Pioneer Ideals and the State University," *Indiana University Bulletin* 7:6-29, June 15, 1910.

between the ideal and the practical, between knowledge and action, between theory and practice, and between the scholar and the worker.

The practical effects of the frontier upon American character may be observed in many aspects of American life, but in none has the consequence been more serious than in education. Unfortunately, not all phases of the frontier have been favorable to the rigorous intellectual character now essential to survival.

We have proclaimed equality of educational opportunity as a national policy, but we have permitted the grossest discrimination against individuals because of the accident of where they were born. We know that our survival may depend upon excellence of intellectual and moral qualities, but we have permitted the "side shows" of education virtually to swallow up the whole circus. We have recognized the significance of excellence in teaching, but we promote our faculties and pay them largely according to the quantity of their publications. And one must admit that literary excellence is not always the criterion by which manuscripts are selected for publication.

We have proclaimed equality of educational opportunity, but we have designed college curricula to serve only a small number (probably no more than 16 per cent) of American youth. The dichotomy between knowledge and action is evidenced in our failure to recognize the facts that all citizens in a democracy need knowledge, and that all of them need to be competent in a particular work.

As a national policy we have proclaimed the desirability of maintaining a balance between science and technology on the one hand, and the humanities and social studies on the other. In practice, the Federal Government provides large subsidies for science and technology but neglects the humanities and social studies. Many universities pursue their humanistic objectives under impoverished conditions yet find it difficult to use all the funds available for scientific and technical fields.

The Challenge of the New Frontier in Higher Education. We need a renaissance of humanistic learning. The materialistic accomplishments of western nations have been of such proportions that all men are within striking distance of an education appropriate to free men; but it remains for the United States, because of its great resources, to open the door to the dawn of a new educational renaissance. A specific (or unique) frontier for higher education will be found in each institution, but collectively, it is a national and an international frontier and, indeed, may become a universal one. The frontier is the border between anarchy and lawful government regulating the relationships between nations;

it is on the periphery of the most advanced knowledge in social, economic, political, and moral responsibility, and the resistance to action in these fields.

The frontier is on every field of action that is unguided by knowledge. It is the distance between the Declaration of Independence and anything less than freedom for all men. It is in every sphere of national and international life where the Bill of Rights remains a theoretical, rather than an actual, protection of minorities as well as majorities, of the possibly guilty as well as the clearly innocent against unlawful prosecution. It is everywhere that disease, poverty, and ignorance remain the curse of men.

The frontier is also in every country of the world that values American freedom above American dollars, in every place on earth where American help can speed the creation of a new university. It is the bridging of dichotomies between knowing and doing, between action and direction. It is the sea of ignorance between desirable individualism and indispensable social control. It is at the point of decision necessary to direct and control materialism as a means of producing better human beings.

The frontier is at the line of action which, through man thinking, eventuates in man as the means and the end of democratic societies. It is a frontier of hard work that recognizes the indispensability of creative, intellectual, and physical activities in the development of man as a unified organism.

There is a frontier in education wherever administration becomes an expensive end rather than an economical and efficient means to the achievement of educational objectives. There is a frontier to be conquered so long as approximately fifty institutions in America receive nearly 90 per cent of all financial support which the Federal Government provides for higher education.

The frontier will be found wherever poetry, literature, music, art, critical thought, and intellectual ideas are forced to become functional, save as a springboard to further creative and intellectual activities and for the enrichment of the lives of individual participants.

Finally, the greatest frontier in higher education is the rediscovery of man himself, the complete understanding of the nature of man as an individual and as a member of the social group, as the basis for man's survival. Such a challenge leads to the limitless frontier of the mind of man, for as Voltaire[16] stated so well:

---

[16]Will Durant, *The Story of Philosophy* (Garden City, New York: Garden City Publishing Co., Inc., 1943), p. 186.

Twenty years are required to bring man from the state of a plant, in which he exists in the womb of his mother, and from the state of an animal, which is his condition in infancy, to a state in which the maturity of reason begins to make itself felt. Thirty centuries are necessary in which to discover even a little of his structure. An eternity would be required to know anything of his soul. But one moment suffices in which to kill him.

The challenge of our times is to add a rigorous intellectual ingredient to the bone and muscle of the physical frontier. The consequences of the physical frontier have not been a revolt against learning, but rather, a revolt against intellectual life divorced from work and from action. Out of this revolt must emerge an intellectualism capable of doing the world's work. Reaction against a passive intellect has paved the way for a dynamic renaissance in education.

Implications of the New Frontier.

1. Although it is possible that only 30 to 50 per cent of the high school graduates in the United States can succeed in rigorous liberal arts and professional curricula, this nation must gird itself for the education of all youth to live and to work in a society so complex that a high school education will not suffice. This will demand continued expansion and improvement of state and private institutions. It will require the development of new types of state institutions in large centers of population.

2. The changing nature of American life, work, education, and international responsibilities demands that higher education abandon twenty-five centuries of intellectual snobbishness and make the people's business its business. The door of educational opportunity beyond high school must be opened wider. The task calls for full utilization of all public and private colleges and universities

It has been made clear that private colleges have many characteristics of public institutions, for they also perform public functions necessary to the life of American citizens. Moreover, they are saving the taxpayers millions of dollars every year by educating large groups of college-age youth. Many of the most dedicated leaders of American higher education are in private colleges.

3. In financing higher education for the future, our objective should be to make it possible for every capable and highly-motivated student to attend the college of his choice. This demands adequate state appropriations for the state institutions and higher tuition in state institu-

ions for those able to pay. It means generous scholarships based upon ability, motivation, and need, regardless of what college the students attend. Finally, it requires systematized loans to needy students to supplement family and state support.

This scheme of financing is not designed to help a particular kind of college. It is recommended as an implementation of the principle of equality of educational opportunity.

4. Careful studies and plans need to be made concerning the development of statewide community college programs. These could easily be as significant for the sons and daughters of the working people (and especially of the poor people) during the next century as the great land-grant college movement has been during the last century. Community college developments should be evaluated with open minds and a vision of the future rather than a backward glance at educational conditions that should not be perpetuated. The community college, if it exists at all, must become the people's college, opening wide the educational doors to knowledge and to purposeful, productive work for increasing numbers of youth and adults of the nation.

A dynamic community college program in the United States could easily grow to an enrollment of 5,000,000 students by 1975 without enrolling a single student who, under the present system, is destined to attend a senior college. That 5,000,000 would represent additional growth in educational opportunity over and above the normal growth of all senior colleges.

5. Finally, the new frontier in higher education demands a grand design for higher educational development on a national scale. Indeed, the whole nation must underwrite the plan and support it with whatever resources are necessary, including federal funds for buildings, scholarships, and loans to responsible public and private institutions. This should be achieved without government interference but with the only competent professional leadership this nation has for higher education—the leadership on our college campuses.

If we default, we shall drift from one catastrophe to another, always reacting to an enemy or to political pressures. It is possible that the grand design and policy will be a consequence of dynamic action in Moscow, unless the experience and wisdom of age are combined with the initiative and imagination of youth to forge for all mankind the touchstone of the new frontier. Higher education on the new frontier must be a cause as well as a result of a free society. This is man's best chance to replace ignorance and prejudice with reason and understanding as the rationale for international relations among men and among nations.

Summary

The foregoing discussion was intended, not to give the student of college administration precise educational concepts, but rather to illustrate the indispensability of conceptual resources as the foundation for administrative decisions. Growth in the acquisition, refinement, testing, and revision of educational concepts is synonymous with the development of administrative behavior so essential in complex university coordination and leadership.

Development of educational perspective is regarded as being so basic to educational leadership that the first four chapters of this volume are devoted to building up the concepts necessary to an understanding of what it is that needs to be organized and administered in higher education.

Problems for Discussion

In a seminar on Academic Problems in Higher Education in 1963, a few advanced graduate students and the author of this text reached certain conclusions concerning the philosophy and purposes of higher education. Those conclusions provide a synthesis for this chapter and pose problems for further discussion.

Higher Education, as is true of all other levels of education, must be relevant to the essential characteristics of the American social order. That is, the educational system must find its guiding principles and ultimate goals in the aims and the philosophy of the American way of life. It is recognized that the American society is not static and unitary. It is dynamic and continually changing, and our culture will continue to evolve and adapt to different conditions. The American culture is a plural culture that contains groups which represent divergent political, religious, ethical, social, and economic beliefs.

Although the American society is diverse and plural, there are basic areas of common concern and belief. A liberal education should encourage diversity instead of coercing conformity; but at the same time, it should emphasize humanistic values to all people. One of the basic problems of any society lies in the necessity of maintaining basic continuity and cohesion and the necessity of providing needed adaptation. Therefore, higher education must mediate between the past and the future so that change will not be too rapid. It must, however, evaluate, encourage, and help to direct needed changes that must arise as the result of shifting conditions.

In pursuit of this philosophy, a liberal education should contribute to the following specific purposes:

1. To develop in students the methods of critical inquiry and the use of the main tools of thought and expression.

2. To know and understand the dynamic arts and sciences of man.

3. To provide experiences and to encourage expression in creative activity.

4. To establish the habit of continuous scholarly growth.

5. To prepare students for productive work and effective citizenship.

Questions

1. In what important particulars do you agree or disagree with the philosophy and purposes stated above?

2. What reasons can you offer for your agreements and/or disagreements?

3. How would administrators and faculties translate the above purposes into action programs related to outcomes?

Bibliography

CONANT, JAMES B. *The Citadel of Learning.* New Haven, Conn.: The Yale University Press, 1956.

DUFF, SIR JAMES. *The Scale and Scope of British Universities: Haldane Memorial Lecture, 1961.*

DURANT, WILL. *The Story of Philosophy.* Garden City, New York: Garden City Publishing Co., Inc., 1943.

EDDY, EDWARD DANFORD JR. *Colleges for Our Land and Time.* New York: Harper & Bros., 1957.

EMERSON, RALPH WALDO. "The American Scholar," an oration delivered before the Phi Beta Kappa Society at Cambridge, August 31, 1837. *The Harvard Classics, Essays and English Traits,* Vol. 5, ed. Charles W. Eliot, LL.D. New York: P. F. Collier & Son, 1909.

KANT, IMMANUEL. *Perpetual Peace.* New York: Columbia University Press, 1939.

A Master Plan for Higher Education in California, 1960-1975. Sacramento: California State Department of Education, 1960.

MYERS, EDWARD D. *Education in the Perspective of History.* New York: Harper & Bros., 1960.

NEWMAN, JOHN HENRY. "The Idea of a University," *The Harvard Classics, Essays English and American,* Vol. 28, ed. Charles W. Eliot, LL.D. New York: P. F. Collier & Son, 1910.

STOKE, HAROLD W. "National Necessity and Educational Policy," *Current Issues in Higher Education, 1959*. Washington, D. C.: Association for Higher Education, 1959.

TURNER, FREDERICK JACKSON. "Pioneer Ideals and the State University," *Indiana University Bulletin* 7:6-29, (June 15, 1910).

VANCE, MAURICE M. *Charles Richard Van Hise*. Madison: The State Historical Society of Wisconsin, 1960.

WHITEHEAD, ALFRED NORTH. *The Aims of Education and Other Essays*. London: Williams and Norgate, Ltd., 1950.

Chapter

2

Policy Perspective in Higher Education

Understanding of higher education in our times requires perspective based upon a synthesis of earlier movements and present tendencies. The essence of perspective is the projection of the past and present into the future. Wise decisions in higher education depend upon an understanding of the history of higher education and the relationship of the present to the future.

The twentieth century has already brought a radical expansion of educational opportunities at all levels in the United States and in most other countries of the world. The most rapid growth since 1930 has been at the college level. In 1960, the enrollment in higher education in the United States was approximately the same as was the enrollment in secondary schools in 1914. This enormous increase in enrollment has been occasioned by several factors, among which the system of electives pioneered at Harvard by President Elliot, and the concomitant expansion of curricula beyond the level of high school work, have played a significant part. Indeed, there is an inclination on the part of many American citizens, and perhaps a considerable number of educators, to classify all education beyond the high school as higher education. Such an inclusive definition, which may be used in determining college enrollments, needs to be kept clearly in mind when one compares American and European systems of higher education.

This inclination to dignify all formal education beyond the high school as higher education may have had more advantages than disadvantages for the United States, because this concept ushered in a vast horizontal expansion of the curricula and opened wide the doors of colleges and universities to a great range of students with respect both to ability and to professional and vocational interests. Such a policy may have played a significant role in the achievement of the high standards of living and of education which characterize the United States in the twentieth century.

A more sophisticated concept of higher education would classify it into two categories: the advancement of learning and advanced education. The former represents the search for truth and is more likely to be identified with research or the vertical expansion of knowledge in a given field. The latter, advanced education, varies in terms of the philosophical position of the individual concerned. It may include all education beyond the high school, or it may be limited to the traditional liberal arts.

It would be a great convenience to assume that higher education is the search for truth and that such truth is the same everywhere and at all times. With this view, problems with respect to policy would be of minor consequence. Whether the American people have been right or wrong, technically speaking, this view of higher education has certainly been rejected.

One cannot escape the inevitable conflicts with respect to definitions and policies in a nation which encourages diversification and dissent to the extent that has characterized the United States. There are in the United States two divergent and articulate groups with respect to policy for higher education. The first would hold that higher education and, possibly, the upper years of secondary schools should be characterized by highly intellectual activity, abstract reasoning, and the mastery of a fixed body of knowledge; that the enrollment should be severely limited at the college and university levels and sharply curtailed at the secondary level; and that higher education is for a limited few, an intellectual elite. Perhaps one of the principles that has made this group a potent force in the determination of educational policy has been its resistance to the functionalization of education. Those parts of the curricula that have been subjected to the fewest changes have been the liberal arts, which tended to be unrelated to the rapidly changing professions and occupations. They have a tendency to be the constants in the foundation for all higher education.

Lamont
Townsend

A second group would hold that higher education should be responsive to the social, economic, and political needs of the masses; that functional curricula should be included; and that higher education should be limited only by the individual's ability to profit from education beyond the high school. This group has probably influenced greater changes in American education than have occurred in any other country in the world. It could easily go too far if it were not for the restraining influence of the first group.

Higher education is the rationalization and distillation of man's abstract concepts, empirical discoveries, and perceptual constructs, through formal and informal acculturation or interaction between masters and scholars. The young are always being initiated into the social order. Learning, growth, and development are continuous. They take place mostly outside the school and involve ideas, perceptions, and abstract concepts as well as skills. Reduction of these to an organized process involves formal education. Pursuit of the process by young adults on an intellectual level involves higher education.

This notion of higher education is identified with the process by which ideas are discovered, evaluated, and perpetuated. The function or process of higher education determines origin. Structures have always varied, and should, to accommodate the function. Structure—organization, administration, and control—relates to the means and not to the substance or ends of higher education. To identify its origin with structure would be tantamount to identifying the origin of government with the inauguration or inception of a particular governmental structure. On this question, the author takes issue with other writers who have dealt with this problem.

Rashdall and Haskins maintain that the university is a creature of the Middle Ages—"as much so as constitutional Kingship, or Parliaments, or Trial by Jury."[1] Rashdall believes that "Ideals pass into great historic forces by embodying themselves in institutions."[2] This view holds that a university constitutes a corporate body. It might be any corporate group, but in the case of a corporation of masters and/or scholars, Rashdall lists three specific characteristics: (1) that the school attracted or at least invited students from all parts, not merely those of a particular country or district; (2) that it was a place

---

[1]Hastings Rashdall, *The Universities of Europe in the Middle Ages,* Vol. I, ed. F. M. Powicke and A. B. Emden, (Oxford: Clarendon Press, 1936), p. 5.
[2]*Ibid.,* p. 5.

of higher education; that is to say, that one, at least, of the higher faculties—theology, law, medicine—was taught there; (3) that such subjects were taught by a considerable number—at least by a plurality—of masters.[3] Moreover, the status of *studium generale,* by the thirteenth century, was achieved solely through papal or imperial sanction. Old institutions, like Oxford and Padua, secured this status by custom—a concession to age.[4]

College administration is a means toward the achievement of educational goals. Hence, it is imperative to take issue with those who define higher education in terms of its type of organization and administration. A more pertinent criterion is function. Consistent with this point of view, definitive criteria for higher education, when operational, would include: (a) transmission of the heritage, a process which changes and refines the heritage; (b) the search for new truth through formal and informal means of objective and perceptual research. These criteria are the essence of the process of higher education. They deal with its purposes and the means by which they are achieved. The definitions of Rashdall confuse means with ends, form with substance. An understanding of present higher education requires a careful consideration of its antecedents in previous societies.

The Genetics of Policy

Greek and Roman Influence. Greek philosophy began with inquiry into the nature of the objective world and soon turned inward on man himself, becoming humanistic, a quality that has been enhanced through acculturation—the blending of one culture with another.

Through trade channels, the Greeks acquired the Semitic alphabet from the Phoenicians, about 1400 B. C. They revised it and added vowels, standardizing it about 403 B. C., thus establishing a basis for teaching and learning. This, with their democratic tradition, is considered one of their greatest contributions to western civilization.[5]

Formal education probably began about the seventh century B. C. First laws regulating it were enacted by Solon in the sixth century B. C. While it was started originally as training for scribes, priests, and accountants, its purpose soon included the training of citizens. Education first became state controlled and conducted for civic reasons in

[3]*Ibid.,* p. 9.
[4]*Ibid.,* pp. 8-10.
[5]William A. Smith, *Ancient Education,* (New York: Philosophical Library, 1955), p. 128.

Sparta, where it was established, maintained, and controlled by the state, with the method and content determined by military needs.[6]

Old Athenian education was similar to that of Sparta, but the emphasis was on the intellectual rather than on the military. Curricula were not fully regulated by the state and included gymnastics, letters (Homer's *Illiad* and *Odyssey*), and music. The emphasis was on itinerant teachers rather than on formal schools.

Following the Persian Wars (500-449 B. C.), Athens emerged as the intellectual center of all Greece, mistress of the seas, and a world power.[7] Poets, philosophers, and teachers flocked to Athens. Most illustrious were Pericles, Anaxagoras, Thucydides, Aristophanes, Hippocrates, and Socrates. With the establishment of democratic institutions and the rise of individualism during an age of enlightenment, higher education emerged for the first time. Its emphasis was on the teaching of letters rather than on the teaching of music, and two distinct types of schools developed: (1) the rhetorical, to prepare young men for public careers and (2) the philosophical, to continue the philosophical tradition of Socrates. In the first type, the emphasis was upon advanced learning; in the second type, the emphasis was upon the advancement of learning. The first rhetorical school was established by Isocartes about 390 B. C. and drew students from the entire Greek world. This type of school persisted into Roman times.[8]

The classical period in Greek history ended with the Battle of Chaeroneia in 338 B. C. when Philip of Macedonia, father of Alexander the Great, terminated the supremacy of the Greek city states. The Hellenistic period dates from 338 B. C. until the Council of Nicea in 325 A. D., which is considered the beginning of the political influence of the Christian era.

According to Jaeger, the Greeks of this early period refined and expanded the learning of the Asiatics. They established the concept of intellectual methods, a technique originated by the traveling teachers known as Sophists. In the fourth century B. C., organized structures of higher education appeared; these structures have influenced the development of higher education for twenty-three centuries.

Four institutions of this period that contributed most in terms of their later influence were:

---

[6]*Ibid.*, pp. 129-131.

[7]H. G. Good, *A History of Western Education*, (New York: The Macmillan Co., 1960), p. 23.

[8]Smith, *op. cit.*, pp. 140-142.

1. Plato's Academy, established about 387 B. C., which was in continuous operation until 529 A. D. Justinian closed the institution
   in that year because members of its faculty refused to become
   Christians.
2. Aristotle's Lyceum, established about 334 B. C.
3. The Gardens of Epicurus, established in 306 B. C. This institution,
   like the Lyceum, was absorbed later by the Academy, but only
   after it had run for some centuries.
4. The School of the Stoics, the Stoa, established by Zeno, the founder
   of Stoicism. This was an impressive school of philosophy for many
   centuries; however, it has been difficult to learn much of its design
   or organization as an institution of higher education.

These institutions offered a series of lectures for both resident and
non-resident students. They did not have formal courses, diplomas, or
degrees, nor did they constitute corporate bodies. However, their instruction in law, philosophy, and rhetoric was outstanding even by
modern standards. These basic higher education functions were performed in Hellenic Society.

These schools did not examine students because they had no responsibility for preparing individuals for specific careers. They did
have buildings in which students resided and therefore engaged in informal educational functions. This factor probably was a source of
impetus for modern-day extra-curricular activities and for the modern
student personnel viewpoint.

The curricular emphasis was primarily general education. Specialized education, as we know it, emerged in the nineteenth century.
Independent medical schools operated during this period, but there
were no law schools and no theological schools.

Organizational patterns included staffs of teachers working under
the general direction of the leader who carried the title of scholarch.
Teachers taught a wide range of subjects instead of specializing in
one discipline. They received their support from private benefactors.
Plato, for example, endowed his own Academy. The academies were
not corporate entities, but were proprietary entities in which each
scholarch named his own successor who was to be responsible for the
institution and its support.

It is conceivable that the Academy and the Lyceum, even though
they did not meet the technical definitions of a university, were
among the world's greatest centers of higher education, particularly

in consequence of their impact upon the development of future centers of learning.

Aristotle's Influence, 384-322 B. C. Aristotle spent most of his career as a teacher. He taught the liberal arts, and, in keeping with his concept of an educated man, he covered a wide range of disciplines. He was a student under Plato, who was in turn the devoted disciple of Socrates, the greatest of the three.

Aristotle was 28 years of age when Alexander the Great (son of King Philip of Macedonia) was born, and he was engaged by Philip to teach Alexander when the boy was thirteen years of age. He remained with Alexander until Philip's assassination. Undoubtedly, Aristotle opened Alexander's mind to the quality of Hellenic culture, for in his future conquests, he, Alexander, attempted to bring about cultural unity in the Eastern Mediterranean world, dominated by the expanding civilization of Greece.

As stated earlier, Greek centers of learning did not have any responsibility for preparing students for specific occupations. Their leaders believed that only the intellectual and social elite should receive higher learning. They originated the practical arts for the biologically, intellectually, and socially degraded workers and slaves who were unfit for citizenship. Aristotle defended slavery under all conditions as a psychological, biological, and social reality. He believed that the producers of material necessities of life were the men of least wisdom, men who were at the bottom of the social strata, and who were unfit for citizenship. The next stratum included the group who produced objects for recreation and pleasure. Because they were associated with practical arts, they, also, were non-citizens. The next stratum was comprised of the inventors, although they, too, were not educated. The educated man dealt with causes, principles, and theoretical concepts. Thus, only the educated man was capable of achieving the highly vaunted state known as "virtuous." Aristotle's position seems currently pertinent, because there are some advocates of his view in the present decade of the sixties.

As Alexander the Great went out to expand the Macedonian conquests from India to Egypt, he took with him a fervor to unite this vast area under the influence of Greek culture. But he broke with his teacher, Aristotle, over the question of what to do about the conquered people. They were born for slavery, according to Aristotle, but Alexander argued that they should become a part of the great heritage.

If anyone doubts the magnitude of Aristotle's contribution to higher education, an examination of the content of higher education curricula in the European universities of the thirteenth to the sixteeenth centuries should dispel such doubt. Without the discoveries of Aristotle, the curricula of the universities of those centuries would have been seriously impoverished. For example, in the fourteeenth century, the professors in the University of Paris had to swear that they would not be inconsistent with the truth as revealed by "Aristotle and his commentator Averroës."[9]

An example of the way in which higher learning was spread through Aristotle's student, Alexander the Great, was the founding of Alexandria, Egypt, in 332 B. C. This city became famous as a center of learning. At its peak, the Alexandrian Museum is said to have possessed 500,000 scrolls, including Aristotle's library, a collection larger than that of any other library prior to the nineteenth century. Other educational institutions, representing other philosophies, clustered about the Alexandrian Museum. These institutions, which flourished as a result of the conquests of Alexander the Great, were regarded as a part of the Hellenistic period. They were particularly strong in the area of research.

The ideas of Aristotle have been a continuous part of higher education since he lived and taught at the Academy. "During the dark centuries between the Hellenistic period and the Middle Ages, the flame of Aristotle's teaching was kept alive in Constantinople, then in Arabia, North Africa, Spain, and finally to the European world."[10]

Dynamic Research of the Hellenistic World. The Greco-Egyptian dynasty (Ptolemy I, 367-285 B. C. and Ptolemy II, 309-246 B. C.) hypothesized that the earth was the center of the universe and that all other heavenly bodies moved in systematic rotation around the earth. This theory was in opposition to the theory of the universe advanced by Aristarchus about 270 B. C. and validated by Copernicus eighteen centuries later.

Archimedes, 287-212 B. C., discovered the law of specific gravity and the principle of the lever. Other inventions of this period included the steam engine, the hydraulic organ, and algebra as a method in mathematics.

Hipparchus, in the second century B. C., did basic research in astronomy, catalogued over one thousand stars, and formulated a sys-

---

[9]Sir John Edwin Sandys, *History of Classical Scholarship*, Vol. I, (New York: Hafner Publishing Co., 1958), p. 604.
[10]Benjamin Jowett, *Aristotle's Politics*, (New York: Random House, Inc., 1943), p. 17.

tem of latitude and longitude. He is credited with having invented trigonometery about 150 B. C.

In medicine, there were discoveries concerning the functions of the nervous system and firm progress on the circulatory system. The Alexandrian scientist, Herophilus, learned to dissect the human body, an advance not seen elsewhere prior to the fourteenth century. Beginnings were made in engineering, chemistry, and in a system of grammar.

Four reasons seem to have contributed to the decline of higher education in the Hellenistic world: (a) isolation of scholars from the practical world; (b) inhibiting influence of state control on the initiative of teachers and scholars; (c) use of slavery rather than science and technology as a means of solving the problem of manpower; (d) tendency of Christian philosophy to turn the attention of men toward spiritual rather than scientific goals.

Roman Influence. Constantinople, founded in 330 A. D. by Constantine the Great, was one of the greatest centers for preserving and transmitting the Greek heritage to the West until it was eclipsed by the Italian cities in the twelfth and thirteenth centuries. It was captured by the Turks in 1453. Higher education in Constantinople included what would be called today universities and professional schools, which kept alive Hellenic and Hellenistic traditions and knowledge. There were schools of rhetoric and philosophy, as well as advanced law schools with highly structured admission requirements, curricular organization extending over four or five years, and examinations for licenses to practice. The work in medicine was carried on by hospitals and monasteries through less formal organization. Famous teachers were given appointments for life, substantial income, and exemption from taxes and military services. Many served as public lecturers and advisors to the government, perhaps beginning the Wisconsin idea.

The most important research achievement of Byzantium was the consolidation of the Roman legal heritage in the Justinian Code, one of the greatest achievements of legal history. Justinian the First, emperor from 527 to 565, closed the Athenian schools of philosophy, the Academy in particular, primarily because their professors refused to become Christians. He may have been motivated, however, by a desire to push the Constantinople universities into world pre-eminence.

From the libraries of Byzantium, Western Europe received many of the original versions of the writings of the Greeks of the Hellenic period. In 1204, however, the Latin Christians destroyed untold quantities of such writings just as they had destroyed such writings in Alexandria centuries earlier.

Islamic Contributions to Higher Education[11]

One of the early ideas of Islamic education was the notion that learning could take place at any time that the teacher met with his student. This could transpire in a mosque or even under a tree. The lesson given by the teacher might be given orally or it might be written on a piece of skin or even on the leaf from a palm tree. Whenever there were Christians or Jews in the various communities, literacy prevailed, primarily because of the Bible, and in turn these literate people taught young students to read and to write.

This type of education was started in Arabia in the city of Al-Taif, and was in vogue prior to the beginning of Islam. The Islamic influence flourished from the seventh century A. D. Mohammed made his famous pilgrimage from Mecca to Medina in 622. He encouraged his people to learn to read in order that they might later read the Koran.

In the wars that took place between the Moslems and non-Moslems in the Arabian Peninsula, prisoners were given their freedom in one of two ways, either by purchasing their freedom or by teaching ten Moslem children to read and write.

The teacher of children in the mosque was not paid a salary but was to be rewarded through the concept of service and in the "hereafter." Throughout the early history of Islamic culture, the mosque was regarded as a school because the principal motivation for learning was a religious one in character. There was a long evolutionary period prior to the professionalization of teaching. But as more people were engaged in teaching and the need for learning to read and to write increased, the title of teacher was adopted, and the center for the school was moved from the mosque to a place in the village called Maktab or Kuttab, meaning something closely akin to the elementary school in America.

It was in the mosque that men practiced oratory in order to become skilled in this discipline. With the rise of the Kuttab, the mosque tended to become the center for a different and higher kind of learning. The mosque had the same relationship to Moslem culture as the

[11]Salih Abd-Alaziz, *The Development of Educational Theory*, (Cairo, Egypt: Government Press, 1947).

forum had to Roman culture. In the mosque as the cultural center, religion, politics, and laws were taught side by side. Language, literature, grammar, and rhetoric were taught in relation to religion. In later periods, these subjects became progressively separated. There were two principal divisions of the curricula: religious subjects and humanities. The curricula was also classified into rational sciences and transmitted sciences, or instrumental sciences and final sciences. The instrumental sciences were regarded as rational, while the final sciences were transmitted sciences, and these were religious in nature. Instrumental or rational sciences included linguistics, music, geometry, astronomy, philosophy, syntax, morphology or grammatical inflection, rhetoric, versification, logic, arithmetic, and the calculation of the Islamic lunar calendar. The transmitted or final sciences included theology, jurisprudence, the art of reciting the Koran, and the science of reading the Koran. Medicine was also introduced as a special discipline in the mosque.

Students were organized in circles, and sat on the floor. A course carried the name of the professor of that course. It was possible for teachers to conduct multiple sections of a course at the same time. Students were free to choose the professor with whom they would study. The Caliphs, who were the rulers of Arabia, decided at a certain period in history that it would be feasible to ingratiate themselves with the school teachers; hence, they began to present gifts to the teachers as a type of pay. This habit gave rise to the practice of payment of teachers for their services. Moreover, land and other types of property were bequeathed to the mosque, the income from which was to be used to defray the expenses of the mosque, including the payment of teachers.

There was a library in each mosque to provide students with such books and manuscripts as existed in these early days. In addition, there was a medical dispensary and a physician. These services were available without cost to the teachers, students, and people who went to the Mosque to worship. The important mosques which served as centers of learning were in Damascus, Palestine, Bagdad, Cordova, Karawlyn in North Africa, and Cairo. In these mosques, the first educational activities were at the elementary level, followed by a period when the highest achievement was at the secondary school level, and, finally, when some of them became centers of higher education.

The reader should understand that in no case did elementary, secondary, or even higher education indicate the same disciplines associated with these levels of education in modern times. The three levels indicate only that education in the mosques evolved through three stages. The first phase included teaching that was carried on from the inception of the mosque itself. The second stage, or secondary level, was identified with a period when teachers began to teach different subjects on more formally organized bases, not only in the mosques but also in centers outside of the mosques. The third period was one of specialization through which it became possible for students to specialize in a particular discipline. The centers of higher learning provided the students with an opportunity for general education basic to the study of the more advanced stages. Entrance and course requirements were much more liberal than in modern universities. Three major Islamic centers of learning were:

Bait al-Hikmah in Bagdad, 825 A. D. It is not known exactly who established this institution. Some scholars indicate it was the Caliph Al Rashid. Others maintain that it was the Caliph Al Maamoon. It is sufficient to know that one of these members of the Abbesides dynasty was motivated to establish this great center of higher learning which much later contributed significantly to the Renaissance in Europe. This institution represented the height of Moslem interest in Greek culture and philosophy, and its significance resides in the fact that through Islamic institutions, the Greek culture and philosophy were preserved for western civilization.

It is probable that Bait al-Hikmah, in its original state, was not intended to be a center for higher education but rather, to be a center for the translation of the classical manuscripts from other cultures, including particularly the Greek culture. These translations concerned medicine, philosophy, and wisdom.

One of the best known professors who taught in Bait al-Hikmah during this period was Khuarazmi. He was famous as a mathematician and an astronomer as well as for his writings in the area of algebra. He was regarded as a competent scientist.

The Caliphs added famous books translated into Arabic to the library. These volumes were in the areas of astronomy, medicine, and Islamic subjects, and included Roman books. Some of the volumes were brought in via Accra, Turkey, and other places. Caliph Al Maamoon added books in several languages, including Arabic, Greek, Syrian, Persian, Indian, and Coptic.

In the beginning, perhaps the essential objective of Bait al-Hikmah was the translation of learned books and manuscripts from Syrian, Greek, Indian, and other languages to Arabic. It was these translations as well as other generous gifts of books and manuscripts from the rulers which developed the library and contributed significantly to the status of Bait al-Hikmah as a center of higher education.

Manuscripts were translated and laboriously transcribed in Arabic by long hand. The scholars who were able to do this were at a great premium. Among other subjects, Bait al-Hikmah emphasized mathematics, philosophy, astronomy, and wisdom.

After Al Maamoon, the history of Bait al-Hikmah is not distinct, although it is possible that it continued right on down to the end of the eleventh century. This provides the continuity in the transmission of Greek culture by way of Islamic institutions into European universities originating in Italy in the eleventh and twelfth centuries.

Institutions in the Islamic society were under the control of the Caliph, and in the tenth and eleventh centuries, the Caliph began to impose restrictions upon academic freedom. Again a religious orthodoxy inhibited the further advancement of higher education.

Higher education in the Islamic society was related more closely to the efforts of individual professors than to institutional efforts. This shows the absence of tight organization and administration in a sense comparable to that which exists in modern institutions. Teaching was centered in the professor rather than in the institution. It was customary for a scholar, when giving his credentials, to enumerate the professors with whom he had studied rather than the institutions where he had studied. There were no institutional degrees, but rather, only certificates issued by the professors indicating that a student had studied a particular discipline with a particular professor. Students selected their teachers in terms of the reputation and standing that the professor had in other parts of the Islamic society, a rigorous system of evaluating instructors.

University of Cordova, 912 A. D. A second great institution of the Islamic world was Cordova, in Spain. During the Dark Ages, England, France, Germany, and Italy had a combined population of fifteen to twenty million people; but Muslin Spain had thirty million inhabitants. Next to Constantinople, Cordova was the largest city in Europe. Its ruler, Abd-Al-Rahman, founded the university during his reign from 912 to 961. It has been estimated that there were six hundred subsidiary colleges connected with the University of Cordova. The library was reported to have contained more than one-half million volumes and was, therefore, the greatest repository of learning which had existed up to that time.

This old center of learning has been permitted to decay until only the foundations and general outline of the buildings are left overlooking one of the most beautiful valleys in Spain. This most westward penetration of Islam into Europe was violently uprooted following the fall of Granada to the Spaniards in 1492.

Al-Azhar University, 970 A. D. A third example of the great Islamic force in perpetuating higher education is Al-Azhar in Cairo. This institution, established by Caliph Moizz of the Fatimid dynasty, originated in 970 in a mosque known as Al-Azhar Mosque. It is still in operation. Its students come from all levels—elementary, secondary, and higher education. This structure embraces three colleges—Origin of Islam, Arabic Language, and Laws of Islam.

Al-Azhar has a president who is appointed by the President of Egypt. The president in 1960 held the doctorate from the Sorbonne.

From the tenth century, it has been a custom for the professors to sit beside the pillars of the mosque, and for the students to select the ones with whom they desired to study. The principal technique of teaching has been the discussion method. Professors have given the students certificates at the end of the courses. This system has continued until the twentieth century.

Islamic institutions in general have carried on research in Greek philosophy, mathematics, astronomy, optics, chemistry, literature, and medicine, in addition to their major attention to theology. They have placed considerable emphasis upon the special preparation of clerks, teachers, judges, and officials of government for the vast Empire.

It is generally recognized that the greatest contribution of Islamic centers of learning has been in the translation of works from earlier cultures which have provided the continuity in the great western tradition. These translations consist of important Greek works preserved in the libraries of Syria for four hundred years following the ruins of Alexandria.

Islam had inspired no scientific movement, but when her monasteries were captured by the Persians and the books examined, a new era opened for science. This interest led to the translation into Arabic of eight books of Plato, nineteen of Aristotle, ten of Hippocrates, twenty-six of Galen, plus those of Euclid, Archimedes, and Ptolemy.

The Arabs discovered the great works of antiquity. They studied, augmented, translated, and transmitted this great knowledge to the West through Moslem Spain. By the end of the thirteenth century, Arabic science and philosophy had penetrated Europe, and Spain's work

as an intermediary had been accomplished. The imposition of a fundamentalist religious dogma upon the Islamic universities caused them
to return to the study of tradition, in which they are still engaged.

European Influences

During the height of the Islamic Empire, there was extensive interaction among the people of the Mediterranean through trade, commerce, and traveling scholars. Moreover, the great crusades from the
eleventh to the fourteenth century when Europe was engaged in
attempting to capture the Holy Land from the Moslems, provided
myriad opportunities for the people of Europe to come in contact with
Islamic culture and, indirectly, with the more ancient culture of
Greece. Through this acculturation, Europeans modified and enriched
existing cultural patterns.

This section dealing with the European heritage which has contributed to the development of higher education in the United States
will be limited to a few institutions in Italy, France, England, Scotland, and Germany.

Salerno School of Medicine. Some authorities believe that the famous medical school at Salerno was in operation as early as the ninth
century.[12] The date and origin are uncertain, but this adds to the
uniqueness of Salerno as the first European medical center.[13] If Salerno
existed in the ninth century, it was probably under the influence of
Arabian and Jewish doctors.[14]

The great discoveries of the Greek medical leader, Hippocrates
(the father of medicine), were recorded in Greek writings. They were
enlarged upon to a certain extent by Galen, who was born in Asia
Minor in 130 A. D. and who is known to have studied at the University in Alexandria and at other centers of learning in Asia Minor.
For the period immediately preceding the great revival of learning,
beginning in the eleventh and twelfth centuries in Europe, Constantinople and Alexandria were centers of Greek authority and culture.

There is more mystery than factual history concerning the origin
and the early development of Salerno. Haskins states:

> . . . a school of medicine had existed as early as the middle of
> the eleventh century, and for perhaps two hundred years thereafter
> it was the most renowned medical centre in Europe. In this "city

---

[12]Rashdall, *op. cit.*, p. 76.
[13]*Ibid.*, pp. 76-77.
[14]Lowrie J. Daly, *The Medieval University, 1200-1400*, (New York: Sheed
and Ward, Inc., 1961), p. 94.

of Hippocrates" the medical writings of the ancient Greeks were expounded and even developed on the side of anatomy and surgery, . . . Of the academic organization of Salerno we know nothing before 1231, and when in this year the standardizing hand of Frederick II regulated its degrees Salerno had already been distanced by newer universities farther north. Important in the history of medicine, it had no influence on the growth of university institutions.[15]

Salerno is interesting as a case study because it preserves the unbroken thread of higher learning from the Greeks to the shores of the United States. Because it was in a seaport city, it was easy for this school to remain in contact with Constantinople and Alexandria. Indeed, historians agree that the Greek language was undoubtedly spoken by a few people at least throughout the period of the Dark Ages in this port city of Salerno. It was famous for mineral waters and as a health resort, and this may have had something to do with its becoming a medical center and attracting physicians. The works of Hippocrates came to Salerno in Greek and, in some instances, in Arabic and later were translated into Latin.

[Works attributed to] Hippocrates, Galen and other Greek physicians had been translated into Latin as early as the sixth century: and, though these early traditions are said to have disappeared, the Graeco-Latin medical tradition was no more extinguished by the ages of darkness which followed than Roman Law was extinguished in the north by the barbarian invasions.[16]

In 1231, Frederick II, King of Sicily, gave Salerno its first official status when he made it necessary for anyone who would teach or practice medicine to be examined by the masters of Salerno.[17] He also constituted it the only medical school in the Kingdom of Naples.[18]

The University of Bologna. Many contributing factors influenced the inauguration of the University of Bologna about 1000 A. D. For example, the city of Bologna was a great center for the gathering of students from northern Italy beyond the Alps. "Far from home and undefended, they united for mutual protection and assistance, and this organization of foreign, or Transmontane, students was the beginning of the university."[19] In this sense, the students had followed the pattern of guilds which had become a standard type of organization

[15]Charles Homer Haskins, *The Rise of Universities,* (Ithaca, New York: Cornell University Press, 1957), p. 6.
[16]Rashdall, *op. cit.,* p. 78.
[17]*Ibid.,* pp. 83-85.
[18]*Ibid.,* pp. 83-85.
[19]Haskins, *op. cit.,* p. 8.

for articulate groups, whether workers or scholars. The term referred to groups such as barbers and carpenters, including both students and masters.

Other factors contributed to the organization and to the characteristics of the University of Bologna. First, it is known that the Germanic invasions had not eradicated Roman law in this part of Italy. On the contrary, Roman law continued to be the dominant system of government for the conquered peoples of Italy.[20]

Prior to the Germanic invasions, lay teachers, or non-ecclesiastical teachers, had been more prevalent in Italy than in other countries of that period. Throughout the Dark Ages and in the period of the revival of learning, this concept of the lay teacher, free from sectarian domination, prevailed.[21] The organization of the students of Bologna into a university which became famous for the teaching of law through lay instructors was a natural consequence of conditions that had existed for centuries in northern Italy.

At Bologna, students were free to bargain with the officials of the community regarding the rents on buildings, as well as other conditions, including disciplinary cases. If they failed to reach satisfactory arrangements with the city authorities, they were free to move to another community not having the problem of buildings in which any investment other than rent had been made.

A second significant provision under which Bologna operated regarded the status of professors. Unless professors were otherwise endowed with economic resources, their sole income was from the fees paid by their students. This gave the students a power over the professors unequalled in any subsequent period in the long history of higher education. For example, Haskins states:

> We read in the earliest statutes (1317) that a professor might not be absent without leave, even a single day, and if he desired to leave town he had to make a deposit to insure his return. If he failed to secure an audience of five for a regular lecture, he was fined as if absent—a poor lecture indeed which could not secure five hearers! He must begin with the bell and quit within one minute after the next bell. He was not allowed to skip a chapter in his commentary, or postpone a difficulty to the end of the hour, and he was obliged to cover ground systematically, so much in each specific term of the year. No one might spend the whole year on introduction and bibliography![22]

[20]William Boyd, *The History of Western Education,* (London: A. and C. Black, Ltd., 1928), p. 136.
[21]*Ibid.*, p. 135.
[22]Haskins, *op. cit.*, p. 10.

The earliest rectors of student-controlled universities were elected by the students to serve at the discretion of the students and under the rules and regulations prescribed by the students.

It appears that organizations of students, such as the case at Bologna, may have grown from the natural inclination and need for students away from home to get together in order to solve some of their common problems. According to Rashdall,[23] these early societies had no authorization from the king, bishop, or municipality, any more than such permission is required for the establishment of a debating society or cricket club among modern students. The first recorded instance of granting state payment to a professor at Bologna was in 1280, and in 1289, two permanent chairs were endowed, with salaries of 150 and 100 lire respectively per annum. Even in these cases where the republic was paying the salaries, students elected the professors on an annual basis. By 1381, there were as many as twenty-three salaried doctors of law, receiving payment varying from 100 to 620 lire.

> The appointment of the Doctors and the general management of the Studium in its relations to the State were eventually entrusted to a board known as the "Reformatores Studii." In the course of the fourteenth and fifteenth centuries such a body (under that or some similar name) was established by the City Government or Prince in all Italian Universities, and the real control of the University more and more passed to this body of external Governors, which by the sixteenth or seventeenth century succeeded in destroying the Student autonomy or reducing it to a shadow.[24]

Here one may see the beginning of lay boards of control over institutions of higher learning, a practice that became dominant in the United States several centuries later.

In summary, it may be stated that Italian universities were the finest examples of student-dominated institutions found anywhere in the Middle Ages. Twentieth century Italian students and students in universities modeled after those in Italy are inclined to demand more of a voice in the affairs of their universities than is characteristic in universities founded upon British and French principles. In the next chapter, which deals with power structure, it will be especially interesting to contrast the dominant French, Italian, and British influences which prevail in the middle of the twentieth century in countries where universities were founded upon these European antecedents.

---

[23]Rashdall, *op. cit.*, p. 162.
[24]*Ibid.*, p. 213.

University of Paris. It is believed that the University of Paris existed as a society of masters as early as 1170. Rashdall believes that the University of Paris originated between 1150 and 1170. French education during the eleventh and twelfth centuries was almost exclusively a function of cathedrals and monasteries. A practice instituted during this period was the employment of a teacher attached to the church to teach scholars. There was an increasing tendency to make this individual a member of the ecclesiastical groups or to place him under ecclesiastical authorities. As the position developed, it took on the title of Chancellor, whose original duties were analogous to those of a Royal Chancellor, i.e. to keep the Chapter seal and to draw up the letters and documents which required sealing; and, as this function demanded an amount of learning which was not a matter of course in those days, it was natural enough that the supervision of the schools, and again the care of the library, should be entrusted to the same functionary.[25]

The Chancellor has sometimes been referred to as an ecclesiastical superintendent of education. Rashdall states:

> The control of the Chancellor on the one hand, and the right of the competent teacher to a gratuitous license on the other, formed the basis of the French educational system. The control of the Chancellor distinguished it from the early Italian system: without the corresponding right, a University of Masters could never have grown up at all.[26]

The University of Paris grew out of the school of Notre Dame, whose Chancellor alone had the power to license teaching in the diocese. This gave him control over the granting of university degrees which here, as at Bologna, were originally teachers' certificates.

Paris ceased to be a cathedral school perhaps before the end of the twelfth century. By 1231, the Pope extended certain privileges and imposed certain restrictions upon the university. The most important provision in the *Bull Parens Scientiarum* of 1231 was the one that regulated the discretion of the Chancellor in conferring the license and permitted masters and students:

> . . . "to make constitutions and ordinances regulating the manner and time of lectures and disputations, the costume to be worn," attendance at masters' funerals, the lectures of bachelors, necessarily

---

[25]*Ibid.*, pp. 281-282.
[26]*Ibid.*, p. 284.

more limited than those of fully fledged masters, the price of lodgings, and the coercion of members.[27]

Other significant provisions of the *Parens Bull*[28] required the bishop to be reasonable in his jurisdiction over scholars and prohibited his having innocent instead of guilty scholars arrested or to imprison for debt or to impose pecuniary penances. The Chancellor was forbidden to have a prison at all; scholars were to be imprisoned in the bishop's prison only, and bail was to be allowed in all cases.

By 1231, there were four faculties at Paris, each under its own dean. There were faculties of theology, medicine, canon law, and arts. The masters of arts, being the largest of the four faculties, was comprised of:

> . . . "four nations": the French, including the Latin peoples; the Normans; the Picard, including also the Low Countries; and the English, comprising England, Germany, and the North and East of Europe. These four nations chose the head of the university, the rector, as he is still generally styled on the Continent, whose term, however, was short, being later only three months.[29]

No discussion of the University of Paris in the Middle Ages would be complete without careful attention to the great scholar, Peter Abelard, 1079 to 1142. He was undoubtedly the outstanding scholar of all Europe during the first half of the twelfth century.[30] Having a position in the cathedral, making for close relationships between ecclesiastical (meaning papal) and university authorities, Abelard's inquiring mind naturally led to difficulties. In the finest tradition of academic freedom, he was a dissenter and a nonconformist. He believed in the investigation of all subjects, including philosophy and theology. A questioning mind with respect to theology, at a time when it was regarded as heresy to proclaim the scriptures to be rational or irrational, was indeed out of bounds in a society whose principal intellectual challenge consisted in the rationalization of Aristotelian viewpoints with Christian orthodoxy. Abelard did not believe in blind faith as a basis for understanding. He argued that faith emanated from understanding.

Abelard was one of the first scholars who embraced the concept that a rational individual should be able to interpret the scriptures for himself. He was a forerunner of the great reformation which at a later date would encourage the subjection of theology to inquiry. Abelard

---

[27]Haskins, *op. cit.*, p. 15.
[28]Rashdall, *op. cit.*, p. 339.
[29]Haskins, *op. cit.*, p. 16.
[30]Rashdall, *op. cit.*, p. 58.

was willing to be put out of his classroom, to be condemned by his elders and his own great masters, to suffer the humiliation of being required to burn his book with his own hands, and to be imprisoned in a monastery and have his sentence approved by the Pope, in order to maintain his unquenching spirit of freedom to subject theology, as philosophy, to the spirit of inquiry.[31] Moreover, he had the distinction of teaching throngs of students from all parts of Europe and of seeing twenty of his disciples become cardinals and at least fifty become bishops. Abelard believed in presenting both sides of the most fundamental questions of his day, because questioning led to inquiry and inquiry to truth. It may be stated that the heresy of one generation virtually became the orthodoxy of the next.[32]

The Origin of Oxford University. Oxford was organized, under a faculty system, by an exodus of English scholars from Paris, in 1168. It was modeled after the faculties of Paris but was not supervised by the Papacy or by the local bishop as was the case in Paris. At Oxford, students followed a four-year course of study under a tutor for the bachelor's degree. A first examination included grammar and arithmetic; and a second included rhetoric, logic, and possibly music. Three years of study beyond the bachelor's degree were required for the master's degree, during which time the student read the prescribed books on geometry, astronomy, and Aristotelian philosophy (physical science, ethics, and metaphysics). The curriculum of most of the universities of the Middle Ages consisted of the so-called seven liberal arts. These included the trivium (grammar, rhetoric, and logic) and the quadrivium (arithmetic, geometry, astronomy, and music). To the liberal arts, both Cambridge and Oxford added the philosophical studies based upon the teachings of Aristotle.

While Oxford is almost as old as the University of Paris, its influence was in no way comparable to that of Paris as a center of learning during the Middle Ages, primarily because of a language barrier. During this period, French was spoken by the nobility and intellectuals of England and Scotland. There was no common English dialect. Peasants and others spoke several Anglo-Saxon dialects. Chaucer's *Canterbury Tales* gave literary status to one of the dialects later in the thirteenth century. Henry V made Chaucer's work of great significance by adopting the same dialect as the official language of the country in 1413.

---

[31]*Ibid.*, p. 57.
[32]*Ibid.*, p. 59.

First Universities in Scotland. Scotland's thirteenth century war of independence and her growing difference with England over loyalty to papal authority (following the Schism of 1378), together with the development of early fourteenth century difficulties in Paris, brought about, in 1410, Incepit Studium Generale Universitatis Sancti Andree.[33]

The organization and administration of Saint Andrews followed practices of both the Italian and the French universities. Student election of certain officials, an idea borrowed from Bologna, but greater status for masters in keeping with the emphasis at Paris, plus greater authority for the bishop characterized the compromising elements in Saint Andrews' earliest charter. There were four nations. The president of each nation appointed a representative to vote on the election of a rector. In case of a tie, the decision lay with the retiring rector.[34] This was a scheme for avoiding the usual influence of the Faculty of Arts, which dominated the University of Paris.

The curricula in Scotland's universities consisted of the trivium and quadrivium plus natural, moral, and metaphysical philosophies.

Professors were considered to be both college and university teachers, a practice adopted from Germany. This brought about almost complete integration of college and university, a sharp contrast with practices at Oxford and Paris where the tutorial system developed college instruction unrelated to the university and its degrees. Authorities in contemporary universities in Scotland continue to emphasize the university as a unit rather than a collection of independent colleges.

German Contributions. A significant development in the liberalization of thought and experimentation was the establishment of the University of Leyden in 1575, and the University of Halle which opened in Germany in 1694. Halle, a Lutheran University, included the four traditional faculties of law, medicine, arts, and theology; but it soon adopted modern methods and a more dynamic view of the role of the university. It dispensed with Latin as the language of instruction. Thomasius, a professor of law, and Franck, in theology, challenged Aristotelianism. Others introduced experimental science, starting the inductive approach to research in contrast to the traditional deductive system of relating everything to some generalization from Aristotle.

Both Leyden and Halle lost their initiative to the University of Berlin, established in 1809. It became the leader of all universities in the world, and it was in the German universities that the most promi-

---

[33]*Ibid.*, Vol. II, p. 302.
[34]*Ibid.*, p. 307.

nent American educators took their advanced degrees during the latter part of the nineteenth century and the first of the twentieth.

The turning point in the development of modern universities was the acceptance of the hypothesis that generalizations and basic principles, in all areas of learning, derive from facts and experimentation rather than from debate or authority. Quest for certainty has become synonymous with freedom of inquiry. The long struggle to permit the flourishing of ideas dates from Socrates to the present, and it will never cease. America's kaleidoscopic heritage from the cultures of Greece, Rome, Islam, and Europe is beyond imagination or calculative dimensions.

Summary of European Influences. Medieval scholasticism dominated the curricula of European universities until in England, Henry VIII, king of England from 1509 to 1549, broke with the papacy and established the Church of England with himself as its head; and in France, Francis I, king of France from 1515 to 1547, began to force literary subjects of the new learning upon the universities.

First reforms of the curricula brought about the addition of classical languages of Greece, Rome, and Israel. Scientific subjects, in general, were excluded until the sixteenth century. Mathematics gained emphasis through the discoveries of the astronomer Kepler; through the works of Copernicus, Galileo, and Descartes; and through Trinity College's Sir Isaac Newton in the seventeenth century.

The domination of the church with headquarters in Rome was almost complete, and in many instances students and/or professors appealed to the Pope against cruel regulations on the part of the Chancellor or local bishop and thus achieved liberalization of control. The Pope also granted students exemption from local governmental authorities, a fact which made the universities almost completely autonomous corporations.

The competition between church and state for the control of higher education was intense throughout many centuries. This struggle continued in Europe and in America, with the church usually dominant, until the nineteenth century. Many of the most learned authorities held that the universities should limit their activities to training competent parish priests and should not engage in controversies.

Period of American Transculturation—1636-1850

The process of imposing one culture upon another may be referred to as transculturation; while the interaction of cultures, by which two or more cultures are changed, is called acculturation. The first American institutions of higher learning were established, not on the basis of interaction between the indigenous American and European leaders in higher education (a process of acculturation), but by a sincere attempt on the part of European-educated Americans to transfer the European system, and particularly that of Cambridge and Oxford, to New England. There was a strong desire, of course, to preserve and transmit the European heritage, the only higher education heritage which colonial leaders had known, experienced, and accepted.

Most professors in European universities up to the Reformation, and for sometime thereafter, were clerics, and the institutions which they staffed were sectarian institutions, e.g. they were dominated by religious groups. This idea, therefore, was dominant in the thinking of New England settlers and particularly the Puritans. Harvard College, for example, was established in order to maintain literate ministers of the gospel. However, this was not the only purpose in establishing Harvard. During this period, the influence of church authorities upon civil authorities was dominant. Therefore, another significant objective of Harvard College was to assist in the preparation of civil leaders under the proper guidance of sectarian influence.

Moreover, the first compulsory school law of Massachusetts, written in 1647, contained the "old deluder" clause, which implied that where it had formerly been the policy of Satan to keep people ignorant of the scriptures by keeping the scriptures in unknown tongues, he now followed with equal success the policy of keeping the people illiterate so that they would not be able to read the scriptures.[35]

The Reformation, with its concomitant emphasis upon one's own responsibility for salvation, a position defended earlier by Abelard, plus the printing of the New Testament in the English language, greatly influenced the pattern of early education in New England at all levels—the elementary schools, secondary schools, and Harvard University.

The Founding of Harvard College. Harvard College was founded in 1636 by the General Court of the Massachusetts Bay Colony. It was molded after the Emmanuel College at Cambridge where many of the early settlers had studied. The founders of Harvard stated its purpose as follows:

---

[35]E. P. Cubberley, *Readings in the History of Education*, (New York: Houghton-Mifflin Co., 1920), p. 299.

After God had carried us safe to New-England, and we had builded our houses, provided necessaries for our liveli-hood, rear'd convenient places for God's worship and settled the Civil Government; One of the next things we longed for, and looked after was to advance Learning and perpetuate it to Posterity; dreading to leave an illiterate Ministry to the Churches, when our present Ministers shall lie in the Dust.[36]

The dominant influence behind the establishment of Harvard was the Congregational Church, but Harvard was also intended to provide a classical education for the sons of wealthy colonial landowners and merchants.

There was no evidence that Harvard was being established to encourage the flourishing of new ideas in New England, for during the same period when Harvard College and the first compulsory school laws of Massachusetts were being inaugurated, Roger Williams was being forced out of the state because of his inclination toward nonconformity with the established church. At the very time that Massachusetts was writing the first compulsory school law in the English speaking world to perpetuate a religious orthodoxy, Roger Williams was leaving this fundamentalist environment in order to establish a state based upon religious freedom, a result of the reformation which had to be won all over again in America.

The General Court of Massachusetts established the overseers of Harvard in 1642, and by 1650, a charter was granted which established a corporation that included a president, five fellows, and a treasurer. These officers ran the College under the general control of the Overseers. In a few years, membership in the corporation was limited to individuals who were not engaged in teaching and research.[37]

The curriculum of Harvard included the trivium, three subjects of the quadrivium (arithmetic, geometry, and astronomy), ethics, ancient history, Greek, and Hebrew. The seventh of the liberal arts, music, was not included. Latin was the language of instruction. Science was not included, the classical languages being emphasized instead. All students took the same courses during the early years, and most of the courses were taught by the president. During the seventeenth century, Harvard's enrollment was only twenty to fifty students, ranging from

---

[36]*Encyclopaedia Britannica,* Vol. 11, (Chicago, London, Toronto: William Benton, Publishers), pp. 230-231.
[37]Frederick Eby, and Charles F. Arrowood, *The Development of Modern Education,* (New York: Prentice-Hall, Inc., 1940), p. 173.

thirteen to eighteen years of age. Students were classified according to social status of parents, as measured by wealth and occupation, with sons of clergymen, magistrates, and gentry ranking first, second, and third respectively.

Founding of William and Mary. William and Mary College was founded in 1693 under a charter granted by King William and Queen Mary. The principal church affiliation was Anglican. The Crown authorized a board of visitors to act as a temporary corporation for governing the institution. The college was to have a president and six professors.[38] The plan called for the Bishop of London to be the Chancellor and for the institution and its resources to be transferred to the president and professors when it was completed. The transfer was made in 1729, and all professors subscribed to the Articles of Faith of the Church of England, the established church of Virginia, and toook an oath of loyalty to the British Crown.

There was great dissension between the board of visitors and the faculty over control of the college, and in keeping with earlier French traditions, the faculty appealed to the Bishop of London against the board's decisions. The board of visitors continued in control following the revolution.[39] The purposes of William and Mary, according to its charter, were to provide a seminary of ministers for the churches of Virginia; to educate youth in good manners; to propagate the Christian faith among Western Indians; and to establish a place of universal study of divinity, philosophy, languages, "arts and sciences."

By 1799, William and Mary had only six instructors: two in divinity; one in logic, rhetoric, and ethics; one in physics, metaphysics, mathematics; one in Latin and Greek; and one in the area of teaching Indians. It was during this period that Thomas Jefferson attempted to make William and Mary a state university and to broaden its curriculum to include law, medicine, and other specialized areas. Jefferson wanted to replace the study of theology and the Bible with ancient languages and ecclesiastical history. His plan included modern foreign languages in the place of classics, and he encouraged a major emphasis upon the sciences and social sciences instead of Aristotelian philosophy. Jefferson's idea was to prepare young men for leadership in public and practical affairs and professional service rather than for narrow scholarship or religious sectarianism. His attempt to make William and Mary a state university failed, and this led to his great efforts in

---

[38]*Ibid.*, p. 174.
[39]*Ibid.*, p. 174.

the establishment of the University of Virginia as the crowning achievement of his career.

The Founding of Yale. Jung Pierpont and two other ministers, all graduates of Harvard, asked Connecticut Colony for authority to organize a collegiate school in 1701. The reasons for founding Yale were, in part, a reaction against liberal tendencies at Harvard: "At the time of the founding of Yale, a theological dispute, which ultimately divided the Congregational church, alienated certain clergy of New England from the support of Harvard. Yale was founded by the party opposed to liberal theology."[40] Cotton Mather was among the leaders who established Yale. His father, Increase Mather, was dismissed from the presidency of Harvard in 1701.

Yale was founded in protest against the liberal element in the established Congregational Church as represented at Harvard. Its first governing board consisted of ten ministers and excluded the president until 1745. This approach to administrative control, followed by many other institutions, was designed essentially to preclude any center of power save that of the church.[41]

The purposes of Yale, as set forth in 1701, were to instruct youth in arts and sciences for employment in "both church and civil state."[42] As late as 1754, President Clap stated: "Colleges are Societies of Ministers, for training up persons for the Work of the Ministry."[43] Clap made it virtually impossible for non-Congregational students to attend Sabbath services of their own choice prior to 1765. Religious freedom was not an automatic privilege of the pioneers who came to the shores of New England. America had to proclaim its own reformation against one orthodox group after another who claimed to possess a monopoly on salvation.

Administration of the college adopted some English ideas and initiated others which were distinctly colonial. The first presiding officers were called rectors, not presidents, and assistants were tutors or ushers, not fellows. Yale possessed none of the characteristics of a corporation. Trustees were not incorporated until 1733. Incorporation made possible self-government, holding of land, receiving of gifts, and the making of rules and regulations. Trustees continued to take the oath to King George.

[40]*Ibid.*, p. 176.
[41]R. Freeman Butts, *A Cultural History of Western Education*, (New York: McGraw-Hill Book Co., Inc., 1955), p. 318.
[42]John S. Brubacher and Willis Rudy, *Higher Education in Transition*, (New York: Harper & Bros., 1958), p. 8.
[43]*Ibid.*, p. 8.

About the time that trustees were incorporated, they began to list students alphabetically in the catalog instead of according to their social status; and the college laws were printed in English instead of Latin, although commencement orations were given in Latin until 1787.

The Dartmouth College Case. In or near the year 1754, Eleazar Wheelock founded what came to be known as an Indian Charity School on his plantation in Connecticut. His concern was to teach reading and writing to the native children and to utilize the local Indian language in the spreading of the Gospel according to the Congregational Church. His endeavor met with such success that he was able to send into the wilderness both missionaries and school masters of the native race. It was in this institution, a rather informal and meager elementary school, that Dartmouth College had its inception.[44]

Wheelock, at first, operated the school at his own expense and with some help from a few of his neighbors who enthusiastically supported his efforts. In a few years, he had gained the confidence of the Indians to such an extent that the school grew to a size which rendered this means of support inadequate. In order that he might continue his work without turning away prospective students, Wheelock sent Nathaniel Whitaker, a fellow Congregationalist minister, to England in an attempt to solicit the needed funds. Whitaker was accompanied by Sampson Occum, an Indian minister whom Wheelock had trained.

This effort apparently met with considerable success, for, while in England, Whitaker thought it advisable to obtain a group of trustees for the fund which he had raised, to choose a permanent campus for the institution, and to seek a charter from the Crown. He secured the services, as trustees, of the Earl of Dartmouth (for whom the colllege was apparently named), one Baron, and several Esquires and Gentlemen, all of whom were among the principal donors. This group, acting on Whitaker's request, considered possible sites for the campus and decided that the school would be located in western New Hampshire on the Connecticut River. This selection was, in large measure, influenced by offers made by several proprietors in that area of rather substantial donations of land.

Thus prepared, and with the help of the governor of New Hampshire, Whitaker prevailed upon George III to create the corporation which became Dartmouth College. In the year 1769, a charter was granted, the creating paragraph of which was as follows:[45]

---

[44]*Ibid.*, p. 8.
[45]Alpheus T. Mason and William M. Beaney, *American Constitutional Law,* (Englewood Cliffs, N. J.: Prentice-Hall, Inc., 1959), p. 359.

Know ye, therefore, That We, considering the premises, and being willing to encourage the laudable and charitable design of spreading Christian knowledge among the savages of our American wilderness, and also that the best means of education be established in our province, do, of our special grace, certain knowledge, and mere motion, by and with the advice of our counsel for said province, by these presents, will, ordain, grant, and constitute, that there be a college erected in our said province of New Hampshire, by the Name of Dartmouth College, for the education and instruction of youth of the Indian tribes in this land, in reading, writing, and all parts of learning, which shall appear necessary and expedient, for civilizing and Christianizing children of pagans, as well as in all liberal arts and sciences, and also of English youth and any others.

Further provisions[46] were also made in the charter. Wheelock was appointed President and given the immediate care of the education and the government of students. He was further given "full power, authority, and right, to nominate, appoint, constitute, and ordain, by his last will, such suitable person or persons as he shall choose to succeed him. . . ." The President was to account annually to the English trustees of the fund. Twelve trustees of the college itself rather than of the fund previously mentioned were appointed by the king. These trustees were given the usual authority—to receive, to acquire, to hold, and to dispose; to pay salaries and to pay charges; to enact laws for the government of the college and of its students; and to grant degrees. All trustees, officers, and employees of the college would take an oath to support the Crown. The trustees were given the power to remove the successor whom Wheelock might appoint and to choose further presidents as the need arose. The Board of Trustees was to be a self-perpetuating body; whenever a vacancy occurred, it was to be filled by an appointment made by the remaining members. Eight of the members were to be "resident, and respectable freeholders" of New Hampshire. Seven were to be laymen. No student was to be excluded because of his religious beliefs.

While Eleazar Wheelock lived, he operated the school much as he pleased and had no apparent trouble with the trustees. In his will, he appointed his son John as his successor.[47] John Wheelock was a military man, rather than a clergyman or scholar. He soon became involved in a losing quarrel with the local Congregational Church. Partially as a result of this, he lost control of the faculty. Further, he was faced with a group of trustees who wished to assert their preroga-

---

[46]*Ibid.,* pp. 359-364.
[47]Brubacher, *op. cit.,* p. 34.

tives. The situation deteriorated to the point that Wheelock appealed to the New Hampshire legislature to support his position on certain matters in opposition to the position of the board. He did so in an anonymous and apparently vituperative attack on the trustees, who then dismissed him from the presidency.[48]

The Jeffersonian Republicans, who were then out of power, seized upon this controversy as a political issue, and to some extent, were victorious in the election that followed.[49] They made it their early business to attempt to assert state authority over the college. To some extent, this action may have been merely the fulfilling of a campaign promise, but it was directly related to a deliberate policy of the party throughout the nation to bring private schools under public control. In order to make the changes the legislature desired, it was, of course, necessary to amend the Charter. In 1816,[50] an act with the following provisions was passed:

1. The name was changed from Dartmouth College to Dartmouth University.
2. It was provided that the board of trustees would be increased from twelve to twenty-one members.
3. A board of overseers of twenty-five members was created to inspect and to confirm or to disapprove the actions of the trustees.
4. The governor was given the power to appoint the members of the board of trustees and the board of overseers.
5. The governor was required to inspect the university and to report to the legislature at least once each five years.
6. All trustees, officers, and employees were required to take an oath to support the constitutions of the United States and of the State of New Hampshire.
7. The president was required to report annually to the governor.
8. The principle of religious freedom was reaffirmed.

Soon after the legislature took this action, the trustees of the college met and refused to accept the act. There were several issues at stake here, but the principal one was that of the power of visitation. This had been a vexatious problem to many of the early colleges in this country. They were afraid that if they took charters from the King they would be subject to Royal visitation and, thereby, to interference

---

[48]*Ibid.*, pp. 34-35.
[49]*Ibid.*, p. 35.
[50]Mason, *op. cit.*, p. 364.

from the Church of England; but, on the other hand, if they took charters from the provincial legislatures, a practice of very doubtful legality, they might be subject to political influence. In the case of Dartmouth, however, this issue had not arisen, for under English law, the founder of such a corporation had the power of visitation, a power which, upon his death, passed on to his heirs.

There was some doubt that Eleazar Wheelock technically qualified as founder, but this was a matter of no great importance because, in granting a charter, the King appointed trustees, and all power of royal visitation passed to them. Under this arrangement, the college was able to be its own master.

Under the amended charter, the State itself, through the power of appointment, through the board of overseers, and through gubernatorial visitation, came to have almost absolute authority. Dartmouth University was, in fact, a state institution.

John Woodward, the secretary and treasurer of the college, was friendly to John Wheelock's point of view and took certain property of the college and held it for the university; appeals by the college trustees that it be returned were ignored. An action was then brought in the state courts to compel its return. As was expected, the courts of New Hampshire, being largely Republican in membership, ruled in favor of the university.[51] The college trustees then sued out a writ of error to the United States Supreme Court, the issue here being solely whether or not the amendment to the charter was in violation of that portion of the United States Constitution which forbade any "law impairing the obligation of contract."[52] This problem resolved itself into essentially only one question: Did a contract which was protected by the Constitution of the United States exist? That there had been at least the form of a contract and that, if binding on the state, it had been violated, were points which were not seriously disputed.

It was first necessary to decide whether or not the college was a public or a private corporation. It was well settled that no one could have a vested interest in a public corporation; no contractual relationship existed. In such an instance, the legislature could do entirely as it saw fit, could effect a change or an abolishment at any time it wished. It was argued by the university that the corporation was public because it had accepted funds from the state and because its

[51]Brubacher, *op. cit.*, p. 35.
[52]*Dartmouth College v. Woodward*, 4 Wheaton, 518, 4 L. ed. 629, 1819.

objective, education, was a matter of public interest. The court ruled that neither of these arguments was valid, that the corporation was organized with private funds, that its acceptance of state money did not alter its character, and that the mere fact that it was of service to the public in educational matters did not render it a public school.

It was further contended that the Revolution destroyed the interest of the Crown and thereby invalidated the contract, but it was held that, at the end of the Revolution, the State of New Hampshire succeeded to all assets, liabilities, and responsibilities which had pertained to the Crown and that, therefore, the state was a legal party to the charter. Relative to this matter was the argument that because the English Parliament at one time had the authority to abrogate the charter, the New Hampshire legislature had succeeded to this right. It was ruled that even though the Parliament was omnipotent, and even though the legislature of New Hampshire could have, between the Revolution and the effective date of the United States Constitution, abolished the corporation at any time, the adoption of that Constitution prohibited any such action thereafter.[53]

The additional contention was made that no living being had any vested interest in the charter and that it, therefore, did not exist; but the court held that the trustees had the duty of protecting the intentions of the donors and were, therefore, representative parties to the contract.[54]

Daniel Webster, attorney for the old trustees and his Alma Mater, in his most celebrated plea before the Supreme Court, invoked the constitutional sanctity of contract and argued further that "the college would lead a precarious existence if it were to be subject to the fluctuation of public opinion or the rise and fall of political parties."[55] Chief Justice Marshall, a Federalist, upheld the sanctity of contract and private status for the college.

On the basis of these conclusions, coupled with the assertion that the constitution was broad enough to cover instances of this type, the judgment of the New Hampshire court was reversed.[56] The immediate result was that the university ceased to exist and the college structure remained unchanged. Of more far-reaching importance was its effect in (1) strengthening the doctrine, set forth in the Georgia land case,

[53]*Ibid.*
[54]*Ibid.*
[55]Brubacher, *op. cit.*, p. 36.
[56]*Dartmouth College, op. cit.*

of the inviolability of a contract to which a state is a party, to later legislative acts of that state and (2) its effect in establishing the contractual character of a charter of incorporation. These precedents, though they have been weakened by the development of the concept of police power and somewhat obscured by that of due process, are still of some authoritative significance even today.

Of further tremendous import is the influence that this decision had on the maintenance of the independence of private schools at all levels. There is probably no exaggeration in the statement that, if the judgment in the Dartmouth case had been adverse to the college, nearly all private schools, particularly those of college level, would have disappeared within a few years.

University of Virginia. When Jefferson, in 1779, attempted to redesign the College of William and Mary in order to make it the state university, his ideas were not accepted. A state university being the goal of his total educational scheme, he turned his attention and efforts toward the development of the University of Virginia in Charlottesville. The Dartmouth decision increased his determination to erect the capstone of his educational plan.

The following ideas were dominant in Jefferson's plan for the University of Virginia: (1) opportunity for specialization and course election; (2) public instruction; (3) secular and nondenominational orientation; (4) universal education for masses combined with opportunities for advanced learning for the gifted; (5) a lay board of visitors appointed by the governor and confirmed by the legislature; (6) generous support from the State; (7) no religious influence in selection of trustees and professors; (8) special state scholarships for poor students; (9) a university according to Euorpean standards; (10) a curriculum covering law, medicine, anatomy, moral philosophy, natural history, natural philosophy, and ancient languages; (11) a faculty recruited almost exclusively from overseas, mostly from England; (12) intellectual independence from the north; and (13) active support for the advancement of scientific agriculture.

It seems clear that even Jefferson was torn between the necessity to transplant European higher education (through European professors) and the need to develop a uniquely indigenous university. The latter would have been impossible even in Jefferson's day; therefore, a compromise was reached—an institution partly European, partly American.

Summary of the Period of American Transculturation

Throughout the period of the seventeenth, the eighteenth, and the first half of the nineteenth centuries, there was a bitter struggle involving exponents of sectarian and secular control, state and private control, and functional or liberal and traditional liberal arts curricula. There had been little consideration for any group except the socially elite and the religiously orthodox. The deep significance of the reformation, the renaissance, and the industrial revolution had not permeated higher education.

Following the Civil War, there was increasing emphasis upon science and technology as means of exploiting the great natural resources of the nation. The Morrill Act of 1862 and the subsequent founding of the great land-grant colleges marked the end of transculturation. Indeed, it was the beginning of America's most unique contribution to higher education—a system which increasingly has reversed the process of transculturation to the point that free men and societies in dozens of nations less fortunate than ours, in the development of their resources, are turning to America as a fountain of ideas and skills basic to economic, political, and social development.

The American Idea of a University (Acculturation)

Cornell University. Cornell University was a great pioneer in the new type of higher education, having been given impetus by the Morrill Act. Its founder proclaimed: "I would found an institution in which any person can find instruction in any study."[57] The first president, Andrew Dickson White, made it clear that he intended to carry that motto into action. He enumerated the following dynamic ideas for the progress of Cornell: (1) completely nonsectarian; (2) close contact with the public-school system; (3) equality between courses of study; (4) emphasis upon scientific study and scientific method in all areas of learning; (5) adaptation of the university to American people and their needs rather than to English or German needs; (6) five-year rather than life terms for trustees, with one trustee elected each year by the alumni; (7) freedom from authoritarianism of every kind, without extending this freedom to Marxists and anarchists; (8) faith in an intellectual elite; (9) public control of higher education; (10) selection of students and faculty without race, sex, and religion as criteria; and (11) vocational training with a strong cultural em-

---

[57]Brubacher, *op. cit.*, p. 158.

phasis. The establishment of Cornell carried Jefferson's idea of a non-sectarian, multi-purpose, scientific, and cultural institution one step closer to meeting the unique needs of its society.

The University as Service to the State. One of the dynamic ideas which America gained from late nineteenth century Germany was the concept of a modern university as a service to the state. Combined with the authority and resources to challenge tradition, conceptual approaches to learning and investigation, and the substitution of scientific research as the methodology of discovery, the idea of service in a newly developing agricultural and industrial society was a potent motivation for a frontier university.

The "Wisconsin Idea" was the synthesis of the trends in many countries and universities toward a unity of knowledge and action. According to Professor Richard T. Ely, the people of the state would not permit the university to become an ivory tower.

Research at Wisconsin has been so closely identified with the economy of the state that the farmers know almost to the dollar how much the university has contributed to their progress. The amount runs into billions of dollars if one takes the total contribution over a period of sixty to seventy years. Thus the campus and state boundaries are coterminous.

The great idea was placed into operation with the appointment of Charles R. Van Hise as president in 1903. The following are a few of his ideas for reforming the university and, in consequence, the state: (1) the university should serve all the people of the state; (2) it would synthesize the essential qualities and distinguishing characteristics of the English College and the German University; (3) liberal arts, applied science and research would be combined to complement each other; (4) the university would move forward as cause and effect of society rather than as following the traditional role of conserving and transmitting the cultural heritage; (5) there would be no boundaries upon the scope of the university's intellectual effort; (6) the university was to become part and parcel of the very fiber of its society—engaging in finding solutions to problems of education, government, health, economics, and sociology, as well as teaching thousands of people through correspondence courses by the year 1910.

Under the Wisconsin Idea, there was a partnership between the university and government, with the progressive legislation, so characteristic of the era of Robert LaFollette, Sr., springing from scientific research rather than from conceptual dogma. "The Wisconsin Idea amounted in essence to the extensive use of the state university for political reform, economic and social improvement, and human welfare."[58]

In combining the English College program in general education (an essentially undergraduate curriculum) with the German concept of a university (concerned primarily with graduate research and productive scholarship), and using the total results for social, political, and economic progress, Wisconsin made extensive progress in breaking with Europe and Colonial America. Cornell and Wisconsin, although involved in a process of acculturation during the last part of the nineteenth century, were emerging as something different from any European or hitherto American university. The period of transculturation was terminated; acculturation was to continue indefinitely. Today, however, universities around the world are being acculturated by American universities. We should be extremely modest about this, for we have been acculturated by twenty-five centuries of higher education from other countries.

By 1887, the legislature of Wisconsin appropriated $12,000 for farmers' institutes, and in 1887-88, a total of eighty-one institutes drew 50,000 farmers.[59] This program prompted Turner to write four years later:

> The improvement of the agricultural condition of the state effected by the University in thus extending its activity is remarkable. . . . industries of communities have been changed from unprofitable grain raising to horticulture, dairy farming, etc., with accompanying prosperity and a rise in land values . . . progress . . . in . . . dairying, horticulture and improved stock raising, is in no small degree the work of the Institutes. Farmers are becoming more intelligent and more prosperous. They participate freely in the discussion, they learn self help and cooperation at the same time, and become interested in public concern.[60]

Frederick Jackson Turner believed that the universities of the Middle West would replace the open frontier as a great motivating force for democracy by producing trained and responsible leadership.[61]

President Van Hise demonstrated, in action and in theory, a depth of insight and perception unique in any age. He believed that the

---

[58]*Wisconsin Legislative Reference Bureau*, (Madison, Wisconsin: University of Wisconsin Press), 1912.
[59]Merle Curti and Vernon Carstensen, *The University of Wisconsin; A History, 1848-1925*, Vol. I, (Madison: University of Wisconsin Press, 1949), p. 713.
[60]*Ibid.*, p. 713.
[61]Brubacher, *op. cit.*, p. 170.

University had three main purposes: to contribute to the undergraduate's preparation for his life work and for intelligent citizenship; to advance knowledge; and to take knowledge to the people and to aid in its application to the economic, social, and political problems.[62]

Professional Education. Our early concepts of the graduate school of Arts and Science were as closely related to German practices as the American college was to its British prototype. Thousands of American scholars went to German universities during the nineteeenth and early years of the twentieth centuries. Among distinguished university presidents who studied in German universities were Eliot of Harvard, White of Cornell, Angell of Michigan, Folwell of Minnesota, Hall of Clark University, Butler of Columbia, Adams of Wisconsin, Barnard of Columbia, and Gilman of Johns Hopkins.

Johns Hopkins University. The first typical German University in America was Johns Hopkins. Leadership in higher education during the nineteeenth century had passed to Germany. The Anglican religious test for degrees continued at Cambridge and Oxford until 1871, a situation closely akin to sectarianism in America. The Reformation was being debated, but it had not been generally accepted on either side of the Atlantic. This fact contributed to the rise of German universities and to the eclipse of English, French, and American universities until the issue of academic integrity and religious freedom had been resolved. The universities of Halle, Gottingen, Berlin, Breslau, Bonn, and Munich were committed to scientific research and freedom of research and learning to a degree unknown in other countries.

The principal characteristics of Johns Hopkins were: (1) It was designed to meet a national rather than a sectional need. (2) Its curricula consisted of typical German disciplines grouped under a Department of Philosophy—language, mathematics, ethics, history, and science. (3) There was a great emphasis upon securing outstanding German-trained faculty members. (4) Research and productive scholarship were emphasized. (5) It was non-sectarian, Darwinian, and pragmatic. (6) Conceptual knowledge was challenged. (7) Gilman, in his inaugural address (1876), challenged the university to account for less misery among the poor, less ignorance in schools, less bigotry in the temple, less suffering in the hospital, less fraud in business, less folly in politics. (8) A system of generous fellowships brought, among the first distinguished students—Josiah Royce, Walter Hines Page, Woodrow Wilson, Joseph Jastrow, John R. Commons, Albion Small, J. McKeen

---

[62]Curti, *op. cit.*, Vol. II, p. 87.

Cattell, John Dewey, Frederick Jackson Turner, and Herbert Baxter Adams. (9) A lay Board of Trustees controlled the University. (10) During Gilman's administration, a great Medical School which was becoming internationally known by 1900 was organized.[63]

By 1896, ten of Johns Hopkins' Ph. D.'s were at Harvard, thirteen at Columbia, and nineteeen at Wisconsin.[64] By 1926, it was stated that nearly one-fourth of all distinguished scientists in America were graduates of Johns Hopkins. What Virginia, Cornell, and Wisconsin had done for college work in general, Johns Hopkins had achieved for graduate education. The pattern thus established did not become typical in America, but the emphasis upon research, scholarship, and high standards provided a goal for all graduate schools and launched the idea in America for graduate-level work as distinct from work of the colleges.

Normal Schools. At the most crucial stage in his fight for the establishment of the University of Virginia and in his efforts to secure financial support from the legislature, Jefferson stated that, should it become necessary to abandon the university or the common schoool program, the common schools should receive priority.

The development of universal education paralleled the building of normal schools. In Massachusetts, where the first normal school was founded in 1839, the compulsory common school law had been passed almost two hundred years earlier; but its implementation followed the Civil War.

The men who developed the normal schools were usually dynamic leaders in the fight for universal public education. They regarded the building of rural schools as the only means by which their institutions could flourish. Most of the university leaders were skeptical of the value or need for the normal schools, but no group of institutions contributed more to twentieth century growth of American universities than did the normal schools. They provided the broad base for universal public education so necessary for a qualitative college-age population.

The first twelve state normal schools in the United States, with dates of founding, were: two in Massachusetts in 1839 and a third one in 1840, one each in New York in 1844, Connecticut in 1849, Michigan in 1849, Massachusetts in 1854, Rhode Island in 1854, New Jersey in 1855, Illinois in 1857, Pennsylvania in 1859, and Minnesota in 1860.[65]

---

[63]Brubacher, *op. cit.*, pp. 176-178.
[64]*Ibid.*, p. 179.
[65]Cubberley, *op. cit.*, p. 587.

Summary of the Genetics of Ideas In American Higher Education

Based upon this inadequate chronological study of ideas in higher education, stretching from the ancient days of Greece and Rome to the present, it is possible to glean certain movements, ideas, or philosophies which have motivated the development of higher education in the United States. Early colonial institutions were clearly a response to a religious motivation to prepare leaders, meaning for the most part ministers, for existing churches. However, this was by no means the only objective in the establishment of colonial institutions. Both in America and in Cambridge and Oxford, which had so greatly influenced the development of colonial institutions, the "gentleman's son" was taking his place by the side of the serious scholar. The founders of our early institutions, and particularly great statesmen such as Jefferson, recognized the significance of higher education for the development of the kind of leaders needed in all aspects of American life.

Soon after the adoption of the Federal Constitution, it became increasingly obvious that the state should assume basic responsibility for the support of higher education. This idea, originating on a modest scale, such as the founding of the University of Virginia, eventuated in consequences far beyond anything that Jefferson and other advocates of the idea anticipated.

Concomitant with the acceptance of the idea that higher education was the responsibility of the state was the recognition of the fundamental role of private colleges and universities, greatly enhanced by the Dartmouth decision, which proclaimed the sanctity of college and university charters as legitimate and legal contracts not to be broken by the state. Thus the great flourishing of private and public institutions of higher learning side by side with what has become an increasing degree of cooperation is one of the unique ideas in American higher education. A whole volume could be written on the process of acculturation which has gone on between public and private institutions in the United States. Moreover, both public and private institutions undoubtedly are infinitely stronger and more susceptible to research, scholarship, teaching, and service functions than they would have been had either type of institution gained a complete monopoly upon the higher education responsibility in the United Staates.

Equality of educational opportunity at the elementary and secondary levels and later at the college and university levels has been one of the most revolutionary ideas of modern higher education developed in the United States. In no other nation in the history of the world has such a high percentage of college-age youth been afforded the privilege of higher education at public expense. Generic to the charters of practically all state, and many of the private, institutions has been the concept of higher education, not for an intellectual elite, but for all citizens capable of benefiting from such preparation. This fundamental idea, sometimes confused with equalitarianism, has been basic to the development of American democracy. Intelligent leaders from Jefferson to present great educational statesmen have never confused equality of opportunity with equality of achievement. Whereas the former is at the very root of the idea of democracy, the latter is utterly incompatible with it.

The land-grant college movement is one of the unique ideas which America has contributed to higher education. From the days of the Greek city states right down to the middle of the nineteenth century, the practical arts were regarded as appropriate only for slaves and lower levels of workers, while the liberal arts were regarded as the sole curricula for the education of free men. The definition of free men, however, was in sharp contrast to a definition which would be acceptable in this country. Free men in the Greek city states and in the universities of the Middle Ages were regarded as men of leisure who could devote their whole life to learning for its own sake. In many instances, of course, they were the sons of tyrants or existing rulers. Their contempt for the laboring class was exceeded only by their ignorance of what was good for the total society. In the land-grant college movement in the United States, the doors of higher education were opened wide, for the first time in history, to workers in mechanical arts, in agriculture, and in industry; and these students were permitted to study alongside those students whose primary interests were in the liberal arts. This, too, represented a process of acculturation unique anywhere else in the world.

The concept of the university as a service agency for the total society, although not originating in America, has been implemented to a greater extent in the United States than in any other nation.

The university as both a cause and a result of society is no longer a debatable issue in the United States. Colleges of agriculture, for example, have revolutionized farming since 1920. They did not wait for modern practices to develop on the farm and then to be perpetuated by the universities. Constant research on improved methods of cultivation, selection of seed, control of insects, and farm mechanization have gone forward as fundamental research projects at public expense. These, in turn, have changed not only the economics of farming but have greatly influenced the sociological composition of rural communities. What has happened in agriculture, of course, has been paralleled by similar progress in engineering, industry, and all technological pursuits.

The area yet to be subjected to rigorous scientific analysis, experimentation, and synthesis is in the realm of social sciences. It is this area that has had the greatest inhibiting influence upon the acceptance of the concept that universities should pioneer in promoting desirable changes in society. Basic research is needed in this area, and great opportunity exists here for the flourishing of philosophical ideas which give rise to rigorous scientific research in any area.

The identification of education with citizenship has been a great driving force in higher education. This has led to the development of many plans for general education, an attempt to relegate what formerly included the total curriculum of higher education to the first year or two of college work. We may never be able to find a satisfactory solution to the problem of general education until we recognize and institute practices to carry out the fundamental contribution of all learning to the area of general education. Moreover, basic to this concept is that, in America, all education is fundamentally vocational or cultural in nature, a recognition of the social equality of all useful work.

Summary

Higher education in the United States is a product of twenty-five centuries of intellectual struggles. It has drawn freely upon the ideas of many antecedent cultures—Greek, Roman, Islamic, and European. A full understanding and appreciation of this great heritage should contribute to the development of leadership for higher education in America.

Americans should be the humble recipients of all of the struggles that have been made by previous societies. In some cases, America has been worthy of its heritage; in many respects, we have fallen short of our potentialities. The world now looks to America to help develop schools and centers of higher learning in evolving countries on every continent. In that great enterprise, we have the opportunity and the responsibility to repay our debt to the rest of the world for the heritage which came to America.

Education, applied to the common tasks of men, has made it possible to develop the intellectual and creative talents of American youth. Higher education, as a result and as a cause of modern society, is a revolutionary idea of intellectual dimensions desperately needed as an instrument for increasing man's humanity to man. The idea has been present but mostly dormant since the dawn of civilization. The challenge to higher education in our time is to make the idea operational in the relationships of men and nations.

Questions for Discussion

1. In what respects is the process of acculturation increasing or decreasing in American colleges and universities?
2. What are the sociological implications of transculturation?
3. What was the unique contribution of Islam to higher education?
4. Why do authorities disagree concerning the historical origin of universities?
5. Trace the influence of Plato's Academy to its closing in the year 529.
6. Contrast early Italian, French, and English Universities.
7. Contrast the early contributions of private colleges and universities in the United States and in Latin America.
8. What events brought about the rise of state universities in the United States?

Bibliography

BOYD, WILLIAM. *The History of Western Education.* London: A. and C. Black, Ltd., 1928.

BRUBACHER, JOHN S., and RUDY, WILLIS. *Higher Education in Transition.* New York: Harper & Bros., 1958.

BUTTS, R. FREEMAN. *A Cultural History of Western Education.* New York: McGraw-Hill Book Co., Inc., 1955.

COMPAYRE, GABRIEL. *Abelard and the Origin and Early History of Universities.* New York: Charles Scribner's Sons, 1902.

CUBBERLEY, E. P. *Readings in the History of Education.* New York: Houghton Mifflin Co., 1920.

CURTI, MERLE, and CARSTENSEN, VERNON. *The University of Wisconsin; A History, 1848-1925*, Vol. 1. Madison: University of Wisconsin Press, 1949.

DALY, LOWRIE J. *The Medieval University, 1200-1400.* New York: Sheed and Ward, Inc., 1961.

Dartmouth College v. Woodward. 4 Wheaton, 518, 4 L. ed. 629, 1819.

DORF, PHILIP. *The Builder; A Biography of Ezra Cornell.* New York: The Macmillan Co., 1952.

EBY, FREDERICK, and ARROWOOD, CHARLES F. *The Development of Modern Education.* New York: Prentice-Hall, Inc., 1940.

GOOD, H. G. *A History of Western Education.* New York: The Macmillan Co., 1960.

HASKINS, CHARLES HOMER. *The Rise of Universities.* Ithaca, New York: Cornell University Press, 1957.

HOFSTADTER, RICHARD, and SMITH, WILSON, editors. *American Higher Education, A Documentary History,* Vol. 2. Chicago: The University of Chicago Press, 1961.

JOWETT, BENJAMIN. *Aristotle's Politics.* New York: Random House, Inc., 1943.

LAURIE, SIMON SOMERVILLE. *The Rise and Early Constitution of Universities; with a Survey of Medieval Education.* New York: D. Appleton & Co., 1887.

MASON, ALPHEUS T., and BEANEY, WILLIAM M. *American Constitutional Law.* Englewood Cliffs, New Jersey: Prentice-Hall, Inc., 1959.

McCARTHY, CHARLES. *The Wisconsin Idea.* New York: The Macmillan Co., 1912.

MORRISON, S. E. *Founding of Harvard College.* Cambridge, Massachusetts: Harvard University Press, 1935.

MYERS, EDWARD D. *Education in the Perspective of History.* New York: Harper & Bros., 1960.

RASHDALL, HASTINGS. *The Universities in Europe in the Middle Ages.* Vol. 1, edited by F. M. Powicke and A. B. Emden. Oxford: Clarendon Press, 1936.

RICHARDSON, LEON BURR. *History of Dartmouth College,* Vol. 1. Hanover, New Hampshire: Dartmouth Publications, 1932.

ROGERS, WALTER P. *Andrew D. White and the Modern University.* Ithaca, New York: Cornell University Press, 1942.

SALIH ABD-ALZIZ. *The Development of Educational Theory.* Cairo, Egypt: Government Press, 1947.

SANDYS, SIR JOHN EDWIN. *History of Classical Scholarship,* Vol. 1. New York: Hafner Publishing Co., 1958.

SCHACHNER, NATHAN. *The Medieval Universities.* New York: Frederick A. Stokes Co., 1938.

SMITH, WILLIAM A. *Ancient Education.* New York: Philosophical Library, 1955.

TURNER, FREDERICK JACKSON. "Extension Teaching in Wisconsin." *Handbook of University Extension.* Edited by George Francis James. Philadelphia: 1893.

VANCE, MAURICE M. *Charles Richard Van Hise, Scientist Progressive,* Madison: State Historical Society of Wisconsin, 1960.

WALDEN, JOHN WILLIAM HENRY. *The Universities of Ancient Greece.* New York: Charles Scribner's Sons, 1909.

Wisconsin Legislative Reference Bureau. Madison: University of Wisconsin Press, 1912.

Encyclopaedia Britannica, Vol. 11. Chicago, London, Toronto: William Benton, Publishers, pp. 230-231.

Chapter

A Frame of Reference
for the Administration
of Higher Education

The Nature of Policy

The basic concepts of democracy must be understood before one can establish the proper function of education in the democratic society. This chapter attempts to analyze man's basic nature, the nature of society, the role of the state, and the concepts of democracy. Such an analysis should lead to a better understanding of the principles and policies which guide the university in a democratic society. These concepts are not presented as ultimates but as examples of the process involved in developing one's rationale for administrative action.

Policy in higher education is a process by which responsible individuals determine the direction which action shall take. It involves a philosophical interpretation of institutional goals and the procedures by which they are achieved. Policy determination is an extremely complex process. It must be in harmony with the most enlightened concepts of social processes, procedures, and methodology of a free society. One of the most appropriate examples of a free society is the American university whose processes are in harmony with its avowed objectives.

The Nature of Man and Society

Man, whether primitive or civilized, is by nature a selfish as well as a social being. He is selfish in that he is less concerned immediately with that which affects others than with that which affects himself. He

74

is social in that he is willing to cooperate with others for the common good of the groups of which he is a member.

Evidences of man's selfish nature are found on every front. The clash between private and group interests permeates many American homes, schools, churches, civic, and community organizations. This tendency is evident in the relationships between labor and management, farmer and industrialist, and in the public controversies between various sections of the country. There is evidence of man's selfish nature in the relationship of elected officials to their publics and in the attitudes of many pressure groups, which make it almost impossible for public officials to perform their responsibilities objectively and with intelligence. Pronounced selfishness and greed extend to the international level as a natural result. Yet, for centuries, writers in the field of political theory have stated that man is by nature social. The existence and survival of man require him to cooperate with others of his kind. Frontier societies which tend to accentuate the glory and worth of the individual at the same time demonstrate most clearly the necessity for cooperation among men.

The free society is one in which men are encouraged to identify individual and common purposes and interests as a basis for group control. Men who are socially motivated as individuals within a group, possessing common interests, are to that extent socially controlled. The community that has developed group consciousness, purposes, and interests is less concerned with the need for legal restrictions to maintain group control. Only when men are associated in a cooperative enterprise are they in a position for self-direction.

The extent to which there is widespread communication and sharing of ideas and purposes between various groups of individuals determines the possibility of a larger voluntary society. Efficient communication and rapid transportation are responsible for the development of strong, nationalistic tendencies in contrast to the radical sectionalism which characterized the early period of American history. Restricted communication between small groups inhibits the development of the national society; radical, self-centered nationalism is the result of restricted interaction between nations.

International communication and transportation, together with a sharing of concern for progress toward a world-wide community spirit, will make every individual identify his own welfare with that of all other people. And although a single individual cannot determine the course of society against the weight of convention and the pressure of vested interests, he can, nevertheless, be effective if he can think freely, cooperate, and participate as a member of various groups.

Case Studies in Group Control. In 1953, in a large vocational school in Saigon, Indochina, courses were offered in all standard trade and industrial subjects. One class of about fifty young high school boys seemed especially well motivated. All of them seemed impatient to complete the course as preparation for army ordnance work and to enter the war effort. These students were oblivious to visitors and activities not related to their goal. Although all of their expenses were being paid by the government of Vietnam, the one experience in common that gave each of these boys the same determined expression, that drew them closer together than brothers, that made them of one mind in their desire to join the war effort was the fact that each of them had lost his father in the bloody struggle against communism. Their actions were determined by purposes and experiences that were completely shared. This experience illustrates human qualities that account for unity in a community whose freedom is threatened.

High in the Andes of Peru on the northwest tip of Lake Titicaca is the small city of Puno. The altitude makes it a very difficult and unpleasant climate for people who have always lived near-sea-level. Most of the inhabitants are Indians or Mestizos. Public services and facilities in education, social welfare, sanitation, transportation, and communication are extremely limited. To this city came fourteen Maryknoll brothers, Catholic missionaries trained in New York, who had decided that this would be a good community in which to try out their ideas of helping young people to live better lives. These fourteen men organized the community for action. A school for three hundred students was erected. The missionaries instituted a modern secondary school program including athletics, forensics, and practical arts. Health conditions were improved through adoption of better eating habits and encouraging the growing of more fruits and vegetables. Juvenile delinquency decreased through the promotion of more socially desirable activities such as football, basketball, singing, dancing, and literary societies. The Maryknoll missionaries were continually busy, frequently late into the night, but a community—proud of its heritage and future—was being formed.

An even more interesting community was the one that developed among the fourteen priests who lived together in modest quarters. During a visit with them, it was noted that different members of the group, even during their dinner hour, would arrive from or depart for some extracurricular activities involving students and citizens of the community. Their work was in their conversation. They loved what they were doing and the people whom they were serving. They were happy and well adjusted, even though there was only one other American in Puno—another missionary. This community could never have been developed by people who were not challenged by the opportunity for human service. In the words of Bishop Fulton J. Sheen, it had to be a "labor of love."

In Chiengmai, Thailand, a group of Presbyterian missionaries launched a series of community projects more than one hundred years ago. They were concerned not so much with saving souls as with saving people from hunger, disease, and ignorance. Through cooperative efforts, these American Presbyterians and their Thai friends have developed a large leprosarium, where thousands of people are being cured of leprosy; a very adequate community hospital (McCormick Hospital); an elementary school that enrolls nearly a thousand children; and Prince Royal College, a secondary school of very high standards, from which many leaders of Thailand have been graduated. Thai citizens and leaders refer to the Presbyterian projects in Chiengmai as the first "point four" program in their country, although it has never been supported or controlled by government. It, too, is a "labor of love" based upon man's humanity to man.

In each of the communities described above, there were shared objectives, problems, concerns, ideals, skills and planning; and there were voluntary associations of men which derive from man's inherent nature to be social. For example, men associate in friendship and in antagonism, in recreation, crime, clubs, fraternities, churches, armies, science, art, business partnerships, corporations, political parties, trade associations, trade unions, labor unions, and as employers, producers, distributors, and consumers. The purposes, interests, and human qualities which cause these associations are significant in the development of communities and society. The sum total of voluntary associations of men in small and large organizations constitutes society, which itself is a voluntary organization.

The degree of social control within a group is determined by the number of interests and purposes which the individuals within the group hold in common. Conflicts between individuals within the larger society come about in consequence of the fact that private interests are stronger than public interests. Delegating a difficult problem to the state does not remove it from the possibility of actions based upon selfish motives, because the problem continues to be administered by individuals who have the same qualities as those persons who elected them. Man is less concerned immediately for that which affects others than for that which affects himself, and he becomes socially conscious only when he realizes that his individual well-being is one with the larger social group of which he is a part. If all actions were in the interest of the whole group, the free society would be perfected at once. Such is not the case. Voluntary organizations and group control, based upon common purposes and interests, are not sufficient where individual interests are stronger than group interests.

Radical Individualism. During a visit to an ancient shrine in northern Cambodia in 1953, there arose an opportunity to observe man in a state of anarchy. A middle-aged man and his son came by, close to a party of Americans. The boy was about nine years of age and was carrying a crossbow. Father and son had been hunting for game in the deep forest in order to provide food for the family. They were skeptical of the group from the coastal region and of the two Americans until someone spoke to the hunter in his own dialect. After being assured that these people were from a friendly "tribe," the man and his son joined the group for a picnic lunch.

The hunter's son was in school that day, learning the art of hunting and of protecting himself in a rather dangerous forest. His schooling was informal. He learned everything from his father. There was no demand that the son attend a formal school; indeed there was no formal school in that community. This was rugged individualism, responsible only to the society of primitive man.

There are many places in the world where one can observe the conditions of anarchy, which subordinates the group to the individual. If all men were perfect, anarchy would be a great system, but the system breaks down because men are not social to the point of being governed without law.

The idea of a society conducting its affairs without the apparatus of government can be traced to writings prior to the Christian era. The Stoic philosopher Zano, 342-267 B.C., condemned the intervention of the state in private life and claimed the right of the individual to regulate his own conduct.[1] William Godwin in his *Enquiry Concerning Political Justice,* written in 1793, stated that the injection of government into

---

[1]William Godwin, *Enquiry Concerning Political Justice,* (Toronto: University of Toronto Press, 1946).

society entirely changes the character of human relationships. According to Godwin, man is by nature sociable, cooperative, rational, and good. He felt government of any sort changes the character of human relationships, because those who rule are bound to become arrogant, self-seeking, jealous of their privileges, and unmindful of those whom they should respect.

Henry David Thoreau was willing to accept the motto, "That government is best which governs least." But he went a step further and stated, "That government is best which governs not at all."[2]

The ideal society proclaimed by the above authors would consist of small groups of self-governing individuals, groups from which formal government would be excluded. The absence of government does not, according to the anarchist, mean an absence of order. On the contrary, it is claimed that the state of lawlessness existing everywhere in society is the direct consequence of the legal force imposed upon individuals by the state. As long as one group holds the power to dominate others, the rest of mankind is enslaved. Once this parasitic growth is abolished, the principle of mutual aid will again prevail in the lives of men.

Throughout its peak of popularity in the eighteenth and nineteenth centuries, anarchy remained largely an unorganized movement with a nebulous program and a variety of interpretations. Some supporters advocated revolutionary means while others proclaimed evolution. In the United States a form of philosophical anarchism, represented by Henry David Thoreau, arose as a product of American individualism. Non-payment of taxes, a policy of passive resistance, and a retreat to nature were some of the outward expressions of this philosophy. During the nineteenth century, with its tremendous national and international conflicts, this highly "individualistic" doctrine did make some headway. But by the end of the first World War, little of its influence remained. By this time, life had become so complex and the services required by society so involved that even the most radical thinkers admitted the need for some sort of government. The question remained: how much rule, by what methods, and by whom?

The Antithesis of Anarchy. Totalitarianism is at the opposite end of the political spectrum from anarchy. It takes many forms and is found in many parts of the world. Some examples are absolute monarchy, Nazism, Fascism, and Soviet Communism. Regardless of their

---

[2]H. D. Thoreau, "Civil Disobedience," *The World's Great Thinkers; Man and the State: The Political Philosophers.* ed. Cummins, Saxe, and R. N. Linscott, (New York: Random House, Inc., 1947), p. 297.

titles, these systems have one thing in common—the subjugation of the individual to the state.

In order to understand, if not to approve and appreciate the methodological processes invoked by totalitarian societies, it becomes imperative for the objective scholar to view, analyze, and study their actions from the vantage point of their system of values. What are the basic philosophical premises that guide their actions? At the risk of over-simplification, certain qualities and practices seem obvious: (1) the state is an entity; (2) individuals get status as members of the group; (3) majority decisions, sometimes meaning an edict or proclamation by one man or a ruling group, reject all rights of dissenting individuals or minority groups; (4) individuals have responsibilities to the state that are out of proportion to their rights and privileges; (5) legislative and executive functions may be dominated by the same person or group; and (6) basic freedoms of press, speech, religion, assembly, and vocational choice are restricted, if not prohibited.

World War I was regarded by many as the final struggle between authoritarianism and political freedom. Free societies appeared strengthened and new ones replaced old monarchies. But only a few years elapsed before the emergence of new systems which were to demonstrate that the centuries of struggle against authoritarianism would have to continue; that each generation will have to be on guard lest its freedom be lost.

The rise of dictatorships has a psychological basis as well as a political foundation. Specialization and automatization in modern society have increased the dependence and insecurity of the average person, who may be ready to submit to new authorities which give him security and relief from doubt.

One of the most profound examples of totalitarianism was Nazism which was an economic and political system, although the hold it had over an entire population must be understood on psychological grounds. The readiness to submit to the Nazi regime is attributed to a state of inner tiredness and resignation. Once Hitler was in power, the Nazi party "was" Germany. Opposition to it meant opposition to Germany. The natural, human fear of being alone, coupled with relative human weakness with respect to moral principles, helps any party to win the loyalty of a large sector of the population. Hitler himself stated in *Mein Kampf* that:

> Like a woman . . . who will submit to [a] strong man rather than dominate the weakling . . . the masses love the ruler rather than the

supplicant, and inwardly they are far more satisfied by a doctrine which tolerates no rival than by the grant of liberal freedom; they often feel at loss . . . with it, and even easily feel themselves deserted.[3]

While Hitler and his party maintained absolute control over the German people, these masses themselves were caught up in the potentialities of power over other nations and were driven to a passion for world domination. The alternative to totalitarianism is for the individual to unite himself with others in a loyalty to mankind and productive work.

Democracy's greatest challenge today is presented by another form of totalitarianism — Soviet Communism. Communism is revolutionary Marxism in practice, although many of the conditions Marx fought are found in Russia and China today. Marx opposed nationalism. He would have been appalled by the religious fervor felt for his doctrine. The heart of his teachings was the abolition of all class consciousness in society, which is hardly the case in communist nations today. Contrary to his philosophy—that world revolution would be initiated by the downcast workers of the highly industrialized nations—the only places where communism has grown have been the most backward, largely agrarian nations. Moreover, the workers in modern capitalistic nations have reached a higher economic, social, and political position than at any other time in history. However, that communism, as put into operation by the Soviets, has been a success, by certain criteria, cannot be denied. In 1931, Stalin stated that Russia was fifty to one hundred years behind the advanced countries. Today the Soviet Union is ranked first or second in terms of over-all strength, depending on who is doing the ranking. Ruthless and cold-blooded as communism is, it must be acknowledged as efficient and fast working. Because all resources of the nation can be harnessed to serve the state, goals can be reached rapidly through sacrifice in other areas. The gains have not been in terms of individual freedom but through giving up more and more of personal freedom to a strong centralized state.

Democracy as Synthesis

The American viewpoint is that society, made up of voluntary associations, is superior to the state. The state is the servant of society. It is called into being to protect minorities rather than to suppress them. The American system means a widespread dissemination of

---

[3]Adolpf Hitler, *Mein Kampf*, (New York: Reynal & Hitchcock, 1939), p. 56.

knowledge and development of intelligence as a method of dealing with problems of an independent people. It is the method of cooperation between education and industry, teacher and student, artist and artisan, employer and employee, statesman and citizen. A sovereign individual and a sovereign state are the objectives, but these two objectives are somewhat incompatible.

The concept of the value of each individual greatly influenced and in turn was propagated by Christianity in Western nations and has become one of the greatest motivating objectives (although not always adhered to in practice) of many free societies.

Stated in the briefest terms are the following ideals which have contributed to the American system of values:

1. Our system of government, education, and religion is based upon the objective of the human personality as being of infinite value. The individual is the single most valuable element in a democratic society. He will be regarded as an end. When the individual is regarded as a means, the society in which he finds himself is other than a democratic society.

2. The challenge to free society is to view man, not as he is, but for what he is capable of becoming. If in any aspect of religion and philosophy there is such a thing as a temporary ultimate, in contrast to one that is fixed, it is modern man. Man must be perfected, or he will perish from his own folly.

3. America stands for a state that is the servant of man. The Bill of Rights and the Constitution were designed to protect man against government, to protect minorities and individuals as well as majorities. The political and civil institutions allow the individual, in cooperation with others, full liberty toward modifying or remaking institutions and government. The machinery for implementing these liberties must be readily available and equally accessible to all.

4. Permeating every worthy social and political organization is the function of education, which increases the ability of people to regulate their own affairs. This ideal presupposes a truly liberal education which frees man from ignorance and prejudices toward competing and diametrically opposite ideological systems.

5. Fundamental to freedom are the separation of legislative and executive functions and the orderly process of law, which the legislative, executive, and judicial functions serve by the settlement of differences among men.

6. Stability and the concept of transmission of the status quo in education and in society may lead to intellectual sterility and societal fossilization characteristic of all societies immediately before their decline. There must be freedom to choose from among alternatives, a freedom limited only by moral and social responsibility. This presumes the necessity of available alternatives.

7. Democracy is both a means and an end of society. Liberalism in America is the middle-of-the-way which rejects totalitarianism on the one hand and anarchy on the other. It is the method of intelligence. It will work only to the extent that it encourages social intelligence through a process of education, at all levels, free from tyranny of government and selfish interests—an education which is so vigorous in its promotion and defense of freedom that it is irresistably and miltantly opposed to dictatorship of the right or left.

Liberalism, based upon free exercise of intelligence, is utterly incompatible with communism. The incompatibility arises from the historical fact that communism destroys freedom of inquiry and the right to differ. Hegel believed that no law can be valid without the approval of all; that the minority must yield to the majority. He made a sharp distinction between those in command and those who obey. The core of his political philosophy was obedience on the part of the masses. It is utterly incomprehensible that any intellectual who has experienced the ultimate in freedom of inquiry and expression could embrace a system which has as its foundation the destruction of both.

The state is called upon to protect the minorities against majorities in the voluntary associations of society; but under the democratic process, even the state, so conceived, is no guarantee that minority groups will be justly protected, for those who are elected, even by popular vote, to represent the people, are gifted or afflicted, as the case may be, with much the same virtues and weaknesses as are found among the electorate. Individuals generally are more concerned for private than for public objectives. It was this concern that caused the founding fathers of the American Republic to insist upon the Bill of Rights—to establish certain freedoms that are beyond the reach of government or majorities. Liberalism thus becomes the method of intelligence instead of coercion. It implies widespread cooperation and the development of social intelligence as the means of controlling the selfish nature of man. The problem becomes complicated when one acknowledges the fact that man is as selfish as he is social.

One of the most difficult problems confronting the peoples of the world is the development of intelligent, public spirited leadership so necessary in the solution of the problems of men. Leadership is needed which will be responsive and sensitive in all situations to the public good without destroying individual liberties. It is not sufficient to take a vote to determine the public interest, even through frequent accounting to the people through elections is necessary. More important than counting votes is the requirement that the voters themselves be socially sensitive and responsive to the public good when they exercise the franchise, for they, too, are public servants who need to recognize public or social gains rather than selfish aggrandizement through the ballot.

The tremendous significance of education in the solution of these problems will be discussed later. Suffice it here, however, to point out that education, when controlled by those whose motives are selfish, may be used as an instrument for destroying man's social inclinations.

Education is an effective instrument of totalitarianism, as indicated by the fact that it is the tenth point listed for the development of a communistic state. Admittedly, the educative process in a democratic community is diametrically different from the process of education in a totalitarian society.

The democratic society does not need to be hampered in its effectiveness by controversial issues, divergent viewpoints, or even private and selfish motives. It is through a fusion of all of these that society learns to operate democratically. Society, however imperfect it may be, is the product of great diversity. It is the product of intelligent change and compromise. It should thrive and become strong through change and a mixture of majority and minority viewpoints, providing the motives, purposes, and interests which give it power are derived from a social consciousness rather than from power blocks which are oblivious to larger social issues.

The end of a free society is the development of the finest human qualities possible within every individual, while at the same time helping him to identify himself and his own personal welfare with the progress of society as a whole. In other words, the maximum development of individual capacities will result in the maximum social good to society. The individual must develop increasing social sensitivity and become responsive to his own development, or else society's investment in him may fail to pay any dividends. But society is confronted with the problem of socially undesirable consequences of associations. And while the major choices of association must remain with the individual, this viewpoint does not preclude the possibility of organized control through the state.

The liberal viewpoint requires the careful cultivation of the intellectual abilities of the masses, the true basis of widespread integration of social intelligence as a means of regulating the affairs of men. The protection of the rights of minorities is basic to the survival of democracy, for democratic society is founded upon the theory and the necessity of constructive change. Change, it must be remembered, usually comes about as a result of a militant minority, not as a result of counting votes in any one election.

Nature of the State

The state may be defined as a community which is permanently established for a political end, possessing a defined territory, and independent of external control. It is obvious from the foregoing definition that the United States, and not each of the fifty states, meets the criteria of a sovereign state. The state, then, is called into being, in the words of Lincoln, ". . . to do for the people what they as individuals cannot do for themselves." The degree of organization of the public which the state attains and the degree to which the officers of the state perform their functions of caring for the public interests determine the quality of the state and the justification for its existence. The state is subordinate to society. It is an agency of society for the alleviation of conflicts between individuals and groups which preclude the normal and natural development of a voluntary, democratic system.

The State and Education. The state is a means to an end. It is man's political organization for harmonizing the consequences of the conflicting interests of individuals living together and for facilitating common tasks. If the state is an instrument for achieving and maintaining a free society, then it should engage in activities which promote social intelligence.

Education, socially organized, increases the number of experiences, interests, and purposes which people hold in common and is closely related to the development of the democratic way of life. It is necessary, therefore, for the state to support and encourage education as the only positive method by which it can achieve the objectives for which it was created.

The application of these ideas to the process of policy in higher education should be clear by now. Education is the only positive means by which a free society can be achieved and perpetuated as a dynamic response to man's needs and aspirations. Notwithstanding this accepted principle, it is doubtful whether democracy can be taught effectively as an academic subject. This poses a dilemma: Education is the sole means by which a free society is achieved and perpetuated, yet the democratic way cannot be taught. It is in the solution to this dilemma that education in a free society is differentiated from one that is not free. In the former, freedom is both a means and an end of society; in the latter, this is not true. Therefore, education which increases the shared interests, purposes, and ideas of individuals, leading to a community, must be promoted through democratic means.

The real problem of government, then, is in securing for public office men whose public interests outweigh their private interests, or men who can identify their own private interests in the over-all good of society. The state is the legal organization of society, whose chief function is the promotion of the well-being of the masses. In a democracy, the chief purpose of the state becomes the perpetuation and the improvement of the free society. The state thus conceived becomes the servant, rather than the master, of the people. It is subject to change and new emphases as the people direct.

Functions of the State. The state has two distinct methods for achieving these broad humanistic purposes. The first is a negative approach to the problem, a method which passes rules and regulations governing the relationships among men and punishes the offenders without having too much concern for their rehabilitation. The state thus conceived is likely to become the master of the people through an ever-increasing number of rules and regulations that interfere with freedom of action on the part of the masses. The promotion of a free society may seem incidental to and remote from the state's imperative necessity to maintain world peace, full employment, and general economic well-being. All sorts of schemes will be promoted to obtain for ourselves the security for which World War II was fought. Gigantic military training programs have been adopted and carried out as a basic national policy. The United States has attempted to use its great wealth and resources freely to promote world peace. The state faces a real challenge, one that calls for a positive program of action.

Military establishments, training, strategy, and force, however necessary they may be for a few years, or even permanently, can secure the peace only temporarily. Peace is not going to be ushered in through international force and negative legislation that promise only punishment for the international offender. International control can be secured through the development of common purposes, interests, and objectives on a world scale. This requires the same approach that the development of a democratic local community requires. The Marshall Plan, Point Four, the Columbo Plan, and UNESCO represent a few positive approaches to international or world consciousness. A negative approach makes unlawful the crime and punishes the offender, but it does not alleviate the roots of the trouble. The only solution for the maintenance and improvement of the free society locally as well as at the state, national, and international levels is through a democratic process of education on a universal scale, this process to be implemented by improvement in the economic, social, and political institutions and by respect for religious institutions, which are concomitants of enlightened people. This is the state's positive approach to the solution of its fundamental responsibility.

Conclusions for Higher Education

There is no exception to the use of the education function in any society, whether of the informal type engaged in by primitive families, as in Cambodia, or of the socially motivated and more formally organized type observed in the work of the Maryknoll missionaries in Puno, Peru. Every society, under the philosophy of self-determination, has the right and the responsibility to propagate its heritage—meaning culture, form of government, institutions, technological skills, family unit, religion or lack of it, and general ideological system. And every society has the right to do so without the imposition of any outside influence. It may, for example, close its intellectual doors to influences extraneous to its own objectives. It may practice intellectual isolationism, although this becomes increasingly difficult with each new conquest in media of communication, space, and time. In all cases, the above position implies and approves a degree of propaganda through education. This quality is more obvious in totalitarian societies than in those that use the democratic process. But democratic societies have used and will continue to use every means to perpetuate their system.

Legally, education is not a function of the United States; it is left to the fifty states by virtue of the Tenth Amendment to the Federal Constitution. Philosophically, the United States cannot escape its responsibility for education in these times. It may have been logical in the early history of the republic to leave education to chance; but present conditions, with the ever-increasing demand for intelligent citizenship, require national interest in and support of a minimum program of education for all the people. The issue of racial integration in the schools may yet awaken Americans to education as a national concern.

There is much debate, newspaper discussion, and jockeying on the part of political strategists today concerning the necessity and desirability of increasing the responsibilities of the state in areas of living most necessary to the peace and happiness of the masses of people. This interference on the part of the state in the private affairs of individuals is something which is distasteful to a great many people. Most efforts of the national and state governments have represented the negative aspect of the state. To be sure, many of the generous acts of the state in the alleviation of want and suffering on the part of the masses would seem to be positive state functions; but in most cases, actions tending toward "statism" are necessary precisely because neither the state nor voluntary organizations made up of individuals have had the social intelligence and the will necessary for positive action.

Far too often the same individuals and the same groups in society who oppose so-called "statism" oppose an extension or expansion of public education and oppose the two for the same reason, failing to realize that the curtailment of the latter ends in an extension of the former. Organizations and groups of individuals, including the United States Chamber of Commerce, concede the high correlation between economic well-being and the level of education attained by the masses. The absence of a high standard of education results in a high birth rate, a lack of ideas and skills, and a low standard of living, requiring intervention of governmental agencies to prevent unnecessary human suffering. Likewise, on the social front, voluntary social organizations and control among individuals and groups depend upon a very high level of education. Social control is dependent upon a high level of intelligence. The only way to maintain free enterprise, an ideal to most Americans, is through a higher standard of education which develops the maximum capacity of every individual. The absence of education results in reduced social intelligence and capacity for voluntary control. The absence of voluntary control makes it necessary for the state to step in and accept the responsibilities which the people do not accept for themselves.

It would seem that the only question to be answered in determining the advisability of providing the necessary state and national support for education is whether or not it can be free from state and national control. The very nature of education and its relationship to the individual and the community require that its control be kept as close to the people as possible. Experiences in the United States indicate that responsibility for and control of public education do not lie necessarily with the same level of government. The state certainly has the responsibility for promoting education as a means of developing the free society and of maintaining a high standard of living for the masses of people.

Legally and philosophically, each of the fifty states is in a position to assume a positive program of action because of its legal right to promote education. A state that is responsive to the people cannot be permanently and negatively static, because new associations with far-reaching consequences are continuously being formed, consequences which call for varied negative and positive approaches to protect the public. If education is made a function of the state to maintain the status quo, it will have failed to accomplish a positive good. Education, like growth, implies change. It means a reorganization of experience toward intelligent action, and, therefore, it is dangerous to free societies for the state to accept the education function in order to preserve the status quo. Our society should prosper from a high corporate intelligence.

The high level of competency on the part of individual citizens, a competency achieved through a high standard of education, results in social control of political and economic conditions of life and a balance between the material and ideal. This implies social control based upon widespread dissemination of knowledge, cultivation of the abilities of the masses, and the integration of knowledge and action in the interest of a free society. The relationships prevailing between controlling boards and administrations on the one hand and the faculty on the other will tend to prevail in the relationship between faculty and students. If democracy is to go beyond the realm of theory, it must permeate all of these relationships.

Summary

When the means of education are democratic, the ends will be compatible with the interests and the intelligently conceived needs of individuals.

The determination of policy through democratic process is significant to the total personnel, not only because it sets the dimensions of their activities and intellectual pursuits, but, more importantly, because it provides each member of the university family with an opportunity to help regulate, order, and determine his own life. These privileges, exercised with intelligent responsibility to society and to other individuals, are basic to the flourishing of ideas and intellectual activity, both of which are indispensable to the work of a university in a free society. In more practical terms, this means that all channels of communication between students and faculty on the one hand and administrators and boards of control on the other must be kept open; that faculties must be permitted to organize in ways most fitting, economical, and effective for bringing their collective intelligence to bear upon the direction in which higher education is to go; and that other groups in society, including students, must have this same prerogative. University administrators have the unique and difficult role of forming the synthesis of views and of making final recommendations to the controlling authorities for policy legislation. The problem of control from without will be the subject of another chapter.

In conclusion, it should be noted that the process of policy is akin to fundamental methods by which a free society governs itself. The process is especially significant in an educational institution which serves as a laboratory for preparing leaders for nearly all groups in society. Our frame of reference, therefore, is the full play of intelligence as the method of control and administrative action. No other rationale will suffice in a community of scholars. If the democratic process fails on the university campus, it has little chance of working elsewhere.

Questions for Discussion

1. Why is the nature of man and of society important in the development of policy for higher education?
2. What is society?
3. Why is a free society so complex in its methods of operation?
4. What are the differences in educational policy in a free society as contrasted with a totalitarian society?
5. Define the state.
6. Why does a state support education?

Bibliography

BARZUN, JACQUES. *The House of Intellect.* New York: Harper & Bros., 1959, 273 pp.
DEWEY, JOHN. *Democracy and Education.* New York: Macmillan Co.,, 1916, 434 pp.

DEWEY, JOHN. *The Public and Its Problems*. New York: Henry Holt & Co., 1927, 224 pp.

FRANKEL, CHARLES, editor. *Issues in University Education*. New York: Harper & Bros., 1959, 175 pp.

GODWIN, WILLIAM. *Enquiry Concerning Political Justice*. Toronto: University of Toronto Press, 1946.

HITLER, ADOLF. *Mein Kampf*. New York: Reynal & Hitchcock, 1939.

HOOK, SIDNEY. *Political Power and Its Personal Freedom*. New York: Criterion Books, 1959, 462 pp.

JOWETT, BENJAMIN. *Aristotle's Politics*. New York: Random House, Inc., 1943, 337 pp.

THOREAU, H. D. "Civil Disobedience," *The World's Great Thinkers: Man and the State: The Political Philosophers*. Edited by Cummins, Saxe, and Linscott, R. N. New York: Random House Inc., 1947.

VAN DOREN, CARL. *The Great Rehearsal*. New York: The Viking Press, 1948, 336 pp.

Chapter

Developing a Dynamic Educational Program

A new renaissance of infinitely greater dimensions than anything experienced by the Middle Ages is sweeping the earth, and many of the universities of the world are not even aware of it. Some of them live and have their being in the ancient past, seeking new ways to revive that past instead of applying their most intelligent efforts to give direction to the greatest revolution of all time. Population explosions, the geometric progression in the increase of knowledge, radical shifts in manpower requirements, and the birth of new nations oriented toward independence and freedom have already relegated status quo colleges and universities to obsolescence.

The Changing Economy

The United States Department of Labor predicts that the greatest percentage of increase in employment in the decade of the sixties will be in the professional and technical occupations, service workers, clerical and sales workers, proprietors, managers, and skilled and semi-skilled workers, in that order. There will be no change in the number of non-skilled workers, and there will be a decrease in the number of farmers and farm workers. Major employment opportunities during the decades ahead will be in those occupations requiring education beyond the high school.

One of the most productive agricultural states is Iowa, but that state has not escaped the revolution now going on in manpower requirements. Iowa's transition from an agricultural to a predominantly business and industrial economy has already been made. The income from business and industry in 1959 was more than double the income from agriculture. Between 1950 and 1959, Iowa's non-agricultural employment increased from 603,200 to 668,360, an increase of 10.8 per cent. The number of people living on farms declined from 754,000 to 697,000 during the ten-year period. Agricultural production increased from 2.1 billion dollars to 2.36 billion dollars, but industrial production increased from 2.5 billion dollars to 4.96 billion dollars in the ten years.

Education and training programs, and especially research activities, carefully designed for the nation's needs, can reduce unemployment. The availability of technicians and skilled workers enhances business and industrial development, which in turn increases the economic base necessary for the support of education and other social services. Full employment at any time in the future will depend upon the level and type of education completed. The professional and technical fields nationwide use 16 per cent of the work force. Although the demands in these areas will increase by 40 per cent during the sixties, these fields will still use less than 20 per cent of the total available manpower. Training in industry will continue to play an important part. It should be supplemented by a vigorous program of in-service training made available to adult groups through school programs. Research at the universities can also contribute to industrial development and employment opportunities. Departments engaged in agriculture, business, and industrial research have a great challenge—that of increasing the total resources through research, planning, and education.

The fact that workers are moving from the farm to business and industry causes a change in the type of education required. Moreover, the demands of particular occupations, including the professions, are changing constantly. Doctors, lawyers, teachers, clergymen, engineers, and farmers have experienced revolutionary changes in the nature of their work during the past fifty years. It is virtually impossible to educate an individual for a specific task. Therefore, one of the most important responsibilities of higher education is that of stimulating the individual to continue to learn all his life. This problem of change in the nature of work requires ability to adjust to new situations and new institutions, but it also requires the insight, skill, and ability to change, adjust, and control institutions, including higher education, to make them responsive to a dynamic society.

The intellectual progress of America is a direct result of our ingenuity in creating a vast technology. Every American has the equivalent of one hundred mechanical slaves at his disposal. This has given us unlimited time and resources to devote to intellectual and cultural activities. But the intellectual and the practical are inseparable. The skilled worker, the farmer, and the shop foreman, because of their increasing productive capacity, have freed the scholar to engage in research necessary for further cultural and technological progress. Specialization of these different groups and levels of workers requires the maximum development of the talents of all people if the balance is to be maintained. The real strength of America lies in the talents of the people. Education beyond the high school must be responsive to the needs of increasing numbers and groups of workers, because the demand for workers with limited education is decreasing.

Increasing Demand for Higher Education

The people of the United States want a college education for their sons and daughters, regardless of their vocational choice. They believe that higher education should prepare people to work in all areas of the economy, that it should be responsible to the needs and interests of students, and that it should be made available to all groups in the society. However, almost 70 per cent of the nation's youth go to work with a high school education or less. This creates a great need for in-service training programs to assist workers in adjusting to changing conditions. Development of the individual's talents and experiences leading to effective citizenship and productive work are in keeping with the finest traditions of American democracy, the dignity of man, and the dignity of work.

A review of research on the distribution of manpower indicates certain ratios between different levels of workers. The Vocational Education Division of the U. S. Office of Education has predicted that, by 1965, there may be ten technical specialists, five industrial technicians, and three engineering technicians for one scientist and one engineer in the labor force. This team may be supported by as many as 150 skilled craftsmen. Further industrialization of the United States demands education beyond the high school for technicians who will be needed to assist scientists and engineers.

The American people are concerned about the goals, purposes, and curricula of higher education. There is agreement on the values of the liberal arts or liberal studies. Teaching students to express their thoughts in writing and speaking, to acquire habits and skills of critical thinking, to become effective citizens, and to make intelligent decisions are recognized by people from all walks of life as objectives of a college education. Leaders in higher education should be encouraged by the fact that farmers, craftsmen, managerial groups, and sales workers, as well as professional people, agree on the value of liberal studies; and all groups should take pride in the fact that the leaders in higher education subscribe to a dynamic program in the liberal arts. The liberal arts provide about 80 per cent of the curricula for the education of teachers and form the foundation for all other professional groups.

The attitudes of all groups indicate that the liberal arts are in a strong position in higher education. The arts and sciences of man are not static; they are vibrant and dynamic, unless the force of ideas is lost in an unimaginative process of transmission. The development of the mind rather than the pedantic informing of the mind is the principal criterion of a liberal education. Leaders in higher education believe that curricular revision is second only to finance as a problem in higher education. Faculties and academic administrators in the colleges and universities should revise and reform the liberal arts as the foundation of all higher education adapted to present and future needs of individuals and society. Failure to meet this challenge is almost certain to result in loss of academic authority and responsibility for the curriculum.

Citizens Know What They Want

Research has demonstrated that liberal education would not be threatened even if policy were developed by typical citizens. In a statewide survey of higher education in Iowa in 1960,[1] responses were secured from 3,652 Iowa citizens on policies and programs of higher education. A stratified sample of workers from the following groups was used in the study: professional workers, farmers and farm managers, managers in business and industry, clerical workers, sales workers, craftsmen, directors of agricultural extension, leaders in business and industry, and leaders in the public schools and higher education. The nine groups were asked to evaluate a selected list of objectives of higher education. On the basis of weighted means, the responses were tabulated by group and by total responses. Five goals of higher education in the order of their appeal to the 3,652 respondents were as follows:

---

[1]Raymond C. Gibson, *Resources and Needs for Higher Education in Iowa—1960-1970*, Legislative Research Bureau, Des Moines, Iowa, 1960, p. 19.

1. Learning to express one's thoughts effectively in writing and speaking.
2. Acquiring and using the skills and habits of critical thinking.
3. Developing skill in active, responsible, and effective citizenship.
4. Understanding and enjoying the arts and sciences of man.
5. Preparing oneself for a satisfying home and family life.

With one exception, the nine groups rated "effectiveness in expressing one's thoughts in writing and speaking" and "acquiring and using the skills and habits of critical thinking" as the most important goals, in that order. The one exception was that leaders in education placed critical thinking first, and effectiveness in writing and speaking second.

These same nine groups agreed that the most important emphasis for Iowa colleges and universities was a combination of courses leading to effective citizenship and satisfactory work, rather than education for an elite or than an exclusive liberal arts emphasis. The Iowa survey revealed interesting conclusions concerning the education of various groups of workers.

Education of Craftsmen. This category of workers included foremen, watchmakers, radio and television repairmen, opticians, toolmakers, printers, lithographers, mechanics, machinists, jewelers, and electricians. The 115,274 craftsmen in Iowa in 1960 made up the largest group of workers in the state next to farmers and farm managers. The sample included in this study numbered 352, of whom 98 per cent were men. The education required of these craftsmen ranged from less than high school graduation to four years of college work, with few required to have graduate work. Three months of apprenticeship training was usually required. The educational level completed by craftsmen is typically high school graduation, with a considerable number having attended college.

The craftsman believes he needs skills and abilities to work under stress, to accept supervision and criticism, to work with people, to follow instructions, and to make decisions. He needs skills in the use of his hands; in coordinating eyes, hands, and feet; in observing differences in form and shape; and in operating machines and tools. He believes that additional education would help toward his success and that high school helped his citizenship more than his ability to work. He regards on-the-job, journeyman, and apprenticeship training as very helpful.

The Education of Sales Workers. Iowa had 70,945 sales workers in 1960. The 270 such workers in the sample studied included advertising agents, realtors, sales clerks, salesmen, and brokers, 82 per cent of whom were male.

The typical education required and completed for employment was high school graduation, the most important secondary school courses being the commercial and business, general, and college preparatory. Seventy-six workers noted that some college work, ranging from one year to graduate work was required, and 146 workers had attended college from one year to the completion of some graduate work. The most important courses in college were business or commerce; science, literature, and the arts; and professional courses.

The sales worker regards it as very important to be able to work with people, to influence the opinions and judgments of people, to adjust to various kinds of situations, to work under stress, and to accept supervision and criticism. Speaking and conversing with people, using simple arithmetic, keeping accurate records, making intelligent decisions, following instruction, and making plans and following them through are very important. The sales worker believes that his high school preparation was important in developing habits and appreciations, personal qualities, and effective citizenship. The most important goals of a college education are those of expressing one's thoughts in writing and speaking; being active, responsible, and effective as a citizen; understanding and enjoying the arts and sciences of man; preparing for home and family life; and learning to use leisure time, in that order of importance.

The Education of Clerical and Kindred Workers. Of the 98,321 clerical workers in Iowa in 1960, 355 were included in the sample studied. The sample included attendants in physicians' offices, bank tellers, typists, bookkeepers, cashiers, and secretaries. Eighty per cent were female.

A typical clerical worker has completed a secondary education, as very few clerical positions require less than high school graduation. Commercial or business education was by far the most important influence at the secondary school level, the general course and college preparatory being second and third. Only 33 of the respondents indicated that college preparation was required in their positions, but 120 out of 350 respondents indicated the completion of from one year of college work to some graduate study. The major courses of study followed in college were business and commerce; professional; and science, literature, and the arts.

Clerical workers regard the following abilities and skills as very important: ability to work with people, to accept supervision and criticism, to work under stress, to do repetitious tasks skillfully—using hands easily and coordinating eyes, hands, and fingers, keeping accurate records, following written or oral instruction, making intelligent decisions, and using simple arithmetic.

The clerical worker believes that his high school education was important in the development of personal qualities, habits, and appreciations necessary for wholesome living and for success in his work. At the college level, he favors the combination of courses leading to effective citizenship and satisfactory work. He regards it as more important to offer technical education at the secondary level than at the college level.

Education of Managers, Officials, and Proprietors. In 1960, there were 84,045 individuals in this classification in Iowa, of whom 502 were included in this sample. They were buyers, store managers, restaurant managers, railroad conductors, city officials, federal officials, credit managers, hotel managers, wholesale managers, county officials, and state officials. Ninety per cent of them were male.

Education required for employment was generally high school graduation. The high school courses which they believe to have had the greatest influence were the college preparatory, general, and commercial or business courses. A requirement ranging from one year of college work to some graduate study was indicated by 189 individuals. Of the total respondents, 292 indicated the completion of from one year of college to a certain amount of graduate study. Major courses of study followed in college were business or commerce, professional, and liberal arts.

Managers regard the following abilities and skills as very important: to work with people, to work under stress, to accept supervision and criticism, to adjust to variety and change, to influence the opinions and judgments of others, to make intelligent decisions, to speak and converse with people, to use simple arithmetic, to keep accurate records, to supervise other people, to follow written and oral instructions, and to make plans and follow them through.

Education of Farm Owners and Farm Managers. There were 199,718 farmers and farm managers in Iowa in 1960. Included in the sample for this study were 155 farm owners and farm managers. Thirty-three indicated high school graduation as a requirement for their work; 11 indicated from one to four years of college work; 40 indicated college graduation; and two indicated graduate work as necessary. These requirements follow closely the actual education level completed by the group, 85 out of 138 having attended college from one to more than four years, and 49 having graduated from college. On the high school level, the most significant courses were: the general course, agriculture, college preparatory, and commercial or business, in that order.

Abilities and skills regarded as of great importance by this group were: the ability to adjust to variety and change, to work under stress, to do repetitive tasks, to work in isolation, and to work with people; skill to use the hands, to read various kinds of materials, to use simple arithmetic, to keep accurate records, to make intelligent decisions, and to make plans and follow them through were also named.

Farm owners and managers believe that a college education should meet the needs and interests of the students and prepare them for the professions and for cultural development. They regard a college education as important for their sons and daughters, regardless of vocational choice. They believe that colleges should contribute to good citizenships and to effective work.

Education of Professional, Technical, and Kindred Workers. Iowa had 66,125 professional, technical, and kindred workers in 1960. The sample for this study included 430 accountants, chemists, draftsmen optometrists, surveyors, architects, dietitians, nurses, and photographers, 75 per cent of whom were male. Educational requirements for employment were college graduation, with considerable emphasis upon graduate study, and this paralleled the level of education completed. College preparatory was the dominant high school course; professional and liberal arts courses were dominant on the college level. Present college curricula provide extensive educational opportunities for professional workers.

The professional worker stressed abilities to work with people, to influence opinions and judgments of people, to work under stress and in isolation, to accept criticism and supervision, to speak and converse with people, to make and follow plans, to follow instructions, to use research in solving problems, to supervise people, to make intelligent decisions, to keep accurate records, to use simple arithmetic, and to read various kinds of materials. He believes college work should fit the needs and interests of students and that it should help farm youth to adjust to the shift to business and industry. He believes college work is important to success in life, and that it is desirable for his son or daughter regardless of vocational choice. He believes that college should prepare students to work in business, industry, and government, and that technical and communication skills should be taught to adult workers.

A Message from 1,577 Iowa Leaders in Business, Industry, Agriculture, and Education. Among the leaders in business, industry, agriculture, and education in Iowa, 1,577 were asked the same questions about higher education, and were in agreement on the following conclusions:

1. The great liberal arts heritage is the foundation of all education beyond the high school. All college students should learn to express their ideas in writing and speaking. They should develop skills and habits of critical thinking. They should learn to be active, effective citizens.

2. Higher education should prepare students to work in industry, business, and government. It should be responsive to the needs and interests of students, and should emphasize cultural development. It should prepare individuals for productive work in the professions and in other white-collar jobs.

3. In-service training opportunities should be made available to adult citizens to help them in their work and to give them the opportunity for cultural improvement.

4. Higher education is closely related to success in life, and it is very important for our sons and daughters regardless of their vocational choice.

5. The most critical problems confronting Iowa's colleges and universities are shortages of finance, lack of facilities, and shortage of highly qualified faculties. But lack of guidance and counseling at the secondary school level creates a serious problem for higher education. There is a need to clarify the philosophy, goals, objectives, and curricula of higher education.

Citizen responses such as these should strengthen the hands of boards of trustees, legislatures, and faculties in meeting the demands for higher education. Informed citizens must be involved in the development of public policy for higher education.

Existing Curricula in Higher Education

The present curricula of colleges and universities are related closely to the preparation of professional and technical employees. These groups include only 16 per cent of the total workers in the United States. Present college curricula are functionally inadequate for 84 per cent of the nation's workers. It is realized, of course, that a liberal arts education can be valuable to any citizen, but emphasis in the secondary schools has not recognized the need for vocational education. Junior colleges, with few exceptions, have a liberal arts emphasis. Private colleges are strong in the liberal arts and are likely to continue in that direction. Public policy governing higher education must recognize the educational and vocational aspirations of all students who attend college in the decade of the sixties.

The research on higher education in Iowa does not imply that higher education should be all things to all people. It does raise important questions which leaders in colleges and universities cannot ignore except at the risk of abdicating their leadership. What shall be the policy on curricula as enrollments increase in terms of the percentage of college age youth attending college and as the actual number of jobs requiring only manual skills decreases? What should policy be with respect to new types of institutions with bold new approaches to curricula and degrees? Should the United States program of higher education continue to be responsive to change only when prodded by national emergencies? These and other questions demand a fresh look, new insight, and coordinated planning among all leaders in higher education.

Types of Institutions Needed for the Future

Liberal Arts Colleges. We need the resources of all private and state colleges to meet the demand for higher education in the decades ahead. The liberal arts tradition will probably continue to dominate private college curricula. Citizens should approve and applaud this great resource, provided the purposes, content, and methodology of learning are subjected to constant critical inquiry. Dynamic leadership and faculty responsiveness to the large increase in knowledge will be necessary to maintain the great liberal arts image. The explosion of knowledge demands more attention to the selection of content than ever before in history. This will be the greatest challenge to leaders in academic affairs.

State Institutions. State institutions must flourish. This is necessary in all aspects of the liberal arts, graduate study, and in the preparation of people for the professions. It is crucial in research and in public service. Unless the state institutions are permitted to develop to their greatest potential, even to the point of wholesome competition, many states will be confronted with an educational catastrophe before 1975.

Teachers colleges should become multi-purpose state colleges, with major emphasis upon the preparation of teachers and administrators for the public schools. Expansion into other areas as regional colleges should be based upon research regarding regional needs. This will, of necessity, duplicate many curricula in state universities and in the private colleges and universities. Duplication is not necessarily more costly where enrollments are as large as they will be in most public institutions. The total enterprise of higher education must be mobilized to maximum capacity to meet the demands of the sixties.

Regional Community Colleges. Community college programs will continue to develop and should be based upon certain obvious facts gleaned from a study of trends in education and work in the nation. Approximately 70 per cent of the youth of the nation goes to work with a high school education or less. About 90 per cent goes to work with less than a four-year college degree.

In strictly agricultural communities, it is possible for young people to learn necessary vocational skills from their parents. For this reason, farmers generally have been slow to recognize the vocational value of formal education. However, there are no isolated agricultural communities any longer, and thousands of workers leave the farm each year to seek employment in business and industry. There can be no more difficult social, economic, and personal adjustment for a young person with inadequate educational preparation than to move from a farm to an urban center to work and live.

In all cases, competent workers at all levels, in the technical and professional fields, will have to continue to learn during the rest of their lives. In-service education and training programs will become increasingly necessary as industry and business respond to new challenges, new products, and new procedures, and as the nature of work is adjusted to a technological society.

Senior colleges and universities will continue to be challenged by the increasing demand for liberal and professional education. The demand for professional and technical workers will increase at a more rapid pace than for any other groups during the decade of the sixties. Moreover, every indication points to a greater usefulness for the liberally educated citizen in American society. A liberal education, drawing upon the social sciences, the sciences, and the humanities for the development of an integrated person, will become even more functional in American society. This should be the distinguishing consequence of a society that provides increasing freedom from the drudgery of manual work. The liberal arts, conceived originally for free men, meaning men of leisure, have served well a nation where all men were progressing toward freedom and where all men worked. The challenge of those who will guide the destiny of higher education during the next century will be to make the liberal arts function for free men everywhere.

Trends in college enrollments and in the demands for higher standards of education for increasing numbers and percentages of workers point to the need for greatly expanded educational opportunities beyond the high school. Most workers will need something less than a bachelor's degree. Less than 10 per cent of college-age youth attain the bachelor's degree. The educational demand is for a balance between general education—for cultural development and effective citizenship, and technical education—to prepare individuals for work. There is a serious gap in education beyond the high school, one that needs to be bridged by the comprehensive community college. State legislatures and school authorities have a grave responsibility to launch a unique program suited to future conditions.

Suggested Scheme for Community Colleges

1. State legislatures should authorize the establishment of regional community colleges wherever studies indicate a potential enrollment of five-hundred students within commuting distance of the colleges, especially in communities where no public higher education is available.

2. The three major objectives of the community college should be: (a) general education for effective citizenship and for possible transfer to senior colleges; (b) in-service general and technical education for adult workers in the region; and (c) terminal, general, and technical education leading to an associate in arts or an associate in science degree upon the completion of two years of study beyond the high school.

3. Local authority for the community college should reside in a community college board composed of seven members elected by the voters of the region. Board members should be elected for seven-year terms, one member to be elected each year.

4. The community college board should have the authority and responsibility for determining local policy; for levying a community college tax within the limitations prescribed by the legislature; and for employing personnel to operate the college.

5. The tuition rate should be the same as for in-state institutions, and the local region and state legislature should share the remainder of the costs, both for operations and building construction, with the state's contribution varying in terms of the local region's ability to pay.

6. State-wide policy, planning, organization, and coordination for the community colleges should be the responsibility of the State Board of Public Instruction and the State Department of Public Instruction.

7. There should be an advisory Community College Commission composed of the State Superintendent of Public Instruction as chairman and representatives of the state colleges, universities, and private colleges. The purpose of the Commission would be to maintain close liaison among all segments of higher education.

8. There should be a director of a Community College Division in the State Department of Public Instruction, and he should serve as executive secretary to the Community College Commission. He would have the responsibility for assisting local regions in planning, organizing, and improving community college programs.

The community college program should increase senior college enrollments in both state and private colleges and universities.

Summary

Developing a dynamic educational program responsive to the needs of a changing society can be accelerated through the use of citizen groups combined with professional leadership within higher education. Changing manpower requirements, occupational and social mobility of workers, and the sharp increase in college enrollments from all strata of society demand new approaches to curricula and programs of education beyond the high school. The academic community will either meet this challenge or the citizens in one state after another will take the initiative in making the necessary changes.

America is at the center of the revolutionary renaissance that is sweeping the earth, but we are not the only nation that is confronted with burgeoning college enrollments. In all of the new nations from Africa to Korea, there is fresh hope for freedom based upon the possibility of a college education. And students are not being denied in the old countries of the West. In Great Britain, France, Germany, Italy, in fact, all European countries and in the communist block of nations, higher education has become synonymous with power; enrollments are increasing; and opportunities for education are threatening old class structures.

Mechanical energy has virtually relieved man of all drudgery in the United States. The equivalent of one hundred mechanical slaves for every person in the nation, according to the Twentieth Century Fund, has removed all limitations upon opportunities for advanced education, save ability and motivation. This phenomenon has grave significance for the type, quality, and quantity of advanced education. The concept of the free man in a free society has expanded by an incomprehensible geometric progression since the Middle Ages. The program of higher education must be designed to meet this new challenge.

Questions for Discussion

1. Contrast the conditions that gave rise to the Land Grant Colleges with present conditions. Is there a need for a further liberalization of opportunities for higher education? Why?
2. What are the principal sources of America's strength?
3. In what ways should ordinary citizens participate in developing educational policy?
4. How can the liberal arts be made more dynamic in American society?
5. What is the meaning of a liberal education?
6. How does general education differ from a liberal education?

Bibliography

American Council on Education, Committee on Education beyond the High School, *Strength to Meet Our National Need.* Washington, D.C.: A.C.E., 1956.

BOGUE, JESSE P. *The Community College.* New York: McGraw-Hill Book Co., Inc., 1950.

BRAMELD, THEODORE B. H. *Cultural Foundations of Education.* New York: Harper & Bros., 1957. 330 pp.

BROWNSTEIN, SAMUEL C. *College Bound; Planning for College.* Great Neck, New York: Barron's Educational Series, 1957. 214 pp.

CURTI, MERLE, AND CARSTENSEN, VERNON. *The University of Wisconsin, 1848-1925.* University of Wisconsin Press, 1949.

DEVANE, WILLIAM CLYDE. *The American University in the Twentieth Century.* Baton Rouge: Louisiana State University Press, 1957.

DIEKHOFF, JOHN SIEMON. *Domain of the Faculty in Our Expanding Colleges.* New York: Harper & Bros., 1956. 204 pp.

EHLERS, HENRY, (ed.). *Crucial Issues in Education.* New York: Henry Holt and Co., 1955. 277 pp., LB7-.E33.

FOWLKES, JOHN GUY, Editor. *Higher Education for American Society.* Madison: The University of Wisconsin Press, 1949. 427 pp., LB2301-.N22.

GIBSON, RAYMOND C. *Resources and Needs for Higher Education in Iowa— 1960-1970.* Legislative Research Bureau, Des Moines, Iowa, 1960.

GREENE, THEODORE. *Liberal Education Reconsidered.* Cambridge: Harvard University Press, 1954. 46 pp., LC1011-.G8.

GRISWOLD, A. WHITNEY. *Essays on Education.* New Haven, Connecticut: Yale University Press, 1954. 164 pp., LD6330-.A5.

HAVEMANN, ERNEST AND WEST, PATRICIA S. *They Went to College; The College Graduate in America Today.* New York: Harcourt, Brace, 1952. 277 pp.

HAWES, RAYMOND F., (ed.). *Higher Education and the Society It Serves.* American Council on Education, 1957.

HOFSTADTER, RICHARD AND HARDY, C. DEWITT. *The Development and Scope of Higher Education in the United States.* New York: Columbia University Press, 1952. 254 pp.

HOLLINSHEAD, BYRON S. *Who Should Go To College,* New York: Columbia University Press, For the Commission on Financing Higher Education, 1952. 190 pp., LB2351-.H7.

HUTCHINS, ROBERT MAYNARD. *The Higher Learning in America.* New Haven: Yale University Press, 1936. 119 pp., LB2321-.H85.

Chapter

Organizational Synthesis

Analysis of the Problem

Organization and leadership in higher education are means toward the realization of educational objectives. The objectives of education distinguish educational administration from public administration and from business management. Legal or governmental regulations on the one hand and the profit motive on the other are less valid where the development of human creative talents is the motive. Our society has very appropriately exempted education from political and business criteria of administration. Executive orders, characteristic of government and the military services, and business criteria of profits and losses do not apply where masters and scholars are organized for the purpose of increasing the power to think and to create.

The individual operating in a free society must accept responsibilities that are in keeping with maximum freedom. Freedom and responsibility must be in balance, or else executive orders are likely to replace the informal interacting play of ideas, regulations, and policies self-imposed by the members of a college or university organization.

Values are sometimes compromised by the complex framework of social action imposed by the technological era, whether it be in government, business, or university organization. The woman who works on the assembly line of a modern electronics plant has little understanding of the complex operation and purpose of the organization which she serves. Likewise, a student in a large university may be completely over-whelmed by the myriad lines of organization and power structure which guide student life. The chances are that these problems will become more complex as university organizations become larger.

The key problem is to find a way to establish a framework for college and university administration in increasingly complex institutions without separating centralized planning and authority from educational activities. The design for the organization of college and university administration must place a new emphasis on the role of the student in the academic and organizational life of the university. In this role, the individual student, in spite of the organizational complexities of a modern university, becomes the center of control. He is able to determine and effect the outcomes, growth, and consequences of higher education. Administration then becomes a service function for the implementation of this process and never a primary consideration.

The Emerging Nature of Higher Education. Without education in its broadest aspects, each generation would be required to start from primitive conditions to create its own society and human institutions, which would end with the passing of the individuals who created them. Individuals and human institutions, therefore, exist not only as a result of education but, more accurately, through the process of education.

The tremendous changes wrought by science and technology have placed upon education the greatest task that any human institution has ever assumed. The ongoing life of the human race depends upon the conscious transmission of the values, skills, ideals, and purposes from older to younger members of human society. The gap between the young and the adult has been accentuated in proportion to the progress of science and social institutions. The task of transmission is one that is achieved just as significantly in the incidental activities of education as in the formal. Thus, education, broadly conceived, consists of all of the experiences in and out of school which contribute to the renewal and further refinement of intellectual, social, economic, political, and technical achievements of individuals and society.

In simple agrarian societies, the need for formal organization to guarantee the necessary transmission of the heritage of the race was not acute. When the traditional modes of communication and transportation were circumscribed by fear of social interaction between individuals, there was no need for education to promote common purposes and interests on a national or international scale. Likewise, the responsibility for the development of vocational competencies in the pre-industrial societies was assumed very largely by the older members of each individual family. In such societies, the tendency to follow in the vocational pattern established by the father was much more pronounced, and the tendency for daughters to secure their vocational competencies from their mothers was an accepted tradition. The development of a highly technical society with its attendant specialization and interdependence of individuals has made necessary an entirely different kind of general, as well as specific, technical education for all the specialized occupations so characteristic of modern society.

Broadly and intelligently conceived, therefore, the task of education today is to bring to the world common purposes, interests, objectives, values, skills, and ideals that will make possible voluntary control of the peoples and nations of the world in the interest of an objective that is greater than any nation or any group of individuals—the objective of humanity itself. It is the function of education not only to teach men the values of voluntary cooperation, but to teach them the necessity for institutions and governments at the local, state, national, and international levels to do for people what they as individuals or nations cannot do for themselves, and to increase the capacity of individuals to act for themselves.

The concept of equal educational opportunity incorporates the new discoveries in the field of psychology which indicate that even intelligence is not a static quality in human personality. Intelligence may be changed through the improvement of the environment and early childhood educational opportunities. The advantages of the total environmental influence are significant. They preclude the possibility of education completely divorced from the activities, purposes, and interests which motivate individuals in a society that is functioning in terms of changing institutions as well as people.

The past century has ushered in the most phenomenal progress of science and technology ever witnessed by any people in a similar length of time in the history of man. One man can now do the work of ten, with better health, longer life, and richer experiences than in previous centuries. The control of science and the products of science for the development of better human beings in a better environment constitutes a soul-searching challenge to those who are charged with responsibility for education. Social progress in human relations and government, ability to maintain the peace, and ability to get along with one's neighbors in a world community have lagged far behind progress in science and technology.

The Function of Specialization. Advances in communication and transportation, and development in cooperation and specialization have made it possible for individuals to pursue for a lifetime their own individual interests without concern for the production of the goods and services necessary for existence. Specialization is a necessary aspect of modern society.

The most phenomenal public enterprises in the United States are voluntary cooperative ventures. The development of these voluntary cooperative enterprises is synonymous with the age of specialization. The interdependence of individuals within society and the resultant voluntary cooperation among individuals and groups in providing goods and services with a minimum of government interference represent a society functioning at a very high level and utilizing to the fullest extent the intellectual resources of its component members.

Life in the rural areas of America presents a sharp contrast to what it was at the turn of the century or even in 1935. In many rural communities, prior to the first World War, families were practically self-sufficient. Most of the food was grown on the farm, and enough quantities were conserved for the winter months. The basic foods such as milk, butter, eggs, bread, meat, potatoes, fruits, and vegetables were products of the farmer's own labor.

A new industrial revolution has taken place on the American farm since the first World War. The impact of technology upon farming has changed completely the lives of rural people in America. Mechanization of agriculture through the tractor, combine, corn picker, cotton picker, four-row cultivator, and other specialized farm machinery has made farming a highly skilled profession and has created a more highly interdependent society that includes the farmer. The automobile, rural electrification with all of its attendant conveniences, and better rural schools have brought to the farmer many of the advantages avaliable only to urban and city dwellers prior to the industrialization of farming.

Agricultural research, experimentation, extension programs, and veterinary medicine are as indispensable to the production of farm animals and crops today as the medical profession is to the maintenance of high-level health among the individuals in the community. Improvement in the breeding of livestock and the development of hybrid and disease-resisting seeds have made farming profitable to the farmer who is in a position to take advantage of these technological advances. Likewise, the inoculation of livestock against diseases and the treatment of isolated diseases among animals are necessary and profitable specialized services which education and research have brought to the service of rural America.

Industry, even before the revolution in agriculture, had ceased to be static, simple, or easy. It is extremely technical. Productive capacity, through highly technical farming and mechanized industry, is a result of the discoveries in engineering, physics, mathematics, chemistry, agriculture, and personnel management.

This mechanization of American industry and agriculture, which has made it possible to transfer the major burden of labor from man to the machines, has great significance for, and offers a challenge to, leaders in education. A very high percentage of all energy produced and employed in the United States today is mechanized, rather than human, energy. The ratio of mechanical to human energy was 99.1 to .9 in 1955.[1] The utilization of machinery as a source of energy is a characteristic of the most advanced societies; the most backward communities in the world are those in which the major sources of energy are human beings rather than machines. Every person in the United States has the equivalent of nearly one hundred mechanical slaves working for him. The meaning of these figures for education is incomprehensible, for the nature of man's work is changing radically his opportunities and his need for education.

Industrialization of society, with the accompanying leisure-time opportunities for individuals, has great significance for the development of a program of general education designed to preserve and to improve a technological society. Specialization in all phases of learning is also increasing. The need for specialists in chemistry, physics, botany, zoology, engineering, mathematics, bacteriology, geology, medicine, and agriculture to maintain the industrial machine is obvious. In every phase of the sciences, individuals with superior ability should be permitted to pursue their specialized fields to the maximum of their abilities.

Specialization in personnel administration is likewise indispensable to the continued operation of the industrial machine. Scientific management is as much a part of present industrial society as are the physical, natural, and social sciences which have produced that society. The maintenance of desirable relationships between management and labor requires a more scientific approach to the problem of management. The social studies, humanities, anthropology, sociology, psychology, and phi-

---

[1] J. Frederic Dewhurst, and associates, *America's Needs and Resources,* (New York: The Twentieth Century Fund, 1955), p. 908.

losophy will play an increasingly significant role in the development of a true science of human engineering.

Specialization is necessary to satisfy the personnel demands of industry and agriculture but is even more pronounced in the medical sciences, law, ministry, teaching, and in all phases of the sciences, social studies, and humanities. Opportunities for research and specialization in the social studies must be made available in order to develop social sensitiveness and responsiveness which will change the behavior of individuals in an interdependent society. In a liberal context, all specialized education is vocational. Even the traditional liberal arts were vocational in the cultural context in which they originated, because they served as curricula for professional education.

The inclusion of vocational education at the college level is based upon the elimination of the dichotomy between mind and body, labor and leisure, theory and practice, vocational and cultural, and material and ideal. Antipathy toward vocational education is based upon a philosophical premise as antiquated as those societies in which vocational competence was the sole responsibility of the individual. This dualism between the practical and the so-called academically respectable or cultural subjects represents ultimate intolerance on the part of the classical scholars, who believe that education should be limited to the few and that higher education, in particular, should have no vocational objective save that of preparing for the traditional professions. The proponents of traditionalism fail to realize that their own university education represents the ultimate in specialized professional or vocational training.

If all the colleges and universities in America returned to the classical curricula suggested by many leaders in higher education, the solution to one very serious problem would be found immediately. That problem is the ever-increasing enrollment and crowded conditions in institutions of higher learning. A return to the classical curricula for all students would bring about a general exodus on the part of many of the most able and worthy university students. This would be repugnant to the democratic ideal.

A liberal education for free men in a society where all men are free implies the right of every individual to take advantage of the educational opportunities of the state in his pursuit of that vocation, profession, or business in which he has the greatest chance to succeed for himself and for society. Occupational success and effective citizenship are inseparable. Basic to fulfillment of community and citizenship responsibilities of an individual is vocational, business, or professional success. Education for vocational competency is complementary to general education in developing effective citizenship.

Intellectual sophistication which denies occupational preparation to one group but makes it available in ever-increasing quantities at state expense to other groups, particularly those engaged in teaching, research, idleness, literary callings, and managerial positions, is contrary to the concepts of a free society and utilizes education to divide men against men and groups against groups, in direct opposition to the purposes for which public education was established.

The industrialization of society and the concept of equal educational opportunity demand adequate vocational guidance and preparation. Increased leisure time, which has resulted from the shorter working day, and the difficulty of securing educational experiences from highly specialized industrial positions point to the necessity for improvement in the vocational and general education of the people.

There is no uncompromising barrier between vocational and general education, between practical and liberal, or cultural, education. The barrier, wherever it exists, is based upon the dualism between knowing and doing, mind and body, theory and practice, vocational and cultural, means and ends. Twentieth-century man must help to do the world's work. Vocational success on the part of every individual who pursues a vocation is a means to other worthy objectives.

In conclusion, it may be stated that education must be concerned with teaching men how to make a living and how to live. The former is practical and vocational; the latter is cultural. However, the two are inseparable and are mutually indispensable in the fulfillment of the individual's responsibilities to himself, his family, and society.

The Function of Public Service. The attainment of a high level of scholarship, interest in, and development of research activities on the part of a university staff offers to the region served by an institution the possibilities of a myriad of services. If education is to function among adults as well as among younger students, great scholars and university professors cannot escape their responsibilities for interpreting and applying the results of research and scholarship in the improvement of the general welfare of all the people served by the institution.

This viewpoint would reject the idea that a university is a community of scholars apart from the public served by the institution. The support of research projects in industry, agriculture, the sciences and, more recently, in the areas of social studies and human relationships, will be in direct proportion to the services rendered by an institution of higher learning in all of these fields of human endeavor.

The university as guardian of the classical, traditional truth and as a center for research activities leading to new truths must focus its attention on the problems of men. Truth and research thus conceived transfer the emphasis from knowledge for its own sake to knowledge, research, and experiences as sources of the solutions to current problems growing out of the arts and sciences of men.

The concept of service to the community, state, and nation is one of the distinguishing qualities of higher education in the United States— a quality which we are now sharing with universities in most of the countries of the world. Economic development demands interaction between higher education and American society.

Student Participation. Students are capable of managing their own activities and affairs with a minimum of faculty supervision. The presence of faculty members at most student functions indicates faculty recognition of, and interest in, the educational worth of these activities. All such activities and organizations constitute an important part of the design of a program of higher education.

The concepts of growth, change, progress, and adjustment are among the most significant and basic postulates of the contemporary world. They provide the basis for recognition of the long, continuous growth in education so necessary for living in a modern society. There is no ultimate in the educational program, not even for adults, because the learning process must be a continuous one throughout life. Each success or failure serves but to promote additional experiences in learning. The school does not wish to promote or sanction emotional immaturity or a dependence upon others to solve every problem that arises, but it is concerned with maintaining and teaching open-mindedness and creativity so necessary to growth throughout life.

To what extent do the schools capitalize upon this desire to learn and experience as expressed through the curiosity of individuals? The answer can be found in the philosophy that determines the purposes of the particular institution or instructor. If the professor believes in conformity and uniformity, he is likely to suppress individual initiative as being detrimental to education. If this suppression doesn't take place in the earlier years of the student's education, it generally does in the middle grades, in the high schools, and in the universities. A visit to any school reveals that the number of questions being raised by children is inversely proportional to their ages.

The possibility of teaching democracy in the classroom is open to challenge, but democracy should become the way of life on every college and university campus. Students and staff alike must be permitted to engage in the processes of democracy as a basic method of education and living. The application of democratic processes in education alone is not sufficient. The individual is a product of his total environment, and the influences outside of the formal program of education are just as important in the development of a free society as anything which goes on in the classroom. Employers, administrators, and supervisors in government, industry, and education cannot escape their responsibilities for the recognition of the dignity of man and for the right of every man to help to determine the objectives and conditions of his work.

Remote idealistic objectives will not suffice in the teaching of democracy. Basic to every objective in education is that the students as well as the professors identify the means and methods with the remote objective. The democratic society will not be ushered in through a set of remote objectives that are removed from the experiences of individuals.

Totalitarian methods cannot be used successfully to teach democracy. The administrator of every institution of higher learning has a definite responsibility for keeping the means and objectives of education in harmony. The relationship that prevails between the administrator and his staff is almost certain to permeate the entire institution in all of its relationships. The administrator should set the stage for the intelligent emerging of ideas, objectives, and values from students, staff, and administrators. This is the process of intelligence which places a premium upon thinking, research, and objectivity as a basis for formation of policy rather than upon resorting to expediency and administrative direction. Society, the state, boards of regents, administrators, staff, and students have the responsibility for working militantly to keep the processes of education democratic, to keep the methods of education in harmony with the objectives.

Administration Defined. School administration is a service function for the implementation of the basic process of education. It is a service, the end result of which must be measured in terms of the effectiveness of institutional objectives. This emphasis is upon the administration of a philosophy of education rather than upon the development of a philosophy of administration. Its chief goal is desirable change in behavior or the growth of those participating in the learning process. It is concerned with the utilization of human effort, the staff of the institution, in the development of human qualities found in students.

Organization should be established in consequence of specific functions, rather than be fitted into a static theory of management. Administrative structure should contribute to the coordination of university functions. This principle is as fundamental in the small college as it is in the large institutions, for major universities with the greatest enrollment have no monopoly on compartmentalization. There are, for example, small colleges where every departmental chairman reports directly to the president; this, in general, means freedom for each department to ignore all other departments because it is impossible for the president to coordinate them.

Specialists in a university, as in industry and government, constitute a centrifugal force which causes an organization to disintegrate. The disintegration of knowledge is the objective of the specialist, but the consequences for a university can be tragic where there is no counter force to hold the institution together. This is the challenge of leadership: to bring about the integration of specialists in developing unity out of diversity.

Implementing the Administrative Organization. No administrative design, regardless of its theoretical efficiency and logical premises, provides any guarantee of a democratic and educationally sound operation. Just as the skilled labor of many workmen is required to build a house according to the architect's plans, so does administrative design require the contributions of many people in order to translate the design into educational results. The variables which cannot be anticipated in administrative organization and design are people, of whom no two are alike. An administrative design without provision for variation in terms of personalities can exist only in theory. When design becomes an ultimate from which no deviation is permitted, it becomes a dogma no longer capable of serving the unique functions of an educational program. The administrative design, philosophical premises, and purposes of education take on significance in terms of people.

The design must accept the students as they are and make provision for teaching and learning situations which eventually will bring about that kind of behavior which is most self-satisfying and socially purposeful and useful. Thus, purposes, philosophies, and administrative techniques must be sensitive, responsive, and dynamic in terms of students' needs in a particular situation. The design must vary, likewise, in terms of the institutional staff; for, although it is desirable to employ staff members for specific functions, in practical situations it becomes necessary to assign functions in terms of the capabilities of available personnel. This type of compromise is not always necessary. It is not necessary in a new situation or when vacancies are being filled.

Individual members of the staff are assigned functions and responsibilities in response to the establishment of a new policy, a new program, or a new course of study. The assignment of responsibility should be accompanied by the necessary authority for carrying out the responsibility. These two go hand in hand, and a widespread sharing of responsibilities among the staff of an institution presupposes assumption on the part of the staff of the necessary authority for the efficient performance of their responsibilities.

Significance of Communication. Indispensable to the implementation of the administrative design is a system of free communication which makes easy the flow of ideas and suggestions from the bottom to the top, as well as from the top to the bottom, in the educational hierarchy. The only way that administrators can act with intelligence in administering a program for students and staff is to know the thinking, objectives, and problems of those for whom the program is being administered. It is infinitely more important to maintain the flow of ideas from students and staff to the administrators than to try to force the dissemination of ideas from the administrator to all others involved. Every means at the disposal of the institution should be used for the two-way dissemination of ideas, problems, and thinking. The radio, the school newspaper, telephones, committee meetings, faculty meetings, convocations, and all other media of communication should be used to implement the achievement of educational objectives and to make more intelligent the decisions with regard to general policy and administrative procedure.

Administrative decisions usually involve the exercise of judgment. Sound judgment depends upon knowing the facts, possessing the necessary discriminating taste and attitudes for making right choices, and having the courage to make correct choices regardless of the consequences. Widespread participation of the staff in keeping the administration informed concerning the objectives, desires, and interests of those who are working at the operational level is equally necessary in the rendition of sound judgments on the part of the administrator. It is incumbent upon administrators of an institution to see the program as a whole. They must be convinced that an institution is greater than the sum of its parts and greater than any one individual or than all of the individuals connected with it. This attitude is necessary in order to be objective in making administrative decisions, which, to be educationally sound, must be based upon ideas, facts, values, and the spirit of service which are in harmony with the general educational objectives of the institution. Communication, then, is basic to the rendering of intelligent decisions.

Summary of Functions. Functions of modern universities are generally grouped under three categories: instruction, research, and service. These functions are nearly always competitive in terms of budget, personnel and general status. A discussion of the nature and significance of each will appear in a later chapter, but the three functions are enumerated here in order to provide a basis for discussion of internal organization and synthesis.

There are few, if any, precedents for internal university organization by the three broad functions indicated. At the end of this chapter will be found an organizational chart based upon the three divisions of a university's program. The remainder of this chapter will be devoted to internal controls.

Internal University Administration

The management of a small college or university, like the management of a small industry, is facilitated by the close personal relationship existing between administrators, faculties, and students. Good relationships can be built up when the principal administrators know all of the staff and most of the students. In a small college of less than one thousand students, the president sometimes assumes the total central administrative responsibilities. He may have a financial clerk, an academic dean, and two or three clerical employees. The registrar, who keeps all student records, may be a professional person, and counseling and guidance are left in the hands of the faculty.

A small college requires each administrative employee to assume many different responsibilities. This is especially true of the president who employs, evaluates, and supervises the faculty; serves as the institution's public relations officer; makes the budget and presents it to the Board and to the legislative authorities; makes myriad public speeches; supervises maintenance personnel; and handles the most difficult student problems.

Central administration in large and small universities differs in degree rather than in kind. Much research is needed to classify administrative functions in higher education. Classification and delineation of functions of administration were of little consequence as long as one man was responsible for the total central administration, but classification is now indispensable to the division of work and consequent employment of specialists in a large institution. Four areas of classification are outlined in the following pages.

Academic Affairs. The first function of central administration is to provide leadership and coordination in developing the academic program. This area is generally called academic affairs. Upon visiting universities around the world, one noted that many of them have no coordination among faculties. In extreme cases, it was found that faculties could have been located in different parts of the country without any change in organization or function. But universities so completely decentralized are weak, because they are divided in their objectives and in their basic strength which lies in unity. Strength is only one reason for an integrated academic program. A great university is more than the sum of its parts or faculties, because when the faculties work together, they can achieve purposes that would be impossible to achieve if they worked as completely independent units.

The principal function of the office of academic affairs should be the improvement of university curricula and faculties toward the solution of problems in research, teaching, and service.

University administration is a service function for the implementation of learning. Its chief goal is desirable change in the behavior or growth of those participating in the learning process, including both students and professors. It is concerned with the utilization of human effort on the part of the faculties in developing human qualities found in students. This implies an institutional organism that transcends narrow faculty objectives.

Such a goal requires educational leadership at the level of the president. Since academic growth and development and the improvement of the economic, professional, and social status of the faculties are basic to the building of a great college or university, it is fundamentally sound for the president to delegate the detailed responsibilities for these functions to a dean of academic affairs or dean of faculties. Delegation of responsibility is necessary to facilitate action and normal growth, because limitations of knowledge, time, and energy dictate a certain organizational stratification. Limitations upon human capabilities, and especially upon the span of control, preclude complete centralization of executive responsibilities in a university.

University functions preclude complete decentralization to the point of relieving the president and his assistants of any responsibility. Effective central university administration is essential, not only for the total program but for strong individual faculties as well.

Student Personnel Services. The universities were founded, have grown to their present status, and exist today for students. They attest to the prestige of higher education among the people. In these times of increasing specialization when society, as well as the individual, has a need for the development of the human talents, the admission, guidance, counseling, testing, and placement of students according to their abilities and respective fields of specialization are functions that are inseparable from the basic purpose of the university. Student activities outside of formal courses likewise need to be encouraged and to receive consideration in planning physical plant development.

In general, student affairs include the administering of testing and counseling programs which determine admission to the university; supervising or counseling students who live in residence halls; maintaining academic records for all students in the university; administering assistance and loan funds; cooperating with the medical staff on problems of health; providing systematic testing programs in connection with orientation and placement of students; organizing adequate guidance services; assisting students in planning wholesome cultural, recreational, and social activities; helping students become effective leaders in managing their own organizations and activities while in the university, as valuable experiences in preparation for adult citizenship; assisting all faculties of the university in programs of academic counseling and guidance; and assisting students in securing gainful employment both while in the university and, more especially, at the time of graduation.

The magnitude and significance of these problems indicate that the administrator for student affairs should have the title of dean or vicepresident. Initially, the central office staff should be composed of specialists in counseling, psychology, and general administration, with adequate clerical personnel to maintain records and to assist with office management and appointments. If the staff is permitted to grow as the service grows, there will be fewer mistakes and greater efficiency and economy.

Business Management. One of the principal functions of central administration is that of business management. Higher education employs more than 300,000 people in the United States and has an annual budget in excess of $4 billion. This would be big business in any country, and the expenditure of a reasonable per cent of the total to guarantee efficiency and economy of operation is obviously necessary and desirable.

Business management of a university must be guided by a great purpose, and that purpose is to help create conditions favorable to learning and teaching. Business management, like all university administration, is a means to an end. Development of a strong business office is justified only because the basic objectives of the university (the education of students) can be achieved more effectively in this way.

The university should have a business manager in charge of all business affairs. His functions should include: (1) coordinating all divisions of the university in the preparation of the total budget; (2) assisting the president in presenting budgetary requests to the governing board and to the legislature; (3) providing technical information and advice on budgetary allocations to different divisions of the university; (4) making all university purchases and payrolls; (5) accounting for all university funds; (6) managing all university property, and accounting for the income therefrom; (7) maintaining and managing all university buildings and grounds; (8) assisting the officials of the university in translating the ideals, philosophy, purposes, and programs of the university into realistic costs which are intelligible to the people as well as to fiscal authorities; (9) coordinating and supervising all university construction; (10) making monthly reports to all divisions of the university on the status of their budgets and making an annual report to be published for public dissemination; (11) managing retirement funds; and (12) employing civil service personnel and establishing working relationships with all divisions of the university in supervising such personnel.

Development and Public Relations. A fourth function of central administration is the highly significant area of development and public relations, which includes university planning, development, and fund-raising; public relations, including alertness to the possibilities of interpreting the policies, objectives, and future planning of the institution; sensitivity to the varied publics, internal and external, including the alumni; and the general area of communication or public information. The latter includes supervision of all university publications and maintaining close relationships with mass media in order that the people may understand and participate in the program of the university. The entire program is designed to serve as a basis for university growth and service.

In view of the strategic demands of this central function, an appropriate title for the person responsible for these functions would be director or vice-president for public relations and development.

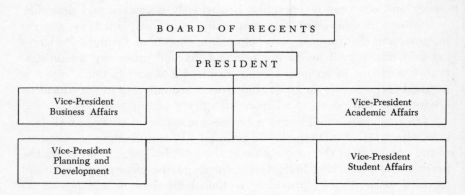

Figure 1. Internal Organization

Figure 1 presents the type of central organization characteristic of rather large universities in the United States. This represents a logical division of the heavy responsibilities centered in the presidency—a division made necessary in consequence of ·the growth in scope and size of individual institutions.

In general, this type of organization has grown from the top down, as a result of increasing administrative problems and the tendency toward

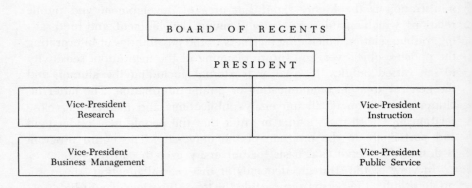

Figure 2. Functional Organization

scientific management. Specific divisions and responsibilities of the four vice-presidencies and the presidency will be the subjects of the next seven chapters of this volume.

The above scheme represents an attempt to synthesize functions and organization. It is not a radical departure from generally accepted patterns, but it does imply certain relationships not always provided for in organization. Business affairs remain the same as in the previous chart and will be developed fully in a subsequent chapter.

Research is recognized as a significant problem to be incorporated in central administration. Under existing schemes of organization, research is not integrated, and different segments or divisions of universities are engaged in both basic and applied research, involving related problems, but without any coordination. Implied in the vice-presidency for research is the possibility that this area is separate and distinct from instruction. Outstanding personnel in the two areas should have equal status, and many individuals in both should be rewarded for superior competencies.

Figure 2 recognizes the basic nature and relevance of instruction in higher education and gives it status apart from, and independent of, research. Outstanding teachers, consumers and disseminators of research, should not be penalized for excelling in one function rather than being mediocre in one and just good in the other. This does not deny the possibility of excellence in both instruction and research, but it does deny the necessity for excellence in both as a prerequisite to promotions to the higher professional ranks in an institution that regards both instruction and research as major aspects of its total program and objectives.

Another departure from the traditional pattern would be the placing of the dean of students under the vice-president for instruction, thereby recognizing the interdependence of all aspects of education of which guidance, counseling, admissions, records, and teaching are related parts, any one of which loses its effectiveness when isolated from the others. This scheme recognizes the responsibility of the total staff, including various counseling specialists, for the total educational program, including the student personnel program.

Perhaps the most challenging change in the second chart is in the area of service. There are myriad service functions, which have grown according to the degree of dynamism found in purposes and programs, impinging upon modern universities. These services include concerts and lectures, extension programs, consulting services, adult education, conferences, field services, and public relations and are related to education, health, agriculture, industry, and cultural affairs.

Under existing programs, these services are not coordinated. Almost every division of a modern university is involved in these activities. The hypothesis presented here is that these services cut across the whole university, and to be effective, they should be coordinated at the level of a vice-president.

The vice-president for service should coordinate university development, public relations, and the university press. This conclusion is based upon the hypothesis that service, public relations, and development in-

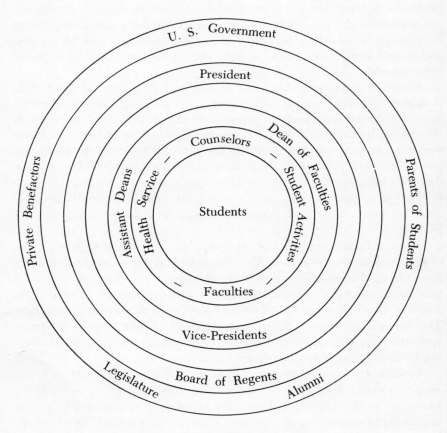

Figure 3. Educational Direction

volve a two-way process, or interaction, between those who are in the university, those who are served by the university, and those who serve and support the university.

In the third stage of organization (Figure 3) there is a greater deviation from the typical or existing schemes. The title, Educational Direction, implies two rather significant departures from tradition: that education and its direction should receive first consideration in the organization of higher education.

Ultimate direction of education (meaning growth, learning, teaching) lies with the student. He fixes the curricula, decides what he will remember and use, what habits, attitudes, and appreciations he will form, and what direction his general behavior will follow. In these decisions and growth the student will be influenced (perhaps to a greater extent than he realizes) by his total environment within and outside of the university, but the ultimate control over his education and his destiny lies with the student.

This philosophical position of placing the final decisions, outcomes, growth, and consequences of higher education upon the student is the only position compatible with adherence to free enterprise and democracy. Groups do not learn, and professors cannot learn, for the group or the individual. Only an individual can learn, and an undue emphasis upon group processes and group action may make conformists out of individuals and destroy private enterprise in education.

Now, there is nothing wrong with group process and socialization in their place; but if education is to continue to serve as a bulwark of freedom, it must be an enterprise that encourages individual initiative, distinctiveness, and integrity against slavery to the group which is the bane of anarchy and the thesis of communism.

The possibility of directing learning varies inversely with the distance from the center circle in Figure 3. Professors are closest to the students and have the greatest influence, next to the students themselves, upon learning. Next come the deans, vice-presidents, president, regents, and the outside publics, in that order. They are on the periphery of education. Even parents are in the outside circle, indicating that they are no longer in a position to determine what is learned.

Now, in the determination of policy, in the broad sense, the chart tends to reverse itself. Broad policy flows in from the society served, is sifted by the legislature, publics, regents, president, vice-presidents, deans, and faculty prior to formulation into curricula and courses, the latter being functions of the faculty because of their proximity to the students.

If one believes that those who must abide by decisions should have a part in making them, then a way must be devised to permit ideas, aspirations, and considerations of policy to move outward from the center of the circle, as well as inward from the outside. Synthesis can be achieved through this balance.

Summary

Administrative organization should reflect institutional functions, objectives, and services. It should differentiate between external and internal control, between development of policy and execution of policy. In the final analysis, it is almost impossible to divide policy and administration. This fact arises in consequence of the American determination to keep control of education close to the people, a practice that requires many policy decisions at the operational level. This is a form of strength but may not always seem efficient.

Policy and administration cannot be separated. The former is a determination of philosophy, direction, goals, and programs. Administration is the process of providing educational leadership and of activating learning and teaching. Every member of a university faculty is helping to carry out the executive function if that function is related to the basic objectives of teaching, research, and service.

Questions For Discussion

1. Contrast the role of the specialist with that of the generalist in higher education.
2. What are the functions of administration in higher education?
3. How can organizational synthesis be harmonized with necessary specialization?
4. To what extent do educational functions determine organization in institutions known to you?
5. Why should students assume increasing responsibility for their education?
6. What is the relationship between purposes and evaluation in higher education?

Bibliography

Bauer, Ronald C. *Cases in College Administration*, New York: Teachers College, Columbia University, 1955.

Britton, William E. "Objectives of Higher Education in America," *American Association of University Professors Bulletin*. 42: (June, 1956), 256-267.

BRUBACHER, JOHN S., and RUDY, WILLIS. *Higher Education in Transition.* New York: Harper Bros., 1958.

CORSON, JOHN J. *Governance of Colleges and Universities.* New York: McGraw-Hill Book Co. Inc., 1960.

CHAMBERS, MERRITT MADISON. *The Campus and the People,* Danville, Illinois: The Interstate Press, 1960.

DEWHURST, J. FREDERIC, and associates. *America's Needs and Resources.* New York: The Twentieth Century Fund, 1955.

DODDS, HAROLD W. *The Academic President—Educator or Caretaker?* New York: McGraw-Hill Book Co. Inc., 1962.

Educational Policies Commission. *Higher Education in a Decade of Decision.* Washington, D. C.: The Commission, NEA, 1957.

FOWLKES, JOHN GUY, (ed.). *Higher Education for American Society.* Madison, Wisconsin: University of Wisconsin Press, 1949.

GLENNY, LYMAN A. *Autonomy of Public Colleges; The Challenges of Coordination.* New York: McGraw-Hill Book Co. Inc., 1959.

HALL, WILLIAM WEBSTER. *The Small College Talks Back; An Intimate Appraisal.* New York: Richard R. Smith, 1951.

HUGHES, JAMES MONROE. *Human Relations in Educational Organization: A Basic Text in Personnel Administration.* New York: Harper Bros., 1957.

McCONNELL, T. R. *A General Pattern for American Public Higher Education.* New York: McGraw-Hill Book Co. Inc., 1962.

MOOS, MALCOLM, and ROURKE, FRANCIS E. *The Campus and the State.* Baltimore: Johns Hopkins Press, 1959.

RAY, GORDON N. "Conflict and Cooperation in American Higher Education," *Financing Higher Education; 1960-70,* ed. Dexter M. Keezer. New York: McGraw-Hill Book Co. Inc., 1959, pp. 103-117.

RUML, BEARDSLEY. *Memo to a College Trustee.* New York: McGraw-Hill Book Co. Inc., 1959.

STOKE, HAROLD W. *The American College President.* New York: Harper & Bros., 1959.

TEAD, ORDWAY. *Trustees, Teachers, Students: Their Role in Higher Education.* Salt Lake City: University of Utah Press, 1951.

WOODBURNE, LLOYD S. *Principles of College and University Administration.* Stanford, California: The Stanford University Press, 1958.

WRISTON, HENRY M. *Academic Procession.* New York: Columbia University Press, 1959.

Chapter

6

The Lengthened Shadow:
A Configuration

Problems of the President

The principal directions of college and university expansion since the end of the second World War have been bulging budgets, buildings, and bureaucracies. The building of increasing layers of administrators has been a natural consequence of mounting enrollments and budgets. The corresponding sagging in faculty status, a result of the decreasing economic position of college faculties, has been the rule rather than the exception during this same period. Mr. Schoenfeld[1] has noted that during the lush period following the second World War, when financial stress was so greatly relieved by the Federal Government, faculties' salaries continued to decline in relationship to the growth of the American economy.

During the post-war period there has been a shifting emphasis in higher education, a shift growing out of an increasingly unselected college population, beginning with the admission of G.I.'s on a wholesale basis, a fact which tended to convince many American families, previously without the benefit of higher education, that going to college is a good investment of time and resources.

The tendency toward universal higher education, as was the case with American secondary education, has not been accompanied by a corresponding shift in the objectives and curricula of higher education.

---

[1]Clarence A. Schoenfeld, *The University and Its Publics* (New York: Harper & Bros., 1954), 284 pp.

128

Indeed, imaginative leadership in this direction has been the exception. The one thing on which the American people seem to agree is that they do want their sons and daughters to go to college. The problem of adjusting college curricula and activities to the needs and interests of individuals entering all types of vocations and professions is a challenge to, and a responsibility of the faculties and administrators of American higher education.

Urgent need for modification of the curricula as opposed to the conservative position that the traditional liberal arts are always sufficient for university students, began to be debated with mounting convictions, if not intelligence, immediately following the launching of Sputnik I. Education as an instrument of national policy and national defense is being advocated by many of America's most responsible college administrators. This view, growing out of Russian rather than American policy, reached a crescendo of enthusiasm at the American Higher Education Conference in the spring of 1959 when President Stoke of Queen's College proclaimed that either higher education will become a principal instrument of national policy or that the Federal Government can, will, and should develop a system of higher education which will be an instrument of national policy. The whole theme of that same conference was aglow with Sputnik influence—the race against time, new perspectives, and imperatives. The tone of the conference implied that the whole profession of higher education should immediately go into orbit lest we be outdistanced by the Russians. Outdistanced in what and to what purpose was not made clear. Moreover, it is doubtful that orbiting around one of the planets is the best posture for critical thinking about American higher education for the decades ahead.

Education is an instrument of national policy, meaning almost blind nationalism, in most of the under-developed countries of the world. It is almost exclusively a result of the societies which it serves. Nations which have never experienced the Renaissance, Reformation, Industrial Revolution, or the fruits of a vibrant system of higher education devoted to dynamic and constructive change in social, economic, and political institutions, are sending their students and leaders by the thousands to study and experience the great educational experiment in which Americans have expressed such rapt confidence. They have been discovering, however, that a materialistic objective may be achieved quite as effectively, and perhaps even more so, at the point of a bayonet as at a meeting around a democratic conference table. Should America and other Western democracies abandon their great educational tradition, won through the intellectual struggles of twenty-five centuries, and make higher education a tool of political institutions or an instrument of national policy without regard to the unique functions of higher education which transcend temporary emergencies, wars, and national and international policy?

The emphasis upon buildings, budgets, and bureaucracies is rapidly converting institutions of higher learning into fund-raising organizations rather than into instruments of social, economic, and political change. It is not unusual for a private university to have as many as thirty-five people engaged in the enterprise of raising funds to support the institution. There is a great conflict going on between the development officers and the public relations directors, the principal struggle revolving around the question as to which representative is to be closest to the president. Which group is to have supervision of the other group or which group is to be subordinate are problems that have developed into one of the central power struggles within the total complex of higher education. These jurisdictional struggles for power within higher education make one question whether or not there are any central, long-range objectives which have captured the imagination, devotion, and intelligent efforts of the great bureaucratic administrative organizations now responsible for the management of American colleges and universities. The only way that this can be achieved is for both groups, and all other groups, to lose themselves in a cause that is greater than either and, indeed, greater than all of them put together. Perhaps one of the criteria of top leadership is whether or not this concept can be developed and implemented.

On the question of the problem of public relations in the management of institutions, the general secretary of the American Association of University Professors, Dr. Ralph Fuchs[2] states: "Public relations considerations are, in my view, the most serious existing obstacles to satisfactory internal functioning of colleges and universities." Other noted men have stated that the most serious problem confronting American colleges and universities is an oversupply of public relations officials.

Dr. Robert Esmond[3], in his doctoral thesis, discovered that, for a public relations officer, the most difficult group within institutions of higher learning is the faculty. A summary of the research and literature dealing with the area of public relations and faculty administrative rela-

[2]American Council on Education, *Faculty-Administration Relationships* (Washington, D. C.: The Council, 1958), p. 23.

[3]Robert Esmond, *Identification and Exploratory Analysis of the Problems of Selected College and University Public Relations Directors,* (Unpublished Doctor's thesis, School of Education, Indiana University, Bloomington, 1959).

tions leads one to believe that many groups are working at cross purposes in the area of higher education. This certainly poses one of the most difficult, if not the most important, problems facing the American college president.

These struggles for recognition on the part of subordinates of the president indicate one of the most significant problems with which any new president is confronted. They illustrate the need for intelligent decisions on the part of the president. A decision represents the weighing of alternative actions and their consequences. In many situations there is limited time for making very important decisions.

Many individuals can contribute research and facts necessary to decision making, but the final act is generally performed by one person, the individual who is held responsible for the consequences.

The most important decision that a college president makes is how he will spend his time. Hundreds of organizations and individuals get to the president through the mail, by phone, and by personal conferences. All of them are attempting to dictate to the president how he shall spend his time, and this encroachment upon his time is without any concern for the educational consequences. The president must recognize his responsibility to decide for himself how he will use his time.

It is imperative that there be a balance in the division of the president's time among academic affairs including student services, business affairs, and public relations and development.

This whole volume is oriented toward democratic administration, but strong executive leadership is completely in harmony with democratic ideas. Faculties and administrators are generally striving for representative leadership rather than for executive decisions by the faculty.

President Stoke of Queen's College[4] advances the thesis that American college presidents as a group determine to a greater extent than any other group in America what happens to higher education. This extraordinary responsibility placed upon approximately two thousand of the more than three hundred thousand academic employees of these American institutions brings to a climactic point the concept of the "university as the lengthened shadow of a great man." At a time when most traditional concepts with respect to university management are being rejected by the administrators themselves, if not by the faculties, one wonders how the professionals in administration, pleading for a profession of administration, can conscientiously maintain such wholehearted confidence in the lengthened shadow concept.

---

[4]Harold Stoke, *The American College President* (New York: Harper & Bros., 1959).

The Criteria of Leadership

In all of the difficulties, perplexities, social revolutions, and catastrophes which face American higher education in the decades immediately ahead, two criteria above everything else may be used to evaluate the effectiveness of leadership in this field. First, the American college president must be willing and able to release the creative talents of a total staff, including not only administrators but academicians as well. In the development of policy and in the implementation of policy, group judgment is possible and compatible with executive action centered in individuals. To the extent that group policy and means for the implementation of policy have been developed, individual executive action without recrimination and without friction becomes possible and desirable. To separate internal policy from executive action is to separate means and ends. Policy is a philosophical consideration of the ends of education. Administration is a means by which these ends and objectives are achieved. To separate administration and educational policy leads to an artificial dichotomy with inconsistencies in the relationship of theory and practice. If democracy is both a means and an end of American society, it is both a means and an end of American education. To proclaim faculty autonomy in the development of educational policy and divorce it from administrative action in the implementation of policy is to imply that the faculty may set the goals and objectives which guide the actions of administrators. Plato defined a slave as one whose actions are determined by goals established by another. Is anyone naïve enough to believe that American college administrators are to be enslaved by their faculties or that they should be? The development of policy is a team responsibility, and the college administrator has a right to be heard as a member of the group. Machinery for the implementation of policy, in order to bring together means and ends, should be established through group judgment. Executive action should be centered in individuals in order to conserve the time of both faculty and administration.

The professors in most of the major institutions of America are virtually bogged down in a maze of bureaucratic administrative and paper-pushing responsibilities. There are professors in American universities serving on more than one hundred different committees. The need for strengthening educational leadership by releasing the creative talents of the total staff is quite obvious. This cannot be achieved by entangling professors in a myriad of administrative responsibilities which rob them of time to carry on their more important duties. It is not the details of administration in which professors want to be involved. They do want to be involved, however, in the determination of philosophy, purposes, and programs for the achievement of the great mission of higher education.

The second criterion by which American college administrators may be evaluated is their ability to channel the creative talents of all members of their organizations into constructive endeavors greater than any segment of the university and greater than the sum of all the segments put together. Any college administrator can release the talents of his staff. It does not require administrative genius to turn people loose, but the real measure of educational leadership lies in the ability of the administrator to direct the creative talents of all members of the university and community toward goals and purposes which transcend all groups and all individuals. To do this without inhibiting the creativity of individual staff members is the challenge which the American college president must face up to in the decades ahead.

The two criteria of leadership would be incompatible in any except a free society. Ours may not have achieved that status as yet, but no temporary emergency should force us to abandon the effort in that direction.

Responsibilities and Opportunities

The selection of the president is one of the most important single responsibilities of the board of control, and custom makes it desirable and necessary to place in the president responsibility and authority for administering the policies established by the board. The college president has a dual responsibility. He is employed by the board of control which determines his responsibilities, authority, term of office, and salary. At the same time, he has the responsibility for administering the institution in the interest of the students, which calls for the utilization of the faculty and material resources to that end. This requires the fullest cooperation among all personnel involved in administrative and staff responsibilities. These responsibilities point to the same objectives—the education of students, service to the community, and research. Moreover, the president has the responsibility for the maintenance of high staff morale and cooperation necessary to the achievement of established objectives. These broad responsibilities require the delegation of authority necessary for carrying them out. The president's office is concerned with four major divisions of administrative responsibility. They are: (1) academic affairs, (2) student affairs, (3) business affairs, and (4) public relations and development.

The board of control, administrative officers, and the faculty may find it relatively easier to agree upon the ultimate objectives of the institution than to reach consensus concerning the choice of means for the realization of objectives. The most serious choice which any president is called upon to make is between the principle of democracy, so essential to the process of education, and the principle of efficiency, so attractive to administrative specialists, economy blocks, and successful businessmen who are inclined to measure institutional greatness in terms of dollars saved rather than dollars translated into educational objectives.

The principle of efficiency sometimes places a high premium upon luxuriously equipped and extravagantly staffed administrative offices, quite often at the expense of adequate academic personnel, instructional supplies, equipment, and libraries. Efficiency in this sense is an appeal to the casual observer who does not look beyond the central administrative offices. The practice, for example, of employing a disproportionately large number of administrative personnel in comparison to the number on the academic staff represents a distorted vision of the objective of education and an exalted view of the significance of administration.

Maintaining a balance between academic personnel and personnel engaged in administrative, clerical, secretarial, and maintenance responsibilities calls for restraint, discretion, superior judgment, and courage. If it is easier to establish a new Civil Service position in order to maintain a high level of administrative efficiency than it is to establish a secretarial or academic position in a department where the members of the staff are overworked to the point of inefficiency, there is either a distortion of objectives or a lack of courage on the part of the president and the deans.

The presidency is, in a real sense, an exalted position. It deserves to be so only to the extent that the incumbent uses his position of exaltation, responsibility, and leadership as an increased opportunity for service to those with whom he works. The lengthened shadow of the great man as the measure of an institution's greatness no longer suffices. If the greatness of an institution is measured in terms of human personalities, the shadow will consist of the configuration of all individuals carrying institutional responsibilites. It will include students, alumni, teachers, janitors, department heads, deans, presidents, boards of control, and citizens who give sustenance and support to the educational enterprise.

Faculty Participation in Administration. The configurated shadow referred to above suggests the possibility of widespread participation in the administrative problem of a college. This concept is based upon the inherent rights and dignity of human beings, rights which take on significance to the extent that human beings are permitted to share the responsibility for the regulation of institutions and the policies which control and limit the activities of their lives. The concept is based upon the democratic notion that members of a faculty have a capacity for regulating their own affairs. Every instructor in a classroom, with the responsibility for teaching a group of students, has a unique opportunity for exercising qualities of leadership. To protect the individual staff member in his right to pursue and teach the truth wherever it leads and, at the same time, to refuse to academic personnel the privilege and responsibility of participating in the over-all leadership responsibility for the institution is inconsistent with the stature attached to the position of professor.

The concept of faculty participation, however, implies a social sensitiveness and responsiveness in harmony with the responsibility of helping to determine policy and procedures affecting a large group of people. Members of the academic staff who are inclined to have no concern for the problems and objectives of the institution outside of their own departments are ill-equipped for the assumption of the responsibility of institutional leadership. Specialization has, in many instances, led academic people to believe that they are not qualified to provide leadership outside of their own fields of specialization. Institutional leadership, however, cuts across many departments, activities, and individual interests. The development of social sensitiveness and responsiveness on the part of the faculty implies an understanding of the broad implications, philosophy, and purposes of the entire institution. Moreover, it implies a willingness to participate in the formation of such policies and their administration in the daily lives of students and faculty.

Broad participation in the responsibilities of administration requires, on the part of every member of the staff, the recognition of various public groups on the same campus. These public groups present diversified interests among individuals within the same group and among various groups. These conflicting interests and their ultimate synthesis offer the members of the staff one of the greatest opportunities for teaching and learning in a practical democratic situation. It calls for the maximum sharing of interests among individuals within a group and among various groups on the same campus. Faculty advisers, student officers, and administrators have the responsibility for utilizing student and faculty organizations as laboratories for experiences in a free society.

It is easier to agree upon the objectives of the faculty or student organizations than to secure group consensus regarding the means for the achievement of established objectives. Fundamental differences in the philosophies of individuals teaching on the same staff, and of students, are responsible for the divergent viewpoints with respect to the means for achieving commonly accepted objectives. Without this individuality on the part of students and members of the staff, the very lifeblood of a university would be dissipated through the immediate achievement of a concurrent majority so deadening to the intellect as to make a university education practically superfluous. A university must thrive on the differences that exist among individuals, because these differences provide the stimuli for constructive and intellectual experiences of the most satisfying nature.

The privilege of the faculty for the assumption of leadership responsibilities within an institution implies a like responsibility for participation in the larger community of which the institution is a part. The professor's primary responsibility as a leader is in the classes which he teaches or in the research in which he is engaged; for the objective of educating the students or assisting them in the achievement of an education is the basic ineluctable purpose of a university. No staff member, however, can be adequate to the challenge of teaching unless he is a participating member of a larger community outside of the university. Authority for the regulation of conditions affecting one's own destiny carries corresponding responsibility for the development of a wider knowledge and sensitiveness regarding the community served by the university.

Rights of Minorities. Faculty participation in institutional leadership implies the rights of minorities as well as the desirability of different viewpoints with respect to the procedures and means which should be used in determining policy and in the administration of that policy. No freedom is quite so basic to students and members of an academic staff as the freedom to differ. This freedom to represent a minority viewpoint must prevail, not only in the classroom and among members of an academic department, but it must prevail in the relationship of the faculty to administrators as well. It may be easier for individual professors in many colleges to advocate communism than it is to differ with the top administration of those same institutions. The pursuit of truth, wherever it leads, all too frequently is limited to the classroom and laboratory.

It must apply with equal validity, seriousness of purpose, and institutional responsibility at the administrative level and in all of the relationships between administrators and the faculty.

Leadership versus Centralized Control. Centralization of administrative authority in the hands of a few or one central administrative officer in an educational institution is based upon the distorted notion of the divine rights of kings, the relationship of the slave to master, and the gradation and stratification of men by class, according to the positions which they happen to hold; or it is practiced in the name of administrative and institutional efficiency or on the theory that rules, regulations, and statutes, established by the legislature and the board of control for governing the institution, require centralization of administrative functions in the hands of a single individual.

It makes no difference which of these concepts is responsible for centralization of administrative responsibility. All of them are equally erroneous and have the same result in practice. The inevitable result is the frustration of intellectual initiative, resourcefulness, and morale of the members of the academic community. No one on a staff denies the fact that the central administrative officer has almost complete authority for the administration of the institution. Possessing the authority, however, does not preclude the possibility and desirability of decentralized administration. Over-centralization is a hazard to democracy—antidotal to education.

Centralization of authority in a single individual tends, in most cases, to produce within that individual the concept of indispensability. Authority and power become primary objectives, notwithstanding the fact that they may constitute a menace to the institution as a whole. Executives, in this case, develop the concept of superiority of rulers or leaders over those who follow. The pursuit of this idea is almost certain to result in absolute control, the suppression of minorities, and the purging of those unwilling to sacrifice their intellectual freedom for a mess of pottage.

Centralized establishment of policy and administration in an educational institution have the inevitable and unfortunate consequence of enslaving the minds of those on the faculty, if not the minds of the student body. Totalitarianism in an educational institution is more fatal than in any other situation because it is most likely to preclude the development, on the part of the individual students, of that initiative, resourcefulness, and intelligence necessary for the achievement of a free society. Centralized authority and control, as well as the image of presidential indispensability, are frequently a result of intellectual abdication on the part of subordinates of the leader.

The totalitarian concept of administration must be rejected for any educational institution. Even on the basis of the criterion of efficiency in industry and government, streamlined administrative organizations and the centralization of authority and administrative responsibility in individuals are no longer the most productive of desired results. Under constitutional government, the election of a chief executive by the people does not imply unlimited powers on the part of that executive. The legislative and judicial branches of the government, as well as the constitution and statutes, serve as safeguards against an encroachment upon the rights and privileges of the masses. Nowhere, however, is the need for the exercise of intellectual freedom, initiative, and resourcefulness more prevalent than in an educational institution, which proclaims as its major function the preparation of young people to assume with intelligence their civic responsibilities in a dynamic and free society.

Production standards of an educational institution are not quantitative; they are qualitative. The greatness of an institution is not measured in terms of the efficiency with which it produces college and university graduates but in the intellectual, cultural, civic, and economic efficiency of those produced. This is a qualitative standard. Inasmuch as these qualities can hardly be taught academically, it is incumbent upon educational authorities, and particularly upon the college president, to establish a dynamic and democratic society on the campus in order that efficiency in the processes of democracy may grow out of the experiences of students participating in a free society under competent and devoted leaders. Every student organization, for example, is as a rule assigned a faculty adviser. At no other time in life will the graduates of an institution have available to them the sympathetic counselors and advisers so characteristic of student life on a university campus. If the processes of democracy are incompatible with the effective operation of a university, they are not likely to work in any other situation.

The President as an Educator

The president of a university or college is responsible, first of all, for synthesizing the thinking and purposes of the staff and students in order to give unity of purpose to the university. The implementation of purposes, indeed the understanding of purposes which motivate the actions of students and faculty, requires a high level of scholarship on the part of the president. He must be familiar with the values, tastes, ideals, purposes, and ideas which have characterized civilization at different periods in history, but more especially the societies of current civilization. Familiarity with these great concepts carries with it the discernment of the relationship between education and the preservation and improvement of the American way of life.

The president of an institution, to fulfill his responsibilities as a leader of students and faculty, must be a student of philosophy. This does not indicate a deep and abiding absorption with metaphysical concepts, but rather, a concern for the problems and perplexities which confront men and women in society and a careful, systematic, and intelligent analysis of the role which a university can play in finding a solution to those problems. This calls for a knowledge of history and a familiarity with literature, political science, and the great philosophers; but above all, it calls for an empirical and dynamic search for originality in bringing the great intellectual resources of a university and its scholars, students, and libraries to focus upon the building of a more democratic and humane society. For every book on administration which the president reads, he should read ten in the fields of philosophy, social studies, humanities, arts, and the sciences.

Philosophy and purposes which permeate the faculty, students, and administrators of an institution are dynamic because the problems which individuals face are dynamic. Therefore, the philosophy necessary for the administrator is not fixed. It evolves in terms of the changing concepts concerning the ultimate objectives of higher education and of the changing customs and habits of the people served by the institution. Dynamic leadership on the part of an institution requires that it assume responsibility for determining the direction in which society will move. Change in social customs and mores is inevitable. Society is dynamic. The antiquated notion that an educational institution should perpetuate the society in which it happens to operate is inconsistent with the dynamics of democracy and the intellectual orientation of those who teach and learn in a modern university.

No president may anticipate unanimity with respect to philosophy and purposes. Unanimity is neither desirable nor necessary. Institutional agreement on the broad, general philosophy and objectives which justify higher education's existence is highly possible, but within the framework of this broad, general policy must lie the opportunity for students and members of the faculty to experience self-realization as individuals. This does not come about as a result of changing one's philosophy of life to conform with a deadly uniform pattern for all individuals. It is achieved through the recognition of the individuality of staff members and students and the right of each to pursue his own philosophical and educational objectives in life without censorship on the part of those who disagree.

The great leader is that individual who has the understanding, sympathy, insight, and intellectual ability to synthesize the aspirations, purposes, philosophies, ideals, and values of students, faculty, and laymen for the development of a democratic community. In the final analysis, the emerging, dynamic philosophy which determines the action of an educational institution represents a community of interests, a diversity of thinking, and different levels of achievement. The lengthened shadow of an educational institution's leadership is a configuration of many individuals—their purposes, planning, actions, and achievements. The leader's own stature is in direct proportion to his ability to synthesize the leadership qualities of all others in building an effective and integrated community of scholars devoted to the search for truth, and freedom to follow the truth wherever it may lead.

Selection of the Staff. The second great responsibility of the chief administrator is the selection of a competent staff. Administration has been defined as the selection, assignment, stimulation, guidance, and evaluation of human effort in the development of human qualities. This becomes the chief responsibility of academic administrators.

In 1946, at a dinner honoring President Frank D. Macillroy upon his retirement from the presidency of Mankato State Teachers College in Minnesota, the honored guest took advantage of the occasion to give some friendly, pertinent, and serious advice to a few men who were beginning their careers as college presidents. He suggested that the greatest contribution which any president can make to his institution is to employ outstanding academic personnel and then to give them a chance to dream and to make their dreams come true. His experiences convinced him that no president is capable of achieving worthy institutional objectives except through a competent faculty.

The employment of outstanding young men and women to teach in an institution is not sufficient. It is necessary that the president use his position of leadership in the state college, or in a private college if that happens to be the status of the institution, for achieving those personal objectives necessary for faculty welfare, morale, and effectiveness. Salaries and security of employment are closely and significantly related to these objectives. It is a generally known fact that many professors follow the teaching profession, not because of the financial remuneration which they receive, but because of the compensating experience of being a part of the success and achievement of hundreds and thousands of young men and women who have been the recipients and beneficiaries of their ideas and teaching. This is great. It is noble. It is characteristic of great teachers. It makes one proud to be a part of the teaching profession. But the theory that a vicarious sharing in the successful economic and personal achievements of one's students should compensate for an inadequate salary is indefensible in any institution, and, for the teaching profession at large, constitutes a national scandal.

The payment of salaries commensurate with the long years of preparation and experience necessary for effective university teaching will go a long way toward the building of a great faculty. It is the responsibility of the president to use his position of leadership in the community, in the state, and with the board of control to secure for the staff salaries commensurate with the high calling of university teaching.

Promotions on the salary scale should bear close relationship to the quality of the service rendered by each individual staff member. A single salary schedule which rewards mediocrity and penalizes superiority is contrary to the American system of competition and reward according to merit. There is no place for the single salary schedule where there is recognition of individual worth and dignity.

Significant as tenure, security, salary, and general conditions of employment may be, they are not sufficient for the employment, growth, development, and maximum efficiency of a great faculty. The most basic possession of any staff is intellectual freedom—that sharing in a community of scholars which welcomes and encourages minority reports, dissenting viewpoints, and moral and intellectual stability that come from a free exchange of ideas. Responsibility and integrity are the foundation of academic freedom.

Security Versus Freedom

In the middle of the nineteenth century, De Tocqueville noted the emphasis which Americans placed upon freedom and security. It was not a security, however, provided by some social agency or unit of government. It was rather a security won through and by the freedom which every individual in America enjoyed under the Constitution and the American system of government. These nineteenth century Americans believed that there could be no security except through freedom and that fredom and its intelligent exercise would lead inevitably to security.

No really great university professor who is cognizant of the processes by which free societies have evolved—and particularly of the significance of a free exchange of ideas in the establishment of society—is willing to surrender any part of his intellectual freedom (freedom to follow the truth wherever it leads) to administrators, boards of control, or anyone else.

The decision on the part of a few administrators and boards of control to require a loyalty oath of every professor because of the existence of a few crackpots on university staffs is a serious threat to all university men of integrity in the United States, a threat made more serious by the fact that the crackpot is willing to deny his membership in the Communist Party, a denial made easy by the fact that he is accustomed to misrepresenting the truth. To the professor who has embraced the truth and the thrill of eternal search for its refinement, questioning his integrity by the requirement of an oath of allegiance is a threat not only to academic freedom but to security and morale as well. No loyal American professor would regret the disappearance from the earth of the Communist Party. The experienced university man knows all too well, providing he has studied any history at all, that outlawing his right to hold membership in the Communist Party may be followed by a challenge to his freedom to belong to any party save that which is in power. However, the precedent which would be established by such action would pave the way for drastic infringement upon all political and social freedom.

It is the responsibility of the faculty, the administration, and the board of control of an institution of higher learning to maintain America's heritage of academic freedom, strengthened and sustained by civic and moral responsibility on the part of every individual who is a part of the university community. To deny the faculty responsibility and authority for the determination of policy with respect to academic freedom is to lose the basic requirement for security, staff morale, and human dignity. Real security and freedom call for the recognition on the part of the administrator of the social significance of all human effort. The administrator must see all men as important parts of the great symphony of humanity. Each one as an individual can contribute very little to society, but all working together and recognizing the interdependence and interrelationships that exist are entitled to that dignity and respectability commensurate with the status of a human being.

Interpretation of the Institution to the Public

It is fashionable these days for public institutions of higher learning to employ expensive public relations men, to set up swank public relations offices, and to spend tremendous sums of money for public relations or propaganda purposes. Expensive alumni coordinators employed to corral wealthy and influential graduates; specialists in public relations and alumni relations; specialists on legislative problems; and specialists on the proper propaganda for athletic enterprises seem to be infinitely more significant in the hierarchy of higher education than fine professors, libraries, and laboratories.

With this concept or interpretation of the program of the public institution, one must take most serious exception. All private citizens should be extremely apprehensive about the policy of spending huge sums of public funds for the purpose of keeping the public sold on the services rendered by an educational institution. The best public relations program—particularly in terms of those who support an educational enterprise—is the result or consequence of the educational enterprise itself. The educational achievements of thousands of graduates, the profits that come to farmers as a result of agricultural experimentation, the improved business techniques resulting from research and experimentation, progress in medicine, and all of the services which a great educational institution makes available to the publics which it serves constitute the only criteria by which the institution should be evaluated.

This type of interpretation offers the president of an institution his greatest opportunity for leadership, for he has the chance to utilize his own energy and personal responsibility in the interpretation of the social consequences of a great cooperative enterprise. The chief justification for a high degree of scholarship on the part of the president is not that he may hold his own with academicians or to excel at the faculty-student convocation, but that he may be conversant with the purposes and accomplishments of the institution, thereby making it possible for him to perform more effectively his responsibility for interpretation to the public.

The president should not be alone; indeed, he cannot be alone in this responsibility. Every member of the staff, academic and civil service, from the janitor to the president, is an ambassador of interpretation and good will for the institution. Everyone plays a significant role in making the institution a happy place for its students. The most effective public relations program should begin with the Freshman class and continue through to a constructive and dynamic alumni association.

Therefore, every professor who stands before a class and lectures, or who works with students in the laboratory or on research projects, or who advises individual students in their graduate work is a public relations official, interpreting the institution to its most important clients. Enlisting the enthusiasm and cooperation of the faculty in performing acceptably this significant function is perhaps the greatest test of the president's qualities as a leader.

Requirements of the Presidency

Perhaps there are no qualities more uniformly necessary for positions of leadership than boundless energy and enthusiasm for one's work. These are not enough, of course; but regardless of the ability, intelligence, and scholarship possessed by the college president, unless he has that willingness to work long hours, unhappiness and failure are almost certain to be the result. Professors may measure their week's work in terms of student-credit hours or student-clock hours of teaching plus the necessary time for preparation and for counseling of students. The good professor always puts in an adequate amount of time, but he can usually determine with reasonable accuracy the number of hours which he will need to work in any given week. The same is true with respect to civil service employees who follow a rigid schedule of a definite number of hours for each day in the week. These schedules, on the part of the professors and most civil service employees, make possible the establishment and maintenance of regular office hours and well-organized recreational programs.

Such is not the case, however, for the top administrators in an institution of higher learning. Their most difficult tasks frequently begin at the end of their regular day's work. Evening programs, dinner meetings, and speeches rob him of time which should be spent with his family or in reading and in intelligent reflection. No one should take the presidency of a college or university unless he is willing to accept additional responsibilities which, at times, seem like an imposition. The administrator needs to get to the office early and stay late. The rigors of the position, therefore, call for boundless energy, versatility, endurance, and persistence.

The college presidency is certainly no position for a man of faint heart, because it requires strong convictions, fearlessness, courage, and that intelligent loyalty to principle, illustrated in one of Lincoln's classic statements when he was a member of the Illinois Legislature:

You may burn my body to ashes, and scatter them to the winds of heaven; you may drag my soul down into the regions of darkness and despair to be tormented forever; but you will never get me to support a measure which I believe to be wrong, although by doing so I may accomplish that which I believe to be right.[5]

A college president must be a man of deep humility and human sympathy. It is a generally accepted social phenomenon that power corrupts. The college or university president is not immune to this corruption. Few individuals in positions of leadership command as much respect and loyalty on the part of subordinates as is accorded to college and university presidents. This has come about, as stated earlier, because of the great-man complex with respect to the building of educational institutions. The university president must guard constantly against the loss of humility and sympathy. It is fortunate for the institution if he deserves the respect and admiration generally accorded a college president. It is unfortunate if he permits power to corrupt to such an extent that his own prejudices become convictions and are used to inhibit that configuration of leadership which can be provided only through the joint efforts of all academic and administrative personnel.

It is one thing for the leader of a group to display showmanship on public occasions as, for instance, at large social functions, to extol the qualities of the faculty and students who constitute a great educational enterprise; but it is another thing, and more significant, for him to display human sympathy in more private situations as, for example, to put at ease and to lend a sympathetic ear to the staff member who enters his office and explains to him the impossibility of paying the grocery bill and of providing the other necessities for his family on his present salary.

The president needs time for reading, for vision and reflection, and for the development of that breadth of viewpoint which encompasses the entire institution with all of its social and economic consequences in the society which it serves. The problems and perplexities which confront the faculty and students and other individuals who are serving in and are served by the institution must be attacked in terms of a vision and an intelligence that transcend means and make direct connections with the larger philosophy and objectives as guiding principles of action.

---

[5]Carl Sandburg, *Abraham Lincoln, The Prairie Years* (New York: Harcourt, Brace & Co., 1927), p. 195.

Summary

The college president of boundless energy, vision, intelligence, humility, sympathy, convictions, and courage, working in cooperation with other great leaders in their own right, has an opportunity to construct a community of scholars representing a cause greater than any individual, yes, greater than all of the individuals connected with the institution. The leader who can thus lose himself in a great cause of which he is a part and, at the same time, who can maintain that clarity of vision, singleness of purpose, and loyalty to convictions so necessary to continuous progress, is in a position to do for hundreds of individuals what they cannot as individuals do for themselves and thus can participate in one of the most satisfying enterprises which man has been able to design.

No one should attempt such a work unless he is deeply and passionately interested in contributing energy, intelligence, and vision in the service of others. He must accept the philosophy that to save a life one must lose his own in the service of his fellow men. In this challenge the president has the opportunity to form the synthesis of great scholars and great disciplines. This is the challenge of leadership.

Leadership is the most appropriate substitute for executive orders; the former is most difficult and demanding for executives, but the latter is only a challenge to faculty resistance. Educational leadership is a difficult role for the caretaker type of administrator, but it is the only avenue to faculty stimulation and guidance.

Questions For Discussion

1. How do the decisions of a college president differ from those of a corporation president?
2. Some authorities believe that the Board of Control of a college or university should appoint a president as chief executive and hold him responsible for everything that happens. Do you agree or disagree? Why?
3. Why would the configuration hypothesis be more appropriate in higher education than in business or government?
4. How would the academic discipline of a president influence his approach to administration?
5. What is the role of the faculty in helping the president and his assistants carry out institutional policy?

6. Is it possible that students should be more significantly involved in administrative decisions?
7. Who should participate in the selection of the president?

Bibliography

AMERICAN COUNCIL ON EDUCATION. *Faculty-Administration Relationships.* Washington, D. C.: The Council, 1958.

DODDS, HAROLD W. *The Academic President—Educator or Caretaker?* New York and London: McGraw-Hill Book Co., Inc., 1962, 294 pp.

ESMOND, ROBERT. *Identification and Exploratory Analysis of the Problems of Selected College and University Public Relations Directors.* Unpublished Doctor's thesis, School of Education, Indiana University, Bloomington, 1959.

HUGHES, RAYMOND M. *A Manual For Trustees of Colleges and Universities.* Ames, Iowa: Iowa State College Press, 1951, 178 pp.

LAW, GLEN CHARLES. *The Urgency of New Leadership in Higher Education.* Philadelphia: Ivy-Curtis Press, 1962, 123 pp.

SANDBURG, CARL. *Abraham Lincoln, The Prairie Years.* New York: Harcourt, Brace, & Co., 1927.

SCHOENFELD, CLARENCE A. *The University and Its Publics.* New York: Harper & Bros., 1954.

SIMON, HERBERT A. *Administrative Behavior.* New York: The Macmillan Co., 1958, 259 pp.

STOKE, HAROLD. *The American College President.* New York: Harper & Bros., 1959.

WOODBURNE, LLOYD S. *Principles of College and University Administration.* California: Stanford University Press, 1958, 197 pp.

WRISTON, HENRY M. *Academic Procession.* New York: Columbia University Press, 1959, 222 pp.

Chapter

7

Academic Problems—Personnel

Functions of the Academic Staff

The members of the academic staff, utilizing the laboratories, class-rooms, and other instructional aids and assistance which the institution provides, represent the ultimate effort of an educational institution in meeting its basic responsibility. The faculty has the responsibility of working directly with the students; therefore, it works at the focal point of education. It determines in a large measure the effectiveness with which this responsibility is met. Boards of control, administrators, deans, directors, and division heads have unique opportunities to contribute to the effectiveness of the educational process or to hinder that process, depending upon the breadth and depth of their vision and the intelligence with which they analyze their responsibilities. All administrative officials, boards, finances, and the physical plant should constitute services to the instructional program, and the academic staff has both the privilege and the responsibility of translating these means into opportunities for learning.

The basic process of teaching and learning requires the transmission of the heritage of society to the students and the use of this heritage in developing students who can solve life's problems by continuing to learn. This process involves content, society, individuals, and method. Effective organization of the content as well as its functional utilization in ultimately changing the behavior of students are the responsibility of the faculty. Basic to the democratic principles in school administra-

148

tion is that those who must abide by decisions should have a part in making those decisions. The teacher-learning situation is one that affects professors and students alike. To deny these two groups the major responsibility for the effective organization of the curricula would be a violation of the principle of democracy so necessary for the achievement of the purpose for which educational institutions were established. It is not enough for boards of control and administrative officials to delegate to the faculty the responsibility for curricular organization and change. Intelligence and enthusiasm must be enlisted, and needs of students must be considered when students are the ones most affected by decisions influencing the curriculum.

Effective utilization of the intelligence of students in curricular planning is inevitable, because, in the final analysis, the student determines his curriculum. A student's curriculum includes all the experiences which the institution makes it possible for him to receive. In order that these experiences might have educational significance, the student must discern their educational and functional consequences in his own living. No one else can do this for him. No one can determine, define, or limit the educational curriculum of a given student without enlisting his cooperation and utilizing his past experiences as a basis for reconstruction and improvement of intelligence.

The administrative organization, the catalogue, and faculty committees may indicate no evidence of the utilization of students in determining the educational curriculum of an institution, but the faculty member and his students determine the educational objectives, the content, and the evaluation of the various courses that make up academic departments.

The establishment of departmental majors and minors is a clear-cut responsibility of the academic staff of each department. One limitation which the administration can justify with respect to curricular improvement and expansion is the requirement that budgetary limitations must be respected in setting up new courses which may involve additional personnel and cost.

Determination of Educational Policies. The role of the faculty in developing, implementing, and evaluating curricular activities of the institution is more obvious and more generally accepted than the responsibility of the staff for general educational policies affecting the entire program of an institution. A university or college campus implies a community of scholars engaged in educational activities of a high order. It implies a maximum of voluntary control of policies, ac-

.tivities, and procedures affecting the various members of the community including students. It is difficult to conceive of any situation involving human experiences where democratic procedures are more significant, necessary, and possible. If the members of a community of scholars are not competent to govern themselves, to determine the purposes, philosophy, and procedures for guiding and determining their activities, and finally, to make an evaluation of the total process, then democratic procedures have failed. If it is necessary to resort to totalitarian methods of control, to benevolent executive orders in determining the curriculum, and to the theory of the indispensability of the leader in the formation of policies affecting a wide range of intelligent people in an educational institution, where in America, or in any other part of the world, can one expect to find the processes of a free society in operation?

The general policies, purposes, curricula, degrees, majors, minors, and educational objectives must be determined by the democratic participation of all members of the staff and the students. Delegating such responsibilities commensurate with intelligence and leadership ability expected of university professors and students represents America's best method for the teaching of those democratic principles and qualities of leadership so necessary for the maintenance of her position as leader of the nations of the free world.

Organization, however democratic, generally constitutes a limitation upon freedom. This is an issue not only among individuals but among nations as well. The issue of the United Nations, and the great question regarding the possibility of its acceptance on the part of highly nationalistic nations, is the compromise of national power in the interest of greater security.

Joining a college community either as a student or as a professor places necessary restrictions and limitations upon one's activities which might otherwise be avoided in a different group or community. This limitation upon freedom with the concomitant responsibility for learning to work effectively with others and with other groups is an essential experience in the development of leadership.

To surrender to the dogma of efficiency and to practice totalitarian methods, because they may represent an easier approach on the part of administrators and faculty, will defeat the very purposes for which educational institutions have been established. Faculty and student participation in the formation of general educational policies affecting these two groups is as necessary to the process of education as are budgets, buildings, equipment, and libraries.

The Library. The library is both a teaching and a research facility and as such is the center of the educational institution. By acquiring, organizing, and preserving books and other materials, the library is the chief door to knowledge in the academic community. By facilitating the transmission of ideas through printed and audio-visual materials, it contributes to the teaching function of the institution. Through the use of its tools, its materials, and its specialized staff, the library supports the research of both faculty and students and aids in the publication of the results of research. It contributes to the instructional function of the institution by providing faculty members with specialized knowledge of subject bibliographies and other teaching and research materials.

The faculty members not only depend upon the library for support in their many roles but should have a responsibility to the library as well; should help integrate the library program with that of the whole institution and work toward the correlation of the curriculum and methods of instruction with the library resources; should aid in the selection of materials in support of the programs of research and instruction; and should encourage students to use the library, both by precept and example, and work with the library staff to develop good habits of reading and study on the part of the students.

Libraries should be planned for maximum utilization on the part of many groups. A central library for a large university may be less desirable in terms of function than departmental or college libraries. However, modern techniques in the use of electronic equipment could be applied to the designing of library resources in such a way that bringing the books to professors' offices instead of having everyone go to the library could be allowed. Pneumatic tubes connecting the library with every academic building would cost very little compared to the erection of additional reading rooms.

Higher education is in need of major advances in the application of imagination to the designing of educational facilities. The library would be the best place to begin.

Counseling and Advising. Counseling and advising of students are not extraneous adjuncts of the educational process. They are necessary to the process and cannot be separated from it. They can no more be placed in a central office than can the function of teaching. Learning is an individual matter. Every individual learns for himself. Groups do not learn. There is 'no such thing as a group mind capable of comprehending acts and designing educational objectives. These are processes of the individual and not of groups of individuals. Teachers need to keep in mind the fact that learning is a personal and individual matter. This calls for personal and individual approaches to the problem of teaching. Counseling and advising offer the opportunity for making the processes of education meaningful to every student.

Responsibility for Research. The research activities of an institution spring from its basic responsibility to discover and disseminate the truth. Man's eternal quest for new truth and light illuminates darkness, eliminates ignorance, and challenges scholars to press forward in a never-ending search for the ultimate. The research function of great scholars is one for which educational authorities should be willing to pay without having students subsidize the research program at the expense of neglected and ineffective teaching. These three important abilities—teaching, counseling, and research—are sometimes found in the same individual; more often, they are not qualities of the same individual.

It is educationally and financially unsound to employ a great research worker to teach unless he is also a good teacher. It may contribute to the effectiveness of both functions to have the same individual participating in research and teaching, but educational authorities must recognize their responsibilities for research and be willing to pay for research rather than curtail the teaching function to support research. Many great research workers have no interest in teaching. They and the institutions should not be penalized by their being required to teach.

All great teachers have an interest in research. It keeps them alive. They are sometimes so busy teaching students that little time is left for research. These great teachers, devoted to the welfare of their students, should not be required to engage in research activities unrelated to their teaching, so as to justify advancement in rank and salary. Teaching and research are two compelling responsibilities of universities. Neither should suffer at the expense of the other. They represent abilities that are quite different. Some staff members are fortunate enough to possess both to a high level of competency. Administrators should not expect always to find superior abilities in both research and teaching in the same staff member. There should be no embarrassment to any member of a university staff over the fact that his major interest is in one rather than both of these areas of a university's activities.

Responsibility for Standards. In addition to the functions of overall educational policies, curriculum development, teaching, counseling, and research, the faculty has the responsibility for determining thresholds for the admission of students, for establishing of scholarship and performance standards, for administering examinations and deciding upon a system of grading, and for determining requirements and eligibility for the various degrees which the institution offers. The faculty has the responsibility for controlling the institution's policy with respect to athletics, and for participating in such areas as public relations, social activities, and student discipline. Most of these functions are administered by individuals, but the broad general policies should involve the faculty, subject always to general policies of the governing board of trustees and to the leadership of the administration.

Responsibility to Community. A basic responsibility of every educational institution is service to the region which supports it. The opportunities for service to people of the region which supports an institution are limited only by the resourcefulness, initiative, and intelligence of the members of the staff and administration. Participation on public school forums and in civic and cultural organizations of the community and to become part of, and active participants in, the larger society is a privilege and an opportunity for the members of a university or college faculty. Professors and school administrators would be the first to admit that educational institutions should play a part in bringing about desirable changes in society. They must be the first, therefore, to accept the responsibility for bringing the benefits of the educational institution to the larger society. Not all faculty members have the desire or the capacity to participate in community activities. Their efforts may be used to better advantage in a different direction.

Personnel Programs

Faculty Welfare. There will be no attempt made here to reduce to averages and medians the salaries that should be paid to the staff of an institution of higher learning. The variations in the cost of living and economic conditions from one section of the country to another preclude the possibility and necessity for uniform salaries throughout the nation. Salaries are important, however, in the long-range program of recruitment of the staff and retention of those individuals capable of making the greatest contribution to the improvement of an institution. One of the greatest weaknesses of teaching as a profession is the fact that top salaries in most institutions, and especially in the public school systems, are far too close to beginning salaries. The incentives for growth, development, and service are not so great where the maximum in salary can be reached soon after appointment.

Following one session of the legislature in a certain state, funds were made available for an average increase of 12.5 per cent in all salaries paid academic members of the staff of an institution. The Board of Regents specified that there should be a 7.5 per cent increase in salary for everyone, the other 5 per cent to be used for merit increases according to the discretion of the college. The directors of the divisions were notified of this arrangement through a meeting of the administrative committee. It was easy for each director to determine the number of dollars available for salary increases in his division. He, in turn, invited the chairmen of the academic departments in his division to make recommendations concerning the salaries of the various members of the departments. Recommendations came from the department heads and the division directors to the dean and the president. With the help of the business manager and the academic dean, discrepancies between divisions were corrected, and final conferences were held with each of the division directors and, in many cases, salaries were increased even above those recommended by the department chairmen and the division director because of the availability of funds. On the basis of the best judgment of those concerned with the supervision and improvement of the academic staff, increases ranging from a minimum of 7.5 per cent to approximately 33.3 per cent were allocated, the highest percentage of increase going to two full professors who were being paid no more at that time than the highest paid instructors.

It is reassuring to the staff to be represented by members of its own departments and divisions in the determination of policies regarding salaries. The position of the administrator is infinitely stronger when this procedure is followed and the best judgments of three or four people are exercised in determining meritorious increases. While the single salary schedule with the automatic increases is easier to administer, it rewards mediocrity and penalizes outstanding ability to the detriment of faculty morale and educational accomplishment. Merit increases, on the other hand, involve the exercise of judgment.

The determination of effective teaching is extremely difficult. Such judgment is likely to be somewhat subjective, but the leaders in educational institutions are employed and paid to make valid decisions. When the administrator's judgment is made in cooperation with that of men and women who are close to the teaching situation, merit increases are probably given with less likelihood of error than that which is inevitable in the single salary schedule and automatic increases. School officials who advocate higher salaries should accept the responsibility for the improvement of the quality of teaching and reward quality on the basis of merit. Fringe benefits are becoming increasingly significant. These include tenure, retirement, insurance programs, sabbatical leave, sick leave, and teaching conditions.

Tenure Regulations. Tenure is a significant means to securing and holding competent academic staff members. In most institutions of higher learning and in public schools as well, teaching personnel receive permanent tenure after a reasonable probationary period.

In certain universities, for example, instructors receive permanent tenure at the end of seven years, assistant professors receive permanent tenure at the end of five years, and associate and full professors receive permanent tenure immediately upon appointment at those ranks. Instructors serving their first year in an institution should be notified well in advance of termination of their contracts; instructors serving after one year and up to seven years should be notified six months in advance of the termination of their contracts; and assistant professors should be notified twelve months in advance of termination of their contracts.

Permanent tenure and security in employment are, to some extent, compensating factors in the teaching profession which, in most respects, does not offer the financial rewards offered to men with comparable preparation in business and the professions. Permanent tenure is extremely important in the achievement and maintenance of academic freedom on the part of the faculty. Tenure contributes to an effective citizenship status so necessary if staff members are to enjoy the same rights, privileges, and responsibilities as other citizens in a community. But tenure should always be based upon competency, integrity, and responsibility.

Outstanding faculty members are seldom concerned personally about the achievement of permanent tenure, but most of them would not want to be associated with an institution that denied this status to the faculty under definitely prescribed conditions. Therefore, an acceptable policy with respect to tenure is basic to the long-range recruitment and holding of outstanding university professors and other personnel.

Some institutions which do not have a system of academic rank permit all academic staff members to achieve permanent tenure with the beginning of the fourth year. This practice which seems so democratic has many of the weaknesses of a single salary schedule. If an institution competes for top personnel, it may find it necessary to consider the employment of staff members who hold permanent tenure in other institutions. Rank and tenure are much more significant to experienced staff members who are changing positions than to younger men and women who usually are not concerned about permanent tenure when they accept their first teaching positions. If these younger teachers are preoccupied with tenure and retirement, they may be undesirable candidates or risks.

Termination of the appointment of an instructor or an assistant professor on probation should receive careful consideration of the chairman of the department, of the division in which the instructor works, and of the academic dean. The president may take an interest in this problem unless the institution is so large that he can give only perfunctory attention to such matters. It is the policy of many institutions, of course, to employ instructors without any thought of keeping them. Where this is the case, the candidates for positions should certainly know the policy of the institution and of the employing authorities with respect to this matter.

Termination of employment of staff members on continuous appointments should be for specific causes or on charges stated in writing, and provisions should be made for the staff member to be heard, not only before the administrators concerned, but before the governing board as well. Such a staff member should, in all cases, be accorded the courtesy of an adviser or counsel of his own choosing. Full records of all proceedings should be filed, and faculty committees should be used extensively in determining the competency of members of the academic staff. It is much better and more rewarding to develop a man than to break one. Proper counseling and understanding may result in the former.

Retirement Provisions. Nothing is more important to long-range faculty welfare than an adequate retirement plan which makes it possible for an institution to attract and hold outstanding men. College boards of trustees and administrative officers repeatedly verify the fact that well-designed plans for retirement and for providing income after retirement help them to develop more progressive personnel policies. A good retirement plan makes it much easier to select and hold competent people and also makes possible the orderly retirement of those who have reached a certain age.

The important decisions that need to be made in the establishment of a satisfactory retirement plan have to do with college objectives and administration and should be made by the institution's governing board on the basis of research and recommendations in which both faculty and administrators have participated.

Every individual for whom the institution provides permanent employment should be covered in the retirement plan. The plan should include faculty members of all ranks, administrators, and all civil service employees. Participation should be compulsory. Most retirement plans take advantage of the fact that a whole group of individuals in a particular situation or institution is being covered by the same provisions. For the plan to be most effective, all employees eligible for participation should be required to participate as a condition of employment. The cost should be shared by the employee and the institution. In situations where salaries are, of necessity, too low, as in states that impose constitutional or statutory limitations upon academic salaries, the entire cost of the retirement plan should be borne by the state or by the state institutions. In other situations where salaries are adequate, the plan should be strengthened if each staff member is required to contribute toward his own retirement, even though there is a tax advantage to the staff member in having the college pay the total cost.

The increase in the cost of living since 1939 has made most insurance and retirement programs hopelessly inadequate unless these programs have responded to the higher costs of living, or unless the benefit allowances vary with the cost of living. Retirement of college and university staff members is a problem which is national in scope. It will never be solved satisfactorily until there is a system of reciprocity which would make it unnecessary for a staff member to lose time or credit toward retirement in changing from one institution to another or from one state to another. There is great mobility among teachers, and the loss of retirement status causes many good people to leave the profession. Teachers Insurance and Annuity Association and social security are helping to alleviate this problem, and every institution should have both of these or else something comparable for faculties.

Insurance Programs. Closely allied with the retirement plan of an institution is its insurance program. Group plans have been designed covering life insurance, sickness, hospitalization, and general medical expenses. These plans are available through Blue Cross and

Blue Shield and other companies on an expanding basis. Life insurance on a term basis is a fundamental aspect of the welfare provisions for the families of staff members. Such programs are provided at a relatively low premium rate by the insurance companies and by the Teachers Insurance and Annuity Association. In recent years, the United States government has made available to civil service employees a program of term insurance, equal to the annual income of the worker, at a very low rate, although many employees are certain to lose on such policies that have no cash or surrender value. Term insurance at Indiana University amounts to three times the academic salary up to a maximum of $36,000 insurance. Major medical insurance at the same university pays up to $15,000 for any member of the participant's family.

Sabbatical Leave. Significant for the in-service education of staff members is a carefully designed plan for sabbatical leave which makes it possible for individual staff members to spend a year away from their duties for study or travel. Carefully planned leaves of absence on the part of conscientious staff members who really use the opportunity for improvement, either through further study, research, writing, or travel, pay high dividends to the institution as well as to the individual. In most cases where a staff member takes advantage of his opportunity for sabbatical, the institution benefits as much or more than the staff member himself. Any institution which is considering a revision of its plan for sabbatical should give thought to the possibility of granting leaves of absence for shorter periods of time at full pay instead of permitting a full year's leave at half pay.

Not nearly enough staff members take advantage of the opportunities for sabbatical because, as a general rule, it is impossible for them to maintain their families on one-half of their regular salaries. Sabbaticals are designed for the improvement of the staff members which, in turn, results in increased service to the institution. Neither of these outcomes can happen unless the staff member actually takes a leave of absence in order to benefit from the plan. As currently devised in most institutions, the plan does not work because most individuals do not take advantage of it. Therefore, it is suggested that sabbaticals be made available or be permitted for one quarter or for one semester with full pay. This would insure more widespread participation on the part of the staff members.

In addition to sabbaticals, the benefits to both the institution and to the individual of shorter leaves of absence to attend professional meetings must not be overlooked. A policy should be worked out, and funds provided, for professional travel which would make it possible for academic personnel to attend important professional meetings each year. Sabbatical privileges should be extended to include the president, vice presidents, and deans. No group in American higher education would profit more from the opportunity to study or travel than administrators. Some colleges are now following the policy of extending sabbaticals to administrators.

Teaching Load. Rapidly increasing enrollments and corresponding staff increases are not unique. Wherever this is happening, the problem of staff load arises. How many staff members should an institution have for two thousand students? Is the student-teacher ratio significant? Some administrators say it is; others say it is not. Should the teaching load be determined on the basis of clock hours of teaching per week, student clock-hours per week, credit hours, or student-credit hours per week? What is the relationship between a credit hour in special departments such as music and art, physical education, industrial arts, and a credit hour in a regular academic department? What is the relationship between an hour spent in a chemistry laboratory and an hour spent lecturing to the same students? To what extent should coaching athletics and directing intramural activities count toward a staff member's teaching load? What is the relationship between an hour spent on administrative problems and an hour used in the teaching of a class? In an academic department that has four staff members giving an undergraduate major and an undergraduate minor and providing certain courses in general education required of all students, what part of his time should the departmental chairman spend on administrative duties? In a large division, such as the division of humanities with thirty staff members, how much of the time of the director of the division should be devoted to teaching? How much time should be devoted to administrative responsibilities? Should the counseling of advisees be considered a part of the teaching load? What is a reasonable teaching load in terms of any one or more of the criteria listed above?

Should the total responsibility of the staff member be measured in terms of a certain number of hours per week? For example, The American Association of Colleges for Teacher Education has recommended that a forty-hour week constitute the service load of faculty members. All of the time required of each faculty member to fulfill his obligation to the institution should be included in computing the service load. This time should include such things as instruction of classes, preparation of class materials, grading papers, keeping records, conferring with students, doing research work for the college, working on committees, supervising college activities, and performing administrative duties. These and other problems relating to the teaching load should be studied carefully by the faculty of every institution. In the final analysis, it is advisable that the faculty set the standard for determining a satisfactory service load.

Functions of Dean of Faculties

Academic affairs should be centered in the office of the dean of faculties, and all faculties should be co-ordinated by this office. The dean of faculties has a challenging opportunity and a great responsibility in setting precedents for a functional pattern of service, which the office should perform for the president and for the faculty as a whole.

The dean of faculties should service as a liaison person between the president and the faculty. In so doing, he serves the president by relieving him of a multitude of routine and official duties that must be performed to insure faculty welfare as well as professional growth and advancement. He also serves the president by keeping him informed of faculty activities, problems, and achievements; and he serves the president by implementing the policies of the board of trustees and the president, policies which concern the faculty. He serves the faculty by presenting their requests, opinions, and problems to the president. He creates for them a climate conducive to intellectual and professional achievement and removes, insofar as he is able, the elements of insecurity.

A great deal of consideration should be given to the selection of the person who is to fill the post of dean of faculties at a university. Ideally the person should have the following qualifications: He should be a well-educated man who has an earned doctorate generally in an academic department. He should be someone with academic experience who either knows, or will quickly learn, the faculty, the philosophy of the institution, and the culture and ideals of the people. He should be personable and able to get along well with others, should have executive or managerial ability, and should be dedicated to the growth and advancement of the institution.

Qualities Necessary for Dean of Faculties. The dean of faculties should possess the following qualities: (1) ability to engage in objective research on major issues and problems; (2) ability to present conclusions based upon careful study, either in writing or orally; (3) ability to plan a course of action; (4) adroitness in representing the president to the faculty and the faculty to the president; (5) broad knowledge and negotiating ability; (6) patience and persistence; and (7) loyalty toward policies of the board and the faculty.

The dean of faculties has an excellent opportunity to synthesize the ideas and thinking of the faculty and to let them function democratically, on the basis of merit rather than authority. This relationship is always more likely to achieve results acceptable to the academic staff. At the same time, the dean of faculties can assist the president in maintaining his responsibility to the board and can exercise leadership within the framework of policies, procedures, and precedents established by the governing board, the administration, and the faculty.

The dean should be appointed for an indefinite length of time or, if for a stated length of time, long enough to assure him opportunity to establish and carry out a program of policies and procedures. The appointment might carry a provisional clause which would provide for his replacement if he failed to perform his duties and carry out his responsibilities in a satisfactory manner. His salary should be commensurate with the duties and responsibilities he assumes. It probably should not be too far below that of the president nor too far above salaries paid to top professors.

As a university grows in enrollment, the duties and responsibilities of the dean of faculties increase from year to year. In time, as his position becomes well established, he will need assistance that should be provided through establishing the office of an assistant dean of faculties or associate dean of faculties. It would appear to be inadvisable to establish such assistance until the position of dean of faculties is firmly established. The dean of faculties should be very ably assisted by a well-qualified administrative secretary.

Following is a suggested list of duties and responsibilities that form the basis of the position of dean: record keeping and official procedures connected with all faculty appointments; record keeping and official procedures connected with faculty resignations, leaves-of-absence, and sabbatical leaves; records of personal data and vital statistics concerning the faculty; administering the budget for faculty salaries, and the issuance of salary letters; record keeping and official procedures concerning approved and official faculty travel; compiling and editing a faculty bibliography; requiring yearly professional activity reports from each member of the faculty and compiling the data from them into a report for the president; implementing the establishment of a faculty council; encouraging and giving recognition to faculty achievement in writing and research; implementing the establishment of policies relative to faculty academic freedom; implementing the establishment of policies by working with the president, the board, and faculty representatives, relative to the duties and powers of the faculty, such as their authority in regard to structuring the curriculum, conferring degrees, student conduct, and faculty conduct; implementing policies and procedures regarding faculty promotions in rank; implementing the development of a faculty retirement plan; implementing the establishment of policies relative to teaching loads and class size; implementing the establishment of a faculty club; establishing and working with a committee, if needed, to develop policies relative to faculty benefits at the university such as special library privileges, special rates for athletic events and other program events the university may sponsor, and faculty parking areas; establishing a committee to develop and implement policies relative to professional ethics of faculty members and their relationships with one another; establishing and working with a committee, if needed, to work with the business administrative officials of the university in establishing such faculty benefits as group insurance, sick leave, medical care, and hospitalization; establishing and working with a committee, if needed, to arrange for faculty use of university recreation facilities; establishing and working with a committee, if needed, to work with problems on family housing; establishing and working with a committee to develop a faculty handbook.

The specific duties and responsibilities of a dean of faculties may vary from one university to another, because such duties and responsibilities must emanate, to a degree, from the particular administrative structure of each institution. An able dean of faculties, however, will ever be alert to recognize the many situations in which he can, through his position, serve his own university.

The dean of faculties needs an efficient, capable administrative secretary. The assistance of such a person is essential in establishing and maintaining the office in the administrative organization on a firm foundation of recognition and respect. She might well be a person who has previously worked in some of the university administrative offices and who knows the faculty, as well as the administrators and their policies. She should come to her new position with a minimum of five years of successful secretarial experience. Ideally she should have a bachelor's degree. She should be attractive, personable, tactful, and discreet. She should have managerial ability, as she will need to direct and manage other workers who may be needed in the office, such as a receptionist, typist, or clerk-typist.

She will need to be able to conserve the time of the dean by answering for him many routine questions on procedures and policies. She must see that information and materials going from the dean's office go through the proper channels to the proper places at the proper times.

She should be paid a top secretarial salary and should have from three to four weeks of vacation time during the year. She should not expect to work only a stated number of hours; for there may be occasions, during rush times, when she will need to work extra time in order to do such things as completing reports and taking notes at meetings.

A capable administrative secretary can do a great deal to promote the pleasant atmosphere that should characterize the office of the dean of faculties at all times. An outstanding administrative secretary will, like her employer, always have the welfare of the institution at heart.

Specific Line Responsibilities. In a small college, it may be necessary to assign many line responsibilities to the dean. These sometimes include recruitment of personnel, health service, library, concerts and lectures, the news service, and student personnel services. Freeing the president from the details of operation through line and staff assistants makes it possible for the president to be available to any member of the staff, to any civil service employee, or to any student who needs to bring problems directly to him.

The organizational chart is significant only as a point of reference in order to maintain proper relationships between operating heads, staff officers, and the chief executive. The implementation of any organizational plan is promoted rather than hindered by the functional approach to operation, which disregards, for most practical purposes, line responsibilities and relationships. An educational institution, as a community of self-governing scholars, should be the last organization in the world which makes it necessary for individuals to stop and consider line organization before contacting other individuals who may be able to bring intelligence and experience to bear upon the solution of their problems.

Organization and administration produce fruitful results, not so much in terms of plan of organization as in terms of the competence of personnel. The chief concern and major responsibility of the dean of faculties is the development of effective academic relationships among line and staff personnel, in order that the institution and the students may receive the ultimate benefit from an effective utilization of all personnel.

It is the responsibility of the dean to work closely with the librarian and the library committee for the improvement of library facilities, the acquisition of additional volumes, and the strengthening of the library in new fields in which the institution offers instruction. The dean and the librarian, along with the library committee, have considerable responsibility for planning any new library buildings. Academic personnel as well as library personnel should play a significant role in determining the facilities to be incorporated in any new building.

Unique Staff Opportunities. The dean of faculties plays a significant part in all administrative and academic activities of the institution. As a chief adviser to the president on academic matters, he has an opportunity to influence decisions without taking the responsibility for the consequences of those decisions. There are many times when the president would be very happy to cast himself in that role.

The dean is in a unique position to become well acquainted with the strengths and weaknesses of the members of the academic staff. They should look to him as a representative of the faculty, a man working at a very high level, with whom they should be able to discuss their problems in all candor and frankness. Regardless of how anxious the president of an institution may be to achieve this relationship with his staff, it is seldom accomplished. The president, particularly in small colleges, cannot escape the fact that he has final responsibility for the employment, promotion, and the termination of appointment of staff members. To be sure, these responsibilities may be shared with chairmen and deans, but, in the final analysis, the president of the institution must take the responsibility for making the recommendation to the board of control.

The dean is responsible directly to the president for co-ordinating the thinking of the faculty with respect to needed curricular changes and revisions. Frequently, this responsibility on the part of the chairman of a curriculum committee is considered more or less a mechanical problem of putting together appropriate courses with correct numbers and correct credit hours for building majors and fulfilling requirements for graduation. More significant, however, than any mechanical problem of building a catalogue is the responsibility of the curriculum committee for assisting in the determination of institutional philosophy, purposes, and the general educational program. This is perhaps the dean's most significant opportunity for leadership, but most deans give very little attention to this problem.

Selection of Academic Personnel

Administration has been defined in this book as the selection, assignment, stimulation, guidance, and evaluation of human effort in the development of human qualities. The dean of faculties, as an administrative officer, is greatly concerned with the selection of the academic staff and must have in mind the criteria for the selection of such staff as well as the method of selection and the sources of personnel.

Criteria for Selecting Academic Staff. The process of education implies that there is an important body of content in society that is worthy of preservation; that knowledge of society and its relationship to education constitute an important possession of anyone preparing to teach; that the ability to teach requires familiarity with the fundamental aspects of human growth and development; and, finally, that the process of education may be enhanced by a deliberate study of the methods and techniques by which content may be transmitted to the learners. These requirements which seem to be necessary in the preparation of public school teachers are equally significant in the preparation of college and university teachers. The employing authorities, therefore, and the candidates themselves are concerned with: (1) the evidences of scholarship on the part of those who would enter teaching at the university level; (2) emotional stability and maturity conducive to a wholesome relationship with university students and professors; (3) successful experiences; (4) creative ability; (5) interest in teaching and in community service; and (6) critical and discriminating ability in meeting new and difficult situations. Creative ability as used above may be reflected in painting, musical composition, creative poetry, and historical, philosophical, scientific, and educational research. A great university needs to pay particular attention to the selection of personnel at the lower ranks in order to insure great teachers in later years.

Regardless of departmental specialization, the prospective teacher of university students should have broad humanistic interests sufficient for the times in which he lives; he should believe in and practice education as a process of continuous growth; he should be interested in the problems and perplexities of his own day; he should have an enthusiasm for working with students, an interest that makes him really want to teach; and, finally, he must be committed to the idea of a free society in all his relationships in order that he may contribute to the fulfillment of the high purposes of perpetuating and improving the cultural heritage.

Method of Selection. The responsibility for helping to select staff members is one of the significant functions assigned to any member of the university community. The process of selecting staff members is almost as important to the institution as the choices that are finally made. The process is significant in terms of the number of people who participate. The members of the department in which the new staff member is to be located have the greatest possible interest in the qualifications and personal characteristics of the individuals selected. The departmental chairman and the dean of faculties, therefore, become the key people in determining the qualifications, specific responsibilities, areas of specialization, and courses to be taught by the new member of the staff. This information serves as a kind of job analysis which, in all cases, should determine the minimum academic and professional qualifications necessary for entrance into the college.

In addition to the chairman and other members of the department, the director of the division or the dean of the college in which the individual is to teach should be consulted and may be the key person in the recommendation of academic personnel, because of responsibility for the administration of the budget and personnel. There may be no departmental budgets. Positions are sometimes listed in the divisional or college budget, and the divisional chairman or dean takes the initiative in securing the necessary funds for the position involved and is very much concerned with the selection of personnel.

The academic dean in the small institution does not, as a rule, have the responsibility or final authority for appointment but is consulted as a staff officer in the final selection of academic personnel. Final authority and responsibility for the recommendation of staff members rests with the president, who submits the recommendations to the Board of Regents for final approval. This step is necessary in order to give legal status to the employment of individual staff members. Thus, the president, the academic dean, the director of the division, and the departmental chairman constitute an official team for the selection of academic personnel. The Board of Control may reject a nomination, but it should never initiate an appointment except to fill a vacancy in the presidency.

It is desirable that departmental chairmen in departments of three or more staff members be elected by the staff of each department. In smaller colleges, the dean or president may appoint chairmen. Terms of two to three years seem most desirable.

Sources of Personnel. Authorities responsible for employing teachers should utilize the resourcefulness and initiative of experienced staff members in locating and employing desirable candidates for new positions and vacancies. University professors, for example, who represent specialized departments, as a rule hold membership in the learned societies and organizations representing their professional specializations and interests. These societies and organizations constitute one of the most reliable sources of academic personnel and are frequently willing to notify employing officials of outstanding young men and women who have finished their graduate work, have taught a few years, and are entitled to promotions.

The graduate schools of the great universities are the best source, at least from the standpoint of quantity, of recruits for the academic staff. It is not unusual, of course, to employ staff members who have recently completed their graduate work but who have had broad, extensive, and adequate teaching experience. All graduate schools, and university professors who advise students on their advanced graduate work, should not only encourage, but insist, that those who plan to enter teaching register with the teacher placement offices in order that adequate credentials may be accumulated and made available to employing authorities. Officials who have the responsibility for operating the place- ment services in universities should make available to employing authorities not only those candidates who are looking for positions, but also the more experienced personnel who are entitled to promotions. This is a responsibility of every university administrator and professor: to assist worthy men and women to find the promotions to which they are entitled and which are necessary to keep them in the teaching profession. The professor who advises doctoral students should be alert to employment opportunities for his students.

In addition to the two sources mentioned, candidates themselves take the initiative in applying through acquaintances on the staff, and these represent good sources of new personnel. Finally, there are the commercial placement agencies which may provide strong candidates, although this source is looked upon as a last resort by many employing authorities.

There are other sources of personnel, of course. For example, an undergraduate institution which sends many of its finest students on to graduate schools is likely to enjoy the opportunity, in later years, of having those individuals return as members of the academic staff. Careful selection of able alumni to fill a reasonable percentage of the positions on a staff constitutes a great source of strength and solidarity for the institution and serves as encouragement for outstanding young men and women to pursue the teaching profession by studying at the graduate level.

Staff Improvement. Guidance and evaluation of human effort imply a constant concern for the improvement of the faculty as well as of the administration of an institution. This is a joint concern on the part of the members of the faculty, the dean of faculties, operating deans, chairmen of departments, and the president. Improvement of instruction is a responsibility which, in the final analysis, must be accepted by the members of the faculty. Methods of improvement cannot be imposed from above; they must grow out of the conjoint experiences of staff members and administrators working toward a common goal.

University professors of education, who for years have been concerned with the improvement of teaching, have been the first to admit the difficulty in determining what constitutes effective teaching. This, then, is the basic problem in launching a program for the improvement of instruction in an institution. If the members of the academic staff and the administration understand the meaning of effective teaching, the possibility of working toward that goal with increasing effectiveness is definitely improved.

No one in an institution of higher learning is in a better position to evaluate objectively a member of the staff than are the colleagues and students of that individual who work with him every day. Therefore, in any effective program for the improvement of teaching, faculty members and students must play an increasingly significant role. The dean of faculties is in a unique position to work effectively on this problem.

Evaluation of staff members serves the purpose of determining eligibility for promotions in rank or increases in salary. Such evaluations should be used also to help in the improvement of the individual staff member and should be held in strictest confidence. For it is the antithesis of democracy that divisional and departmental chairmen and the dean know of the weaknesses and shortcomings of an individual staff member without using that knowledge to help him make necessary improvements.

In one situation, a faculty committee was appointed to study the methods of improving teaching and counseling. The findings of the committee were reported to the entire faculty by the members of the committee. These recommendations carried infinitely more prestige with the staff than if they had been handed down by the president or by anyone else outside of the staff. The policy of individual staff members with respect to grading of students was studied, and it was discovered that the percentage of failures ranged all the way from 3 per cent in one department to 14 per cent in another department. Members of the staff began to think critically and objectively about the implications of this wide range of failures. Many individuals who considered it in their favor to fail a high percentage of students changed their viewpoints as a result of faculty discussion of this problem.

Another committee reported on unique methods used by individual staff members for effective teaching. The use of audio-visual materials, mimeographed outlines, syllabi, and materials provided by the instructor, as well as student participation in classroom discussions and activities involving joint student-professor planning and evaluation were reported to members of the staff. Many of these methods were securing excellent results as evidenced by the fact that, under a system where attendance at class was voluntary, students in certain classes were eager to be present for every meeting and were requesting permission to make up those experiences missed through necessary absence from class.

At still another committee meeting, the question of office hours for the counseling of students was discussed. A significant conclusion was that it is extremely important for members of the staff to be punctual and reliable in maintaining office hours and appointments as indicated in their schedules. Recommendations on these problems coming as they did from members of the staff were more effective in establishing better habits of counseling and better methods of teaching than if they had come from the administration. Out of the faculty discussion came many suggestions for more intelligent utilization of all of the services which the institution offered and particularly of the services in the realm of student counseling.

The role of the dean of faculties in the improvement of teaching implies the responsibility for counseling members of the staff with respect to graduate work and the securing of advanced degrees both of which seem to bear some relationship to the quality of teaching. The dean should take the responsibility for reporting significant research which may bring about improvement in the methods of teaching. It is possible for an individual to teach year after year without making any significant improvement. To reward the individual for many years of unsuccessful experience is not good economy, and it is poor educational administration. Experience is significant only to the extent that it brings about a reconstruction of one's thinking and experiences in future situations and results in more intelligent actions. One's colleagues and administrative superiors should assume some responsibility in the prevention of failure, year after year, and should help their fellow staff member to develop his responsibilities as a teacher, a counselor, or as a specialist in research.

The dean should encourage productive scholarship on the part of the staff. The writing of articles, books, reviews, monographs, and the reading of papers before learned societies represent significant experiences in the improvement of one's effectiveness as a member of the teaching profession. It is essential that an institution give proper recognition to those individuals who, through persistence, sacrifice, and intelligent use of their time, bring recognition to themselves and the institution through productive scholarship. It is doubtful that anyone can achieve the ultimate as a great teacher without becoming a productive scholar in his own field.

Another method by which members of the academic staff may improve their status as teachers, counselors, and effective members of the college community is by serving on committees concerned with the problems and perplexities faced by the institution, its staff, and its students. Staff members have benefited greatly by serving on the curricular committees, various committees dealing with general education on an institution-wide basis, and on committees in their own divisions. Serving on a curriculum or a general education committee which cuts across all academic departments offers the staff member an opportunity for gaining a broader perspective regarding the scope and functions of the entire institution. Such committee reports have significance for the staff as a whole and for the implementation of constructive changes, but perhaps the greatest significance attached to such studies is the improvement of individual staff members who make the studies.

Rank and Promotions. In maintaining and improving staff morale, no aspect of the faculty welfare program seems more important than the methods by which increases in rank and salary are achieved. The members of a department in which a staff member works and, particularly, the departmental chairmen who should be closer to the individual staff members than any other administrative officers, should play a significant role in evaluating and recommending for promotions in rank members of the academic staff. This is particularly a responsibility of professors, associate professors, departmental chairmen, divisional directors, and deans.

It does not suffice that justice may prevail, notwithstanding the fact that the promotion is made by the president of an institution. More important than anything else is that the staff member has the assurance that individuals who work in the same field or department and are intimately familiar with the qualities of the work being done have an opportunity to make recommendations to the dean and to the president, whose actions with respect to such matters are usually final. In the case of a larger institution where there are deans for the various colleges, the approval of the president is likely to be perfunctory, and the real authority for making promotions lies with faculty and deans.

Promotions in rank should never be used in lieu of increases in salary. The two should stay in balance, and an increase in rank, to carry significance, should in most cases carry an increase in salary. However, an overlapping of salary at the interval between ranks is not only necessary but highly desirable.

The thing against which the administrator must constantly strive is failure to render justice because of his failure to know each member of the staff individually. The administrator must recognize the fact that individual staff members differ very greatly in their abilities to present their own cases for promotions and increases in salary. Some of the most valuable people on any university staff are individuals who must be discovered by departmental chairmen, deans, and presidents, because many of the greatest academic personnel would never recommend themselves. The judgment of no single individual on a university campus should be considered infallible or final. The judgments of many individuals should be sought in any attempt to evaluate a given person's efficiency and worth.

The deans, divisional directors, and departmental chairmen share in the opportunities and responsibilities for making recommendations and evaluations in connection with the appointments and promotions of staff members. Employment of academic personnel involves joint agreement among departmental and divisional chairmen, deans, and the president.

Promotion of a staff member from one rank to another is first of all a faculty responsibility, but it involves departmental chairmen, deans, and the president.

Salaries and rank are the concern of all members of the faculty, and the president should establish the habit of discussing with the entire faculty questions of salary increases, faculty rank, and welfare. The more freely and openly these questions are discussed between members of the staff and the administration, the more likely are the members of the faculty to accept, in good faith, the final decisions on the part of the administration and the board of control.

Graduate Programs and Research

All graduate programs and research should be coordinated by the dean of the graduate school who may also serve as director of research and report to the dean of faculties or the president. One graduate school in a major university is more likely to produce coordinated research than will a program decentralized by schools and colleges.

Staffing a centralized administrative graduate office for each school of a major university increases administrative costs by a factor almost equal to the number of independent schools and colleges offering graduate work.

Essential educational functions of graduate education are carried out by departments and professors. Proliferation of administrative offices by schools and colleges decreases the support for substantive graduate work and research.

Since graduate schools emphasize research, it seems wise in terms of economy and efficiency, as well as for excellence in results, to make the dean of the graduate school also the director of research for the entire university. Graduate schools generally have no separate faculty, but utilize the faculties of all schools participating in the graduate program.

The fifteen years (1960-1975) offer an opportunity unparalleled in American history for giving new scope and direction to higher education. The role of the college teacher will be paramount in the new situation. The influence of those who prepare college teachers may determine the quality of higher education for the remainder of the twentieth century. Because of these facts, it seems necessary that the following questions receive careful study: (1) What changes in objectives, curricula, organization, and administration may be anticipated as a result of the increasing demand for education beyond the high school? (2) What new personnel needs are indicated to meet the above changes? (3) What new opportunities are available to improve the quality of college teaching and research as future staff requirements are met?

Major universities, in the process of preparing future college faculties, will have a unique opportunity to reshape higher education during the sixties, when more than one-half of the 1970 college staff will be appointed. By 1970, the opportunity may be gone for another generation.

The question, therefore, is whether the 140,000 new faculty members appointed between 1960 and 1970 are to be indoctrinated in maintaining the status quo (which is certainly a success story for higher education), or whether institutions are to analyze present problems and future consequences in shaping institutional programs and personnel needs.

A university brings together great leaders, administrators, and educational statesmen to operate the university. But it is possible that they may not perpetuate themselves and their ideas through younger leaders who will follow. The perpetuation cannot be confined to the local campus because the influence is a world influence. Superior teaching is not limited to any particular college. To draw upon all colleges of the university in the improvement of college teaching is to guarantee the success of the enterprise.

Economy in Curricular Organization

This section presents three schemes for the most economical use of undergraduate faculties and the minimum course offerings in relatively small liberal arts colleges.

Model I. Minimum Enrollment and Minimum Budget. What is the minimum enrollment and the minimum budget necessary for an undergraduate liberal arts college to operate within its tuition income? If one assumes that such a college has no endowment and that it receives annual gifts of about $75,000, what tuition rate is necessary? This question poses the problem of frugal use of two scarce resources—personnel and finances. A suggested list of departments grouped by division is presented here. These departments are the same ones that appear in the bulletin of one of the best-known liberal arts colleges in the Middle West. The list of departments would be longer in colleges not so well-known.

Division of Humanities

Philosophy	English
Art	French
Music	German
Speech	Spanish

Division of Social Sciences

History	Business
Geography	and
Sociology	Economics
Political Science	

Division of Education

Psychology
Education
Physical Education

Division of Science & Mathematics

Physics
Chemistry
Biology
Mathematics

The divisional grouping of departments in a small college should result in more efficient use of the faculty and a better return on budgetary allocations. It makes it easier to use faculty members with multi-discipline competencies, and this is necessary where the typical department has only one faculty member.

If the above departments must operate with the absolute minimum of academic personnel, one person for each department would be required. Two extra staff members should be assigned to each of the divisions, with the exception of education and psychology, which would need at least one extra person. These extra positions would make it possible to staff departments somewhat in terms of the demands for general education.

A total of 27 faculty members would be required: 10 in the humanities, 7 in the sciences, 6 in the social sciences, and 4 in education and psychology. If a ratio of 20 students to each faculty member is maintained, the enrollment would be 540 students.

Unless a college is so well-endowed that financial support is no problem, 500 students should be the minimum to justify continued operation.

The total offering of the college would be 162 courses or an average of 6 for each member of the faculty. If each of 27 instructors offered

TABLE 2

NUMBER OF COURSES AND CREDITS FOR A COLLEGE OF 540 STUDENTS			
Course	Number of 4-Credit Courses	Number of 3-Credit Courses	Total Semester Hours
Philosophy	4	3	25
Art	6	4	36
Music	6	4	36
Speech	4	3	25
English	4	4	28
French	4	4	28
German	4	4	28
Spanish	4	4	28
History	4	4	28
Geography	4	4	28
Sociology	4	3	25
Political Science	4	3	25
Business and Economics	6	4	36
Physics	4	4	28
Chemistry	4	4	28
Biology	6	4	36
Mathematics	4	4	28
Education	2	4	20
Psychology	4	4	28
Physical Education	3	5	24
Total	85	77	568

3 courses per semester, all courses would be offered every year; however, there would be too many sections of certain required courses to make it possible to offer all courses every year. Moreover, institutions with very large faculties seldom offer all listed courses every year. The curricula shown above indicate the extent to which the whole problem of course offerings can and should be simplified in small colleges.

TABLE 3

BUDGET AND PERSONNEL FOR 540 STUDENTS	
Expenses	
Salaries by Position	
President	$20,000
Secretary	4,000
Dean of College	15,000
Secretary	4,000
Secretary-Registrar	4,000
Clerk	3,000
Business Manager	10,000
Accountant	7,500
Secretary	3,600
Director of Public Relations	10,000
Secretary	3,600
Librarian	10,000
Assistant	6,000
Clerk-Typist	3,000
Faculty (27 @ average of $10,000)	270,000
Six faculty secretaries @ $3,000	18,000
Library Books and Audio-Visual Materials	25,000
Research	20,000
Supplies, Equipment, and Expenses	25,000
Operation and Maintenance	65,000
Student Aid and Scholarships	55,000
Auxiliary Services (self-supporting)	
Contingency Fund	23,300
Total	$605,000
Income	
Tuition—$1,000 per student	$540,000
Annual Gifts	65,000
Total	$605,000

The central administrative staff for a college of 540 students would consist of the president, dean of the college, business manager, and the director of public relations. A secretary-registrar, with the help of one clerk-typist, would perform the functions generally assigned to the office of the registrar and would report to the dean of the college. This office, with the help of the dean, would be in charge of the admission of students. The dean of the college would coordinate student personnel services and would utilize the faculty for the counseling of students, with the department of psychology assuming responsibility for counseling of individuals requiring psychological therapy.

It should be noted that no funds have been budgeted for auxiliary services. These would include residence halls, food services, student union, and other enterprises which should be completely self-supporting.

The budget for supplies, equipment, and expenses would be controlled by a committee representing the entire institution and would be financed on the basis of need rather than on a departmental basis.

The entire budget of the institution, including $23,300 in the contingency fund, would be provided by two sources: (1) $540,000 from tuition, based upon a tuition charge of $1,000 per student for the academic year; and (2) $75,000 from annual gifts.

It should be noted that salaries averaging $10,000 for each member of the faculty would be considerably higher than those generally prevailing in liberal arts colleges of this size. If the salaries averaged only $8,000 and the contingency fund was cut to $2,300, the entire operating cost could be paid from tuition. However, in an institution of this type, it would probably be easier in the long run to meet the operating expenses if the higher salaries were paid, because it is anticipated that there would be a close relationship between the level of faculty salaries which undoubtedly influences the quality of the educational program, and financial support from all sources, including tuition.

This plan for the organization and support of a small liberal arts college is vulnerable to the charge that many liberties have been taken with respect to the staffing of the administrative offices and the faculty; that the curriculum has been almost ruthlessly pruned; and that the budget has been arbitrarily allocated to various functions. These charges are quite correct, and indeed many variations from this plan would be necessary in any given situation; but this scheme represents precisely the kind of planning, staffing, budgeting, and curricular organization which could save several hundred small private colleges from disappearing from the American scene within the next fifteen to twenty years.

Model II. This model has been projected on the assumption that departments should have an average of 2 faculty members each, which would mean 40 faculty members for 20 departments. Faculty salaries would amount to $400,000 if the $10,000 average were maintained. This type of institution would need a minimum of 800 students. Tuition could be reduced to $900. If gifts amounted to $75,000 annually, the total budget would be $795,000 or $190,000 more than under Model I. An increase of 13 faculty members would cost $130,000 which would leave $60,000 for additions to the administrative staff, including a full-time dean of students, one or two more staff members for the library, and one more person in the business office. With prudent use of the faculty and tuition income, the budget could be balanced with only $75,000 in gifts.

Model III. Another scheme for the relatively small college is based upon a minimum of 3 faculty members for each department. This would require a faculty of 60. The enrollment would need to be 1,200. Faculty salaries would increase by $200,000 over those for Model II.

The college with 1,200 students should balance its budget on a tuition charge of $800 plus $100,000 in annual gifts, because administrative costs should change very little over those for Model II, and scholarships and student aid could decrease as the tuition is lowered. The total budget would be $1,060,000. Gifts and grants could be used to improve the quality of the educational enterprise.

All three schemes would be dependent upon frugality in the use of buildings as well as other resources, because the temptation to expand physical facilities beyond needs must be resisted. Low percentage utilization of space can be a serious drain on the entire operating budget.

Summary

Faculty personnel policies reflect the basic philosophy that controls an institution of higher learning. The advancement of learning and advanced education demand faculties and students of many talents and different types of motivation. The university, from its inception in medieval times, has served as a haven for dedicated scholars even when they were rejected by intellectually unsophisticated citizens at large. If the university ever ceases to be a place where the scholar, who has no commitment except to advance learning is welcome, then the name "university" will no longer be an appropriate descriptive title.

Personnel policies in many small colleges, and even in some larger universities, are such that dedicated scholars are virtually required to engage in popularity contests in order to keep the wolf away from their door. No set of rules and regulations laid down by a board of control, no beautiful criteria for promotions carefully written by faculty committees, can obscure the real personnel policy of an educational institution as expressed in the allocation of its financial resources and the impact of such allocation upon the quality of research, instruction, and public service emanating from the various departments. The inescapable fact is that the budget of a university represents the translation of educational philosophy into dollars and cents. In the critical period which America is now entering with respect to higher education, the ingenious educational leader will be the one who finds ways of allocating the highest percentage of the budget to focus directly upon the objectives of teaching, learning, and research.

Questions for Discussion

1. How can the faculty participate most effectively in developing educational policy?
2. Who should make the ultimate decisions on curricular development?
3. Are faculties generally a dynamic or a conservative force in developing educational policy?
4. What aspects of public administration principles, as developed by Leonard D. White, are appropriate to higher education?
5. Are job descriptions necessary for academic administrators and for faculty members? Why?
6. What are the most important functions of an academic dean?
7. Work out a scheme for academic promotions. What criteria should be used?
8. How should the graduate program of a university be organized?
9. What departments should be included in an undergraduate liberal arts college?
10. How should the educational dollar be divided?

Bibliography

BARZUN, JACQUES. *Teacher in America.* Boston: Little, Brown and Co., 1945.
BLEGEN, T. C., and COOPER, R. M. (ed.). *The Preparation of College Teachers.* Washington, D.C.: American Council on Education, 1950.
BURNS, NORMAN. (ed.). *The Administration of Higher Institutions Under Changing Conditions.* Institute for Administrative Officers of Higher Institutions. Chicago: University of Chicago Press, 1947.
BUXTON, CLAUDE E. *College Teaching, A Psychologist's View.* New York: Harcourt, Brace & Co., 1956.

CAPLOW, T., and McGEE, R. J. *The Academic Marketplace.* New York: Basic Books, 1958.

CORSON, JOHN J. *Governance of Colleges and Universities.* New York: McGraw-Hill Book Co., Inc., 1960.

DEVANE, WILLIAM CLYDE. *The American University in the Twentieth Century.* Baton Rouge: Louisiana State University Press, 1957.

DIEKHOFF, JOHN S. *The Domain of the Faculty in our Expanding Colleges.* New York: Harper & Bros., 1956.

Educational Policies Commission. *Higher Education in a Decade of Decision.* Washington, D.C.: The Commission, 1957.

FOWLKES, JOHN GUY. (ed.). *Higher Education for American Society.* Madison: University of Wisconsin Press, 1949.

FUSSLER, H. H. (ed.). *The Function of the Library in the Modern College.* Chicago: University of Chicago Press, 1954.

HARDEE, MELVENE D. *The Faculty in College Counseling.* New York: McGraw-Hill Book Co., Inc., 1959.

HUGHES, JAMES MONROE. *Human Relations in Educational Organization.* New York: Harper & Bros., 1957.

HUTCHINS, ROBERT MAYNARD. *Some Observations on American Education.* Cambridge, England: Cambridge University Press, 1956.

JUSTMAN, JOSEPH, and MAIS, WALTER H. *College Teaching: Its Practice and Its Potential.* New York: Harper & Bros., 1956.

MARSHALL, MAX S. *Two Sides to a Teacher's Desk; Dedicated to Students, Teachers and Bystanders.* New York: Macmillan Co., 1951.

Personnel Services in Education. The Fifty-Eighth Yearbook of the National Society for the Study of Education, Part II. Nelson B. Henry, editor. Chicago: University of Chicago Press, 1959.

RIESMAN, DAVID. *Constraint and Variety in American Education.* Lincoln: University of Nebraska Press, 1956.

RUML, BEARDSLEY. *Memo to a College Trustee.* New York: McGraw-Hill Book Co., Inc., 1959.

TEAD, ORDWAY. *The Climate of Learning; A Constructive Attack on Complacency in Higher Education.* New York: Harper & Bros., 1958.

WILSON, LOUIS ROUND, and TAUBER, MAURICE F. *The University Library; The Organization, Administration, and Functions of Academic Libraries.* New York: Columbia University Press, 1956.

WOODBURNE, LLOYD S. *Faculty Personnel Policies in Higher Education.* New York: Harper & Bros., 1950.

Principles of College and University Administration. Stanford, California: Stanford University Press, 1958.

WRISTON, HENRY M. *Academic Procession.* New York: Columbia University Press, 1959.

Chapter

8

Academic Problems—Curricula

Dynamics of Liberal Education

Liberal education is functional knowledge applied in releasing man's mind from prejudice, ignorance, and fear. Combined with professional education, it results in vocational competency. The former contributes to being—the latter to doing. They are inextricably complementary.

No ultimates in liberal education have developed anywhere in the world. The arts and sciences of man are dynamic, not static. The trivium (grammar, logic, rhetoric) and the quadrivium (arithmetic, geometry, astronomy, and music) constitute the almost sacred tradition of many liberal arts colleges. Designed originally for free men (meaning men of leisure, clothed with the authority of totalitarian rulers), the liberal arts have a romantic, if not a functional, appeal to the academic community.

In a nation such as the United States, where the virtues of universal education and useful work are embraced, the ancient trivium and quadrivium have naturally been severely distilled and refined or watered down (depending upon one's prejudices), especially by the great and the near great state universities whose sensitivity to Ancient Greece has been slightly less than that accorded to rural legislators and to athletics.

Pronouncements by those who design teacher education curricula reach the ultimate in the virtue of diversity with respect to liberal or general education, as evidenced by institutional requirements ranging from 15 per cent to 85 per cent of the four-year undergraduate curricula.

Other institutions, particularly in Europe, Asia, and Latin America, regard general, if not liberal, education as a function of elementary and secondary schools and do not accord it any space in university curricula.

It is postulated here that in America, failure to agree upon the objectives of liberal education has made it impossible to formulate any universal program or to reach any significant agreement on areas of study and courses.

Objectives and Definition. What are the objectives of general education? Is it mastery of a body of knowledge; the question of basic tool subjects necessary for further education; the development of citizenship competencies; acquisition of a value system; mastery of philosophy; self-realization; or vocational skills? All of these and other objectives have motivated leaders in the establishment of liberal education curricular requirements. The problems of the space age make all of the above objectives inadequate, confusing, and impossible to translate into human behavior.

Education is progressive, dynamic, and personal. It is different for each individual. It cannot be separated from intelligence, because advanced education implies ability to improve one's selection of alternative courses of action with each new experience. If this principle is operative, one may be expected to act more intelligently with each intellectual experience. The emphasis must be upon the development of the mind rather than upon informing the mind. The liberal arts involve knowledge which liberates the mind from intellectual oppression. But knowledge alone is insufficient. Intellectual liberation is a result of many factors, one of which is knowledge. The ability to think, to anticipate consequences, and to control and determine one's own objectives are also basic.

A tentative definition is that liberal education is a process by which one synthesizes all experiences, knowledge, dispositions, habits, and interests in resolving life's problems. This calls for getting outside of the self; looking at one's prejudices, habits, real interests, and possible consequences of a given course of action; and calling upon past decisions and knowledge to render an integrative judgment.

If this view is accepted, there needs to follow a radical departure from current practices in liberal education. This is an inductive process, yet it is treated deductively. Elementary schools are devoted exclusively to what some authorities refer to as general education or mastery of the fundamentals. The first years of secondary schools are devoted to general education with some specialization in the senior high school; and most colleges and universities have general or liberal education courses in the first year or two, with specialization in the last two or three years.

This procedure is deductive in that it implies ability to make an intelligent synthesis prior to being educated. Liberating, integrating experiences and competencies should come at the end of whatever educational stage is involved rather than at the beginning of the stage.

Appropriate experiences in the last year of the undergraduate program would involve integrated studies composed of the physical and biological sciences, on the one hand, and the sequence composed of sociology, psychology, history, and philosophy on the other. A third area could be in the participative arts—music, art, drama, and dance. These could form a continuous program throughout the last two years of undergraduate study and would represent an interdisciplinary approach rather than isolated departmental courses.

This program rejects the concept of the tool subjects as liberal studies. For example, the mastery of English, elementary mathematics through trigonometry, spelling, writing, and speaking are sometimes regarded as general or liberal education. This kind of policy has led most students to regard general education as a necessary evil to be dispensed with as soon as possible and with the least possible effort, in order to move on toward basic objectives. All deficiencies in tool subjects (communication skills for the most part) should be removed early in the college student's career, but they should not be confused with liberal education.

Liberal education courses should be offered toward the end of the student's degree program regardless of the degree he is seeking. To meet the requirements for majors and minors, advanced courses could be taken concurrently with liberal courses. The objective is to help the student integrate knowledge and experiences—a process that is impossible prior to the acquisition of knowledge and experiences.

Is there less or more need for liberal education today than in previous societies? Is there less need for a balance between education for citizenship and education for the professions? Should some students turn to science for the ends and means of living, while others try to find both in the arts, or commerce, or political science? Should a university try to provide both liberal and professional preparation?

In recent years institutions of higher learning as well as business, commerce, engineering, and other professions have indicated an increasing concern for the liberal education of students. The University of Tokyo and all other Japanese universities, for example, now require two years of general education of all students. The same is true of the University of the Philippines. The argument here is based upon the thesis that history, philosophy, literature, the arts, ethics, and religion should be the sources of the ends of living and that science and technology should provide the means for achieving the good life.

If the mission of the university is concerned with professional and technical training aimed at further industrialization, then liberal education is of the greatest importance, for man is both the means and the end of industrialization. If the university really is to assist in this economic development, it will need to increase and refine the wants and tastes of the people through liberal education by permitting scientific, technical, and engineering schools to provide the skills for their achievement. Otherwise, the new skills will be developed without clearly defined purposes and long-range objectives, and spiritual qualities will give way to materialistic ends.

The Nature of Liberal Education. Liberal education emphasizes the responsibilities of citizenship without minimizing the rights of the citizen. It points the way to the maximum sharing of interests and purposes among people without destroying their individuality. It builds brotherhood among men by emphasizing the ways in which men are alike rather than by exaggerating their differences. It should attempt to alleviate the strife among nations and among men through the study of the science of man and the art of peace, rather than the science of war and the devious glory of conquest.

The re-orientation of higher education represents revival of the fundamentals, made functional through experience. It means a new emphasis for the liberal arts—a liberal arts education that is functional for free men in a society where all men are free and where the dignity of work is recognized. It recognizes the social, economic, political, moral, and vocational interdependence of individuals.

The core of the curriculum for liberal education is found in the sciences, the social studies, and the humanities. Courses in these fields, properly integrated and articulated, constitute a new science that is rapidly emerging because of the imperative need for individuals to study, live, and work together on the basis of mutual understanding and respect, rather than old and new world prejudices which have led to inevitable conflicts and wars between individuals and between nations.

It is reasonable to anticipate the development of the science of man as the basic liberal education need of the twentieth century. The essential quality of education, a quality which justifies its public support, is its contribution to local, national, and international citizenship.

Research and discoveries in the world of matter have been so great that man today is threatened with destruction by this Frankenstein monster of his own invention. This situation has arisen because the emphasis has been upon the increase of knowledge concerning the material resources of the world. The mind of man should be the next great conquest of science; and the discoveries of science should be implemented by moral direction, placing man in the proper relationship to his physical environment.

This is the new challenge to scientists, philosophers, and teachers —to rediscover man that he may be able to cope with the intricate society in which science has placed him. To meet this new challenge, higher education must continue to foster the mastery of truth as an instrument of effective living; must rededicate itself to the maximum development of leadership; and must instill in all of its students a fervor and zeal for justice and service to mankind. The science of man must become as important as the science of the physical world in the universities' research projects. Areas of the curricula having particular significance for the development of the science of man are philosophy, psychology, sociology, and anthropology. Even the members of state legislatures in 1959 were demanding this new emphasis— to balance research in physical, biological, and social sciences.

Contribution of Social Studies. "Since wars begin in the minds of men, it is in the minds of men that the defenses of peace must be constructed." This auspicious preamble to the Charter of the United Nations Educational, Scientific, and Cultural Organization constitutes a propitious challenge to the professors of social studies in any institution of higher learning. Deliberate focusing of curricula upon the cosmic problem of world peace makes imperative the development of a greater degree of understanding among individuals. Prodigious as the task may seem in a world of heterogeneous individuals and societies, nothing less than the development of universal understanding can form an acceptable objective of the social studies in these extraordinary times.

The whole world is a community; and conscious, deliberate promotion of common purposes, interests, and understanding among individuals as a basis for peaceful living is a general objective of all education. It is specific and paramount with the social studies. In a world of informed, intelligent peoples, communication between ministers, diplomats, and heads of states is not sufficient to develop or maintain a peaceful world community. Consciously shared and integrated purposes, objectives, and ideals on the part of the masses are necessary for the development of harmonious relationships among the nations of the world.

Industrialization and specialization which have made the nations of the world economically interdependent are utterly inconsistent with radical nationalism as the basis of political, social, and idealogical loyalties among people. The objective of one world at peace, ennobled and necessary as it may be, will remain forever a remote possibility until world consciousness transcends jingoistic nationalism.

The development of a universal society so necessary in an interdependent economic world is practically impossible because of the difficulty of achieving common understandings, purposes, and conjoint living among world citizens. The world requires the common sharing of purposes in the solution of community problems. It requires understanding at the intellectual level, and this should be an objective of the social studies.

While this objective of local, state, national, and international understanding is a unique function of the social studies, it is by no means limited to the social studies. It is a responsibility that impinges upon every aspect of college and university life. It is a fundamental part of extra-curricular, as well as the formally organized curricular, phases of education. Research, vocationalism, professional competencies, and all other areas of learning must be accented in the direction of greater human understanding at all levels of society.

Social studies are concerned with the preservation of the ideals, the values, and the history of the various cultures because of the significance which these hold in the development, refinement, and constant changing of present cultures. Familiarity with traditions of past civilizations is not a looking backward for the objectives of education, but the assessment of past cultures for an intelligent solution and more sagacious approach to present cultural problems.

Wisdom and logic, while constantly undergoing changes as a result of further experimentation, are themselves the conscious accumulation of the most intelligent reactions of the past as a basis for the exercise of intelligence in the solution of current and future political, social, and economic problems. Preservation of the social and political heritage of the past through history, political science, and economics; the continuous sifting, winnowing, and refining of data for the solution of current problems; and a constant sensitivity to our responsibility to future generations make possible that continuity of experience and intelligence by which the continued progress of civilization is assured.

The Humanistic Tradition. Almost a hundred years ago, Cardinal Newman expressed the humanistic objective of a university education when he stated: "It aims at raising the intellectual tone of society, at cultivating the public mind, at purifying the national taste, at giving enlargement and sobriety to the ideas of the age, and refining the intercourse of private life. It is the education which gives man a clear, conscious view of his own opinions and judgments, a truth in developing them, an eloquence in expressing them, and a force in urging them. It teaches him to detect what is sophisticated and to discard what is irrelevant. It shows him how to accommodate himself to others, how to throw himself into their state of mind, how to bring them before his own, how to influence them, how to come to an understanding with them, how to bear with them. He is at home in any society—he has common ground with every class; he knows when to speak and when to be silent; he is able to converse—he is able to listen."[1]

Literature, religion, music, art, drama, and philosophy are particularly associated with the dissemination of ideas, values and high purposes sufficient to motivate and redirect the course of human behavior. The humanistic concept should result in an increasing spirit of cooperation and respect among the various faculties of the institutions that subscribe to the unity of the individual and the equality of all socially desirable vocations and curricula. The humanities express man's humanity to man.

No one can comprehend the significance of ideas, values, and convictions intelligently preserved in literature, art, music, philosophy, and drama in the determination of the attitudes and actions of a people. The vibrant current of humanistic values has soared or waned according to the aesthetic sensitivity of men since the onrush of that sweeping revival of values expressed in the Renaissance of the fourteenth, fif-

---

[1]John Henry Cardinal Newman, *The Idea of a University* (London and New York: Longmans, Green & Co., 1888), pp. 177-178.

teenth, and sixteenth centuries, a period which marked the transition from the medieval to the modern world.

The Renaissance continues in the modern world at an accelerated pace. Nothing is static except change, but values, ideas, philosophies, and historical perspective continue to give direction to dynamic societies of the twentieth century.

Classical works of art, music, literature, and philosophy constitute a dynamic aspect of the higher education curriculum. The challenge to those who have responsibility for curricula in the liberal arts is to draw upon the works of masters in all fields, both for their own sake and as a challenge to the development of standards in contemporary institutions. A balanced curricula must be based upon consideration of the disciplines, society, and the individual.

Music, literature, religion, philosophy, and art probably constitute the chief agencies for the development of intelligent, aesthetic appreciation. Their responsibility is not confined within departmental limitations. They contribute to the formation of aesthetic standards and values for all experiences. As such, they constitute a functional phase of the curricula in the same sense as do highly vocational or specialized courses.

Aesthetic appreciation and relevant values are basic in the achievement of successful living. Every subject that is taught has the inherent qualities necessary for the development of imagination and appreciation, provided that the students and professors look beyond the achievement of immediate skills to the socially desirable consequences of the subject in the development of successful living. This concept is basic to the humanization of the sciences and vocational subjects and to the development of interaction among the individuals who represent the component parts of the curricula. All subjects should either have immediate value or be a means to a perceivable end. The assignment of isolated, self-sufficient values to specialized subjects results in educational distintegration, compartmentalization, and failure to recognize the interdependence between vocational and humanistic studies.

Education in its broadest sense, encompassing the whole environment of the individual—home, church, schools, community activities and experiences—may lead to the solution of some of man's problems. Limited to the formal classroom situation, it can never do so.

Liberal education is concerned with values and ideas. The values, ideas, purposes, and loyalties of any people in any culture form a significant part of the content of education. When knowledge of the past is used as a basis for securing or knowing the values and ideas which motivated the people of other cultures at other periods of history, such knowledge becomes functional in the determination of procedures, techniques, goals, and values for the improvement of present society. Drawing upon the past for a wider intelligence in the solution of current problems and anticipating the consequences of present action is the method by which the continuity of experience is developed and values are refined and maintained.

The great sweep of history with its all-encompassing story of man's inhumanity to man is indispensable to the humanities curriculum. World history, the fine arts, world literature, and the history of philosophy, with emphasis upon the development of different philosophical systems —general in their approach and integrated through joint planning on the part of professors involved—constitute the core of the humanities curriculum for liberal education.

The unifying influence of music as a universal language is obvious. Men do not need to speak the same language in order to appreciate the beauty of music. Competency as a performer is not required in order to develop musical appreciation. The same is true with respect to art. The history of art as an expression of the feelings, emotions, and values of peoples of different cultures and of contemporary cultures is indispensable to the development of understanding among heterogeneous individuals and nations. Artists, like musicians, have developed common symbols which reach beyond differences of race, nationality, or language and thus constitute a great unifying force on an international scale.

History is the connecting link between all of the segments of the humanities courses and should be used effectivly in literature, philosophy, art, and music. Philosophy provides the synthesis so necessary for the integration and articulation of all of the humanistic studies.

Humanities provide satisfying experiences necessary for emotional stability. Clear, precise thinking on the part of individuals requires good language habits. No ability which man possesses is of greater human significance than the power to express ideas clearly and to set these ideas before other men, either by oral or by written communication. The ability to perform on a musical instrument or to paint a satisfying picture, to write a poem or to make an acceptable speech— these abilities contribute to the well-being of the individual and have lasting educational values. The development of skill in these various activities is not usually a major objective in the liberal education courses, but students should be permitted to elect dramatic art, fine arts, music, and speech to meet the requirements of liberal education in the humanities. These areas of study have even greater significance for those who aspire to positions of leadership in higher education.

Liberal Education Values of Science. Development of the scientific method in the solution of problems, as well as openmindedness, objectivity, intelligent observation, and accuracy in interpreting and recording data are among the values which science can contribute to the liberal education of all students.

Properly presented, the sciences satisfy the inherent curiosity of students to find out things for themselves and to learn through experience. Science is the only branch of knowledge which is concerned with material objects and processes which lend themselves to exact measurement and description. This quality is not always appreciated nor understood by those outside the field of science and, indeed, may be challenged by those who believe that science has humanistic responsibilities as do the social studies and the humanities.

The method of science is indispensable in the solution of world problems, but the products of science itself must be humanized by placing the emphasis upon the development of better human beings in a better environment. The age-old conflict between scientific objectivity and political dogma should give way to the emerging science of man, using the same openmindedness and scientific approach which have characterized the progress of science.

Education is a process of growth requiring increasingly intelligent action and decisions with each succeeding experience. It is dynamic, progressive, and continuous. The theory of the universe, developed by Copernicus, Galileo, *et al.*, unleashed the creative intelligence of man through scientific inquiry. The surrender of the idea of static substance paved the way for great progress in the realm of the physical world. Of even greater impact was the revolution in the realm of ideas and theory of certainty. The dogma of knowledge as revealed by God dampened the spirit of inquiry for centuries.

Copernicus, Bacon, Dewey, and other dissenters changed the emphasis from limited and fixed ultimates as the only challenge to intelligence and learning, to unlimited search for methods and consequences. The new theory has greatly influenced man's conquest of the universe.

Liberal education in the sciences is concerned with the ability to profit from history, to synthesize facts and experiences, and to apply intelligence and imagination to present conditions in order to anticipate consequences of present actions. It means control of methods and techniques in order to control outcomes and harmonize means and ends.

The impact of the methods of science upon the development of logical thinking divorced from fixed entities, which, prior to Francis Bacon and the age of experimentation in science, tended to enslave man's thinking and progress, should become a vital objective of liberal education in the sciences. Case studies of scientific principles at the most simplified and primitive stages offer the student and professor alike an unusual opportunity to gain a more intelligent insight into the struggles of men of science to overcome philosophical, religious, and social dogma so utterly inconsistent with the dynamic qualities of unhampered scientific inquiry. They lend meaning to the spirit of, and the necessity for, free inquiry. They refute conformity as a virtue.

Case studies on the historical development of scientific principles and concepts offer myriad examples of successful and unsuccessful experimentation in all aspects of science. They reveal the tendency for experimentation to stimulate new ideas, techniques, concepts, and further experimentation where the mind is free.

Scientific inquiry is concerned not only with conditions under which certain phenomena occur but with consequences as well. Ends and means should be related, and it is out of success and failure in trying different methods and applying different principles that generalizations and concepts emerge.

One of the best ways to develop in students the desired methods of scientific inquiry is to involve them in problems and abstractions, the solutions to which require the use of experimentation. Student participation in establishing hypotheses, testing procedures and techniques, evaluating results and conclusions, and formulating new objectives is more important than the accumulation of facts and ready-made generalizations resulting from performing routine laboratory experiments.

Ability to think critically and to abandon authoritarian learning are both positive goals that are closely related. Critical thinking is especially necessary for the application of the fruits of science to physical and mental health, communications, aesthetics, general problems of living, and improvement of the general social order. The transfer of scientific method to the social field is an objective which must be achieved if the true spirit of inquiry and intelligence is to determine solutions to social problems.

Limitation of Laboratory Experiments. It is time to challenge the mechanical repetition of traditional laboratory experiments as being the basis for liberal education in the sciences. Laboratory work is a significant means to the achievement of desired objectives, but not so important for liberal education as for specialized courses leading to careers in science. Slavery to the laboratory method is based upon the false notion that progress in science consists in demonstrating as many known facts as possible within the shortest possible time, notwithstanding the fact that most of the demonstrations of experiments, as performed by students, follow step by step the methodology and procedure established by earlier experimenters as recorded in the standard textbooks. Moreover, the results must be identical to those achieved in the thousands of laboratories where the experiments have been performed in previous years. This is not the method of scientific inquiry.

Science education, with emphasis upon the problems of living and an understanding of the environment, has many advantages over the strict laboratory approach for those who teach undergraduates. Experiences approximating methods followed by scientists would place less emphasis upon fixed experiments.

The first step in releasing the student and the professor from this slavery to the laboratory method, at the exclusion of other desirable methods of learning (notably those followed in the legal professions, in philosophy, and in history), is to take the emphasis off the accumulation of a set body of facts unrelated to the problems at hand and irrespective of the liberal education needs of the students. Experimentation in education needs to sever its chains from a bondage that limits research by recognizing but one method.

In progressive programs for liberal education in the sciences, there is a trend away from the teaching of fact as its own end and, likewise, a noticeable trend toward a more critical selection of the content which should constitute the science curriculum for liberal education. This trend is one which is now advocated by the departmental specialists in the sciences wherever those specialists have given serious and critical consideration to the role of science in the education of all students.

There are many departments and institutions, however, where allegiance to the status quo in the teaching of scientific experiments, without regard to differentiation among students and their particular needs, is as great today and constitutes as serious a limitation upon the effectiveness of science as did the allegiance and loyalty to mystical pronouncements and philosophical dogma of the ancient and medieval periods of history. The static curricula in science as well as in any other area of learning are utterly incompatible with dynamic education and the progressive continuity of experience.

The history of science reveals that most of the methods which have been used, and most of the techniques, have been failures. The student who studies a basic scientific principle divorced from its historical development and setting misses this basic experience.

The Dilemma of Science. The acceptance of science as a basic part of the pattern of liberal education imposes upon scientists a responsibility uniquely different from that of discovering new scientific principles and advancing quantitative knowledge. Science is responsible for the tendency toward a materialistic society. The adaptation of the basic scientific principles to the practical arts has relieved man of the responsibility for providing energy necessary for the production of goods and services. This has transformed man's way of living from a self-centered, individualistic family entity to a highly mechanistic society involving and demanding the ultimate in specialization and cooperation.

Dynamic continuity of specialization in the sciences and in the development of new basic principles is indispensable to the perpetuation of society. A continued and ever-increasing emphasis upon specialization will characterize science as well as all other branches of knowledge. Acceptance of science as a part of the liberal education curriculum, however, constitutes a new responsibility for the scientists. The impact of science upon culture has been so great that it is now deemed necessary that every college graduate should be familiar with the historical development of scientific principles and with an understanding of the social implications of these discoveries.

Moreover, the program of liberal education in the sciences, like that in all the other divisions and departments of the university, is a humanistic program. General education, in order to have its deepest possible significance, requires an integration of knowledge, which recognizes and perceives the basic relationship between all activities of men and the basic unity of man as well as knowledge. Scientists with highly specialized departmental interests represent, as a general rule, the ultimate in the disintegration of knowledge. Society demands this of all scientists who represent departmental specialities. Academic respectability and achievement of rank, tenure, and desirable increases in salary all too frequently depend upon departmental specialization and, unfortunately, are not used to encourage a liberal education background. This constitutes the dilemma in science. Professors are highly specialized because the colleges and universities have demanded no less. Colleges and universities have demanded no less because society is now founded upon the principle of specialization.

This principle of specialization on the part of university professors and its demand on the part of employing administrators come close to the heart of the problem in liberal education. Integrated studies are desired. In general, professors are specialists in disintegration of studies and knowledge.

Perhaps the most difficult, if not the most serious, problem which must be encountered in the development of an integrated program for liberal education lies in the reform of graduate schools in their approach to the basic preparation of those employed to teach special, as well as general, departmental, and divisional courses. Specialization at the graduate school level, with its high research ability, limited departmental interests, and a minimum opportunity or inclination to broaden the graduate student's educational horizon, is the rule rather than the exception.

Proposed Solution. The first step in the alleviation of the difficulty in the program of liberal education in the sciences is the radical reform of graduate schools in the preparation of professors in all departments of science, particularly those professors whose objective is to teach courses for liberal education. Liberal education in the sciences at the undergraduate levels is indispensable for scientists themselves. Departmental disintegration and specialization must be balanced by appropriate courses with liberal objectives, not only for the professors of general courses but for the specialist as well.

College and university administrators have the inescapable responsibility of providing salary schedules, tenure regulations, salary increments, and retirement provisions that encourage scholars to pursue liberal education in the sciences as a teaching career without their having any embarrassment as to academic respectability or fear concerning the opportunities for promotion. The history, principles, problems, concepts, habits, attitudes, patterns of behavior, and methods of science should become the common motivating intellectual objectives of every member of a science division. These common objectives and problems and agreements upon basic scientific principles offer one possibility of integrating the present scientific personnel.

These reforms and changes can be accomplished with the enthusiastic cooperation and support of the profession of science. They can be accomplished in no other way. Evidences of the necessary interest and motivation on the part of scientists are available wherever scientists themselves have studied their own problems in relationship to the objectives of liberal education.

The offering of general courses in earth, physical, and biological sciences, for the present at least, will in most cases require the joint efforts of professors with departmental specialities. If, on the other hand, introductory courses designed as prerequisites to advanced training in the various departments of science continue to substitute for liberal education requirements, it will be necessary that the emphasis be taken off the accumulation of a set body of facts and be placed instead upon a more intelligent understanding of the principles of science and their broad implications in society. It will be necessary further that members of the staff be motivated by common objectives, problems, and principles if these introductory, specialized courses are to constitute a synthesis of man's progress in the sciences. This may not be the best solution. It represents a possible improvement.

Remote Objectives. The discoveries of modern science offer mankind the greatest opportunity in history to transfer the emphasis from materialistic means to the more socially desirable or undesirable ends, depending upon the use and adaptations of the products of science. Science has made possible the tremendous production of goods and services so characteristic of present societies. If this production becomes the end rather than a means to a larger objective, "materialistic" is a just criticism of the system. Science must be humanized, and its products must be humanized. The consequences of science must be tested by the criterion of the production of better human beings in a better environment.

The nature of science should be studied with conscious effort toward an understanding of its relationship to social, economic, and political problems and progress. The relationships between science and other activities of man become clear only as the student is able to integrate all areas of learning, utilizing the literature of science in the same way that he utilizes history and political theory, art and music.

Liberal education in the sciences requires the conscious development of ability to think; intelligent understanding of the basic principles of science; the development of socially desirable habits, attitudes and appreciations; the establishment of desirable patterns of behavior based upon social sensitivity to one's personal, civic, economic, and political responsibilities; and, finally, the development of that quality of suspended judgment, openmindedness, and objectivity, characteristic of the approach to scientific problems.

The erroneous concept of the neutrality of science with respect to issues involving values must give way to social consciousness and responsiveness on the part of scientists and students of science in a dynamic society, the solution of whose problems depends upon the synthesis of a general and specialized intelligence of all citizens.

Science and Society. Scientists, therefore, constitute one of the great voluntary constituents of society. They are of, by, and for society and not apart from society. In most periods of history, they have shared ideas and discoveries on an international scale to a greater extent perhaps than has any other group outside of the fields of literature, art, and music. Scientists represent a group of individuals closely interwoven because of the common purposes, objectives, and activities which motivate their actions. Their contribution to the democratic process, however, like all other groups, depends upon their interaction with and their contribution to other voluntary organizations within society.

Need for Academic Improvement

The people of the United States believe that higher education is a great means toward constructive change and progress. In general, higher education has lived up to this challenge. American colleges and universities are only in part a result of society. They are, in truth, a cause of American society.

The agricultural resources of the nation, the level of cultural achievement, the standard of living, and the health of the people are the direct result of research, teaching, and extension services carried on for a century by the universities of the nation.

Faculties have sometimes been complacent in the management of academic affairs. They are known everywhere for their opposition to serious changes in curricula and programs. Higher education helps to effect change everywhere, but it has difficulties in changing itself. The largest public relations problem is inside the colleges.

A courageous approach to the problem of learning is needed. Learning is an individual and highly personal matter. At best, the professor can only stimulate and guide learning.

New techniques of teaching and learning are imperative. Breaking the sound barrier of ignorance in communications media must be applied to learning. Courses and content must be pruned to permit new and healthier growth. Distinguished professors should be relieved of clerical and administrative tasks in order that they may have contacts with more students. The education function requires many people working at different levels. Libraries, laboratories, and extra-curricular facilities must be used so as to permit students to assume increasing responsibility for their own education. College faculties must apply the good business and professional principles which they have taught to so many other groups. The whole process of higher education must be subjected to rigorous research in order to accelerate and improve the process of teaching and learning.

The responsibility for excellence in teaching, learning, and research, the principal functions of a university, belongs to the faculty. The ends of higher education are in the development of people and the advancement of knowledge. Administration, budgets, public relations, committee work, and clerical activities are means toward achieving these ends.

Henry Wriston believed, after thirty years of being a college administrator, that the ideal faculty man very appropriately regards administration, committee assignments, and haggling about the wording of regulations "as distasteful."

While one may agree with the academic viewpoint on academic affairs, boards of trustees and administrators have the realistic problem of relating a university to its publics and to society in order to get the support required by the faculty. Adequate support is necessary for improvement.

Administrators and faculties are not two opposing camps. The dramatic discoveries of learning, teaching, and research must be in the public image of universities. In this sense, administrators are dependent upon the faculties for success in gaining institutional support. Faculties need the skill of administrators in the organization and management of academic affairs. The two groups are interdependent.

Distate for administration on the part of academic personnel sometimes results in a policy of drifting and stagnation. To make matters worse, institutions frequently follow the questionable practice of appointing heads or chairmen of departments on a permanent basis. This sometimes blocks needed changes in a department for the remainder of the chairman's term.

If administration is distasteful to the best of academic people, then periodic change of departmental chairman may be necessary to promote and to protect academic excellence.

Upon resigning from his position as dean of the College of Arts and Science at the University of Wisconsin to go back to being a professor, Dr. Mark Ingraham[2] stated the following reasons for his decision:

> Perhaps most important, I do not sympathize with certain tendencies in our current civilization which to a greater and greater extent control our universities as well as other social institutions. I shall mention two.
>
> The emphasis on science and technology leads to an imbalance in our culture. It also leads to competitive pressures that go far to determine the policy of any university.
>
> A hierarchy in American intellectual life, descending from mathematics and the physical sciences through the biological and social sciences to the humanities, is unfortunate.
>
> I say this in spite of my love of mathematics. A hierarchy in reverse order would be equally bad. I believe that the opportunity, recognition, and pay of an individual in a university should be determined by the quality of his character, mind, and accomplishments rather than by the fields of his interest.

Summary

A strong liberal arts program would achieve the following purposes: (1) provide a liberal education which is indispensable to the preparation of educated men; (2) strengthen the professional schools by providing a broad cultural and technical foundation necessary for effective living; (3) make it possible for present and future students, majoring in the arts, sciences, and literature, to gain that broad cultural and liberal education so necessary for citizenship and for an understanding of the great history and cultures of the world.

Mankind has the resources and skill to produce a world society free from disease, illiteracy, hunger, and fear; a world in which the new inexhaustable energy does man's drudgery and allows all men time for meditation, art, and aesthetics; a world where shared interests and

---

[2]Source: A letter from Dr. Ingraham on the occasion of his retirement as Dean of the College of Arts and Science, University of Wisconsin, Madison.

social purposes govern; and a world where the mind of man may at last be devoted to the creation of beauty and the promotion of love.

Mankind has the resources and skill to destroy all great cities and centers of industry, to disrupt communication, to kill the sources and contaminate existing supplies of food, to wipe out most of the population, and to reduce all civilization to a state of abject anarchy.

The dispositions, habits, and thinking formulated by the young in the classrooms of life will determine whether man follows the path of creative activity and peace or whether, in a continuation of competition for power, he destroys all human values and life itself. The former path is the one dictated by reason and by all principles of morality; the latter is dictated by a lust for power, completely devoid of moral responsibility.

This is an issue in which the teachers of the world will play a paramount part. Parents, teachers, and all who teach the young may, through united effort, be able to direct the energies of man from hatred and war to the virtues of reason, love, and peace.

What has all this to do with college administration in general and with academic administration in particular? The answer is "everything." College administration is synonymous with educational leadership. Unless it goes beyond the mundane housekeeping functions of buildings, budgets, and general bureaucratic management, it does not touch educational consequences. The first consideration of those who administer academic affairs must be ideas, values, philosophies, and directions which form the components of their educational compass. Otherwise, the administrator becomes the means by which a giant educational enterprise moves, without inhibition, in all directions. Dynamic leadership in higher education will always be dependent upon the ability of the leader to integrate the best ideas and thinking of the academic and administrative personnel.

Questions for Discussion

1. In what specific ways are the liberal arts a more dynamic force in our society than in previous cultures?
2. What rationale can one develop for an inductive rather than a deductive approach to general education?
3. What are the methods by which individuals learn?
4. How do individuals think?
5. What is the relationship between knowledge, thinking, and action?
6. Is educational synthesis becoming more difficult? Why?

Bibliography

BARZUN, JACQUES. *The House of Intellect.* New York: Harper & Bros., 1959.

BRONOWSKI, JACOB. *Science and Human Values.* New York: J. Messner Co., 1956.

CAPLOW, THEODORE, and McGEE, REECE J. *The Academic Marketplace.* New York: Basic Books, 1958.

CONANT, JAMES BRYANT. *Education in a Divided World.* Cambridge, Massachusetts: Harvard University Press, 1948.

CURTI, MERLE EUGENE. *American Paradox.* New Brunswick, New Jersey: Rutgers University Press, 1956.

GOODE, WILLIAM J., and HATT, PAUL K. *Methods in Social Research.* New York: McGraw-Hill Book Co., Inc., 1952.

NEWMAN, JOHN HENRY. *The Idea of a University (The Harvard Classics, Essays English and American,* Vol. 28, ed. Charles W. Eliot). New York: P. F. Collier & Son, 1910.

SNOW, CHARLES PERCY. *The Two Cultures and the Scientific Revolution.* Cambridge, England: The University Press, 1959.

STILES, LINDLEY J., and others. *Teacher Education in the United States.* New York: Ronald Press Co., 1960.

WHITEHEAD, ALFRED NORTH. *The Aims of Education, and Other Essays.* London: Williams and Norgate, Ltd., 1950.

Chapter

9

Student Personnel Services

Purposes—Principles—Programs

Background of Personnel Services. The foregoing chapters have attempted to delineate a rationale with respect to administration as well as to teaching. The thesis has been advanced that the methods of education must be in harmony with the objectives; that a democratic relationship must exist between staff and administration and between the students and professors.

Germane to the achievement of this relationship is the student personnel program which has the intelligent support of the entire academic and administrative staff, for, in the most comprehensive sense, student personnel services impinge upon all institutional services (curricular, extracurricular, and personal) which are made available to students. This statement does not imply that guidance is the whole or the Gestalt of which education is a part. No more distorted viewpoint of the role of guidance can possibly be presented; however, many specialists in guidance have defined their functions as encompassing the entire process of education. Guidance is one aspect of education with which all competent professors and administrative employees should be concerned. Delimiting the process of guidance is necessary for the determination of specific functions and adequate staff for carrying out those functions.

Before attempting to determine what is the most desirable administrative organization for student personnel services, it is necessary to analyze the functions and responsibilities that fall within this category.

201

Ideally, this approach should be used in determining the administrative organization for all facets of an institution.

Student personnel services are among the many unique aspects of American education. These services are almost completely unknown in colleges and universities in Europe, Latin America, Asia, and Africa.

Following the war between the States, women began to clamor for the privilege of admission to institutions of higher learning which previously had been limited to men. This brought about great concern for the social, moral, and physical welfare of women who were to be admitted. The doors began to open. The first solution to the problem was the appointment of a lady principal, warden, lady assistant, or matron, who supervised the social, physical, and general well-being of the students. These officials were the forerunners of advisers and deans of women, the latter title being used first at the University of Chicago.

The first counseling services made available for women were concerned primarily with the social activities—a concern which developed out of a fear for the consequences of permitting young men and women to attend the same institutions. With the admission of women to institutions of higher learning came the desire and the need for analyzing the consequences of college education for homemaking and for other vocational competencies. The American Association of University Women, since 1882, has been very active in this aspect of the counseling program.

The influx of students from different cultural backgrounds, with varied but frequently undetermined vocational goals, has made modern institutions of higher learning very different from original colleges and universities on the continent of Europe and in early American society. The changes which have come about in higher education have focused attention upon the need for more adequate guidance and counseling of the students.

The housing of students has been one of the principal student personnel problems from the beginning of higher education in America. In the latter part of the nineteenth century, the paternalistic concept of student discipline and control was challenged by the newer German philosophy of accepting college students as responsible adults. The former view came from the English system where colleges were responsible for developing the intellect and for protecting, if not improving, the morals of students, even though the latter objective was achieved at Oxford by locking the men in their dormitories at 9:00 P.M.

Following the Civil War, the English dormitory system in America began to decline sharply for two reasons: (1) the admission of students destined for careers in business, commerce, and industry as fellows along with those study for the professions; (2) the liberalization of controls as expressed by great leaders of the period such as Francis Wayland, Henry P. Tappan, and especially President Eliot, who believed that only self-control is legitimate for college students.

When dormitory housing as an institutional responsibility began to wane, fraternities, sororities, and palatial houses under a system of private enterprise sprang up to fill the need for living quarters.

Eventually the pendulum swung back, and, at the turn of the century, Woodrow Wilson, who was then president at Princeton University, was demanding that curricular and extracurricular activities be brought back together at Princeton. In 1907, Wilson, in stating his case for housing students in University-controlled residential quadrangles, each with its own dining hall, common room for social intercourse and diversion, resident master, and preceptors, stated: "The only way in which the social life of the undergraduates can be prevented from fatally disordering, and perhaps even strangling the academic life of the University, is by the actual absorption of the social life into the academic."[1]

Fifty-two years later, Henry M. Wriston, who lived and worked with students for almost fifty years and listened to the alarmists of successive generations denounce the current clothing, dance, music, language, curricula, and intellectual softness of students, was moved to proclaim:

> The net effect upon me of that long experience is one of admiration for students. They follow the fads, different fads from those of their elders . . . Their music doesn't go round and round, but up and down. They are not harmoniously concerned with the scarcity of bananas, . . . they are youth growing out of the teens into the twenties—and facing the same old problems—with a new vocabulary.[2]

The scope and complexity of American society, with systems of higher education designed to serve as both cause and effect of that society, led inevitably and necessarily to the elective system, diversified curricula, and heterogeneous student bodies. In such complex institutions, it is virtually impossible, and certainly undesirable, to cast all students in

---

[1]Day, Donald, *Woodrow Wilson's Own Story* (Boston: Little, Brown & Co., 1952), p. 84.

[2]Wriston, Henry M., *Academic Procession* (New York: Columbia University Press, 1959), pp. 194-5.

a common academic and social mold. It is even more impossible to develop college-sponsored and college-supervised conjoint living and studying on the basis of individual differences. With these facts in mind, it is high time that students assume increasing responsibilities for the substantive elements of their educational growth. Otherwise, college and university experience will destroy the last hope of the free enterprise system which, at best, is the untrammeled intelligence of American youth.

Personnel functions were, in the main, always present to some degree. The beginning of these functions on a specialized basis developed out of a disciplinary problem. Because of the role of women in American society, there arose a demand on colleges to provide supervisors for women.

The actual functionary of deans of women developed from this so-called "protection-era." The first dean of women on record was at Swarthmore in 1890, followed by Chicago in 1892, Oberlin in 1894, and Michigan in 1896. The first national convention of deans of women was held in 1903.

In 1882, the Association of Collegiate Alumnae was formed to promote women's affairs in colleges and universities. This organization continued its activities through 1915. During its existence, it conducted research as to whether or not college women were physically and mentally capable of meeting college requirements and whether or not college made women unfit for homemaking.

There followed a realization of a need for counseling of college men. This need developed with an increased range of vocational choice. Classes were no longer small, and faculty could no longer pay attention to the all-round student development. As the population grew, financial, marital, social, and academic problems grew. Increased curricular offerings made decisions without guidance difficult.

The nature of the work of the first men in the field of guidance offered no one set pattern of organization, and in most instances, the services were performed by everyone. The first dean of men was at Harvard in 1890. Discipline was his chief function. The dean's position often grew out of admissions or registrar's duties. Functions of placement, counseling, arranging loans, and student employment were often distributed among faculty members, if these services were offered at all. Early deans were, for the most part, only disciplinarians.

Many contributions were made by the American Council on Education. It contributed more to college personnel work than any other single organization through its early emphasis upon a personnel point of view. Through committees for research, its accomplishments have been significant. Examples of these committees include: the measurement and guidance committee of 1920; the Hopkins survey of student personnel procedures in 1926; the development of cumulative records, rating scales, scholastic aptitude and achievement tests in the early thirties; and the conference on college personnel work in 1937.

Some specific factors which have contributed to the growth of personnel services are as follows: increase in enrollments (from 1900 to 1950, college enrollment increased tenfold; the general population only doubled); wider socio-economic representation in the student body; upsurge of the elective system during the early 1900's and the breakdown of traditional requirements; changing purposes for attending college such as competencies in technical fields, scientific learnings, teacher training, business, and government services; growth of Land-Grant and state-supported universities not bound by old-fashioned traditions; obligations to serve secular public needs with the establishment of state universities; changing admission requirements; size and complexity, which led to business-like and increased administrative activity; separation of student services from faculty supervision and their development as administrative staff functions; liberalization of methods, purposes, and curricula; expanding systems of scholarships, fellowships, student employment, and other financial aid; gradual acceptance of the relative significance of informal education constantly in process outside the classroom; increased emphasis on the total college experience and realization that the environment can be controlled and manipulated to change student behavior; growth of centralized student living and dining services; provisions for health services and growth of social activities; realization of individual differences in ability, interests, background, aspiration, and personality; admission of women on a large scale; and increased student-participation in running their own affairs and participation in college affairs.

Principles of Student Personnel. The movement in student personnel services has not always been based upon fundamental principles. Among those that seem to be generally accepted are the following:

1. Individual differences in the student body are anticipated.
2. The individual is conceived of and treated as a functioning whole, and his development in all areas of living is treated as a unit.
3. Teaching, counseling, student activities, and other organized educational efforts of the institution "start realistically from the point where

the individual student is, not from the point of development at which the institution would like to find the hypothetical average student."

4. As an effective unitary organism, the student needs experiences to fulfill his intellectual, social, spiritual, and physical needs.
5. Student personnel services require the involvement of the entire institution.
6. Those who must abide by decisions should have a part in making them. This principle applies to students as well as to faculty.
7. The process of education requires that both masters and scholars progress increasingly toward the utilization of intelligence as a method of solving problems.
8. Students need to be led to perceive consequences, before acting, as a fundamental approach to intelligent social control.

Purposes of Student Personnel Services. Whether the student personnel program consists of one, two, or twenty persons, the basic functions are the same. Among functions which are generally accepted by college administrators and specialists in student personnel, the following are typical, but the list is not exhaustive.

The student personnel program is designed to achieve these purposes:

1. To assist the faculty in the understanding of students in order that the faculty in turn may be of more value in assisting students.
2. To assist parents in the adjustments that need to be made when sons and daughters enter the university.
3. To help the individual student to understand what he can and should do to strengthen his qualities, to handle his difficulties rationally rather than emotionally, to find suitable channels for his emotions, and to move toward his more acceptable self.
4. To sponsor appropriate experiences in co-curricular activities which will encourage social and cultural sensitivity, appreciation, and stimulation.

Williamson[3] believes that the personnel program should help the student in achieving (1) orientation to his college environment; (2) success in his studies; (3) satisfactory living facilities; (4) a sense of belonging to the college; (5) balanced use of his physical capacities; (6) understanding of himself; (7) understanding and uses of his emotions; (8) lively and significant interests; (9) understanding and control

---

[3]E. G. Williamson, and others, *The Student Personnel Point of View* (Washington, D. C.: American Council on Education, 1949), pp. 6-11.

of his financial resources; (10) progress toward appropriate vocational goals; (11) individuality and responsibility; (12) ethical and spiritual meaning of life; (13) ability to live with others; (14) growth toward satisfying and socially acceptable sexual adjustments, and (15) preparation for satisfying constructive post-college activity.

In general, the purposes seem to be classified into the following categories or broad organizational functions: (1) admissions—orientation, testing, selection; (2) personnel records; (3) counseling—education, social, emotional, vocational, and personal; (4) preventive medicine, health services, and personal hygiene counseling; (5) remedial services —speech, reading, and study; (6) supervision and integration of housing and food services; (7) activities program—social, religious, and recreational; (8) discipline as a positive program of growth toward maturity; (9) scholarship—financial aid, self-help, and veterans' programs; (10) job placement; (11) foreign students; (12) married students; (13) evaluation; (14) measurement and testing; and (15) personnel research.

Principles and purposes for student personnel services must be developed with full recognition of the forces that have actuated and vitalized this new administrative function; but these forces are not the only consideration, because they sometimes represent the militant aspirations of a vested interest which, like all bureaucratic hierarchies, worships magnitude and numbers. Fundamental criteria are found in the larger context of purposes of higher education in America. Direction in which education is moving is the basic foundation for conjoint action. If there is no agreement on ends, there will be no agreement on means. It is not sufficient to speak glibly of teaching, research, and service. These must be translated into operational definitions to carry vibrant meaning for young growing students.

At the risk of over-simplification, one may state that education is a process that spans the whole of life; it is coterminous with life; to break the continuity is to nullify past individual achievement. It is not something to be acquired, after which one may get on with other responsibilities. Education is an exacting taskmaster. The truly educated person can never escape the continuing responsibility, nor would he desire to do so.

Formal education (colleges and universities) is designed to accelerate and promote the process of education. Its mission is to bring the student into contact with the great heritage and achievements of all time and to assist the student in testing the results on life's problems and actions. Developing rather than informing the mind is the central task.

The Educational Policies Commission has summarized the objectives of higher education under four appropriate points:[4] (1) to help realize the dream of individual opportunity; (2) to preserve and enrich the cultural heritage, which, in the American value system, is not an escape from the vicissitudes and practicalities of life but a means of wrestling with them; (3) to add to existing knowledge through research and creative activity; and (4) to help translate learning into equipment for living and for social advance. Higher education is rooted in the service concept. Colleges and universities are thus parts of the foundation of democracy.

Student Personnel Viewpoint

The student personnel "point of view," a term frequently substituted in careless thinking for student personnel services, is a pervasive philosophy regarding the individual, a philosophy that affects the curriculum of the university, its teaching procedures, administrative policies, selection of faculty, and regulation of student conduct—in short the entire program of the institution. The degree to which it is present in a university goes far to determine the effectiveness of the student personnel program.

The origin of the student personnel "point of view" is not identified with any particular place or time. It has been present in all great centers of learning throughout history and was used to a significant degree by Socrates, Plato, and Aristotle.

Wherever and whenever a teacher operates in terms of the needs and interests of students, the personnel viewpoint is invoked. Scholars and teachers, sensitive to personal, social, intellectual, and vocational needs of students, have been present in all great institutions of learning. But not all academic personnel are motivated in this direction. The personnel worker needs to recognize these facts and to work to increase the climate of understanding between masters and scholars rather than to take on the impossible task of performing the substantive function of education through a bureaucratic student personnel task force.

Implementation of the personnel viewpoint demands no less than the development of a community of masters and scholars whose basic objective is intellectual achievement, and if such a task is rejected by the professors in a modern university, student personnel workers might

---

[4]Educational Policies Commission, *Higher Education in a Decade of Decision* (Washington, D. C.: National Education Association, 1957), pp. 6-10.

as well develop to the maximum all the side shows, which as Wilson[5] at Princeton warned would eventually "take over the circus."

The only point at which policy for such a climate of learning can be established for a whole institution is at the level of the controlling board and the president; and the rationale for great frustrations on the part of student personnel workers is that, as a small group, they are often working against the central current of the side shows—athletics, social organizations, and activities devoid of intellectual qualities.

Selection and Admission

The admissions work in colleges and universities is generally centralized in one office and is sometimes coordinated with the position of the registrar. Fundamental causes for the origin of the office of director of admissions were increasing college enrollments and the necessity for selecting students on the basis of their academic backgrounds and aptitudes for the college programs they plan to follow. Rejection of large numbers of applicants during the 1960's tended to make this a public relations problem.

The major services of the admissions office are: to correspond with prospective students and others regarding the offerings of the university; to process all applications for admission; to circulate bulletins and other printed materials about the school; to evaluate the records of prospective students for admission; to provide for pre-college counseling and guidance; to conduct research appropriate to the function of the office; to work closely with the registrar or recorder in matters relating to orientation, registration, student records, and transfer.

This phase of administration is assuming an increasing importance in the success of higher education. There is a continuous phenomenal increase in the number and types of applicants for admission. The problem has become not only that of preventing individuals who lack the requisite ability or preparation from entering but, also, and more important, that of attracting the many able students who do not now receive education beyond high school.

The Educational Policies Commission has enumerated four principles to guide admissions practices:[6]

---

[5]Donald Day, *Woodrow Wilson's Own Story* (Boston: Little, Brown & Co., 1952).

[6]Educational Policies Commission, *op. cit.*, pp. 33-35.

1. Every effort should be made to provide higher education for all youth who are capable of profiting by it.
2. In admissions policies, heavy emphasis should be placed on attracting those who are particularly gifted.
3. Admission efforts should be active rather than passive; the task is one of selective recruitment rather than admission.
4. Continued recognition must be given to students' self-selection for college. Student choice, based on adequate information, is a part of sound admissions policy.

The first contact made by university representatives is often long before the student graduates from the secondary school. College admissions representatives visit schools and talk with students and parents. Increasingly of late, these representatives are guidance trained, and many have had guidance experience in secondary schools. They must be skilled counselors, since so many young high school students are on the threshold of very significant decisions and in need of competent assistance.

For institutions where student tuition is the principal source of financial support, some authorities argue that recruitment is logically a public relations function and that, therefore, it should be placed in that office.

Recent trends in the methods of selection of students indicate that there is greater cooperation between colleges and secondary schools, and that there is a breaking away from the widely practiced system of basing entrance requirements on the number of earned credits in specific subject-matter fields, such as foreign languages. There is accordingly a marked growth in the use of aptitude tests and a student's standing in the high school graduating class. Students with high scholastic aptitude scores and good standing in their graduating classes generally have the necessary ability and motivation to succeed in college.

Research seems to indicate the soundness of the new approach to admissions. For example, the Eight Year Study by the Progressive Education Association came out with a plan of cooperation between a number of secondary schools and colleges in this way:

1. The participating colleges waived their usual subject and unit requirements, and many even went so far as to waive college entrance board and other examinations.
2. The cooperating schools were free to experiment with their own curricula. Their one obligation was to supply sufficient evidence

of the student's readiness for college work. Their graduates had a somewhat greater degree of college success than did the control group of 1,475 students who had taken the traditional college preparatory courses in secondary schools, whether success was judged by college standards, by students' contemporaries, or by the individual student.

There has been extensive research on the kinds of competencies which are good predictors of college success. Certain criteria seem to be gaining acceptance as indications of probable success of students in college. They are as follows:

1. Scholastic aptitude based upon a test such as the American Council on Education Psychological Examination.
2. Critical reading ability as evidenced by the Illinois High School Reading Test.
3. Writing skill as revealed by the General Educational Development Test of Correctness and Effectiveness of Expression.
4. Mathematical ability based upon tests such as the Quantitative Section of the American Council on Education Psychological Examination.
5. Evidence of intellectual interest and effective study habits.

The University of Minnesota, Duluth Branch, made a study of the "general" prediction of academic success, as measured by the over-all honor-point ratio for the first year of college work, and of the "differential" prediction of the success of students in specific courses. In the latter prediction, the criterion was the honor-point ratio in the subject studied.

The study was essentially correlative in character. The first part involved 421 students, of whom 258 were male and 163 female. The second part, concerning differential prediction, involved five sub-groups, ranging from 108 cases (in the prediction of success in zoology) to 410 cases (in the prediction of success in English).

An analysis of the data pertaining to the above groups has led to the development of certain predictive techniques. The validity of these techniques has been tested by an application of them to a subsequent class of students who entered the year following the initial phase of the study. Plumb concluded:[7]

---

[7]Valworth R. Plumb, "The Prediction of Academic Success at the University of Minnesota, Duluth Branch" (Unpublished Doctor's thesis, Madison, Wisconsin: School of Education, University of Wisconsin, 1951).

1. Of the measures studied, the high school percentile rank is the best single index of probable success in the freshman year of work. This statement applies both to the general prediction of success and to the differential prediction of success in specific courses.

2. For predictive purposes, the American Council on Education Cooperative General Culture Examination is the most useful of the tests employed. Its usefulness extends to the prediction of success in specific courses as well as to the prediction of general success. Two other examinations published by the American Council on Education likewise have predictive value, namely: the Psychological Examination and the Cooperative Reading Examination.

3. The factor of sex is definitely related to academic success. The females in this study were decidedly superior to males, as judged by the means of honor-point ratios. The only exception was in the correlation of the mathematics score of the General Culture Examination with the criterion.

4. The location of a student's home was related to his success at the University of Minnesota, Duluth, with students from one zone of residence showing superiority over the students from at least two other zones.

5. A delay of entrance to the University of one year after high school graduation tends to result in lower scholarship of students for the first quarter of work as compared with the scholarship of students entering in the fall following their high school graduation. However, this disadvantage disappears by the end of the first year.

An adequate program of admissions includes a positive approach to the selective admission of students. Most data available, for example, indicate that many students in the upper ten per cent of their high school graduating classes do not attend any college or university. Thus, it becomes the responsibility of an institution of higher learning to provide incentives and encouragement to all students who have outstanding ability and who are likely to profit most from a college or university education. It is the responsibility of student personnel workers to maintain close liaison with high school principals and counselors throughout the region which the institution serves, in order that the program of studies and curricula of the college may be developed and utilized in terms of meeting the changing needs of the young people who will be served by the institution. This is primarily a counseling problem of making known to high school graduates the availability of desirable curricula having significance for their particular aptitudes and interests.

Because of the nature of the work performed by student personnel services, it seems entirely logical to make extensive use of key personnel from this office for the counseling of prospective high school graduates in their own schools—through assembly programs followed by individual conferences with students and also through college-day programs sponsored by many high schools for the purpose of bringing to their prospective graduates representatives of the various institutions of higher learning who are given an opportunity to present the college level educational offerings. No responsibility impinging upon the college staff calls for greater integrity, honesty, and insight than does this opportunity for presenting to the members of a high school graduating class an objective appraisal of the educational opportunities at the college level. It is necessary to send out representatives who would be willing to advise a student to go to another institution if that institution can better serve the needs and interests of the individual concerned.

Another approach is the sponsoring of a superintendents' conference on the campus in the spring. At these conferences, counselors and key academic people are given an opportunity to explain the educational opportunities offered by the institution. This approach makes it possible for the public school administrators to counsel with their own students regarding the opportunities for higher education within the region. Likewise, the practice of inviting the regional high school principals' association to hold its meetings on the campus goes a long way toward improving the liaison between high school and university counselors to the end that the educational objectives of students are more adequately met both at the high school and at university levels.

These conferences with the public school men of the region provide a two-way exchange of information and suggestions regarding the improvement of the entire program of education from kindergarten through college. Curricula may be developed or improved through contact with public school educators and others outside of an institution. Many of the most practical and educationally sound suggestions which have been made for the improvement of education have come from the public school men who are keenly sensitive to the sociological, economic, and vocational environment of the area students.

Public school educators have been most concerned about the shortage of elementary school teachers in recent years. This is a problem on which public high schools and private and public institutions of higher learning have been able to work cooperatively. The problem is not only one of securing a greater number of candidates for teaching, but especially one of improving the quality of teachers through selective admission.

College education is being adjusted to meet the needs of youth. Colleges and high schools are engaged in the same task, and if they work together in harmony to satisfy the needs of youth, then the transition from high school to college will be a relatively simple matter. The nation cannot afford to neglect the education of tens of thousands of its brightest young people who would benefit most from college work. Nor can it afford to let tens of thousands of others drop out of college because of inflexible, outmoded patterns of curricula.

Orientation and Testing

After a student has decided to go to a particular institution, it becomes the responsibility of the admissions office, in cooperation with college officials and the faculty, to provide an orientation program designed to help the student learn as much as possible about the institution and its regulations. It is also the responsibility of the admissions office to give the student an opportunity to take placement examinations which are then used by counselors in placing him in certain classes. The orientation program may consist of a few days during the summer, a week or shorter period prior to the opening of school, or a class for a period of time during the school year. Older students can be of value in the planning of these programs by relating the experiences they had when they participated in the program as new students.

Copies of all information and results of tests obtained by the admissions office should be kept in the office of student personnel services in the form of a cumulative folder for counseling references as well as for general referral purposes.

A bureau of measurement should conduct the group testing program of the university, should administer various tests to students at the request of other agencies, and should cooperate with schools and industries in planning and carrying out testing programs.

Psychological tests and inventories are widely used for securing information about the individual's present abilities and characteristics. They are traditionally classified into such groupings as general or scholastic aptitude tests, school achievement tests, tests of social and emotional adjustment, tests of special aptitudes, and vocational interests tests. It should be clear that whatever information is gathered by means of tests, it must be corroborated by information available from other sources. A test score seldom, if ever, gives an answer itself; and the information that it provides should be related to other information secured from records, inventories, or interviews. The test scores need to be interpreted within the context of this broader pattern of information. Tests are, nevertheless, one of the most valuable single devices for securing information about the individual.

Inventories are frequently classified as tests, but they are not in the same category as psychological tests which call for right-wrong answers. By inventory is meant a personal measure of what a person likes or feels, or how he reacts in social situations. An unwise choice of tests, or unwise use of the results, is worse than not using the tests at all.

Counseling of College Students

Counseling centers in the division of student personnel services function in a variety of ways and offer such aids as the student needs (1) in the choice of curricula in full view of the individual's potential and interests; (2) professional or vocational choices; (3) the analysis and improvement of basic study skills, reading habits, and the budgeting of time. Identification, classification, and possible referral of personal and emotional problems is another area of major concern to the counseling center. Close working relationships and good rapport with the health service, the psychology clinic, as well as the psychiatric and social services, should these be available, are very helpful to counseling centers on present-day college campuses.

Social development, adjustment, and emotional status are observed carefully by counselors as well as by faculty advisers during the entire college career of the student. The health examination is a fundamental aspect of the initial registration of students and is required before registration can be completed. Close liaison between the student personnel office and the health service facilitates the utilization of health data in the counseling program. Likewise, the office of student personnel service and the psychiatric consultant accumulate data which are fundamental to the proper understanding of the student's health status. These data become significant to the school physician. In all such cases, however, protection to the student against embarrassment is paramount. Data of the most personal nature must be made available to qualified guidance and medical personnel, who in turn must be cautious at all times to use such data with discretion and to accord to the student the high ethical respect which usually prevails between a doctor and his patient.

The economic and financial status of students is more readily available to the office of student personnel services than to almost any other office on the campus, by virtue of the fact that this office has the responsibility for determining the need for scholarships and loans and is also responsible for keeping an inventory of available part-time work opportunities for students who choose that method of meeting the cost of their education.

The academic records, likewise, are a fundamental part of the counseling program and must be readily available to those charged with the guidance responsibility.

With all of the above information, the counselor or the adviser to the student should be in a position to help him make intelligent choices in all aspects of his college life.

The counseling program should contribute to the total development of the individual. Significant aspects of this total development are: (1) academic achievement; (2) emotional stability; (3) social sensitivity; and (4) over-all personal well-being. These four objectives of the counseling program will now be considered under the topics of academic achievement, psychotherapy, social sensitivity through student activities, and integrating student experiences. After these considerations, another rather "specialized" function, foreign student advising, will be discussed. This is one function which is most likely to grow and change rapidly in the future.

Academic Achievement

The principal objective of an institution of higher learning is the education of students. Education may be viewed as the total development of an individual; therefore, his academic achievement is but one aspect of that development. However, it is difficult to justify the expenditure of the funds of the student and his parents, as well as other funds provided by the state or philanthropic organizations and individuals, unless the student's academic achievement meets certain standards. Many authorities believe that schools and colleges should limit their responsibilities to the academic function.

Responsibility for the academic success of the students, however, does not rest altogether on the counselors. Faculty advisers, departmental chairmen, major professors, and all other individuals charged with the responsibility of teaching the students must assume a positive approach to the problem of academic success or failure. This means that the instructor is responsible for counseling with the student and for doing everything possible to prevent the embarrassment and waste of time resulting from academic failure and consequent probationary status.

The counselors in an institution need to assist academic personnel in approaching the most difficult cases of academic failure. Student scholarship average is defined as the number of earned honor-points divided by the total number of credits earned and failed. Scholarship averages of one, two, and three are called "C," "B," and "A" averages respectively. The student is expected to make satisfactory progress in the curriculum he has elected. He should report to his adviser as soon as he feels that he is in difficulty. In many institutions an average of "C" is required for graduation. Moreover, any student who fails to earn a certain honor-point ratio during any one quarter or semester may be placed on probation for the succeeding term. Students preparing for certain professions, such as medicine and engineering, are expected to show much higher achievement than the minimum level or else to change to another curriculum. Students who fail to remove themselves from probationary status at the end of a certain time require special approval for re-admission. Only in exceptional cases should a student be permitted to re-enroll after three consecutive quarters or two semesters of unsatisfactory work. Students who are on probation are especially urged to take full advantage of the guidance opportunities in the office of student personnel services.

Intelligent counselors frequently discover the most unsuspected causes for failure which, in many instances, can be corrected. One cause may be a lack of reading ability which precludes the possibility of doing the outside reading assigned. In this case, there should be opportunity for referral to the reading clinic where remedial assistance may alleviate the difficulty if not eliminate it altogether. Sometimes failure is due to a problem of health for which the health service is willing to take some responsibility. Failure often results from an attempt on the part of the student to carry too heavy a schedule, either of academic work or of social and extracurricular activities. This is a problem on which the counselor can be of particular help and assistance. In other instances, failure results from lack of ability or from lack of application on the part of the student. In many situations, failure is a result of poor instruction.

Psychotherapy

Some counseling cases among students indicate a problem which goes beyond changing of environmental factors into the more difficult problems of the emotions—the solution of which requires a high level of specialization on the part of the counselor. One of the basic qualifications for counselors is that they recognize their own limitations and the need to refer certain students to a more highly or specially trained person or department.

Adequate testing programs provided through the offices of the student personnel services should be used extensively for diagnostic purposes and for determining remedial procedures in many instances. As indicated before, however, emotional problems do not subject themselves so readily to the solutions provided by testing. Therefore, it is sound policy to make available a competent psychologist, qualified in the field of psychotherapy, who works part-time as a counselor on the difficult emotional cases. Close liaison should be maintained between the psychologist, the counseling office, and the student health service in seeking solutions to the difficult emotional problems that can be so damaging to the general welfare and success of certain individual students. Personal adjustment in a world of tension must become an increasing objective of education. Psychotherapy service is predicated upon the principle that health services include mental cases and that these must be treated.

Social Sensitivities through Student Activities

One of the most basic advances in the realm of social activities during the past twenty-five years has been the acceptance of the fact, by academic and administrative personnel, that student activities and student life, in general, are a fundamental part of educational growth and development and, hence, bear a significant relationship to, and are a fundamental part of, the curricular offering of an educational institution.

Opportunities for the development of leadership, cooperativeness, social sensitivity, poise, and graciousness—fundamental requisites to success in almost any venture—are seldom stressed in the traditional academic departments. It is no accident, therefore, that the trend toward functionalism in education has ushered in a new emphasis upon the practical application of the basic principles of democracy through student organizations.

These organizations constitute a basic part of the educational program of an institution. As such, they are entitled to the leadership which the institution can offer, for the same reason that academic departments are staffed for the teaching of students. This concept does not imply an overt attempt on the part of the administration or the staff to organize a myriad of student activities. Student organizations, in order to have significance and to possess the possibility of growth consequences, should spring from the students' urge to seek self-realization through active participation in and control over their own social affairs. Sponsorship on the part of the faculty should not be offered in the spirit of domination because of high position in the educational hierarchy. Student organizations in smaller colleges are usually controlled primarily by the student council, with the director of student personnel services acting as an adviser to the student council.

A student affairs council, or committee, should be the policy-forming body for all student activities, ranging from the approval of new activities, programs, and organizations to the dissolution of some when they no longer serve a real purpose. This council ought to have faculty, student, and administrative representation, since all parties are deeply involved in the campus activities scene.

Paramount in the whole student activity picture today is the need for constant evaluation and reassessment of the co-curricula objectives in order to keep the emphasis on the educational values of these activities and also a need for analysis of just how these activities contribute to the growth of the individual student.

Student participation in policy-making and planning seems to be a trend in American higher education today. Curricular building and academic policy-making seem to be the areas in which students make the fewest contributions. Student abilities seem best used in the American college scene in the student activities, student conduct, and welfare areas. Therefore, working with activities and organizations, planning and coordinating as well as initiating all-campus programs of general interest, and sitting in on policy-making committees for all of these seem to be the forte of the college student of today.

Students can and should help to develop policy with respect to extracurricular fees such as student union fees. The Council could be encouraged to take useful responsibility for studying the results achieved from the collection of the fund and to make recommendations concerning its more efficient use in the interest of student activities significant to the students themselves. There is no reason that this fee should be collected without student representation on policy committees dealing with the fund.

In one college, the committee responsible for securing an orchestra for the Junior-Senior Prom succeeded in booking one of the best-known orchestras in the nation at what seemed like a phenomenal sum of money to pay an orchestra for one evening. They proposed to finance the venture by selling a certain number of tickets. In order to make expenses minimal for students purchasing tickets, the Student Council voted to ban corsages for women at the dance. This action alone saved the thousand couples attending the dance approximately $3,000, which was considerably more than enough to secure the orchestra. The question of sending corsages stimulated heated debate throughout various organizations on the campus and particularly in the Student Council, which assumed final responsibility for the banning of corsages.

Student publications, including the college newspaper and yearbook, offer excellent purposeful opportunities for developing creative and managerial abilities of young people in college.

Students usually assume almost complete responsibility for the management of homecoming activities and the homecoming ball culminating the celebration. This annual event calls for very considerable executive and managerial ability on the part of the leaders and requires the cooperation of business and professional men, of the police department for managing traffic, and of many other individuals who participate in the construction of floats and in the organization of the homecoming parade. This is a student activity and provides an excellent opportunity and laboratory for learning to work together in a cooperative enterprise.

These organizations and activities illustrate a few of the educational opportunities available through student organizations. In all of these activities, the director of student personnel services and his assistants, together with other staff members, constitute a corps of experienced people to serve as faculty advisers working with the students in order to assist them in every way possible without actually solving their problems for them. Student participation in campus activities is advocated because students can make a contribution which no other group can make.

The student activities office is created to coordinate the entire student extracurricular and social program. It serves as central headquarters for all student organizations, including fraternities, sororities, and student government. It advises groups and individuals who are interested in entering and building worthwhile activity programs. It acts as a focal point for the interpretation and administration of all social regulations.

The activities programs of colleges have come to be recognized as one of the most important facets of a student's collegiate experiences. Because of this, the student personnel field has paid particular attention to the direction and the worth of students' out-of-class activities. The purpose of the activities program has become recognized as being similar to, if not the same as, the purpose of the more formal academic program. At best, a good activities program supplements, enriches, and strengthens the classroom program. It does this by providing a wide variety of activities conducive to a well-balanced learning experience—activities to promote understanding of social and group forces, to develop personal skills, and to present opportunities to exchange classroom ideas in a social setting.

Many campuses have a central office where all social and assembly activities are registered and placed on the calendar. Because of the large number and variety of activities, it has become necessary to limit certain types of activities to certain times on many campuses.

Usually the dean of students and his staff are not wanting for variety and frequency of student activities. Their real concern is to weave these activities into the general educational program and to make them be of real value to the students.

The scope and value of university activities are often determined by the nature and extent of available facilities. For instance, a good intramural program, one that involves a large percentage of the students in a variety of sports, must have fields and courts on which to play.

Whenever possible, it is also advisable to have natural areas developed for outdoor activities. In a matter of months after Indiana University secured several acres of lake property, one student group had organized a sailing club, had purchased five sailboats, and within a year, had organized a full-scale regatta. Natural facilities also offer much to co-curricular programs involving field trips and scientific field studies.

An auditorium or large assembly hall is a necessity in order to bring to a campus outstanding cultural programs. An even more important use for an adequate auditorium is the wide range of theatrical and musical activities involving student participation.

It is through the provision of adequate and well-planned recreational facilities that higher education can best achieve one of its often-stated objectives, that of worthy use of leisure time.

The student personnel program is concerned with student conduct to the end that the individual will be strengthened and that the welfare of the group will be advanced. In this, the university, in general, and the student personnel workers, in particular, accept responsibility for guiding students toward socially acceptable standards. The regulations pertaining to the college community life should be made with a sensitivity to student opinion. When disciplinary measures are necessary, personnel officers contribute to the preliminary investigation in order that causation factors within the individual personality can be studied and understood as much as possible. In matters of discipline, the student ought to be dealt with as a unique personality; but, at the same time the welfare of the group cannot be sacrificed in the treatment of the individual.

While the handling of student conduct will probably be a concern of student personnel services, the philosophy should always be that of prevention rather than of a therapeutic nature. All programs of the student personnel services have the objective of making the student aware of his responsibilities to himself and to the community. The fact that student misconduct is a result either of ignorance or of incomplete adjustment (in terms of the objectives of the student personnel program of the university) must be the basic consideration in handling all problems. The student must be responsible for his own behavior, and disciplinary action ought to be of an educational value. Disciplinary policy in serious matters should rest in the hands of a group which includes some student members, rather than with one individual; but executive action must be free from groups, as a general rule.

Student Health Services

The student health service administers physical examinations to all students, provides treatment or makes necessary recommendations, arranges for the services of psychiatric help as needed, and maintains student health records.

The medical clinic on a college campus is usually referred to as the health service, indicating the emphasis on health education and prevention of disease. Public health workers believe it is desirable to teach students the part they can take in improving and maintaining good health.

The medical profession recognizes the term "health" as including both mental and physical aspects which are inseparable. A large percentage of persons who are ill suffer from mental health problems. Most of the ordinary problems of students can be handled successfully by the medical staff of a university health service.

Remedial clinic services usually consist of agencies in the areas of speech, hearing, reading, and study. They are operated by academic departments for purposes of service to students and for the training of specialized personnel. Because of the important counseling role of these agencies, the connection with the personnel program should be a close one. Many students with handicaps in the areas mentioned above have related problems in adjusting to the academic and group living situations of college; therefore, to insure adequate treatment of the student's total adjustment problems, an administrative coordination should be carefully executed. Another reason that these agencies should be associated with the student personnel services rather than exclusively with the administration of an academic department is that the services offered to the students in the programs should not become secondary to research and training as far as students are concerned.

Foreign Students

The purpose of foreign student offices is to assist foreign students in obtaining aid in solving problems related to their residence and study in this country; to maintain a file of information regarding study in other countries; and to provide services which involve scholarships, grants, and necessary procedures for enrolling foreign students.

The admission, orientation, and counseling of foreign students has become one of the most specialized of all student personnel functions. There were approximately 72,000 foreign scholars and professors in the United States in 1962. With the advent of the post-war influx of students from all over the world, the need arose for colleges and universities to pay particular attention to the problems attendant to resident foreign students.

The problems involved in having foreign students on a campus are manifold. Getting them to the United States and to the campus, financing them, orienting them to American customs and social institutions, scaling language barriers, introducing the educational programs available to them, and bringing them into the stream of campus life are all challenging problems which require special attention and abilities to solve.

Schools realize the value of having foreign students on their campuses but are often unwilling to do much in terms of drawing out the real values of their presence. Generally, only the large universities have a specialized personnel officer to work with foreign students. Only a few have adequate orientation programs for them, and the vast majority have done little to really capitalize upon their presence in terms of contributions to the educational program.

Phenomenal growth in the numbers of foreign students has paralleled America's increasing role in world affairs. The presence of 70,000 foreign scholars in our midst should offer American colleges and universities one of their greatest opportunities to contribute to international understanding. Every foreign student is, in a sense, an ambassador from his country to the United States; and upon returning to his country, he is a potential ambassador for the United States in his home country.

Foreign students have special problems that need special consideration, but they do not need academic coddling; and, if they do receive it, they go home as severe critics of higher education in the United States.

Foreign students need contacts with American students and with American homes, and they need community and cultural activities that give them insight into the American culture. These are the objectives that, if realized, justify the expense to them, to their governments, and to our government in bringing them to the United States to study.

Housing and Dining Services

Residence halls are an essential part of the organization of the university. Their functions are comparable to libraries, laboratories, and classrooms. The social development of students is a significant responsibility of higher learning. The university residence hall, more than any other unit on the campus, is the place where this process of social development may take place so that, in due time, the student becomes a mature and responsible citizen. The student spends most of his time in his residence. The educational implications are obvious.

The problem of housing and feeding students began as soon as the university was established. The original college housing was largely student-controlled and student-operated, but this control gradually passed into the hands of the institution. By the beginning of the seventeenth century, the management of all residence halls was the responsibility of university authorities. Enthusiasm for maintaining control of housing on the part of the students and the university authorities fluctuated; it went up and down and back and forth between students and university authorities. About the beginning of the present century, the concept of the dormitory as an educational unit once more began to be accepted. There is general agreement that the institution is responsible for the physical, mental, and emotional well-being of the student who lives on the campus twenty-four hours a day. Many institutions are making a determined effort to assure their residence halls' being more of an educational unit.

Housing and dining are not limited to residence halls which are built and maintained by the college. Fraternity and sorority houses, co-operative houses, and off-campus housing are also becoming the concern of the personnel administrator. Much progress has been made in protecting students from inadequate and expensive facilities through adoption of housing codes and their application through a system of "approved" housing lists. The university health service sets up standards for rating the rooming houses, apartments, and private homes used. Many schools regularly inspect private homes, rooming houses, and apartments to check on the adequacy of facilities and to improve oft-strained relations with landlords.

High standards of health and living may be achieved more easily and at less cost in residence halls, under good personnel, than in any other way. To this thought might be added the idea that a college education is not really complete if the student does not live on campus. The commuter student is actually only a part-time student, and "college" will mean less to him than it will to those who live in a residence hall, which may be the most important factor in the social education of the student, or it may merely be a place where the student must stay. It could be a place for gracious living or it could be a prison-like mess hall where the student gets through the process of eating as quickly as possible. For many students, the college dormitory will be the first experience in living on intimate terms with a group of individuals of the student's own age. For many, the term "social responsibility" will for the first time come to have some real meaning.

The recent influx of married students, spurred by the post-war veteran education program, has led to college concern for their living facilities. Those schools with facilities for married students have, as a general practice, provided very little special counseling and programming service for these students. This is perhaps as it should be, because these students are older and more settled in their objectives.

As for fraternities and sororities, administrative opinions differ widely on the question as to whether or not to support their growth. Many college administrators find the activities, restrictive membership, and narrow loyalties of fraternities and sororities to be detrimental to their ultimate educational and social goals. To compromise and do the best job possible with existing conditions has usually been the pattern of administrative decision on this matter. But the policy of encouraging greater student responsibility for his own social development is a good one, whether it be in dormitories or in sororities and fraternities.

The environment that the students are experiencing in the residence hall will be largely determined by the dominant administrative viewpoint with regard to the functions of residence halls:

1. The academic dean may think of it in terms of its contribution to the total educational offering of the institution.
2. The personnel dean will see it as a valuable means of aiding in the total development, particularly in the social development, of the student.
3. The head of buildings and grounds may sometimes think of the residence as one of his major headaches.
4. Some consider it as a means of making money; as a form of education; as a structure of wood, stone, and steel; or as a place where students are housed, fed, and kept under control.

Religious Programs

One of the often-listed purposes of higher education is to offer students the opportunity to select personal, social, and spiritual values which will lead to a mature life. Depending upon the nature of the college or university, the religious program of the school will play a greater or lesser role in the fulfillment of this purpose.

The majority of the small liberal arts colleges in the United States were founded by a specific religious group for purposes of furthering the beliefs of that particular group. Although the development of higher education in American life has erased much of the dogma and religious discipline common to these schools in the past, there still remain such activities as required chapel attendance, sectarian services, and direct financial support from specific church groups. Until recently, many schools discriminated against some religious groups in their admissions policies.

Cast in a different tradition of separation of church and state are the large public universities. More often than not, efforts are made to keep off the campus any religious activity that might provoke public criticism and jeopardize public support.

On nearly all campuses, there are student religious groups that strive to increase religious tolerance and understanding. Perhaps there will be less difference between the two groups of institutions in the future. Private institutions have become more liberal in their policies, as have public institutions, in recognizing the rights of individuals to pursue their own religious objectives under encouragement from college authorities.

Financial Aids

In spite of progress in providing educational opportunity, certain barriers remain for some qualified students. High among these barriers are financial obstacles. Pressures of family need often combine with current high wages for relatively untrained beginners to push an able young person off the educational path and into a vocational blind alley. The financial handicap for gifted students seeking higher education is a tangible fact. The student personnel services show that it can be dealt with constructively by means already established in the American tradition, such as more extensive programs of student aid.

With but few exceptions, financial aid to students is a centralized function of the Student Personnel Office. This centralization is advantageous because of the immediate access to records, easier accountability of funds, and ease of administration. Below are some of the types of aid available in many colleges and universities:

1. *Loan Funds* are usually given on the basis of need. The size of the short-term loan is often limited, but long-term loans may reach upwards of several thousand dollars in some institutions. Many schools charge a nominal interest rate, although some withhold interest accrual until after a student graduates. The N. D. E. A. loan funds have developed an enormous administrative problem for colleges and universities.

2. *Scholarships* are awarded both on the basis of need and of achievement. Some scholarships are limited to certain types of achievement, such as science or foreign language. Others may be awarded on the basis of scholastic promise as indicated from tests or past records. A type of scholarship very common in state universities is a fee remission scholarship. This means exemption from all, or most, tuition fees.

3. *Fellowships* usually are awarded only on the basis of promising scholastic achievement and are more commonly awarded to faculty and advanced graduate students. Fellowships are often offered to those engaged in research. Generally, fellowships, unlike assistantships, require no specified work on the part of the recipient.

4. *Assistantships* are almost always awarded to advanced graduate students. The recipient is to work part time as an instructor, a research assistant, or a professional assistant.

5. *Part-Time Work.* Most colleges and universities have a variety of minor jobs that can be adequately filled by students. Dining hall waiters, library assistants, janitors, clerks, gatemen, and bookstore positions offer occasional or regular work for students. In addition to campus work, many personnel officers make available to the students lists of local community employers.

One other function of a student employment office is that of summer job placement. Job listings of available positions for summer work are made by the personnel office. Many students earn enough during the summer that they do not need to work during the academic year.

6. *Cooperative Housing* is not nearly so widespread as other types of financial aid. This type of housing offers a limited number of students the opportunity to reduce their room and board costs by assuming their own housekeeping duties. Savings through the reduced overhead and labor costs are passed on directly to the students in the form of low room and board charges. Some schools even have arrangements whereby students can either prepare their own meals or else eat a less expensive, but just as nourishing, diet.

7. *Work-Study Plans.* This form of financial aid is less common in the majority of colleges and universities. Basic to this type of aid is a curricular arrangement whereby part of each year or semester or day is spent on campus and the other part in the "field" working on a job corresponding to the major study area. During the working period, the student can often earn enough to defray a large percentage of his college expenses.

8. *Financial Counseling.* In addition to financial aid coming from the college or university, there are many programs for promising students in the form of outright grants and low- or non-interest loans from industry, service clubs, banks, fraternal orders, special educational funds, foundations, and other groups. The scholarships and loans office of the personnel division usually tries to make use of these outside agencies as much as possible.

Records and Grades

One of the most poorly managed aspects of student personnel is that of grades and records. Personnel records on every student of the university should be made available (in a useful form) to those who require such records for carrying out their work. These records should be centralized for optimum use and easy accessibility. In addition to adequate identifying information, records ought to include pre-college information, academic records and achievements, and activity participation. At the end of each term or semester, the records should be brought up to date. Training should be given to those people who will use these records. Information from records should be disseminated to properly authorized persons. The records should be designed so that they are useful in follow-up and research studies after the student has left the university.

No system of record-keeping can be satisfactory if it fails to include the records of the registrar, particularly if the purpose is to have adequate information for a comprehensive counseling program.

Responsibility for Job Placement

The student personnel office is responsible finally for the placement of students in positions at the time of graduation. The recorder, who is responsible directly to the director of student personnel services, maintains—with the cooperation of all other personnel involved in the office—a complete file on each student.

The director should spend considerable time in maintaining proper contacts with public school principals whose graduates enter the institution and who, in turn, employ many of the graduates to teach in the public schools. An assistant director of student personnel services should assume the responsibility for the placement of all graduates entering the teaching profession. In large universities, this function is sometimes left to the School of Education. This is a significant responsibility and one which can be assumed successfully only through continuity of personal and long-range planning and cooperation among the various departments and divisions engaged in the preparation of teachers. Careful planning and intelligent cooperation among all departments concerned are necessary in order to insure an adequate supply of teachers without the embarrassment of having a large surplus in certain departments. Relationships between selection of a particular aspect of teaching as a career, the counseling program, and, finally, job placement are obvious.

The same principles hold with respect to placement in other professions and vocations. The office of student personnel services should provide one counselor who spends practically all of his time in securing part-time work for students and in placing graduates of the institution who wish to enter business or the professions. This is a service which has deep significance for the students while they are in school and at the time of graduation. Employment cannot be guaranteed, but no effort should be spared in placing graduates in positions for which they are qualified. To many students, this is the final test of the institution's interest in them.

The basic principle governing the placement program is to help the student to live more effectively and to earn an adequate living. Citizenship and adjustment in these times of stress are major problems. These two basic objectives combine the vocational and the humanistic aspects of education. The student personnel program may be improved materially by having the placement counselor serve on the general education and other committees concerned with the development of adequate curricula leading to these two immediate objectives of education.

In smaller colleges and universities, the placement function itself is generally centralized and coordinated by a personnel service director. On larger campuses where there are divisional units such as the Colleges of Arts and Science, Business, Education, Music, and other major professional schools, the placement function is managed by each school or college. However, contacts, services, and demands on time become so great that placement becomes a full-time specialized function which is generally a better service when centralized in the student personnel offices.

Placement records include not only academic achievements and credits, but also a chronicle of the student's participation in extra-curricular and social activities. The basic information which is of interest to the prospective employer is accumulated continuously during the entire college life of the student, not abruptly at the end of the four years. The credits, grades, achievements, awards, and faculty recommendations are thus made available to the prospective employer in order that he may know as much as possible about the potentialities of the student seeking employment.

The placement of students in positions of responsibility is an obligation impinging upon every member of the faculty and staff who, through school, business, and professional employers, is in a position to help his graduates make desirable employment connections. This is a service aspect of the college or university that goes beyond the call of duty and transcends the traditional responsibilities of the staff member. Helping the graduate to secure a desirable position brings its own reward.

Organization of Student Personnel Services

If education is a process that begins and ends with life, then most of it takes place outside of the classroom. During the four years that an undergraduate spends in college, most of his time is spent outside of formal classroom work.

Educational growth may be measured by effective changes in behavior. Student personnel services have particular concern for changes effected outside of the classroom and laboratory. Integration of educational experiences is a problem of all institutions and of all individuals. Synthesis is logically facilitated by organizational unity. This is the fundamental basis for unitary, instead of dual, control of educational enterprises. If this thesis is sound for a total institution, it is equally valid for an area function such as student personnel services. Yet, in practice, many, or even most, college administrators who believe in and practice unitary control for the total institution segmatize student personnel services by creating numerous coordinate offices, usually under the direction of a myriad of officials at the top of the administrative hierarchy.

The whole galaxy of student personnel service is a staff function to the president and his line organization of the faculties; but management of the personnel functions is a line organization which can profit from unit control in the same way and for the reasons that prevail for the institution as a whole.

Organization, per se, will not solve the student personnel problem for colleges and universities, but effective organization can be a means toward the achievement of desired goals. The absence of direction or coordination in this area results in compartmentalized segregation of functionally interdependent services. Such an arrangement is neither economical nor efficient, and the education process is not enhanced by it.

Expansion of student personnel functions along the horizontal line under the coordination or direction of an administrator who has other functions more demanding, as is generally the case with the president or even the academic vice-president, segmatizes the different aspects of the program and treats the individual student as if he were a series of individuals rather than an organism.

Horizontal expansion along a line which always goes back to the key administrator of the program is desirable. It keeps decision-making close to the student and also close to the top coordinator. The confusion resulting from inexhaustible strata of administrators kills the initiative of both students and staff in their efforts to effect desirable policy changes.

Plan for Coordination

All student personnel services, including admissions, records, counseling, testing, housing, scholarships and loans, social activities, health services, part-time employment, and job placement, should be centralized under the director or dean of student personnel services. Close liaison should be maintained between the director and the academic dean in order to develop and maintain a student-centered curriculum. The director should serve as a member of the administrative committee, the faculty council, and the president's cabinet and should bring to these groups the indispensable student viewpoints which should weigh heavily in the determination of institutional policy and change.

The administrator of these functions may carry the title of director of student personnel services, dean of students, or vice-president for student affairs. He should be responsible to the president for developing the student personnel program and for coordinating his special staff and members of the faculty in implementing and executing group-determined policy. The program must be developed by, or in close cooperation with, the teaching faculty. This special group of faculty counselors should be carefully selected, trained, and assigned with due regard for their duties. Criteria for selection would be academic status, quality of personal adjustment, interest in and understanding of students, and a willingness to learn new concepts and techniques. Promotion in rank and salary should include the criterion of effectiveness in the counseling process.

Coordination between the academic vice-president and the vice-president or dean of students should be on a team basis but should also be actively promoted and directed by the president. Academic and student affairs are the two areas that should challenge the president more than any others, because adroitness in the management of academic and student affairs generally leads to good public relations and adequate financial support. The last two are means; the first two are ends of education. The president should not delegate his concern and responsibility for the ends too far from the top of the administrative strata.

Student personnel services represent a shift in emphasis in the design of higher education. The new emphasis is upon the development of the best qualities and talents of people. This calls for human engineering.

Ambitious personnel services which are divorced from the basic education of students prevail only where there is a lack of understanding of the relationship between experience, learning, and being. Student activities and their management enhance, rather than compete with, the educational program. The two are united under the president, and no theory or practice regarding the span of control precludes the possibility of having the president coordinate these two fundamental aspects of college life.

Integrating Student Experiences

The development of an integrated personality becomes the goal of every intelligent teacher and student. This is a personal goal for the teacher, as well as an objective toward which he also strives, for those whom he teaches. Articulation is not easily achieved among students or adults. The chief responsibility for its achievement lies with the individual himself. Seeing the relationships between the various courses taken in different departments, which together constitute adequate general education and professional preparation, is a difficult task for the professor and practically impossible for the student except as he or she sees the campus working together as a community, integrating wherever possible the campus scene—classroom and extra-classroom.

In the church-controlled colleges of America, religion provides the central idea around which human personality is articulated or integrated and takes on significant unity and meaning. Public education in the United States has no such central core as religion; and some leaders believe that there exists, consequently, a great vacuum which can be filled only through the unity of religion and education.

The rallying theme of the democracies, particularly in the United States, has become the worth of the individual—the individual as the end of education and government rather than as the servant of government. The dignity of human personality is central in the Hebraic-Christian religion. It is central in a free society; therefore, the integration of these two great forces in American life seems perfectly logical and possible. The ideas, values, tastes, attitudes, and appreciations essential to the development of democracy are also germane to the great religions of the world. The two are not divorced. They already supplement and complement one another in ways that are more effective than the traditional concept of the separation of church and state would indicate. The concept of the Golden Rule in religion is basic in education. The high value which the Hebraic-Christian religion places upon every individual personality, regardless of race, color, or creed, is equally fundamental to the democratic philosophy of education.

The ideas of Christianity are fundamentally revolutionary. Their adoption in practice would bring about kaleidoscopic changes in concepts of social justice, human dignity, and respect for every individual. If the schools of the world would really set in motion the functional application of the ideas of the great religions and teachings of men like Confucius, Buddha, Christ, Mohammed, and Gandhi, education would cause an unparalleled social revolution. Would the power-hungry politicians stand for this?

These ideas are included here to illustrate the potential for development around the goal of respect for the individual and respect for the dignity of all cultures, so basic to public higher education. There are good evidences that these objectives are being achieved in present-day efforts to include students from foreign lands on most campuses, in endeavoring to give them their desired education in the classroom, to share our American way of life with them, and to learn from them on equal terms. Add to these programs a re-emphasis on values in American society—where human freedom is the core of existence—and the ideals of democracy may well be transmitted as a primary goal of modern higher education.

The American system of equality of educational opportunity is equally revolutionary in its emphasis on the complete development of the potentialities of every individual. The liberation of the human spirit through the development of individual intelligence is as basic to Christianity as it is to the democratic process of education. The inevitable result of these two great forces—religion and education—is the establishment of democracy as a way of life among morally intelligent and responsible human beings.

The acceptance of the fundamental tenets of religion, education, and democracy is basic to an articulate program of personnel services. It is basic because nothing short of this will give the personnel worker that confidence in the ultimate worth of the individual so necessary to an objective and intelligent approach to the solution of any student problem, however difficult. An integrated human personality is an objective of personnel work, just as it is an objective of higher education, Christianity, and democracy. It is the responsibility of every individual who comes in contact with students to contribute to the total human development in order that individual students may come to know themselves and to appreciate their responsibilities for the development of proper relationships with other individuals.

Organization and administration of the program are concerned with the development and articulation of human personality. Centralization of all aspects of the student personnel program under a single director, therefore, is a recognition of the unity in human experience. It is a recognition of the unity in educational experience. It is one means of achieving integration of human personality.

The organizational chart shown below indicates that the controlling factor in a functional student personnel program is the student. All

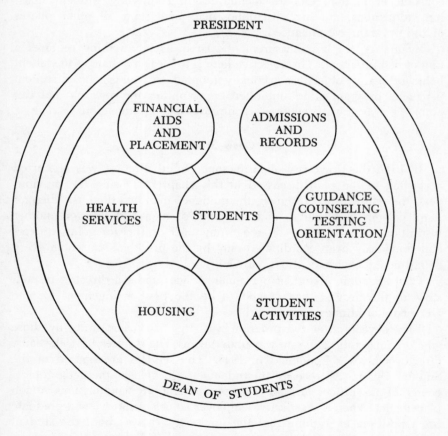

Figure 4. The Student as a Controlling Factor.

actions are in terms of student welfare. Policy stems from this source. Success of the program is determined by its results with the students. Communication of new ideas and changes is from the center of the circle out as well as from the president and board in.

Evaluation and Research

The student personnel program needs to be constantly evaluated in terms of the positive and/or negative effects it has on the students, the effect it has on the teaching faculty, the extent of the students' use of the services offered, the personal relationships of the personnel staff, and the continued professional training of its members. By this constant evaluation, modern techniques in counseling, student housing, admissions, grading, discipline, placement, and all other phases of the program are enhanced.

Evaluation implies measurement. To measure anything requires a unit of measurement. The objective here is to measure changes in student behavior against objectives originally adopted. A well-organized student personnel program offers unlimited opportunities for research that can point the way toward continuous improvement in education.

A Case Study

In 1947, the University of Minnesota, Duluth Branch, was organized according to the plan discussed in this chapter. During the previous year, the registrar had resigned, the guidance man had died, the director of placement had retired, and the dean of men had left for another institution as a professor of geography. All of the foregoing officers had previously been coordinated only by the president, to whom every departmental chairman also reported.

Centralization of student personnel services under a director, responsible to the provost, has proved to be the best arrangement for the University of Minnesota at Duluth.

Eleven years after the program was organized, a re-study by those who organized the program was undertaken. The services have the same director who was appointed in 1948. The services are housed in the Student Union. All records on students are located at the geographical center of the offices and serve every function from admissions to job placement. When a prospective employer comes to interview a graduate for a position, everything that the university knows about the student is as close to the employer as a buzzer on his desk. Earlier journeys to interview prospective professors at big universities where one could find partial credentials in the placement bureau but had to walk a mile to the other end of the campus to see the academic record, convinced the Provost of the University of Minnesota, Duluth, that the only excuse for such an arrangement was administrative ineptness. In student affairs, as in all other aspects of college administration, expensive, inefficient, and clumsy practices are justified by invoking the concept of infinite variety—a legitimate concept when applied to educational ideas and content, but without scientific validity when applied to management.

Summary

The dynamic approach to student affairs as recommended in this chapter cannot be placed in operation in a given institution without due consideration of personnel engaged in these functions; but the whole administrative organization—line, staff, and faculty—exists as a means toward the education of students. The program is larger and more significant than any individual, and only as the individual catches the vision of his own relationship to a much greater cause than status can he make his best contribution. When he realizes this, opposition to effective organization disappears. If it doesn't, perhaps some individuals should. Above all other considerations, it is incumbent upon college administrators to know how to organize such services when the opportunity arises and to have the courage to act boldly when the long-range interests of students demand such action.

Questions for Discussion

1. What unique characteristics of the student personnel problem justify having specialized personnel for this function?
2. To what extent should students govern themselves?
3. What is the role of the faculty in student personnel services?
4. What academic preparation and experiences are most valuable for counselors and for student personnel administrators?
5. How should student personnel services be organized?
6. To what extent should personnel administrators stimulate or initiate student activities?
7. To whom should the dean of students report?
8. Is part-time work to defray expenses a good educational policy for capable, highly motivated students?
9. Why do universities in the United States place more emphasis upon student services and activities than do European universities?

Bibliography

ARBUCKLE, DUGALD S. *Student Personnel Services in Higher Education.* New York: McGraw-Hill Book Co., Inc., 1953. 352 pp.

BARRY, RUTH, and WOLF, BEVERLY. *Modern Issues in Guidance-Personnel Work.* New York: Bureau of Publications, Teachers College, Columbia Univ., 1957. 234 pp.

BROWER, PAUL J. *Student Personnel Services in General Education.* Washington, D. C.: American Council on Education Series, Committee on Cooperative Study, 1952.

DEVANE, WILLIAM CLYDE. *The American University in the Twentieth Century.* Baton Rouge: Louisiana State University Press, 1957. 72 pp.

DIEKHOFF, JOHN S. *Democracy's College.* New York: Harper and Bros., 1950. 208 pp.

EDDY, EDWARD D. *The College Influence on Student Character.* Washington, D. C.: American Council on Education, 1959. 185 pp.

FALVEY, FRANCES E. *Student Participation in College Administration.* New York: Bureau of Publications, Teachers College, Columbia University, 1952. 206 pp.

FEDER, DANIEL D., and others. *The Administration of Student Personnel Programs in American Colleges and Universities.* Washington, D. C.: American Council on Education, Series VI, No. 19, 1958. 46 pp.

FOERSTER, NORMAN. *The Humanities and the Common Man.* Chapel Hill, North Carolina: The University of North Carolina Press, 1946. 60 pp.

HOPKINS, EVERETT G. "The Essentials of a Student Personnel Program," *Educational and Psychological Measurement,* 8: 430-450, 1948.

LLOYD-JONES, ESTHER (ed.). *Student Personnel Work as Deeper Teaching.* New York: Harper & Bros., 1954. 361 pp.

MUELLER, KATE H. *Student Personnel Work in Higher Education.* Boston: Houghton Mifflin Co., 1961. 570 pp.

RIKER, HAROLD. *Planning Functional College Housing.* New York: Teachers College, Columbia University, 1956. 240 pp.

SHANK, DONALD, and others. *The Teacher as a Counselor.* Series VI, Washington, D. C.: American Council on Education, Student Personnel Work, 1948. 48 pp.

STROZIER, ROBERT M., and others. *Housing of Students.* No. 14, Series VI. Washington, D. C.: American Council on Education, 1950. 68 pp.

TEAD, ORDWAY. *The Climate of Learning.* New York: Harper and Bros., 1958. 62 pp.

WILLIAMSON, E. G., and others. *The Student Personnel Point of View.* Washington, D. C.: American Council on Education, 1949. 20 pp.

WILLIAMSON, E. G. *Counseling and Discipline.* New York: McGraw-Hill Book Co., Inc., 1949. 387 pp.

WILLIAMSON, E. G. (ed.). *Trends in Student Personnel Work.* Minneapolis, Minnesota: University of Minnesota Press, 1949. 417 pp.

WRENN, C. GILBERT. *Student Personnel Work in College.* New York: The Ronald Press, 1951. 589 pp.

WRISTON, HENRY M. *Academic Procession.* New York: Columbia University Press, 1959. 222 pp.

Chapter

10

The Economics of
Higher Education

Business Management Problems

Higher education is a complex business operation, but it is also an educational enterprise and a major aspect of public administration. The annual budget for public colleges and universities may reach $7.5 billion by 1970,[1] and costs for the private sector of higher education will almost certainly boost the total to $10 billion. These figures are cited only to indicate the size of the business aspect of higher education.

Notwithstanding the size of the budget and the complexity of the management problem, many seasoned leaders in higher education lash out at the idea of preparing educators for positions of leadership and management either because they believe that it is impossible to do so or else because they believe that it is impossible to select the right candidates for such preparation. Sometimes one gets the impression that good administration may be inimical to higher education. However, the cost to taxpayers, to parents, to foundations, to corporations, and to students will cause these groups to organize and to impose business methods and techniques, if not business executives, upon higher education unless there is self-discipline toward efficiency and economy within the profession.

Education in public administration was resisted by proponents of the spoils system until the great depression gave rise to the "brain trust"

[1]Seymour E. Harris, *Higher Education in the United States: The Economic Problem* (Cambridge: Harvard University Press, 1960), p. 13.

in government, and then war and full employment demanded more intelligent deployment of the nation's manpower. The problem of logistics is now as acute in higher education as it has ever been in government or in industry.

The oldest university in the Western hemisphere, San Marcos University, in Lima, Peru, has followed the practice of establishing a business office for each faculty, and purchasing is decentralized the same way. There is a separate budget for the central office of the treasurer and for the rector, but most funds are allocated to the faculties. The University Assembly elects the rector; San Marcos has had 211 rectors in 407 years. Management has been kept fluid, ineffective, and inefficient.

College presidents in the United States have longer tenure than do the rectors of San Marcos, but the turnover in certain second echelon administrative positions is even more frequent than is the change of rectors at San Marcos. For example, many development officers average two positions per year.

There are, in any college or university, certain housekeeping administrative functions that must be performed with efficiency and economy lest the educational process be seriously impaired. The process of financial control and budgeting is such a function. The budget of an educational institution represents the translation of educational philosophy and purposes into dollars and cents. The translation must be made by those who understand the purposes of higher education, because the budget is a means for achieving educational purposes. For the budget to be developed and fixed by individuals and authorities outside the institutions, and without clearance from within, is to ignore the fundamental relationship between the means and the ends of education.

Growth in higher education during the decade ending in 1970 will be most pronounced in terms of enrollments, personnel, buildings, and budgets. An analysis of these areas of growth provides the basis for understanding the problem of the economics of higher education and for dealing with resultant problems of management.

The Enrollment Explosion. Actual enrollments as reported by the United States Office of Education for the fall of 1962 revealed that the increase over 1961 was 8.1 per cent. Table 1 indicates a total of 4,206,672 degree-credit students, including resident and extension students, part-time and full-time.[2]

---

[2]U. S. Department of Health, Education, and Welfare, "Opening (Fall) Enrollment in Higher Education, 1962: Institutional Data," Washington, D. C.: U. S. Government Printing Office, 1962, p. 2.

TABLE 4

	Total Degree-Credit Enrollment		
Year and Change			
	Both Sexes	Men	Women
Fall 1962	4,206,672	2,603,072	1,603,600
Fall 1961	3,891,230	2,423,987	1,467,243
Per cent change, 1961-62	+8.1	+7.4	+9.3

TOTAL U. S. DEGREE-CREDIT ENROLLMENT, BY SEX, FOR 1962 AND 1961

(Source: U. S. Office of Education)

The Office of Education projected enrollments for 1970 exceed six million students.[3] In terms of the 8.1 per cent increase over 1961, the figures for 1970 are probably conservative, but they are sufficient for projecting minimum staffing needs for the decade. Of the 2,600,000 increase in enrollment during the decade of the sixties, it is estimated that 1,952,777 will be full-time, resulting in a total 4,504,000 full-time students by 1970.[4]

It is anticipated that these conservative increases in enrollment, while requiring 350,000 professional persons (272,000 full-time equivalent) in teaching, research, and administration in 1961, will demand an increase to 362,000 full-time professional workers by 1970. Other projections have placed the enrollment at 6,570,000 and the teaching staff at 553,000 by 1970.[5]

Assuming an average salary of $15,400 instead of the 1961 average of $8,600, professional personnel costs will approach $5.6 billion in 1970. Salaries for non-professional personnel in clerical and operational responsibilities will probably reach $2.3 billion. Total personnel costs will approach $8 billion by 1970.

Supplies, equipment, libraries, operating costs other than personnel, and student aid programs will add at least $3.5 billion to the total current

---

[3]U. S. Department of Health, Education, and Welfare, "Ten-Year Objectives in Education: Higher Education Staffing and Physical Facilities, 1960-61 through 1969-70," 1961, p. 8.
[4]*Ibid.*, p. 2.
[5]Harris, *op. cit.*, p. 115.

expenses for higher education. The total operating budget by 1970 may approach the staggering sum of $11.5 billion.

Physical Facilities. Conservative projections of both enrollment increases and required additional facilities indicate that expenditures for replacement and rehabilitation of existing buildings and new additions to take care of increased enrollments for the decade ending in 1969-70 will be about $19 billion. This figure does not allow for any increase in building costs for the 10-year period; building costs increased by 38 per cent between 1950 and 1960. Similar increases would require total expenditures well over $20 billion for physical facilities for the decade ending in 1970.

Assuming that annual expenditures for physical facilities should level off at $2 billion per year by 1970, the total capital outlay and operating budgets would reach $13.5 billion by 1970. All of these projections are based upon costs regardless of sources of income for both public and private colleges and universities. If the GNP reaches $700 billion by 1970, financing higher education will require 1.9 per cent of the total. While such a percentage would represent a great increase in the proportion of GNP going to higher education, it would be relatively low in comparison to the percentages of GNP going to research and development in 1963.

Ultimate success of programs in research and development, and even in defense establishments, will depend upon excellence in higher education. The consequences to society in general and to individuals defy translation into units of cost and should be viewed more in terms of an investment upon which will depend economic, social, and cultural development.

Frame of Reference for Business Operation

Many states operate under a highly centralized budgetary system for all state services. On the whole, such a system is desirable and necessary. It represents sound public policy and fiscal responsibility essential to the orderly functioning of both legislative and executive branches of state governments. Moreover, the use of the budgetary process and general revenue funds, instead of earmarked taxes, as a method of supporting state services is in keeping with good principles of public administration.

It has been axiomatic, however, that in American society, education cannot be subjected to the same centralized administrative procedures and controls as are imposed upon other functions of government. This principle has resulted in the establishment of school boards to control local schools rather than placing them under county commissioners or city councils. State boards of education determine broad general policy for education in the fifty states; colleges and universities, both public and private, have been placed under governing boards that determine general policies, exercise financial controls, employ personnel, and make periodic evaluations.

There is a rationale for exempting education from the general scheme of public administration which applies to departments of highways, health service, police protection, etc. For example, there is the American notion that education must be diversified, that its control should be kept close to the place at which education takes place, and that the very nature of education in a democratic society precludes the possibility of absentee management. Moreover, the various states have made serious efforts, and with great success, to cushion colleges and universities against partison political control. The flourishing of ideas and of free institutions has been a natural consequence of this policy.

Organization for Financial Management

Authority for financial operations has generally been centralized in the hands of the college president. The business function, as a separate part of college organization, is relatively new in American higher education. When colleges were small, the president performed the business operations with a financial secretary as an assistant.

The unitary type of organization provides for reporting of financial affairs to the governing board through the president. This can be achieved in different ways. The president may present the budget for adoption, translating and reporting the financial status of the college to the entire board or to its executive committee. In some instances, where a team approach to administration is followed by the president, the senior business officer, with the president's approval, may present the budget and the reports. Authority for business operations is delegated to the chief business officer who is responsible to the president for the efficient financial operations of the college. The business officer must keep the president informed as to the financial conditions of the institution.

The American Council on Education divides the operation of the business organization into eight functions: (1) accounting, auditing, reporting, and budgetary control; (2) receipt, custody, and disbursement of moneys; (3) investment of funds; (4) procurement; (5) management of auxiliary and service enterprises; (6) operation and maintenance of plant; (7) supervision of non-academic personnel; and (8) administration of staff benefit programs.[6] These functions should serve as the basis for the functional organization of the business office in a large college or university. In a smaller college the functions may be combined and may be performed by one man working with a staff of one or more assistants or secretaries.

In many colleges and universities, the investment function is performed directly by a committee appointed from and by the board or by an external trust officer or firm appointed by the board. In any event, certain investment functions must be performed by the appropriate internal business officer. Short term investment of accrued funds is an example of this type of investment.

Figure 5 presents the eight functions in terms of an organizational scheme for achieving coordination under the Vice President for Business Affairs. Personnel and staff benefits have been combined under one unit, although these functions may be so complex as to justify specialized administrative personnel.

Figure 6 is a suggested organization for the business management of relatively small colleges. All functions performed under the first scheme would be present in the small college. The accountant would serve as cashier and assist higher officials on problems of investments. The manager of auxiliary enterprises, or the business manager, would serve as purchasing agent; the business manager would be responsible for civil service personnel and staff benefits.

In the small college, it is necessary for individuals to work at more than one specialized function. This is true in business management and equally necessary in student personnel services, academic affairs, and in planning and development. Many specialized administrative functions are seasonal or else require attention for only a few hours per day or week. Such specialized tasks do not justify or require full-time personnel. Therefore, the only way to avoid extravagance in personnel costs is to assign certain individuals more than one specialized task. Efficiency and economy in administration demand careful development of job descriptions and position classifications as the foundations for recruitment of personnel in all aspects of college administration.

---

[6]National Committee on the Preparation of a Manual on College and University Business Administration, *College and University Business Administration,* Volume I. (Washington, D. C.: American Council on Education, 1952).

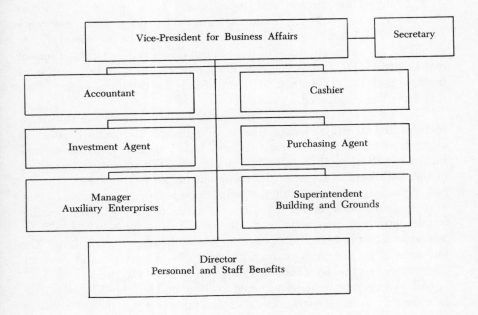

Figure 5. Organization for Business Management.

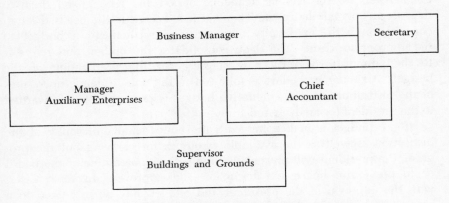

Figure 6. Simplified Business Operation.

Accounting for Income and Expenditures

Accounting for income and expenditures is an important function of business administration; it cannot logically be merged into any other function of the institution. The college or university, whether private or public, occupies a position of trust in the use of public funds. Prudent management and accounting are necessary to fulfill this position of trust through the efficient utilization of funds for the purpose for which they have been budgeted.

The use of systematic budgetary procedures is one of the first steps in the efficient utilization of funds. The budget has been defined as a predetermined plan of expenditures based upon estimated income for a fixed fiscal period. In reality, it expresses the educational program of the institution in terms of the money available to carry that program out. A budget makes possible the projection of the proper use of income during an academic or fiscal period. In other words, it makes possible for the administration and faculty to translate the funds which will be available into the maximum program which these funds can buy. The budget and its preparation should logically be a part of, and be complementary to, the educational philosophy of the institution.

All people who will be affected by the budget should participate, to a degree, in its preparation. To that end, everyone should know its permissions and limitations. The budget should reflect a realistic understanding of the resources available to the college.

The recommended procedure for the preparation of the institutional budget begins with the faculty members who determine their instructional needs for the coming academic period and recommend them to their departmental chairmen. The chairmen reconcile the needs through consultation with the faculty members and recommend a budget to the appropriate dean. The dean consolidates the budget and refers it to the administrative officer responsible for the preparation of the budget. A similar procedure is followed in the non-academic operations of the institution. When a tentative budget is prepared, it is forwarded to the president for analysis and study.

If the budget is in keeping with the educational philosophy of the institution as well as the available resources for carrying out the program, the president will present the budget to a committee of the board or to the entire board for discussion and approval. In some cases, with the approval of the president, the budget may be presented to a committee of the board by the senior financial officer. Traditionally, it is the president's budget, since the president is the senior administrative officer of the institution and the only officer directly responsible to the board for the efficient operation of the institution.

The budget forms the basis for financial control of the institution, but a proper system of accounting must also be devised and used in order that this control may be carried out. An adequate accounting system will provide for proper classification of expenditures, making possible the analysis of costs and determination of expenditures within the institution. The accounting system followed will provide internal reports necessary to proper budget control and use of income. One such report would be a monthly budget report to faculty, department chairmen, and deans so that they may know periodically exactly what funds are available to them for use in the instructional program. In the final analysis, the purpose of the accounting system is to facilitate the instructional, research, and service program of the institution—not to show a profit. Accounting also provides records necessary for reporting the audit and account for financial affairs of the college to the governing board. Most colleges provide for an audit and annual report of business affairs by an external auditing agency. These audits and annual reports provide statements and reports necessary for a year-by-year comparison of business operations of the institution. If standard report forms are followed, they also permit comparisons with other similar institutions.

The annual report usually includes: (1) balance sheet, a statement of the financial condition of the institution and of funds for which it is responsible as of a specified date; (2) general operating statement, showing current income and expenditures during the past fiscal period; and (3) separate operating statements for each auxiliary enterprise in addition to the general operating statement. The three important accounting reports of the institution are a budget, general operating statement, and balance sheet.

The budget is a financial picture showing where the institution is going and what it is planning to do during an academic and fiscal period. The operating statement is a financial picture showing what the institution did during the academic and fiscal period. The balance sheet is a financial picture showing what the institution is worth at a given time. College and university financial experts consider the operating statement to be the most important. An educational institution is a spending agency, not a capital-building agency. This is one of the principal differences in business philosophy between an institution of higher learning and a profit-making institution. This concept does not preclude the use of efficient business methods, nor does it encourage wanton and unnecessary spending.

Higher education in recent years has moved more closely to the concept of free, or at least low-cost, higher education for all who desire and are capable of pursuing an advanced program of education. Consequently, while fees have risen in recent years, higher education is, in great part, a social service for which the beneficiary, on the average, pays only a minimum portion of the cost.

The National Committee for the Preparation of a Manual on College and University Business Administration designates income from educational and general operations, auxiliary services, and student aid as the three major categories. Since the adoption of the Internal Revenue Code of 1954, which permitted transfer of income-producing operations and property to colleges and universities at a tax saving to the donor, a fourth category, non-educational operations for income purposes, may be included.

Educational and general income usually include student fees, government appropriations, allocations from organized affiliated supporting groups, endowment income (net), gifts and grants, sales and services of educational departments, and any other income accrued as a direct result of the operation of the educational program. It frequently includes income derived from organized activities conducted for the purpose of giving professional training to students in the educational departments. The sale of products of farms, dairies, and experimental stations, and the operation of hospitals, dental clinics, and legal clinics are also examples. The primary reason for these operations is for professional training, however, and not for the production of income.

Auxiliary enterprises are those enterprises operated by an institution ostensibly at a profit, or at least on a break-even basis, to provide goods and services incidental to the educational process. These enterprises are ordinarily operated for the convenience of students, faculty, and staff. It is not uncommon for the goods and services to be provided for anyone who needs or wants them. Bookstores, dormitories, student unions, laundries, cafeterias, dining halls, and similar operations are examples of auxiliary enterprises. The inter-collegiate athletic program is also classified as an auxiliary enterprise.

Student-aid income consists of the income from endowments and trusts established specifically for the purpose of giving aid to students for payment of tuition and for other direct educational costs. Designated student-aid gifts and grants are ordinarily included in this category.

Restrictions placed upon grants and funds for fellowships, scholarships, and prizes make it necessary to account for them as income separately from other sources of income.

Accounting for income from independent profit-making business operations as a separate category is growing in popularity. These business activities should not be confused with auxiliary enterprises. They are business enterprises which the college has acquired either through inheritance or through directed investment. Commercial rental property, held outside of the endowment, is the most common example of this type of operation, but colleges and universities own and operate a wide variety of commercial enterprises.

Although present sources of income for support of higher education are varied, colleges and universities are exploring and exploiting additional sources in order to meet the rising costs of operation.

Business Operations and Expenditures. Colleges and universities conduct many business operations which are basically the same as those in other types of organizations. Educational materials, food, furniture, vehicles, medical supplies, and many other goods and services must be purchased. Students must be fed, housed, and entertained. Buildings must be built and maintained. It is the responsibility of the business office to provide for all these functions and to attend to countless routine matters essential to facilitation of the academic program. All must be done prudently and efficiently.

Purchasing of goods and services is one of the principal functions which must be performed by the business officer. When one considers that a small college with only a thousand students purchases hundreds of thousands of dollars worth of goods and services annually and that a large university may deal in millions of dollars, it is easy to see the importance of wise purchasing procedures. Purchasing must be handled efficiently to assure optimum utilization of funds but with a degree of flexibility to avoid impairment of the academic program of the institution. Centralized purchasing, that is, using a system of requisitioning, results in the most efficient use of funds and prevents duplication of effort.

It requires considerable time to acquire dormitories and dining facilities, and since enrollment is expanding so rapidly, it is difficult to keep up with current needs and to provide adequate facilities. But the business office must find means for financing and constructing such facilities. The Federal Housing and Home Finance Administration has helped greatly in this area since 1950 by providing long-range, low-cost financing. Student unions, dormitories, and dining halls may be amortized through the use of income produced by the facilities. Classroom buildings and similar facilities which earn no direct income must be financed through allocations from state governments or through private donors.

Management of numerous auxiliary enterprises is an area of business management somewhat peculiar to college and university management. Most institutions operate service facilities which are not educational in nature but which are related indirectly to the educational process. In modern society, a myriad of services must be provided to make the student happy and comfortable while engaged in pursuing an education. Practically, these enterprises are operated on a profit-making or break-even basis. Since they provide services supplemental to the educational process, the use of income intended for general and educational purposes should not be permitted to finance them. Efficient management of the auxiliary operation is important to make such subsidization unnecessary. In the accounting system, proper allocation of direct and indirect costs to the appropriate auxiliary enterprise is necessary to make sure that subsidization does not occur.

Management of endowment and invested funds places higher education in a unique position of management. The institution occupies a dual position, as both trustee and beneficiary of trust funds. Frequently, the institution has funds placed under its control, the capital fund of which must remain untouched and the income from which is restricted to a specific use. A trust may be established with income to be used perhaps to endow a particular professorship, or to purchase books for the library, or to maintain a building. Careful management and accounting techniques must be employed to assure that the terms of the trust are not violated. College business managers have had many headaches over such trusts. The donor, himself, may pass into the "great unknown," but heirs have a way of cropping up to see whether or not the college is doing what grandpa wanted done with his money.

Institutions of higher learning require expenditures in many areas in order that their programs can be carried out properly. Planning for use of the college's money requires some system for classification of these expenditures. Categories frequently used by colleges to classify current expenditures include: general administration, student services, public service and information, instruction, organized research, libraries, and operation and maintenance of educational plant. This classification provides an analysis of the myriad of expenditures necessary in higher education.

Cost Control and Analysis

No educational institution, regardless of how large or how well off financially it may be, ever reaches a point where it has all the money it needs. One college president put it this way: "Any college with enough money is a college devoid of ideas." Since colleges, regardless of size, must spread a limited amount of money over an unlimited number of possibilities for expenditure, some method of expenditure control must be used. Frequently, expenditure control is made difficult by the apparent inability of separate entities and agencies within the institution to relate their individual financial situation to the over-all financial situation of the institution. In illustrating the financial problem to his faculty, one president summed it up by saying: "If I have only one gallon of paint with which to paint a whole room, I cannot afford to use it all just to paint the window frames."

The budget and periodic reports are the chief instruments of control. However, some basic unit of cost measure may also be employed. Unit cost is the average cost of performing a particular function or of achieving the completion of a particular unit of performance. The cost of instructing one student at a given level for a given period of time and the average cost of one semester hour of instruction are bases for which cost is computed. *Financial Reports for Colleges and Universities* includes the following factors in the computation of unit cost:[7]

1. *Administrative bases*—One of the first factors to be considered is the administrative or academic bases covered. A general cost of the entire university would be of more importance for a first study.
2. *Period of time covered in a cost study*—A given period of time should be chosen for the study (semester, year, etc.), and it is essential that the enrollment and cost be stated for that period of time.
3. *Units employed*—There must be a selection of the units to be used. There are various measures—students enrolled, the student-clock-hour, the student-credit-hour, and the semester-credit-hour. This committee recommended the use of the full-time-student equivalent and the student-credit-hour. The semester-credit-hour is sometimes used successfully.

---

[7]National Committee on Standard Reports for Institutions of Higher Education, *Financial Reports for Colleges and Universities* (Chicago, Illinois: The University of Chicago Press, 1935), p. 178.

4. *Financial data*—It is important that the financial data used be taken directly from the regular financial reports. It is of major importance to know the costs of performing the primary function for which educational institutions are established, namely, the instruction of students. In addition, it is important to know the costs of the activities and functions which are not directly related to teaching but which are important factors in the educating of the students.

5. *Computation of costs*—Any procedure for the determination of costs is complicated because of the problem encountered both in the division of overhead, which are expenses of the institution between the instructional and non-instructional functions, and in the allocation of the overhead charges for instructional functions among the administrative bases of the institution.

Any procedure for determination of costs must solve the problems of (1) division of overhead expenses between instructional and non-instructional functions and (2) the allocation of indirect costs for instruction among various administrative units of the institution.

Determining unit costs is a very difficult part of the business manager's or comptroller's job. There is not a set method which is standard for every college; the system used in each university is devised to fit the needs of the given institution. Industry finds it much easier to develop unit costs systems. The student is not a valid unit because he varies as to the amount of work he carries. The cost of offering a course cannot be based on an allocation of funds from one department without taking into consideration that there are students from other departments taking the course. A business student taking a course in the liberal arts division is an example.

Even though cost systems have their limitations, administrators have found them to be very valuable in the internal administration of the university. A cost study is usually the first step taken when an analysis or survey is being made for the purpose of setting up financial policies. In addition, the results of unit cost breakdowns are used in fund-raising programs in order to point out to the public that the rate of tuition charged is not equal to the cost of educating a student.

There are two procedures for making computations or allocations for unit-costs studies. One procedure, the short method, does not involve the overhead and general expenditures. This procedure can be used for the computation of the cost of the university as a whole. The cost figures obtained from this method are less accurate than are the figures obtained from the detailed procedure. The instructional salary costs and unit costs for the total instructional area may be included in this method.

The detailed method, or long method, for making allocation of unit costs is used in determining the costs for the instructional functions and the non-instructional and non-educational functions. This procedure involves, first, the allocation of charges for overhead and general expenditures between the instructional and all other functions, and, second, the allocation of the charges assigned to the instructional functions among the various administrative units.[8]

Because of complexities in determination of unit costs, limitations caused by the failure to use a uniform classification of expenditures by different departments, schools, colleges, and universities, and the criticisms resulting from improper use of unit-cost studies, many colleges are unwilling to use this method of expenditure control and analysis. Methods to determine unit costs and to develop a standard system for classification of expenditures are areas of college and university business administration which are badly in need of definitive research.

Control of expenditures and determination of costs are responsibilities of the senior financial officer. In doing either one, the business manager must know and understand the philosophy of education of the institution he serves. He must consider the welfare of the institution as a whole when he evaluates each spending situation.

Criteria for Determining Costs. Every college or university must engage in research on institutional costs, in relation to functions performed, as a necessary approach to the development of and justification for operating and capital expenditures. To the extent that institutions use a uniform classification of expenditures and accounting procedures, it is possible to make valid comparisons of costs between different units within an institution and between different colleges and universities. Similar or identical nomenclature in the classification of expenditures can assure valid comparisons only when each functional classification is carefully defined in order that similar procedures can be followed in allocating items of expenditure to the various classifications.

It is patently evident that institutions with the same budgetary divisions or expenditure classification use radically different definitions for items of expenditure. By careful allocation of administrative costs, based upon definitions that are designed to keep administrative costs low, one institution may indicate the cost of administration at 3 per cent of the operating budget, while a second institution with the same system of classification and, indeed, the same actual administrative costs comes out with 10 per cent of the budget in this category.

[8]*Ibid.*, pp. 180-181.

The Government of New Zealand and officials in higher education there have recognized the fact that certain administrative costs are constant regardless of size of a college or university. The formula in operation in 1957 allocated 62,000 pounds to each institution irrespective of its size and then added 1.2 times the cost of academic salaries which were calculated on the basis of one staff member to fourteen students. Academic personnel were proportioned by rank as follows: three professors, five associate professors and senior lecturers, five lecturers, and three junior lecturers. By using the factor of 1.2 times academic salaries, administrative costs were increased beyond 62,000 pounds in proportion to the size of the faculty.

Some state institutions have lost the initiative to state budget officers in the allocation of funds by function. Missouri is a good example; and, although the relationships between the five state colleges and the budget and comptroller's office may be cordial, in general, the college presidents have accepted the decisions of the state budget office on very important educational policies. For example, the basic unit of cost is the instructor, and the state allows one instructor for every twenty-three students. Salaries of instructors are fixed at the national average for all teachers colleges. Total personnel services make up 68 per cent of the operating budgets, and teaching salaries account for 70 per cent of all personnel services or 47.6 per cent of the total operating budget.[9]

At the University of Missouri, the ratio of students to faculty was fixed at 18 to 1 in 1963, and salaries were established at the average for all universities enrolling over 10,000 students. This is a more favorable position than the state colleges enjoy, but neither approach can be justified.

The Missouri Budget and Comptroller's Office has anticipated physical facility needs of all state colleges and universities by using a criterion of 14 square feet of space per student in classrooms and lecture halls, fixed capacities for laboratories, and 34 and 37 per cent student-station utilization for lecture halls and laboratories respectively, based upon a 44-hour week.

The above approach, based upon the number of additional square feet needed each biennium, could result in appropriations for one third or one half of a building because needs have been projected in terms of additional square feet of space based upon enrollment increases.

[9]Raymond C. Gibson, *Expansion and Coordination of Higher Education in Missouri*, A Summary Report to the Governor's Council on Higher Education in Missouri, (December 17, 1962).

The cost of instruction may be determined by using student-credit-hours of instruction as criteria. Table 2 presents comparative costs for the different divisions of an institution using the student-credit-hour as the unit of cost.

In Table 2, the budget was for one semester plus one half the budget for summer session. Student-credit-hours were tabulated by multiplying the number of students in each course by the number of semester hours which the course carried. The sum of all these products plus one half of the summer session student-credit-hours gave the total student-credit-hours by division. The budget was divided by the student-credit-hours to determine the costs by division. Natural sciences, humanities, social sciences, and teacher education were exceedingly low in costs, while mechanic arts and agriculture were excessively high. These budgetary allocations reveal the philosophy of the college better than any statement

TABLE 5

COSTS PER STUDENT-CREDIT-HOUR, BY DIVISION, FOR 1961-62 AT COLLEGE A			
Division	Budget	Number of student-credit-hours	Cost per student-credit-hours
Natural Science	$ 44,522	8,385	$ 5.31
Humanities	49,722	8,590	5.79
Social Sciences	39,212	6,201	6.32
Teacher Education	91,379	8,712	10.49
Home Economics	14,075	679	20.73
Mechanic Arts	26,137	908	28.79
Agriculture	41,076	572	71.81
Freshmen Studies	14,125	923	15.30
Total	$320,248	34,970	Ave. $9.16*

*The average cost per student-credit-hours ($9.16) results by dividing the total budget ($320,248) by the total number of student-credit-hours (34,970).

of purpose. Costs by division or department must be considered as significant in the organization of curricula and courses.

In another college, the range in cost per student-credit-hour was from $4.55 in art to $102.76 in music. In this case, one may justify this great range in costs only by knowing what the costs are and the factors that influence the costs. In this institution, there was considerable emphasis placed upon music, including private lessons; the school of music enrollment was relatively small, and a good faculty had been employed in music. Moreover, the art department, which was lowest in credit-hour cost, was inadequately staffed with part-time professional people, but courses drew larger numbers of students than did the specialized courses offered in music. Music and Christian education ($55.07 per student-credit-hour) were given top priority in this church-related private college.

In 1959, the Indiana State Legislature passed a resolution which mandated the state colleges and universities to present joint requests to the legislature based upon appropriate units of cost on which the four institutions were in agreement. There followed in Indiana exhaustive cost studies which resulted in budgetary requests based upon the cost per student at different levels of instruction and for the different institutions.

The four Indiana institutions are requesting biennial appropriations based upon the anticipated number of students at the different levels. Table 6 was based upon 1962-63 costs. Adjustments for increased

TABLE 6

UNIT COSTS FOR LEGISLATIVE REQUESTS IN INDIANA 1962-63				
Level of Instruction	Indiana University	Purdue University	Ball State Teachers College	Indiana State College
Freshman	$ 656	$ 696	$618	$501
Sophomore	733	834	538	544
Junior	922	1,214	724	722
Senior	976	1,403	882	953
Graduate	1,568	1,693	405	363

costs are made by percentage increases for faculty salaries, staff salaries, supplies, and equipment. Increases are requested for extension services and research, veterinary science and medicine, regional campuses, and for long-range building programs.

The approach which Indiana has used provides evidence to prove the value of effective coordination in approaching state legislatures for appropriations for higher education as shown by completion of a ten-year (1951-61) building program amounting to $81,000,000. Continuous institutional research on enrollment trends, costs, curricula, and building requirements has kept the Indiana citizens and legislators informed concerning needs for higher education. As a result, the state has provided the resources to meet mounting enrollments and costs. Of equal importance have been the results of cooperative planning and effort on the part of the Indiana Conference on Higher Education, composed of both public and private colleges and universities.

It is apparent from Table 7 that the public colleges and universities of Indiana receive most of their funds for capital outlay from sources other than state taxes. Federal government loans for residence halls, athletic facilities, student unions, and other non-academic facilities; grants from the federal government for hospital and medical facilities; and gifts from various sources have provided 68 per cent of the total capital for physical facilities of the four institutions. These data indicate the increasing similarity between public and private institutions in meeting capital outlay expenditures. Private institutions are receiving increasing percentages of their resources from taxes, and public institutions are receiving relatively less from state taxes.

TABLE 7

SOURCES OF CAPITAL OUTLAY IN INDIANA STATE COLLEGES AND UNIVERSITIES AS OF 1962		
Institution	Funds From State Appropriations	Funds From Other Sources
Indiana University	$51,818,614	$136,643,336
Purdue University	41,576,258	74,734,111
Ball State Teachers College	11,075,340	26,594,858
Indiana State College	13,697,398	11,793,365

Utilization of Physical Facilities

There are several approaches to determining efficiency in the utilization of classroom and laboratory facilities. Tabulation of the number of teaching stations and the number of hours utilized per week is one method.

The dimensions of classrooms provide basic data for determining available student stations. Pre-determined capacities of laboratories are generally accepted as standards. These capacities are usually available from building charts in the office of the superintendent of buildings and grounds. In some cases, it may be desirable for deans and central administrative personnel to check the classrooms and laboratories to determine standards.

A student station in classrooms and lecture halls is regarded as 15 square feet of floor space. The number of square feet in a classroom divided by 15 determines how many students the classroom can accommodate. The total for each building is the sum of all student stations in all classrooms and laboratories in the building.

Finally, the registration figures and room assignments for all courses can be used to compute the total number of student-hours of instruction, by building, per week. Then it is possible to determine how many hours per week would be required to use the total capacity of the buildings in order to provide the necessary instruction and laboratory work.

A second approach to determine classroom and laboratory utilization is based upon the classroom rather than student-station as the unit of measurement. In this case, one simply records the number of hours per week that classrooms and laboratories are in use. To reduce the results to a percentage figure, one divides the number of hours of use by an appropriate weekly standard (for example, 40 hours); the quotient will be the percentage of utilization based upon a 40-hour week.

The student-station quotient is a more accurate measure, because an institution could achieve 100 per cent classroom utilization while the student-station utilization might be only 50 per cent, assuming that the classrooms were used 40 hours per week at one half of their total capacity.

Low ratings on student-station utilization is a result, in part, of a disproportionate number of small classes, more importantly a result of poor planning of physical facilities. Planning physical facilities should be based upon research concerning the need for classrooms, seminar rooms, and laboratories of many different sizes. With careful research and planning, it should be possible to increase greatly the utilization quotient and to save hundreds of millions of dollars, if not a few billion, between 1963 and 1975.

Russell found that the median student-station utilization among eighty-four institutions was 11.1 hours per week for classrooms and 10.9 hours per week for laboratories. He also found a close relationship between student-station utilization and institutional size as measured by the production of student-credit-hours, the larger institutions scoring much higher than smaller colleges and universities.[10] The relationship of institutional size to space utilization was so positive that Russell suggested different sets of utilization norms for each of three size-groups of degree-granting institutions, one set for institutions with a regular academic year production up to 16,000 student-credit-hours, a second set for institutions with student-credit-hour production ranging from 16,001 to 48,000, and a third for those with more than 48,000 student-credit-hours.[11]

The administrative opportunity for small colleges is to challenge Russell's thesis by taking specific steps which could achieve much higher utilization quotients regardless of enrollment. For example, the dean of a liberal arts college with an enrollment of 650 students became concerned about the disproportionate number of classes with less than ten students. A careful analysis of course offering by department revealed that two-hundred semester hours of credit could be deleted from the college bulletin without reducing any department below the number of courses and credits required for an undergraduate major. By pruning the curricula and consolidating course offerings, nearly all of the small classes could be eliminated.

Of course, there were certain faculty members who regarded the dean's suggestion as an infringement upon everything from security to academic freedom and as a clarion call for the faculty to man their battle stations. When the heat of the argument had been replaced by a flicker of light, the dean and the faculty discovered that the only way, in the long run, to increase faculty salaries and general status within the limited resources available was to perform the necessary surgery on an antiquated curriculum.

Class size can be increased, credit-hours of teaching reduced, salaries increased, and building utilization increased by reducing the number

---

[10]John Dale Russell and James I. Doi, *Manual for Studies of Space Utilization in Colleges and Universities* (American Association of Collegiate Registrars and Admissions Officers, [Athens, Ohio: Ohio University, 1957]), p .99.

[11]*Ibid.*, pp. 101-2.

of credit-hours and courses in any college. Moreover, the consolidation of certain courses and the elimination of others should result in a better opportunity for the students to get an education. These are high dividends for doing what ought to be done anyway. The price for neglecting this important responsibility for academic leadership could be the closing of many small colleges during these times of increasing costs.

Inefficiency becomes a chain reaction. Too many courses and small classes result in inefficient utilization of physical facilities and faculties. New buildings are erected, and the physical plant frequently is expanded beyond actual needs. Operating costs rise; faculty salaries become relatively lower; the result is financial difficulty under the dead weight of academic and administrative bureaucracies. Unless deans become better administrators and administrators become knowledgeable academicians, higher education will continue to dissipate much of its energy in trying to solve a succession of financial crises.

Problems in Financial Administration. Several specific and persistent problems have plagued college and university business administration since it has become a separate function of administration. Among the more prominent of these problems are business office and academic relations; lack of adequate appreciation of educational philosophy on the part of business personnel; finding and achieving methods of reducing costs, particularly where instructional and research programs are concerned; and the procurement and training of specialized business personnel.

The major area of interest of the business manager is the efficient management of the financial affairs of the college, not participation in development of the academic program. He should always be ready to give sympathetic assistance when so requested, but the president, the academic dean, and the faculty are charged with the responsibility of positive curriculum development. In his position as administrator of the financial program of the institution, the business manager occupies a powerful position of control over educational efforts of the faculty. There have been cases, particularly in small colleges, where the business officer has exercised greater control over what could or could not be offered in the instructional program than has the dean of academic affairs. On the other hand, directors of academic programs have not always understood and appreciated the difficulty encountered by the business officer in "making ends meet" and in directing the financial resources to every area of need on an equitable basis.

The positions of the business officer and the dean of academic affairs need to be reconciled. Both should have the same objective—the development of the total institutional program to its greatest potential. Both need to achieve understanding and appreciation of the problems and efforts of each other. Regular administrative council meetings are desirable and tend to make known to all concerned the fact that every business and financial problem will have its effects on the educational program and that any educational problem will have definite financial aspects. One institution, following the pattern of several business corporations, has its top administrators lunch together in the private dining room of the college each week. Arrangements are made for department heads and other staff members to join the group on a rotating basis. The result has been a greater appreciation and understanding of the functions and problems in each area of specialization.

A second problem is the criticism of the business officer's lack of appreciation of the educational philosophy of the institution and his indifference to the aims of the college and to the efforts of the faculty to achieve these aims. While this criticism may be valid, it should be remembered that the responsibilities of the business officer are of a business character; consequently, he will tend to associate more closely with the businessmen of the community than with the faculty. The acceptance of the business officer by the faculty as a professional associate and his inclusion in discussions of academic affairs can achieve a great improvement in his appreciation and understanding of the educational philosophy of the institution.

College and university business administrators have been very successful in the development of procedures for reduction of costs in furnishing goods and services to the institution. Another major area of cost, that of instruction, is not within the direct province of the business office. Because of the tradition and nature of the instructional program, it does not lend itself readily to cost study, subsequent cost reduction, and improvement in efficiency. Many educators feel that badly needed cost reductions should be effected in instruction as a major area of expenditures in order to meet the demands of rising enrollment and to improve the status of faculty salaries.

The business office is in a position to work closely with those who are concerned with the instructional program by making available cost studies and comparisons of expenditures. Actual cost reductions must be effected outside the business office and at a higher policy-making level. Faculties, as agents in the determination of policy, have to co-operate in order to effect cost reductions. Many proposals for reduction of instructional costs have been made. Beardsley Ruml,[12] in *Memo to a College Trustee,* presents several proposals which he feels would result in a considerable reduction in cost of instruction and ultimately in a rise of faculty salaries. Ruml's plan calls for a sharp reduction in courses, particularly those attended by only a few students. He would abandon the low student-teacher ratio as a measure of college quality. By raising the ratio, installing some very large lecture courses, and reducing the teacher's classroom load, he would cut costs and at the same time free faculty members for individual counseling and research. Ruml also proposes that the semester system be dropped and that the year be divided into four equal instructional terms of eleven weeks, which would result in the utilization of plant and dormitory facilities, and would increase income from tuition. As an incentive for the achievement of economies in the instructional program, he would designate all tuition receipts for faculty salaries. Thus, the faculty would benefit directly from the efficiencies derived from curricular changes.

Certainly, all small classes could not be eliminated since some subject matter must be presented in a small-group situation, but it must be recognized that one way to reduce costs is to eliminate marginal and duplicating efforts which increase costs. The only way to reduce cost is to eliminate unneeded and inefficient cost-causing factors. Much research and cooperation are needed to find a solution to the problem of cost reduction in instruction and in administration.

Qualified business personnel for colleges and universities is difficult to find and to retain. The desirable qualities of college business personnel are similar to those required by commercial operations. Higher salaries offered by business for jobs of similar responsibilities attract college and university business personnel away from these institutions. Many universities recognize this problem and are paying salaries comparable to the responsibilities involved. Some, particularly small colleges, still pay low salaries. The result is constant turnover of personnel in the business office. Little progress has been made in the organization of courses of study for training college business personnel.

Individuals desiring to prepare for a college business career may gain the necessary academic preparation by following a regular program of business administration or accounting and taking elective courses in

---

[12]Beardsley Ruml, *Memo To A College Trustee,* (New York: McGraw-Hill Book Co. Inc.), 1959.

education. Experience in a college or university business office would be advisable and desirable before a person assumed the major responsibility for the operation of a business office. The Universities of Omaha and Kentucky operate summer workshops for college business personnel who hold, or who are about to assume, positions of business responsibility for the colleges which send them to the workshops. Those workshops provide an opportunity for the business personnel to share problems and possibly to arrive at solutions. Perspective thus gained is invaluable to these persons when they are later confronted by similar problems at their home institutions.

The personal qualifications of a person assuming a college management position include honesty, integrity, ability to work with others, and sound business judgment. Insight, initiative, and resourcefulness are particularly important for the business manager of today's institutions in order that he might find means to pay rising costs, to meet the needs of rising enrollments, and to provide the multitude of other services expected. There can be no doubt about the ability of the American economy to support higher education, but optimum utilization of resources must be made by college and university business officers.

Selected Business Procedures and Principles

Edmondson[13] has formulated certain guiding principles and practices for business management. They are as follows:

1. Adequate accounting machines should be acquired where the size of an institution justifies this type of operation.

2. A budget is a control device the purpose of which is to present the administrative personnel of the institution with a financial plan of expenditures expressed in terms of dollars. It is possible, on the basis of past experience, for an institution to project its income and expenditures prudently for a definite fiscal period. Only as such projections become a part of one instrument can the budget be prepared and used as a fiscal control device.

3. If the fiscal period ends with a large fund available for the final month of the fiscal period, the board should require an operating budget and a contingent budget. The operating budget should be

---

[13]Raymond C. Gibson and James H. Edmondson, *Purposes and Organization of A. M. & N. College in Arkansas,* Indiana University Bookstore, Bloomington, Indiana. 1962.

developed along conservative lines in relation to previous experience for income from all sources. The contingent budget should be established to permit the acquisition of items on a predetermined priority basis as funds become available.

4. Absolute fiscal control must be achieved. In order for it to be achieved, however, it must be desired by all persons in the organization. The senior fiscal officer cannot effect proper fiscal control of the organization without complete cooperation. It is necessary that the president of a college cooperate with the chief fiscal officer in achieving such control. Specifically, no one, not even the president, should commit an institution to any type of contract until it has been determined that the expenditure has been provided for, both through the budget and through available funds.

5. All expenditures of an institution, whether inter-institutional, intra-institutional, or student-help, should be equated to cash. They should be budgeted in order to facilitate control.

6. Periodic evaluation of financial forms should be made and changes effected with a view toward simplification.

7. Authority and responsibility for investigation of price and the selection of one vendor as opposed to another should generally be vested in the purchasing agent (within the limits of the state purchasing code for state institutions).

8. No person, other than the purchasing agent, business manager, or president, should have authority to commit the institution to a purchasing contract. The latter should do so only upon the advice and consultation of the purchasing agent.

9. Receiving, storing, and inventorying should be under the direction of the purchasing agent.

10. No purchase should be made without the completion of a written requisition and the issuance of a purchase order. Emergency purchases, which should be kept to a minimum, should be followed up by a verifying requisition and the issuance of a confirming order.

11. Generally, a college should not commit itself to any purchase agreement which extends beyond the current fiscal period.

12. The state purchasing office should permit the acquisition of goods which can be acquired more efficiently and inexpensively locally. This would include printed supplies.

13. The purchase of goods for food services should be placed by bids, with delivery as needed.

14. At least two weeks before the opening of school, the president, business manager, and supervisor of building and grounds should "walk the campus," making a detailed list of pressing small repairs which need to be completed before the students arrive.

15. In small colleges, a "working clothes" superintendent of buildings and grounds should be employed to work as a trouble shooter and supervisor of working personnel. There is no need for an office-bound type of supervisor in a small college. Overseeing is the responsibility of the business manager or his assistant.

16. Direct responsibility and authority for maintenance should be placed in the hands of the business manager. In no event should the plant superintendent by-pass the business manager in his relationship with the president of the college.

17. Responsibility for the business operation of all auxiliary enterprises should be placed under the direction of a manager of auxiliary enterprises. Proper assignment of overhead costs should be made so as to determine the exact costs of the auxiliary enterprises.

18. Costs of operating various instructional and administrative divisions should be studied and compared in order to determine cost criteria and trends.

Summary

The internal planning and management of fiscal affairs in higher education demands the application of fundamental principles and practices which have proved successful in business operations. There is no reason for the business management of an educational institution not to heed the criteria of standards applicable to business enterprises. Failure to invoke sound principles of management and control of the financial resources of an institution is almost certain to result in the imposition of external control which is generally inimical to the best interests of higher education.

The budget of an educational institution represents the translation of philosophy and purposes into dollars and cents. This translation must be made by the faculty and administration who have the responsibility for carrying out the educational program. The achievement of an educational objective is radically different from the production of units of goods and services for profit. Faculties and administrators are entitled to exemption from external interference with and control of the budget only so long as sound business principles are applied to the purely business operations of an educational institution.

Questions for Discussion

1. What factors have contributed to the increasing complexity of business management in higher education?
2. How does the budget of a university reflect its philosophy?
3. Who should plan new physical facilities?
4. Who should set the priority for new physical facilities?
5. Why should classes be scheduled by a central office?
6. What is the difference between student-station utilization and classroom utilization?
7. Why should education be exempted from the procedures that generally apply to other public functions?
8. Justify the practice of placing the business management of residence halls under the business office rather than of centering this function under student personnel services.
9. What criteria should be used to determine unit costs of higher education?
10. What is the relationship between course offerings and space utilization?

Bibliography

Education Policies Commission. *Higher Education in a Decade of Decision,* Washington, D. C.: National Education Association of the United States, 1957.

GIBSON, RAYMOND C. *Expansion and Coordination of Higher Education in Missouri.* A Summary Report to the Governor's Council on Higher Education in Missouri, December 17, 1962.

GIBSON, RAYMOND C., and EDMONDSON, JAMES H. *Purposes and Organization of A. M. & N. College in Arkansas,* Indiana University Bookstore, Bloomington, Indiana, 1962.

HARRIS, SEYMOUR E. *Higher Education in the United States: The Economic Problem.* Cambridge: Harvard University Press, 1960.

HOLLIS, ERNEST V., and associates. *Costs of Attending College.* Washington, D. C.: U. S. Department of Health, Education, and Welfare, Office of Education, 1957.

HUNGATE, THAD L. *Finance in Educational Management of Colleges and Universities.* New York: Bureau of Publications, Teachers College, Columbia University, 1954.

A New Basis of Support for Higher Education. New York: Bureau of Publications, Teachers College, Columbia University, 1957.

LONG, JOHN D. *Needed Expansion of Facilities for Higher Education: 1958-70.* Washington, D. C.: American Council on Education, 1958.

McVEY, FRANK L., and HUGHES, RAYMOND M. *Problems of College and University Administration.* Ames, Iowa: The Iowa State College Press, 1952.

National Committee on Standard Reports for Institutions of Higher Education. *Financial Reports for Colleges and Universities.* Chicago, Illinois: The University of Chicago Press, 1935.

National Committee on the Preparation of a Manual on College and University Business Administration. *College and University Business Administration,* Volume 1. Washington, D. C.: American Council on Education, 1952. *College and University Business Administration,* Volume 2. Washington, D. C.: American Council on Education, 1955.

National Federation of College and University Business Officers Associations. *A Study of Income and Expenditures in Sixty Colleges: 1953-54.* Multilith Report, 1955.

Office of Education. *Biennial Survey of Education in the United States: 1952-54.* Washington, D. C.: Department of Health, Education, and Welfare, 1956.

RUML, BEARDSLEY. *Memo To a College Trustee.* New York: McGraw-Hill Book Co., Inc., 1959.

RUSSELL, JOHN DALE. *The Finance of Higher Education,* Revised Edition. Chicago: The University of Chicago Press, 1954.

RUSSELL, JOHN DALE, and DOI, JAMES I. *Manual for Studies of Space Utilization in Colleges and Universities.* American Association of Collegiate Registrars and Admissions Officers. Athens, Ohio: Ohio University, 1957.

RUSSELL, JOHN DALE, and REEVES, FLOYD W. *The Evaluation of Higher Institutions: Administration.* Chicago: The University of Chicago Press, 1936.

SCHEPS, CLARENCE. *Accounting for Colleges and Universities.* Baton Rouge: Louisiana State University Press, 1949.

U. S. Department of Health, Education, and Welfare. "Opening (Fall) Enrollment in Higher Education, 1962: Institutional Data." Washington, D. C.: U. S. Government Printing Office, 1962. "Ten-Year Objectives in Education: Higher Education Staffing and Physical Facilities, 1960-61 through 1969-70," Washington, D. C.: U. S. Government Printing Office, 1961.

Chapter

11

Business Management

Civil Service Personnel

The business manager, in addition to having the specific responsibilities discussed in the previous chapter, is the logical official to assume a major role in the employment, promotion, and improvement of civil service personnel. He is concerned with salary increases accruing to civil service personnel because these have budgetary implications. His office should keep a central file on job descriptions and should assist department heads and other appointing officers in the development of job specifications for new positions. Academic appointments must clear the business office for budgetary purposes.

The business manager may make all civil service appointments in his own department. This includes personnel for buildings and grounds, service enterprises, the business office, and the food services. Where both counseling and business functions are involved, residence hall counselors should be appointed through joint agreement of the business manager and the director of student personnel services.

An experienced college administrator, A. J. Brumbaugh, has delineated a few principles of college administration which apply to the civil service as well as to academic affairs:

1. The administrative organization of a college or university is a means of facilitating the effective operation of the institution, and not an end in itself. Therefore the administrative pattern should grow out of a definition of the functions to be performed and of their allocation to selected personnel. . . .

2. Related functions should be grouped together and should be centered in one administrative officer. . . .

3. There should be a clear differentiation between policy making and administrative functions. . . .

4. There should be a unity of command, and line relationships should be clearly defined, so that each person in the administrative setup knows who his immediate superior is and what authority is delegated to his superior and to him. . . .

5. The authority vested in an administrative officer should be commensurate with the responsibility delegated to him. . . .

6. There is a limit to the span of control that can be effectively managed by one administrative officer. This limit should be determined and observed with reference to each administrative officer. . . .

7. The facilities and tools of management should be adequate to make possible effective supervision, control, and management. . . .

8. The auxiliary services should facilitate rather than dominate the administration. . . .

9. Democracy in administration is desirable—I could say essential —but it has its limits. . . .

10. Integrity is a *sine qua non* of administration! . . .

11. Change and reorganization should be made as indicated by analysis, special studies, and evaluation. Vested interests or resistance to change should not be permitted to inhibit growth and improvement. . . .[1]

The Classification Movement. The classification movement represents a just demand of equal pay for equal work. In response to such a demand, the United States Senate passed a resolution in 1838 instructing department heads to classify clerks according to the type of labor, care, and responsibility demanded, and relative public value of services from each class. Congress did not take any comprehensive action until 1923.

School administrators, because of the unique place of public education in American society and its independence of other public administrative services, have been slow in accepting or adopting the best personnel procedures. Education's escape from regular channels of administrative control gives the school administrator license only to point the way toward a better system and not to lag behind administrative practices in government and in industry.

The movement for the occupational classification of public service personnel has been rapidly extended since the first classification plan was adopted in the city of Chicago in 1912. Today it is safe to say

---

[1]A. J. Brumbaugh, *Problems in College Administration*, (Nashville, Tennessee: Board of Education, Methodist Church, 1956), pp. 3-5.

that every large jurisdiction in the nation responsible for employment matters through a central agency has a duties classification system for a large part of the service.

The merit system was a very significant step toward classification of positions, because filling positions upon the basis of merit implied the necessity to know what constituted the duties of and qualifications for various positions. Other factors were general demands for increased governmental efficiency and economy.

Significance of the Position for Classification Purposes. The position classification rests upon the fundamental principle that a position exists irrespective of employee. Good principles of public administration reject the idea of making the position fit the employee. It is necessary, however, to recognize the fact that a personnel agency may be handicapped in getting its recommendations carried out because of the characteristics of the employees in certain positions. This is a basic problem which a personnel administrator faces in trying to reorganize an old department. Position is distinct from the employee. It may either be occupied or vacant. It is characterized by duties and responsibilities. As long as these factors are the same, the position remains the same whether or not it is occupied.

The basic units or positions are combined into classes through analysis of their characteristics. A class comprises all positions sufficiently alike in respect to their duties and responsibilities to warrant: (1) requiring the same education, experience, and knowledge; (2) using the same tests to choose qualified employees; and (3) the application of the same pay scale for employees within the class.

A class specification should include the title of the class, the statement of duties and responsibilities, examples of work performed or typical tasks, a statement of minimum qualifications, and, in some systems, a statement of lines of promotion and scales of pay.

The concept of position irrespective of the incumbent is best illustrated by the specifications for a typical position.

Title: Secretary to the President
General Statement: Under supervision, the secretary shall relieve the president of the detailed responsibilities for running the office.
Duties and Typical Activities: The secretary shall take and transcribe dictation, have charge of an executive office and the custody of private files; maintain and receive official and departmental correspondence without supervision; confer with callers; arrange interviews; have charge of certain administrative functions; make arrangements for transportation for the executive or for his distinguished visitors; con-

serve the executive's time by acting as intermediary between him and the public; bring matters to the attention of the executive at the appropriate time, accompanied by such material and facts that might influence the executive's action; keep records; make reports and perform other related work as required.

Entrance Qualifications: The training should be equivalent to that represented by graduation with a degree from an institution of recognized standing; at least five years of clerical and stenographic experience, a part of which shall have been in a secretarial capacity; familiarity with modern office practice; proficiency in English; the ability to transcribe accurately and rapidly dictation of very difficult and complicated material, and to type from plain copy at the rate of fifty net words per minute; clerical aptitude; mental alertness, tact, good address, resourcefulness, courtesy, judgment, pleasing personality, good physical condition.

The position classification may also be used for higher level positions such as the chief business officer.

Title: Vice President for Business Management

General Statement: The business vice president, under the direction of the president, shall be responsible for coordination, supervision, and evaluation of institutional activities involving receipt, budgeting, custody, and disbursement of funds; procurement of goods and services; management of auxiliary enterprises; operation and maintenance of physical plant; administration of civil service personnel and of staff benefit programs.

Duties and Responsibilities: The business vice president shall perform the following functions:

1. Assist the president and faculty in the preparation of the budget.
2. Establish and maintain proper systems of accounting, purchasing, and budgetary control.
3. Serve as personnel officer for civil service employees.
4. Prepare monthly and annual financial statements for the governing board, the president, the academic departments and schools, and for various state and federal agencies.
5. Check requisitions and invoices for goods and services and sign all disbursing checks.
6. Supervise operation and maintenance of physical plant and new construction.
7. Supervise business management of auxiliary enterprises.
8. Supervise fiscal aspects of student loan funds and other student activities.
9. Supervise the storeroom and approve requisitions for goods from the storeroom.
10. Establish and supervise an inventory system for all properties of the institution.

11. Keep a schedule of all insurance for institutional property.
12. Be responsible for all movable physical property of the college.
13. Schedule and make work assignments through appropriate foremen.
14. Inspect and follow up regularly to determine the extent to which work orders are being carried out.

Entrance Qualifications: Formal education to the level of a bachelor's degree plus a year of graduate work, either in business administration or school administration; five years of experience, a part of which must be in educational work; minimum entrance requirements such as social skills in managing personnel, technical skills in management, and the ability to grow through experience.

Useful Operational Practices. Serious personnel problems can be avoided, at least in part, by determining the functions to be performed, writing job descriptions for different positions, grouping the positions on the basis of similarity, and organizing the total operation for efficiency and economy in the utilization of personnel and budgets. A list of practices and principles for the business manager should include the following:

1. The business and related operations must begin with a systematic job analysis of all work to be performed and with the grouping of positions by function.
2. The total staff for the business operation and related functions can and should be kept at the minimum necessary for efficient and economical operation of the educational enterprise and its physical facilities.
3. The budget for the business operation and related activities should be studied and evaluated in terms of central tendencies among similar institutions.
4. Appointments to positions for the business operation must be based on ability to perform indicated work and to progress on the job rather than be based merely on paper qualifications.
5. A system of evaluation of work should be established and in-service programs should be developed to improve the total service. The services of unsatisfactory workers should be terminated after other appropriate steps have been taken. These steps would include evaluation, in-service supervision, and opportunities for self-improvement.
6. Simpler jobs should be filled with personnel available at appropriate wage rates. Under-employment of personnel is undesirable and can lower staff morale.

Recruitment of Personnel. Men of ability do not automatically find their way into the public service, especially when the competition for expert personnel becomes acute. The shortage of professional and skilled employees, in recent years, has resulted in a wholesale exodus of personnel from many branches of the public service, the teaching profession being the best example.

The negative approach to the problem will not suffice for an organization that proposes to be staffed with the kind of personnel recommended for an institution of higher learning. The emphasis must be on finding ways to induce the most competent individuals to enter the service.

A positive program of selection involves the discovery and cultivation of the best sources of personnel, attractive announcements and carefully planned publicity, use of tests of high selectivity and reliability, a good placement program, and supervision during the probationary and training period.

One of the most important functions of the director of civil service personnel is to keep on file, at all times, an adequate number of prospective candidates to whom he can send announcements concerning important positions to be filled. The personnel office is in the market for a certain product. The educational institution should be in a favorable position because its business is the production of competent personnel.

No administrative agency of the state is in a better position than an institution of higher learning to take advantage of the product of higher education. Wherever it is possible to do so, departments, divisions, and colleges of a university should recruit young people with superior training and give them a chance to start in the lower income positions with the idea of developing a career service in the institution. The successful execution of a systematic program of recruitment makes it imperative that recruiting and employing authorities use two accepted criteria in determining qualifications for original appointments. Those two criteria are, first, ability to perform satisfactorily in the position for which the individual is employed and, second, the capacity, initiative, and resourcefulness for growth and development through experience.

It is unwise, from the standpoint of both economy and efficiency, to make it necessary for competent young administrative, clerical, and civil service workers to transfer from one institution to another, or from public to private institutions, in order to secure meritorious promotions. There are situations, however, when a change to another institution is desirable and necessary for the growth of an individual.

All members of a university staff who have responsibility for the employment of civil service personnel should be alert to the possibility of building up a central card file on prospective candidates, with their names and addresses filed under the type of examination each candidate would be interested in taking. When an announcement is to be made concerning a position, the cards could be pulled from the file and mailed to the candidates, who would then make formal application for the position. Notices should be timely: that is, close to the time when action will be taken. Candidates should be notified of openings for which they qualify; the notice should include information which would help the candidate to decide whether or not he is interested; notifications should be reliable; and the program should be flexible and economical to administer.

The responsibility for getting out attractive recruitment literature and publicity should be shared by the director for civil service personnel, the information office, and the appointing authorities. The style of the announcement may be a decisive factor in determining the responses of competent candidates.

The unassembled examination may consist in the submission of a thesis or published writings of the candidate, an education and experience statement, and references from whom the institution can secure confidential evaluations. Upon the basis of these, or in some cases upon the basis of tests used, the most promising candidates may be asked to appear for a personal interview. Such a procedure is a desirable one for filling the important positions in an institution of higher learning.

After an applicant has been tested and certified by the director of civil service personnel, it becomes the responsibility of the operating head, which in the case of an institution of higher learning would be an administrator, a departmental chairman, a dean, or a division director, to install the individual in the position and provide the necessary supervision and help for an adequate orientation program. Supervision of the employee in the early stages of the appointment must be sufficient so as to avoid early frustration because of lack of definition of functions and responsibilities. However, the supervisor must be cautioned against the inhibition of the new employee's initiative and resourcefulness through too much supervision during the early stages.

If the position description is used as a basis for selection and placement, there should be little room for doubt concerning the duties and responsibilities of the new employee. He should know exactly to whom he is to report and the people who are to report to him. He should know the specific responsibilities which he is called upon to assume. Nothing breaks down the morale of an organization more quickly than doubt and suspicion concerning these matters.

As to the desirable age at which employees should be recruited, it is considered generally desirable for a university to recruit its civil service employees at a rather early age, thus capitalizing on the special skill which individuals acquire through experience in the public service. The establishment of a career service is made easier through the recruitment of younger men and women who, through experience and growth, have the opportunities for promotion within the same institution. The disadvantages to the career service in the employment of men and women in middle life, or beyond, are obvious, although flexibility with respect to age is likely to be necessary and sometimes advantageous to the institution.

Civil service positions are less attractive during a period of inflation and prosperity because of the relatively higher salaries paid in private industry. Since World War II, educational institutions have been in an unfavorable position in trying to compete with industry and the federal government for civil service as well as academic personnel. Balance between supply and demand is achieved as salaries in educational institutions, under the civil service system, tend to approach those of industry. The lower beginning salary under civil service is, to a certain extent, offset by the security of position, regularity of employment and of salary increment, and provisions for sick leave, vacations, and retirement. A progressive program of recruitment requires a careful comparison of these advantages with those of other types of employment in order to attract high level personnel for the civil service positions in a university.

In conclusion, it may be stated that recruitment is concerned with the discovery and cultivation of the best employment market, the use of attractive recruiting literature and adequate publicity, employment of up-to-date tests of high selectivity and reliability, a placement program that puts the right person in the right job, and an efficient in-service training program as an integral part of the selection process.

Preparation of the Duties Classification. The responsible administrative officer in the department concerned should, in cooperation with the director of civil service, prepare the specifications for new civil service positions. When a position is already in existence and filled, the revision or initiation of a position description should start with the incumbent, flow from there to the supervisor for consultation and revision, and on to the personnel office. Many states have been slow in establishing personnel bureaus that are competent in setting up specifications for professional and technical positions in all departments of a university. The most desirable situation with respect to this function is for the institution and its operating departments to maintain control over civil service personnel, subject to general policies of the state.

Securing the cooperation of all staff members influenced by an appointment (from the president down to the beginning clerk) in making a duties classification is one of the best guarantees that the system will work. These are the people who will be most concerned about the results and the decisions which will follow. To give them a part in making the duties classification and in formulating the general policy with respect to personnel is the only way to make the system operate democratically.

Operating supervisors and incumbents in positions must have the major responsibility for writing the duties classification for positions in their departments. The personnel agency, under the general supervision of the Vice-President for Business Management, should check job descriptions for general policies and for classification by grade.

In a state that has a strong personnel bureau, the bureau sometimes has the responsibility of writing the initial duties classification for administrative departments of the state, including institutions of higher learning, unless those institutions have their own civil service system. This power, when exercised by the state, is almost certain to lead to difficulties. It is especially important that the state personnel bureau and the personnel officer of the university work jointly and in harmony on the personnel problems in which both have an interest. In any state that does not have a state bureau of personnel, the educational institution should take the initiative in writing and in keeping current the duties classification for all civil service positions within its jurisdiction. By this means, the university points the way to the adoption of good personnel practices, a significant function for an educational institution.

Preparation and Grading of Examinations. Examinations, like the classification of positions, should be the responsibility of the department supervisor and the personnel officer. For example, it is possible in testing for clerical aptitude and ability, to give objective examinations which can be accurately scored and the results of which can be made available to the employing authority for consideration in the final appointment. These examinations can be administered by the personnel officer, by an agency such as the testing service, or by the director of student personnel services whose office is staffed for preparing, administering, and scoring objective tests. Technical preparation and experience are necessary for the construction and administration of such an examination.

The following principles apply to the preparation and grading of examinations: (1) The central personnel office, working in cooperation with line officers, should have the authority for the construction of civil service examinations. (2) The central personnel office, whether it is the state personnel bureau or the office of the director of civil service in the college, should be the legal authority for the grading of examinations. (3) Opinion and expert advice of operating departments should be enlisted in the preparation of civil service examinations. (4) The process of examination should be flexible enough to meet the requirements of the operating departments. (5) Personality is not revealed on most written examinations, and, if dealt with at all, must be judged on the basis of an oral interview.

Appointing Authority. The president's signature should be carried on all appointments which are recommended to the governing board. This does not mean that the president must exercise the responsibility for initiating appointments and for evaluating candidates who may have applied. There are many civil service positions in most colleges which are just as significant as academic positions in the over-all operation. Therefore, it is entirely possible that the president may need to take an active interest in civil service rules and regulations in order to guarantee a high level of competency in several of these key positions.

All recommendations for appointment to civil service positions should carry the signature of the departmental supervisor, the dean, the business manager, and the president. In some cases, the president delegates to the business manager final authority with respect to civil service positions. In very large universities, this is perhaps a sound practice. In smaller colleges and universities, however, it is possible for the chief executive to take an active part in the personnel policies governing civil service workers.

Names Submitted by the Personnel Bureau. The number of names on the register will be determined by the employment market. However, the central personnel bureau should certify more than one candidate when the recruitment policy is such that candidates are available. In most cases, the personnel bureau certifies three names when an appointment is to be made. The principle with respect to certification is that the university director of civil service should certify to the appointing officer the first three names on the register from which the appointing officer may make his selection.

It is appropriate for the operating authority to have the privilege of rejecting the entire register when no candidate seems to meet the requirements of the position. It is believed, however, that if the appointing officer is required to accept one of three candidates certified, he should have the privilege of appointing employees on probation basis for a period of three months to one year.

Methods Used in Making Promotions. One of the most serious problems among competent and highly trained young people entering the civil service, either in government or in education, is the seeming reluctance on the part of appointing authorities to transfer promising individuals from one position to another. It is a necessary practice in many state departments of education and other branches of state governments, as well as in the federal government, that promotional examinations be designed which make it possible for employees to seek promotions through transfer to positions at a higher level when vacancies occur. If a university is to attract competent and well-trained young men and women, it should develop a career service for such people. A career service implies the availability of opportunities for orderly promotions as a consequence of more adequate preparation and experience.

It is the duty of the operating head of any department to encourage and plan for in-service training and growth of employees as a basis for promotion to higher grades in the department.

In-Service Training. Among the methods used for the improvement of employees on the job are the following: departments encourage and arrange for special studies and courses in appropriate institutions; work is supervised by an operating official who helps the employees to improve through experience; and weekly staff meetings, designed to improve personnel operations, are held.

The only in-service training provided in many operating departments is through supervision of the employees. Civil service employees in many institutions are permitted to attend the university on tuition scholarships granted by the governing board. The only restriction is that courses taken must, in some way, be related to the duties and responsibilities of the individual concerned. Most of the operating department heads would welcome a liberal interpretation of the courses which may have practical value for a civil service employee.

There are four purposes of a good training program: (1) training for induction, which means the keying of the employment demands with the product of the educational institutions and prevailing upon the schools to offer training that will result in the types of graduates needed by the employment agency; (2) training for promotion, which is the very heart of the merit system; (3) training for improving efficiency on the job; (4) staff conferences to broaden outlook and training through assignments to planning activities which cut across departmental lines. In all of these programs of training, an educational institution has the opportunity to point the way for other operating departments of the state.

Nothing makes an employee more anxious to progress on the job than the feeling that he is an important part of the organization. It is necessary at the very outset for the employee to know definitely what his job assignment is to be and how he should go about accomplishing his purpose. Individuals must be encouraged to express their own thinking on matters related to their positions and interests. Supervisors should give consideration to these ideas in making decisions which affect other employees. Relationships must be understood. Responsibilities and authority must be in balance. Criticisms and evaluations must be made privately in order that the employee may maintain his self-respect. A good policy to follow with regard to civil service employees is that principle which has been stated earlier concerning the larger problems of administration, namely, individuals who must abide by a decision should have a part in making that decision.

Vacations and Sick Leaves. In most civil service systems, the length of service and type of position held determine the number of days of vacation. All civil service employees should have a minimum of fifteen days of vacation annually with pay. This should be in addition to the legal holidays which are taken by most of the staff. The length of vacation will vary upward to a maximum of thirty days, depending upon the degree of responsibility.

If an institution is adequately staffed with civil service workers, it should be possible to arrange vacations for times when responsibilities and the production load are at the minimum, so as to avoid the necessity of employing substitutes. However, it may be necessary to employ substitutes on a miscellaneous payroll in order to have enough clerical help to maintain the flow of work.

The formulation of a sick leave plan constitutes a more difficult problem because of the element of uncertainty connected with it. Sick leave has been much more systematically adopted for civil service workers than for academic employees in most institutions of higher learning. Many of the best public school systems grant one day of sick leave per month, cumulative up to one full semester. The federal government grants one and one-fourth days sick leave with pay for each month, with the provisions that any balance unused at the end of that month shall accumulate and be available for future use, but with the limitation that not more than ninety days shall be allowed in any one year. Civil service employees should be allowed a minimum of one day per month, preferably fifteen days per year, accumulative up to ninety days or more.

An adequate policy with respect to sick leave should make provision for a relatively long period of leave with full pay, to be followed by an even longer period on part-pay, with the possibility of permanent retirement because of disability.

Economic security is one of the major inducements offered by government employment. This should apply with equal validity in the case of university civil service positions. Generous provisions for vacations, sick leave, and security of employment should be used to persuade outstanding employees to enter and remain in the public service. It is only through such a positive program of recruitment, in-service training, and high level efficiency that the administrator can justify a generous policy on the part of the tax-paying body.

It is a sad commentary upon those charged with public responsibility when the emphasis is upon the security, favorable working conditions, and privileges rather than upon the responsibilities for zealously protecting the public interests through an ever-increasing efficiency of operation. The privileges of sick leave and vacation with pay are earned through the acceptance of responsibilities and as a result of high level performance. This is true in industry; it is true in government; and it should be true in all public institutions of higher learning.

Retirement and Pensions. There are three types of personnel cases which can be met satisfactorily only through an adequate retirement system: the employee made superfluous through reorganization, employees of advanced age, and the disabled employee.

New methods and inventions sometimes result in situations which make necessary a radical change in the duties of a position. Unless the retirement system makes some provision for such a case, desirable changes may be delayed, the employee may continue at full salary on a make-work assignment that is not worth what he is paid, or dismissal without provision for the future may become necessary. An educational institution should never become a charitable institution for those who cannot make a contribution.

Employees of advanced age are almost universally retired on pensions. Every institution of higher learning must develop retirement programs as a requirement for good personnel policies and to facilitate the recruitment of faculties as well as civil service workers. Without a well-supported retirement plan, there is a tendency to keep professors long after they should have been retired. Recruitment of younger staff members, so necessary to the life of a college, is also dependent upon compulsory retirement at the other end of the scale.

A sound dismissal-of-personnel principle would be one that would provide that, after all other measures have failed, termination of employment should be by the personnel office upon the recommendation of the operating head of the department. In the case of an institution of higher learning, the director of civil service, acting upon the basis of established policies, should make the termination upon the recommendation of the head of the operating department. In all cases, there should be adequate opportunity for the employee to have a hearing and to present his case.

Magnitude of Administrative Costs

The most expensive item in the total budget for higher education is personnel. No aspect of college administration offers a greater challenge than does that of personnel administration. How much should it cost to staff adequately a liberal arts college with 1,000 students? How much should be spent for civil service personnel? What should be the total budget? How many employees will be needed in the civil service and academic categories? The standard responses of college administrators to the above questions are: "It all depends upon the quality of the program," or "There are too many variables in terms of teaching, research, public service, etc."

There is a tendency among leaders in higher education to study costs as they are and to assume that costs are always below what they should be. It is possible that a careful analysis of the functions that really need to be performed through higher education, with equal attention to those aspects that can be performed only by the student, and the allocation of personnel and budgets in terms of indispensable functions would reveal the fact that higher education is receiving adequate support even for these critical times. This is the challenge of leadership in higher education—to decide, in cooperation with competent and serious members of the faculties, what needs to be done and then to apply the most advanced principles of personnel and resource management in achieving desired objectives.

A report on salaries in higher education institutions for 1961-62 indicated the proliferation of administrative positions.[2] Among public colleges with enrollments ranging from 500 to 999, median salaries for sixteen administrative positions, reported by five or more institutions, totaled $108,100. The range among these median salaries was from $3,740 for bookstore managers to $13,000 for presidents. Among private colleges with enrollments ranging from 500 to 999, median salaries for twenty-four administrative positions, reported by five or more institutions, totaled $163,320. The range was from $3,760 for the bookstore managers to $12,550 for presidents.

A typical private college with 1,000 students may have a total budget of $1,000,000, excepting auxiliary services, of which, on the basis of the above data, $163,320 may be used for key administrative positions. This would be 16.3 per cent of the total budget; and, if clerical and other subordinate positions are added, the total may be as high as 25 per cent of the total budget. This would not include the staff necessary for operating and maintaining the physical facilities. It is not unusual for the actual administrative costs to exceed 25 per cent of the budget in colleges with less than 1,000 students.

Why should an institution with a budget of one million dollars spend 25 per cent on administration? Why is it necessary to have from sixteen to twenty-four administrative positions in a college of this size? If these questions were answered on the basis of scientific research, the financial problems of higher education could become less acute without damage to the educational program.

It is not unusual to observe an elementary school with an enrollment of 700 to 1,000 student operating with an administrative staff consisting of the principal, a secretary, and the equivalent of one full-time person from the central administrative offices of the superintendent of schools. Administrative costs in such a school may be less than 5 per cent of the budget. And one could make a good case for the fact that elementary and secondary school children, being considerably younger than college

---

[2]W. R. Bokelman, and L. A. D'amico, *Higher Education Salaries, 1961-62.* United States Department of Health, Education, and Welfare, Office of Education (Washington, D. C.: U. S. Government Printing Office), 1962.

students, should have more special services provided for them than are provided for students in a university.

Elementary and secondary schools are generally staffed at a ratio of twenty-five to thirty students to each teacher. Is this because younger children require less individual attention than do college-age youth? The difference is certainly justified in some cases on the basis of research and public services carried on by college personnel; however, there are thousands of faculty members at the college level who engage in less research and public service than does the typical public school teacher.

One possible explanation of the more economical approach to the administration of the public schools is that public school administrators have been professionalized. No one can be appointed to an administrative position in the public schools unless he has credentials indicating preparation and experience leading to administrative competencies.

If the governing boards of higher education would insist upon administrative competencies for civil service or non-academic positions, the results would add greatly to the resources for academic programs. If administrative as well as academic competencies were prerequisites to appointments to positions of president, vice president, and dean, the resultant improvements in academic programs would merit almost any support which conscientious and competent leaders in higher education request.

Summary

The administration of higher education as a discipline and as a profession is of recent origin, but the same may be said about the serious study of public administration in the United States. Professional attention to the field of public administration was almost entirely lacking prior to the twentieth century.[3] Leonard D. White has stated that the serious study of public administration in the United States "dates from the brilliant essay of Woodrow Wilson" in 1887.[4]

Higher education has never experienced the spoils system nor the periodic scandals that have characterized governments at all levels and in all countries. Frugality, prudence, honesty, and integrity have been characteristic of most college administrators, especially of the great ones; but virtue is no substitute for competence in the management of an enterprise that costs as much as higher education did in 1963.

---

[3]Leonard D. White, *Introduction to the Study of Public Administration* (New York: The Macmillan Co., 1958), p. 10.

[4]*Ibid.*, p. 10.

There is hardly such a thing as a large public organization operating without a merit system for personnel administration. Any institution of higher learning that is operating without a merit system and the application of principles of personnel administration is inconsistent with its own teaching. No public college or university should be permitted to ignore sound personnel principles. Exemption from standards developed for other state employees cannot be justified for civil service or non-academic personnel in higher education. Equal pay and status for equal work and qualifications should apply to all agencies of the state.

Academic rank is an indispensable characteristic of personnel policy for faculties and should never be subjected to personnel policies governing civil service personnel. Neither should college administrators abuse the prerogative of academic status by assigning it to civil service personnel, a practice that is frequently followed as a means of increasing salaries or status beyond what the position description would merit. Pay scales should be established in such a way as to permit a clerical employee, as well as a vice-president, to advance in pay and status as a result of experience and increased responsibilities.

One of the principal reasons for friction between departments of administration in state governments and state colleges and universities has been the tendency of higher education to ask for special privileges, even though personnel practices may be less effective and efficient than those followed in government. It is unfortunate that relationships have not improved as state governments have improved personnel practices. In too many cases, state personnel officers, without any knowledge of college administration, attempt to impose controls and policies inimical to higher education; but in other cases, leaders in higher education have failed to place their own house in order.

The development of systematic state budgeting, purchasing, and auditing, plus efficient personnel offices, has increased the tendency to bring higher education under state personnel and fiscal policies. Building agencies, state architects, and coordination of housekeeping functions have moved state officials even further toward encroachment upon the power of higher education officials to regulate their own affairs.

The economy and efficiency movements in government, from time to time, and increased centralization of executive authority in the governor, have caused legislators and citizens generally to question the fiscal policies of higher education. The various Hoover Commissions have accelerated these trends.

The most fundamental reason for the loss of control over college personnel and fiscal matters to state governments is inefficient, wasteful college administration. The supposedly traditional academic distaste for efficiency as compared with the attitudes of modern businessmen whose success depends upon the most efficient deployment of scarce resources have not helped the cause of higher education.

If 100 of the major colleges and universities should suddenly decide to find their challenge in the most efficient and economical use of personnel and budgets, the resultant revolution in higher education would set new standards of excellence and purpose. If college administrators could be motivated to find a challenge in things academic, rather than in problems of budget and personnel, perhaps there would be less difficulty in financing higher education.

Questions for Discussion

1. How do policy and problems for civil service personnel differ from policy and problems related to academic personnel?
2. What is the significance of a position in the recruitment of personnel?
3. Who should write job descriptions for civil service personnel?
4. What are the functions of a central personnel office?
5. Who are some of the individuals who have made contributions in both public administration and in higher education?
6. What criteria should determine whether certain positions should be classified as civil service or as academic?

Bibliography

BOKELMAN, W. R., and D'AMICO, L. A. *Higher Education Salaries, 1961-62.* United States Department of Health, Education, and Welfare, Office of Education, Washington, D. C.: U. S. Government Printing Office, 1962.

BRUMBAUGH, A. J. *Problems in College Administration.* Nashville, Tennessee: Board of Education, Methodist Church, 1956.

MOORE, HAROLD E., and WALTERS, NEWELL B. *Personnel Administration in Education.* New York: Harper & Bros. 1955.

MOSHER, WILLIAM E., PH.D., and KINGSLEY, DONALD, PH.D. *Public Personnel Administration.* New York and London: Harper & Bros. 1941.

TEAD, ORDWAY. *The Art of Administration.* New York: McGraw-Hill Book Co., Inc., 1951.

WHITE, LEONARD D. *Introduction to the Study of Public Administration.* New York: The Macmillan Co. 1958.

WOODBURNE, LLOYD S. *Principles of College and University Administration.* Stanford, California: Stanford University Press, 1958.

Chapter

(12)

Public Relations and Development

The Dilemma in Higher Education

The population of the United States in 1960 was just under 180,000,-000, and it has been estimated that it will reach 225,000,000 by 1975. One of the critical problems confronting present professional workers is the fact that, during the next fifteen to twenty years, they will be called upon to provide services through the professions, industry, government, and research for a population radically out of proportion to the existing number of professional people. The nation will need more specialized and professional talents than it has needed at any period in history, notwithstanding the fact that the supply will be sharply limited.

It has been pointed out in the Rockefeller Report[1] that, between 1870 and 1955, while the population was increasing four times, public high school population was increasing approximately eighty times and that elementary education was becoming virtually universal. By 1975, colleges and universities will have doubled and, in some cases, tripled their enrollments of 1960.

A Look at the Teaching Profession. The demand for teachers in the years ahead must include consideration for the improvement of the quality of the present core of teachers. In 1956, 33 per cent of the elementary teachers did not hold a bachelor's degree, and over 21 per cent of all public school teachers had less than four years of college preparation.[2]

---

[1]*The Pursuit of Excellence,* Special Studies Project Report II, Rockefeller Brothers Fund, (Garden City, New York: Doubleday and Co., Inc., 1958), p. 21.
[2]*Ibid.,* p. 23.

There were 1,454,362 public school teachers in service in the 1961-62 school year, of whom 578,403 were in the secondary schools, and 875,959 in the elementary schools. The ratio of elementary to secondary teachers was eight to five, but the supply of new teachers for the fall of 1962 was divided in favor of secondary over elementary by the ratio of eight to five.

The Research Division of the National Education Association estimated the demand for new elementary and secondary teachers for the fall of 1962[3] as follows:

1. To replace those teachers leaving the profession 125,000
2. To serve increasing enrollments (1,143,514 increase over 1961) 35,000
3. To relieve overcrowding and to eliminate part-time sessions 30,000
4. To give services and instruction not now provided 25,000
5. To replace the unprepared 25,000
6. Total (based upon fall of 1961) 240,000
7. Number of 1962 college graduates expected to enter teaching (74.5 per cent of the new supply) 106,000
8. Net estimated shortage 134,000

Of the 11,184 new full-time teachers employed at the college level in 1960-61, 25.8 per cent held the doctor's degree, 20 per cent had one year of preparation beyond the master's degree, 36.8 per cent held the master's degree, and 17.4 per cent had less than a master's degree.[4] Percentages for the same four categories of preparation for all college teachers in 1953-54 were 40.5, 20.9, 28.2, and 10.4 respectively, for the doctorate, master's plus one year, master's, and less than master's degree.[5]

There were 1,275 unfilled teaching positions and 296 unfilled administrative positions in 1,085 institutions reporting for the years 1959-60 or 1960-61.[6] Of 1,085 institutions reporting, 826 believe that the shortage of qualified candidates for college teaching will become more acute. The greatest shortages were in mathematics, physical sciences, foreign languages, and social sciences.

---

[3]Research Division, National Education Association, *Teacher Supply and Demand*, 1962, p. 21.
[4]*Ibid.*, p. 16.
[5]*Ibid.*, p. 13.
[6]*Ibid.*, pp. 19-20.

The demand for college teachers will increase from approximately 300,000 in 1962 to 350,000 in 1966 and to 390,000 in 1969-70. In a typical graduating class of 9,000 doctoral students, college teaching positions gain only about 2,000 new teachers. Another 2,000 would already be in college teaching.[7]

College enrollments have reached approximately 37 per cent of the 18-21-year age group in contrast to 4 per cent in 1900, but it is probably more difficult to staff the nation's colleges now than it was in 1900.

Competition for Degrees as Status Symbols. While the number of men and women taking the doctorate has shown a slight decline in recent years, the percentage of those who complete the degree and enter college teaching has shown an even sharper decrease. The demand for high level talent in industry, in government, and in research is providing formidable competition for colleges which traditionally hire individuals for teaching. One of the major mid-western universities that graduates about as many doctoral candidates in physics as does any institution in the nation reported that not one of its graduates for the year 1958-59 in the field of physics planned to enter college teaching.

Notwithstanding the tremendous shortage of personnel at all levels of education, the demand for services increases. Curricula at all levels of education have been expanded in every direction. Many constructive critics believe that the elementary schools have taken over traditional functions of the home to the detriment of the fundamental task generally assigned to the elementary schools. Curricula at the secondary and college levels are increasingly analogous to a modern cafeteria, say the critics, with hors d'oeuvres and dessert having been given the status of meat and potatoes. The tendency on the part of students, and perhaps many professors and leaders in the field of education, to regard college attendance and a bachelor's degree as a superficial license of employment rather than the indication of mastery of an area of learning, has militated against the mission of institutions of higher learning for the development of excellence in intellectual qualities as the basis for college graduation. By the same token, the tendency of employers to require increasingly the college degree as a prerequisite to employment and promotions, regardless of what the degree stands for, has mollified this mission.

College teaching itself is suspect in the eyes of many discerning students, alumni, and friendly but concerned, laymen. The emphasis upon

---

[7]*Ibid.*, p. 44.

research and productive scholarship, used loosely and indiscriminately as a basis for promotion in rank and concomitant increases in salary, has forced many great teachers to become mediocre writers in order to keep the wolf from their own doors. Excesses in this direction have led some academic administrators to state quite frankly, although not publicly, that there is a tendency for promotions committees to act upon the basis of quantitative criteria in the evaluation of teaching and productive scholarship. This is undoubtedly a dilemma from which any successful business executive would know how to extricate himself—namely, the recognition of the inevitable and desirable differences among men and women as they pursue areas of specialization. One wonders whether a society can justify discriminating against those who become specialists in the dissemination, consumption, and orderly utilization of research through teaching, particularly in cases where teaching, rather than research ability, is the professor's choice and the area in which he can make the greatest contribution.

Higher Education in Competition for Personnel. It is compulsory that most American youth finish the secondary schools. As indicated before, approximately 37 per cent of all those of college age are now attending some type of post high school institution. Thus, the youth of America who finish the bachelor's degree, the group from which candidates for the advanced degrees are recruited, selected, or encouraged for further study, have already spent from sixteen to seventeen years in the learning-teaching profession. This assumes that children enter school either at the kindergarten or the first-grade levels and advance normally through the completion of the bachelor's degree. With the completion of the master's degree, their tenure in the profession is increased by another year; and with the fulfillment of requirements for the Ph.D., the individual has had twenty years of exposure to the teaching profession. Imagine the teacher of methods in a foreign language class in 1964 using students' time to teach them how to check the class roll!

These graduates at the various degree levels constitute the reservoir of skilled personnel for industry, the professions, government, research, and various private enterprise pursuits. They are the source of personnel for all positions in the total hierarchy of education. Moreover, as a group, they tend to set the tone, standard, and financial support, and through participation as laymen in legislatures, executive positions in government, and on boards of control, they determine the scope and general policy with respect to education at all levels.

This poses a paradox. Leaders in education direct the learning activities of American youth from sixteen to twenty years, a group from whom leaders and workers in the field of education must be recruited; but education seems to have greater difficulty than do other groups in competing for the products of educational institutions. A tentative hypothesis is that the paradox is a direct result of faculty and administrative ineptness in the area of public relations. Every advantage concerned with influencing vocational and professional choices lies with leaders in higher education.

Many leaders argue that the problem is one of financial support and pay scales. Others maintain that teaching is not attractive; that support in the way of physical environment, including facilities for research, study, mediation, and counseling is inadequate; that opportunities for financial advancement are greater in industry and other professions; and that colleges and universities are only a means to a more practical and rewarding pursuit of the good life in private enterprise. The answer to all of these objections is: They are symptomatic of a fundamental ineptness in the area of public relations.

If the status of higher education is eclipsed by industry, with its dynamic products (for example, the four barrel carburetor and the superfluous fin), by the profession of medicine, honorably devoted to the healing of those who are sick instead of to the development of the intellect of those who are well, by farmers engaged in the production of food for human consumption and grocers responsible for the distribution of that food, by lawyers engaged in defending those who are in trouble, by leaders in the executive, legislative, and judicial branches of the government, then education should exchange leaders with the other professions and industry. All of this implies that the great story of education must be presented through modern media. However, that is not true. The first step is to justify being known to the publics.

Now that the dilemma has been indicated and a tentative hypothesis formulated, it is important to turn to the various disciplines for guidance, organization, and philosophical direction in resolving that dilemma.

Developing the Foundation

Perhaps no measure could do more to alleviate the serious shortage of college teachers than for the 300,000 men and women who staff America's colleges and universities and their 4,200,000 students to be motivated once more by scholarly endeavors; to hold formal and informal campus group meetings or sessions to engage in intellectual pursuits to the point of actually becoming disciplined minds rather than disseminators, advocates, and consumers of intellectual and social trivia.

Tead states:

> The lack, if I read the evidence aright, is in the *leadership to press* . . . *learning* objectives with persuasion and courage. This statement may seem surprising to those unacquainted with the campus world; for it is presumed that the purpose of higher education is to educate. The assumption, however, may be naive.[8]

Tead believes that too many young people go to college for the wrong reasons; that entering students find themselves poorly guided, intellectually unequipped, and unmotivated; that learning situations are not meaningful and inviting because faculty members are ill-informed as to how to apply the principles of psychology; that marks and promotions are sometimes inflexible and arbitrary, either too easy or too hard; and that the side shows of athletics and social activities occupy the center of the intellectual scene.

Schoenfeld diagnoses the problem under four points:[9]

> First, the modern American university has become so increasingly preoccupied with its satellite functions of research and public service and their attendant galaxies, from fund-raising to football, that the central function of undergraduate instruction has gone into a partial eclipse. . . . A second reason for the fuzziness in student focus is that student supervision has gradually been delegated to bureaus of specialists who are *in* but not *of* the administration or the faculty. . . . Third, a true student point of view is difficult to develop and retain, and the tangible rewards are slim. . . . Finally, American students have been ineffective on their own part in developing those responsible student agencies and student governments that might be expected to inject the undergraduate point of view into campus councils.

Students in the London School of Economics in 1962 had well-disciplined intellectual habits for earning their first degrees. They stated without reservation that they receive very little help from formal teaching, tutoring, or lectures and that one could pass the examinations for the baccalaureate only by spending sixteen hours per day, for three years, in the library.

The people who send their sons and daughters to colleges and universities and pay the bills are dissatisfied with the quality of under-

---

8Ordway Tead, *The Climate of Learning* (New York: Harper and Bros., 1958), p. 20.

9Clarence A. Schoenfeld, *The University and Its Publics* (New York: Harper and Bros., 1954), p. 11.

graduate instruction; they are also concerned about counseling and housing problems and with crowded conditions that prevail on many college campuses. Budgets are questioned because they are high, and there is a certain mystery, because of lack of understanding, surrounding the nature and importance of academic research.

Schoenfeld[10] believes that public relations, in the proper sense of the term, is primarily a matter of institutional conduct and only secondarily a matter of publicity. In his proposal for solving the problem, he believes that three fundamental principles need to be invoked:

1. Improved public relations is needed as never before if our schools are to continue to merit and receive adequate support.

2. Public relations correctly conceived is no bag of publicity tricks; it is inextricably sound administration in all its aspects.

3. Public relations is not the job of a single individual; every contact between the university and its constituency is an episode in the complex flow of institutional relationships.

In all cases, says Mr. Schoenfeld, the administrator remains the catalyst. In the definition and delineation of the components of the public relations complex, Schoenfeld included boards of trustees, faculties, and administrators.

Another eminent authority in the field of communications, Carroll Hanson, has explained the difficulty in informing the American people concerning the role of higher education.[11] He stated:

> About eighty-nine million American citizens twenty years of age and over have taken no college courses. In many instances, they have never been on a campus. They have never seen a college physics laboratory or a college library, have never weighed the merits of a liberal arts education, and have no concept of a professor's function except through the distortions presented on TV and .in the movies. To millions of Americans, higher education is what happens in the stadium on Saturday afternoon.
>
> This group of eighty-nine million citizens comprises a no-man's land in educational communications, the silent zone of strangers in our midst, and it constitutes one of the toughest communications problems in higher education today. The fact that this problem exists may account, to a large extent, for many of the other pressing problems facing higher education.
>
> Why is this group of strangers a communications problem? Communications experts tell us that, among the four essential ingredients

---

[10]*Ibid.*, p. 3.
[11]Carroll Hanson, "The Strangers in Our Midst" (a public address given at Indiana University, 1960).

for successful communication, one essential is this: a message must employ signs which refer to common experience between the sender and receiver in order to get its meaning across. There must be common fields of experience between the sender and the receiver of a message. The more overlap there is in the field of experience, the easier communication will be. Where there is no overlap, communication is impossible.

It is likely . . . that the problems facing higher education are not causing much excitement among the millions of citizens who have never had any experience with higher education. Evidence of this is weak, but it is found in the experience of many persons who have tried to persuade the mass media to publish and broadcast on the desperate problems higher education faces. The mass media [leaders] are reluctant in many cases, not because the executives do not feel sympathetic, but because they know the mass audience will only be bored by the problems which seem so exciting to some.

Probably the most prized platform in the world for anyone who wants to expound his views is the National Press Club in Washington, D. C. Prime ministers, generals, statesmen, and ambassadors—even presidents—seek access to this platform. But in the history of the club, now over fifty years old, only one educator has ever been acceptable as a speaker. The reason is this: the newspaper men who run the program apply one ironclad criterion. Is the topic interesting to the public?

Role of Students. Perhaps the most significant group in the long-range development, maintenance, and improvement of institutional relations is the students. Indeed, if an institution spent all of its funds on the development of a public relations program, it would not equal in personnel or in effectiveness what every college has for the asking in its student body. This does not imply that students are to be cultivated as propaganda and publicity agents—because these are not the elements of public relations—but as intelligent, participating members of a society of scholars whose positive and dynamic qualities, virtues, and weaknesses are disseminated throughout the community, in the broadest sense, by the members of the society. It does not mean a laissez-faire student body concerned with the maintenance of a society-centered status quo. It means the opposite of that. For, in the words of Dean Weaver,[12] "It is here that we seek to infect young minds with the research virus of intellectual discontent, hoping that thenceforward they will be ever curious, distrustful of dogma and seemingly established fact, constantly probing, and creative."

12John C. Weaver, *Some Dilemmas in Graduate Education* (Lincoln: University of Nebraska Press, 1958), p. 8.

Schoenfeld defined the larger university responsibility by invoking the dynamic viewpoint expressed by Van Hise who stated: ". . . that with the continued support of the state, a university could be built which would provide all the services the state might expect from it, a university as broad as human endeavor, as high as human aspiration."[13]

The public relations program must be based upon all the activities in which a university is engaged. These involve instruction, research, and service to the state which are influenced by the legislature or other sources of funds and the university's relationship to those sources; a board of regents and its activities in the development and synthesis of policy for higher education; the administration and its complex responsibilities in giving direction to policy formation and in the execution of democratically determined policies; the students and their activities, goals, programs, and aspirations; and the alumni association which determines in a real sense the degree of support coming from all other publics. The program here includes social and recreational activities, football and basketball, win or lose.

And, while an institution through its public relations program, of necessity includes every possible interaction which it has with all of its publics, the heart of the program is the intellectual life of the institution. It is doubtful that higher education can ever be an economical investment when its objectives are anything other than the development of intellectual excellence on the part of its students. Social, recreational, and matrimonial activities are an important by-product, if not a fundamental part, of the intellectual development. It is doubtful, however, that these corollary activities, when permitted to gain the dominant role in higher education, can ever be carried on and justified at the expense which is necessary when they cease to be corollaries or by products of the central dominating purpose for which institutions of higher learning were established.

Definition of University Publics. Dewey formulated a workable definition of the public: "Those indirectly and seriously affected for good or for evil form a group distinctive enough to require recognition and a name. The name selected is The Public."[14] According to Dewey, this public is organized and made effective by means of representatives

---

[13]Maurice M. Vance, Charles Richard Van Hise. The State Historical Society of Wisconsin, Madison, 1960. p. 90.

[14]John Dewey, *The Public and Its Problems* (New York: Henry Holt and Co., 1927), p. 35.

who, as guardians of custom, as legislators, as executives, judges, etc., care for its special interests by methods intended to regulate the conjoint actions of individuals and groups.

Now, in an institution of higher learning, many individuals and groups are actively engaged in the process of teaching, learning, research, and public service. Moreover, under a system of academic freedom that encourages the pursuit of truth through research and scholarship, there is being developed a great heritage of private enterprise which is almost nonexistent, or at least rapidly declining, in any other organization in America. Devotion to private enterprise in intellectual matters has led many scholars to become oblivious to the indirect, if not to the direct, consequences of their endeavors. This is in the very nature of intellectual enterprise and freedom which is so characteristic of higher education, with its infinite variety, in a free society.

America has not escaped from the European tradition of the "ivory tower," cloistered halls, monastic life of Cambridge, and intellectual isolationism with respect to the practical, political affairs in which institutions have their being. Is it possible that public relations problems in higher education spring, at least in part, from the tendency on the part of those who are responsible for institutional programs and activities to be less concerned for the consequences of their actions, and for the total programs of institutions in particular, than the various publics would like? This is not to imply that great centers of learning should, in all of their activities and programs, be the result of society or of agencies for maintaining the status quo in economic, social, and political affairs. Indeed, it is incumbent upon universities to provide leadership in modifying human institutions, economics, and politics. But they must operate within the framework of the existing society and the legal and social controls imposed upon them. However, in taking the initiative for dynamic and inevitable changes, leaders in higher education have the responsibility of bringing members of the larger communities into the planning and the actions involving both the preservation of the great heritage and the modification and direction of the inevitable changes.

Without attempting to lay down a formula that would apply to all institutions, it may be stated that the publics of an institution in general include all groups affected for good or for evil by the program of the institution. Resolving the difficulties inherent in such a situation calls for a program of adult education on a scale commensurate with the scope of the total publics affected by consequences of the program of the institution.

The designing of an effective public relations program involves first and foremost the total faculty, students, and administration of a college or university. The development of excellence in scholarship and a devotion to learning as the central idea of the university is the first step. The whole climate of the university should be conducive to learning; this idea should permeate residence halls, student unions, the faculty club, seminars, lecture halls, libraries, and academic offices. If the university is to be a community of scholars, there must be a climate charged with the dynamic qualities of research, experimentation, intellectual stimulation, and guidance and a general devotion to the virtues of scholarship by those associated with the university. This characteristic should become a way of life in American institutions in the last half of the twentieth century, when the very security of the nation is dependent upon excellence of achievement in science, engineering, technology, the humanities, social studies, and philosophy.

Such a program must include intelligent and objective admissions standards; testing, counseling, evaluation, and guidance of all students in general, but of freshmen in particular; and orientation, guidance, and assistance to new academic staff members who are beginning their careers in teaching. It must place an emphasis upon libraries, offices, and books at least comparable to the emphasis placed upon pageantry and football. It must include dynamic, wholesome, competitive athletics, intramural sports, and recreational activities which are so necessary to the mental health of an institution and which act as a nerve center for motivating alumni and friends. Athletics, recreational activities, and social programs must be a part of the academic life of the institution. They gain new dimensions of significance when teamed with the regular academic program. There is much virtue in the farmer's admonition to his son to "work hard if you would really enjoy resting." Students and faculty alike can participate intelligently in useful recreational activities in proportion to their devotion to the austere life of the scholar.

If such a program succeeds, the institution automatically has as many public relations officers as there are students and faculty members on the campus. In their devotion to research, learning, and service, students and faculties fulfill the most essential criteria of superior citizenship—appreciation for the state and the community which have made possible their intellectual environment through which they make systematic progress toward the fulfillment of greater responsibility and intelligent service. The development of such a program is the principal step in the organization of an effective public relations function.

The Process of Public Relations

In analyzing the process of public relations, one must recognize the significance of group pressure, facts, intelligence, emotions, attention, motivation, attitudes, and opinions. Research indicates that facts are not enough for a good public relations program. The process of communication is complex where the publics are as varied as those responsible for the support of higher education.

Results of Research. Asch experimented with fifty groups, each containing eight male college students who were asked to match the length of a line with one of three other lines which were unequal. Decisions were given orally. Prior to the experiment, seven out of eight students in each group were instructed to give obviously erroneous responses. This left fifty students out of the fifty groups free to exercise their own judgments. One third of the fifty followed the distorted estimates of the majority. Among those who dissented, there was serious concern and a certain interfrustration over their failure to agree with the majority.[15]

In another experiment dealing with this same phenomenon, Crutchfield used 159 persons in groups of five. Through the use of slides, various kinds of judgments were tested including lengths of lines, vocabulary items, number series, areas of figures, estimates of the opinions of others, attitudes on issues, and expressions of personal preference for line drawings. Again four out of five of the subjects were instructed to give erroneous answers, and the four were unanimous. One member in each group was confronted with the decisions of the other four members, after which the subjects' reactions were carefully scrutinized. The results indicated group conformity ranging all the way from 30 per cent on the matching of the length of lines to 79 per cent on questions designed to maximize ambiguity.[16]

Results of the final experiment indicated that, at the lower end of the scale, several of the men showed conformity on no more than one or two of the critical items. At the other extreme, however, one man was influenced on seventeen of the twenty-one items. In summarizing the results, Harlow states: "It is only where there is ambiguity and confusion that you can count on the band wagon effect—which means that other factors than the band wagon are determinative."[17]

[15]Solomon E. Asch, *Groups, Leadership and Men,* Harold Guetzkow (ed.), (Pittsburgh: Carnegie Press, 1951).
[16]Richard S. Crutchfield, "Conformity and Character," *The American Psychologist,* (May, 1955), pp. 191-198.
[17]Rex F. Harlow, *Social Science in Public Relations* (New York: Harper & Bros., 1957), p. 69.

The implications of these studies for the public relations man are obvious. An intelligent approach to the changing of group attitudes, motivations, and interests requires careful planning of the project involved; evaluation of attitudes, opinions, motivation, and interests of the individuals who make up the group; and careful presentation of the program with assurance that more than one individual, or rather that a considerable proportion of the individuals, will make a positive response. For example, Harlow states that science has shown that facts alone do not change attitudes; that people are not logical, reasoning beings and that they depend largely on their emotions; and that the ability of the common man to ignore those things which do not strike his immediate interest is profound.[18] Harlow states his conclusions with respect to the methodology of persuasion as follows: (1) The object must be clearly defined. (2) The appeal must be direct and emotional rather than intellectual. (3) Language must be simple and therefore easily understood. (4) Pronouncements must be clearly formulated and repeated over and over again.[19]

The viewpoint of Harlow is supported by Bernays, who states that wishful thinking and simple hopefulness influence the action of human beings far more than rational intelligence. He believes that effective advertising is based upon emotions and not upon intelligence. Bernays believes that strategists in public relations are concerned with truth always but that they are equally concerned with the people's interpretation of the truth—and sometimes they must give this interpretation precedence in their thinking even over the truth itself.[20]

The Educational Policies Commission summarizes the results of research on communication by pointing out certain significant generalizations:[21]

1. The communication of meaning is a complex process because each individual is a complex of different motivations, attitudes, needs, and experiences; and the problem of communication is to get two or more individuals to agree on the meaning of certain symbols. Each individual tends to perceive and to hear what he desires rather than what other people present.

---

[18]*Ibid.*, pp. 69-70.

[19]*Ibid.*, p. 88.

[20]Edward L. Bernays, *The Engineering of Consent* (Norman: University of Oklahoma Press, 1955), p. 97.

[21]Educational Policies Commission, *Mass Communication and Education* (Washington, D. C.: 1958), pp. 48-56.

2. The social context of any communication influences its effect; people perceive and respond to messages because of the influence of other individuals and groups. The response is not generally a direct one.

3. Communication builds on existing attitudes because attitudes are infrequently changed by communication.

4. Communication changes people, not by sharp, well-directed steering, but in a slow and almost imperceptible alteration.

5. Research in education has been concerned greatly with perception, which is the first step in the transfer of meaning.

A review of basic research in public relations and communication reveals the extreme difficulty, complexity, and significance of these problems in society in general, and especially for education, because the whole process of education is bound up with communication. But another essential observation emanating from the literature is that much of the material written for publicity, propaganda, and promotion in commercial enterprises is false or, at best, designed to exploit those who are uninitiated in the significance of propaganda.

Individuals engaged in education cannot ignore the results of research on people's motivation to action; neither can they resort to shady media of publicity, propaganda, and advertising. Therefore, it is incumbent upon leaders in education to present a program of excellence and to disseminate the story through modern media. A good program may fail to gain support if it is inadequately presented to the publics, and even a superior program may fail if ineptly presented.

Organization of the Development Office

E. H. Hopkins, in the Greenbrier report, suggested an organization which would make the chief officer for institutional development one of three men reporting to the president. Under the development office, he would include public relations, alumni relations, and fund raising. He would place student personnel services in the academic category because he feels that personnel is basically educational and that it should be placed under the dean of faculties.

Regardless of whether or not the officer holds the rank of vice-president, a title designed to carry prestige highly desirable in the performance of his job, colleges and universities are establishing development offices at a rapid pace. When the head officer does not hold the title of vice-president for development, he may be labeled director of university relations, director of development, director of public relations and development, or assistant to the president in charge of public relations and development.

Private and church-related institutions which have not had development programs or which have done little with them are beginning to place heavy emphasis upon them. Publicly-supported institutions are somewhat slower; but many, like the University of Michigan and Indiana University, are organizing with great vision. The results at Indiana and Michigan have been truly outstanding.

Institutions of higher learning which receive their support through public funds are not as cognizant of the value of development offices, and many which have not been prepared for them are just now setting the stage for such positions. Many feel that it might tend to relax interest on the part of legislatures, but Chancellor Herman B Wells at Indiana University maintains that there are many highly desirable enrichments of programs which the legislature would not support. He can point to examples such as a magnificent fine arts center, a rare books library, and a beautiful auditorium.

The Greenbrier Conference and study reached certain conclusions which seem basic to the total problem of institutional planning and development.[22] They are as follows:

1. The functions of public relations, alumni relations, and fund raising exist on every college campus, and each function is an essential ingredient of institutional advancement.
2. It is imperative that these related functions be coordinated.
3. While there is no single "best" organizational pattern, there are common principles and practices of good organization and management that apply in all institutions, regardless of size.
4. Each institution must make the decision as to what is the best type of organization for its own situation.
5. There is a great need to upgrade the qualifications of administrative personnel for planning and development.
6. There probably is general agreement that there is a need to increase budgets for public relations, fund raising, and alumni relations.

The challenge of greatly increased enrollments in institutions of higher learning is a rigorous test of educational leaders who are organizing development and public relations offices to explore new avenues for

---

[22]E. H. Hopkins, *The Advancement of Understanding and Support of Higher Education,* American College Public Relations Association (1958), p. 57.

resources and to awaken regular sources of income to their increasing responsibilities for every worthy student.

When foundations, corporations, governments, and individuals combine their resources to support higher education, America can be assured that its youth will be educated, and that the nation will be even stronger in upholding its principles of democracy.

Administrators engaged in action programs must give careful consideration to the implementation of any plan of organization. This is an area of administration which is certain to be a failure unless it is organized according to the best-known principles of management. Poorly organized programs for planning and development sometimes cost more than they contribute. It is easy to spend more money on alumni relations, for example, than is contributed by the alumni.

Dr. Arnold F. Emch has stated the following principles of good organization:[23]

1. A good organization reflects the essential purpose of the institution.
2. All the essential functions must be provided for accomplishing this primary purpose.
3. A good plan of organization clearly defines the essential functions of each division of the organization.
4. A good plan of organization provides single and distinct lines of authority and responsibility from top to bottom.
5. Similar or like functions should be grouped together and performed by employees adapted to a specific type of work.
6. A good organization will adopt the simplest possible structure required to accomplish efficiently the necessary work.
7. The assignment of individual responsibilities will be made with due consideration for the equitable distribution of work loads and the reasonableness of the spans of responsibility.
8. A good plan of organization will provide flexibility of operation to meet special and changing conditions.

Institutional objectives, planning, development, organization, management, and action must be coordinated if public relations and fundraising programs are to succeed.

Planning and development are comprehensive terms that range from the establishment of objectives to means of growth of an institution.

---

[23]Arnold F. Emch, "The Organization and Management of Universities" (An address delivered before the Association of Governing Boards of State Universities and Allied Institutions, 1949).

These are not limited to any one aspect of growth such as physical plant or endowments. They include educational planning and development. To separate the educational program from public relations and development would leave public relations and fund-raising personnel without any program and without any chance of success in gaining support.

Moreover, no good development officer would be willing to work on a dynamic fund-raising program without having a part in planning the utilization of those funds. The two aspects cannot be separated without risking failure in both. The success of leaders such as Russell Bintzer at the Carnegie Institute of Technology, Edgar Cale at Pittsburgh, Art Schaefer at DePaul, and E. H. Hopkins at Duke has been a result of their involvement in the planning of the total educational program and its support.

The elements of an effectively coordinated program seem to require a vice-president, with appropriate staff members for public relations, alumni relations, and fund-raising or development. Adequate clerical personnel and records are equally important.

The vice-president for planning and development must have status next to the president and should be a recognized member of the president's council on total university management.

The Greenbrier Conference, in 1958, concluded that the most significant qualification for individuals who aspire to roles of leadership in planning and development is that of being first an educator, of feeling like an educator, of thinking like one.[24]

Specific qualifications mentioned in the report of the Greenbrier Conference were interest in education, knowledge of the institution, attractive personality, competence, confidence, and self-respect.

The achievements of competent men in this field are indispensable to the growth and functioning of higher education. The results now being achieved attest to the confidence of alumni, businessmen, labor, and ordinary citizens in the future of higher education. Success of planning and development in any institution depends upon understanding and participation on the part of the entire faculty, students, alumni, and administration.

Case Studies on Application of Principles of Communication

Kentucky Public Schools. The first case to be summarized involves a statewide system of public education. The experience was spread

---

[24]Hopkins, *op. cit.*, pp. 20-22.

over a two-year period, 1958-1960, when 174 local citizen committees made an evaluation of the existing school program, determined minimum desirable standards, and formulated an estimate of increased costs and possible methods of financing the program. The Kentucky Council for Education sponsored the study and provided organizational leadership to bring the citizen committees into being.

Studies and research were designed to aid in formulating policies and standards on qualifications and salaries of teachers, classroom conditions, instructional supplies, school transportation, the curriculum, and enrollment trends.

Over 10,000 citizens participated in the studies which eventually were coordinated into a statewide plan. The State Legislature adopted the program as presented, including provisions for obtaining the necessary revenue to finance it, without a dissenting vote in either the House of Representatives or the Senate.[25] The increase in appropriations was 50 per cent over the previous biennium.

Dodson's research involved an evaluation of the method by which the citizens of Kentucky influenced such dynamic support for public education. His principal conclusions herein enumerated have significance for all educational leaders:

1. State education associations should encourage the establishment of citizens committees in local school districts. This can usually be done more effectively if the association cooperates with a state-wide council of some kind rather than takes the lead in insisting on their establishment.

2. Members of the teaching profession should be on the local committees but should be in the minority. This arrangement discourages accusations of teacher domination.

3. Lay people do not want domination on the part of educators, neither do they want acquiescence. . . . .

4. The development and promotion of a state-wide school legislative program through local committees make it easier to secure legislative enactment, since legislators are responsive to the wishes of their constituents. . . .

5. State education associations should beware of becoming tied to political personalities. The results of the study indicate that it is

---

[25]J. Marvin Dodson, *A Comparative Study and Analysis of Selected Procedures in Achieving Desirable School Legislation* (Unpublished Doctor's thesis, School of Education, Indiana University, Bloomington, 1961), p. 6.

unwise for education associations, either state or local, to endorse candidates for office. . . .

6. The warning against public endorsements, however, does not mean that education associations cannot participate in a political election. They can appropriately publicize the statements on education of candidates for public office. . . .

7. It can be concluded that the endorsements of state-wide issues which indirectly affect education fall within the appropriate activities in which an education association can become engaged. . . .

8. It is unwise to use the pupils in an attempt to influence parents to vote for educational issues or for candidates for public office. . . .

9. People are dependent upon professional educators for help on educational matters. Even though the educators are receiving some criticisms at the present time, one can conclude from the results of this study that their opinions on educational matters are respected. . . .

10. We are not living entirely in the age of television. Newspapers rank high on the list as a medium of communication, especially newspapers with state-wide circulation and those with county-wide circulation. . . .

11. There is still no substitute for face-to-face communication or individual contacts. . . .

12. Program planning should involve more than making arrangements for a speaker to address an audience. This is not always the best way to clarify current questions and issues. One can conclude from the study that either a panel or an open general discussion is a better way to clarify problems and to get ideas across.

13. People are interested in the educational welfare of their children. Therefore, in showing how school money is spent, it is well to depict this in terms of number of dollars per child. This information has more appeal to parents and to the public generally than does the amount spent either for teacher salaries or for school buildings. . . .

Charles R. Van Hise at Wisconsin. Van Hise became President of the University of Wisconsin in 1904. His creed, expressed in his inaugural address, was that the university's functions should be "as broad as human endeavor," that the boundaries of the University were the boundaries of the state.[26]

---

[26]Maurice M. Vance, *Charles Richard Van Hise* (The State Historical Society of Wisconsin, Madison, 1960), p. 90.

President Van Hise was a product of the University and an internationally-known scholar in geology. His surveys of the resources of the Great Lakes area were the most authoritative of the early twentieth century.

Under the stimulation of Governor Robert La Follette, President Van Hise and the faculty made strides in the implementation of the Wisconsin Idea. With the University at one end of State Street and the State Capitol at the other, professors served on commissions involving all aspects of the state and made the University an integral part of the economic, social, and political life of the state.

University leaders drafted the Wisconsin Civil Service Law and helped organize the Industrial Commission; served on the Railroad Commission; helped draft the state income tax law and served on the Tax Commission. The State Department of Agriculture, the Public Health Service, the Forestry Board, the Conservation Commission, and the Geological Surveys were greatly dependent upon the University of Wisconsin.[27]

Progressive political interests were defeated in the gubernatorial contest of 1914. Emanuel Philipp, who was elected Governor, and many members of the Legislature were elected on a platform of retrenchment in University funds and programs, if not punishment for the leaders of the University of Wisconsin.

In the 1915 session of the Legislature, Governor Philipp and his followers introduced forty-two bills "to limit funds and the influence of the University in educational as well as in political, social, and economic issues."[28]

Nearly all of the bills designed to curtail the concept of "a service University as broad as human endeavor and as high as human aspiration" were defeated. Most members of the Legislature did not know what hit them, but Van Hise, Frederick Jackson Turner, and other leaders of the University knew. Patently, it was not an army of public relations and development officers. The conscience of a university based upon human aspirations was appropriately the conscience of the people. The program of the University was the people's program, and the voice of the University was the voice of the people.

President Van Hise discovered by research and by insight that every man, including governors and legislators, is a product of the social

---

[27]*Ibid.*, p. 113.

[28]E. C. Wallenfeldt, *A State University President and the Social Psychology of Meeting Legislative and Gubernatorial Opposition: A Case Study of the Manner in Which Charles Richard Van Hise Met Opposition in Wisconsin in 1915* (Unpublished Doctor's thesis, School of Education, Indiana University, Bloomington, 1962).

groups of which he is a part and that his attitudes are shaped by these various groups. He discovered that there were intelligent friends and advocates of the University in every Wisconsin group of any significance. He and the professors provided the alumni and friends of the University with all important facts regarding research, curricula, teaching, and service functions of the University. Friends of the University who were associated with key legislators and with the Governor won the necessary support for the University.

From President Van Hise's experience, one can enumerate specific conclusions:

1. The University had developed a program based upon the needs of Wisconsin citizens.
2. The citizens of the state were aware of the relationship of the University to their welfare.
3. The University was fortunate in having administrators and professors who were competent to carry out the program and to communicate its significance to the people.
4. The citizens became the most effective public relations representatives of the University. No staff of public relations experts could have been so effective as were the citizens in changing the attitudes of conservative legislators.

U. S. Point Four in Peru. In 1950, the U. S.-Peruvian Education Mission was engaged in the development of rural schools and vocational schools at the secondary level, as well as a comprehensive program for the education of teachers. The program was being supported by joint funds provided by governments of the United States and Peru. The director of the joint program, during his first weeks on the job, was requested by the director of information and public relations in the education mission, to include in the budget for the new fiscal year a tenth position in the area of public relations and publications. After careful investigation and conferences with knowledgeable Peruvian and North American educators, it was decided to terminate the employment of eight of the nine people in the public relations office and to transfer the ninth to an office responsible for translating and publishing educational materials for the various cooperative projects.

An outstanding professor of philosophy was employed as associate director of the cooperative Education Mission. The decision was made to place all the emphasis upon the development of a program of excellence in rural education, vocational schools, and teacher education. It was decided to de-emphasize all efforts toward the dissemination of propaganda, pending the development of a good program. Within fifteen months, representatives of mass media made a beaten path to the offices of the Education Mission, and the program flourished in terms of its acceptance and support by the Peruvian citizens and the Peruvian government.

During this same period, the U. S. Director of the Joint Peruvian-North American Mission in Agriculture stated on many occasions that the cooperative Agricultural Mission had, as its director of public relations, the most outstanding newspaper man in Latin America. This gentleman possessed all the technical skills and the social amenities to assist the American director in building an astoundingly favorable image of the Agricultural Mission which, for a period of nearly fifteen years, deserved to be noted exclusively for its extravagance and sharp practices in the use of funds provided by the governments of the United States and Peru. During this period, there were many Peruvians of sufficient intellectual and economic sophistication to discern the fact that the Department of Agriculture of Peru could have provided infinitely greater services through the frugal and prudent use of Peru's contribution to the joint program without any United States funds whatsoever, if the Peruvian leaders could have divested themselves of the American bureaucrats.

As revealed in the American press, the day of reckoning for the well-heeled U. S. Director of the Agricultural Mission in Peru finally came when he was dismissed from his position. A running battle waged between the Department of State and congressional committees over the prudent use of foreign aid funds, and refusal of the Department of State to release the record on Mr. John R. Neal. This would make interesting reading for any contemporary Sherlock Holmes who would like to probe beneath the synthetic diplomatic surface concerning such incidents as the 1958 stoning of Vice-President Nixon within the compound of San Marcos University.

This case illustrates better than any theoretical statement the consequences of Madison Avenue techniques of salesmanship designed to make a fraudulent program palatable to Mr. John Q. Public.

The University of Minnesota, Duluth. In the 1949 session of the Minnesota Legislature, the "high priests" of the University of Minnesota made ruthless cuts in the budget submitted by the administrators of the University of Minnesota, Duluth, and secured approval by the Regents of the University before whom there was no representative from Duluth.

The budget, submitted to the Governor and through him to the Legislature, requested an operating budget of $251 per student for the institution in Duluth. The requests for comparable programs in similar institutions in the state, outside of Duluth, ranged from $450 per student to approximately $600. The citizens and legislators from northeastern Minnesota, into which the University at Duluth was beginning to sink deep roots of public service and higher education opportunities, quite understandably protested the impoverished conditions under which it was proposed to operate the institution. Governor Youngdall called upon the state budget director to make a careful budgetary analysis of all budgets proposed for state colleges and the University. Subsequently, the director of the budget notified the Governor that, if the appropriations followed the requests as submitted by the university officials, the executive branch of the government and the Legislature would be parties to the most inequitable distribution of college and university funds in Minnesota's history. When the complete story became known to the ordinary citizens of Minnesota serving in the Legislature, the budgetary requests of the University of Minnesota, Duluth, were restored, the objections of the "high priests" to the contrary, notwithstanding.

In general, these cases point to the fact that we should never overestimate the information which citizens have concerning such technical problems as higher education, and we should never underestimate the ability of ordinary citizens to make intelligent and prudent decisions once the necessary information and facts have been collected.

Summary

One cannot defend the notion that the coordinating officer or vice-president must come from any one of the three areas to be coordinated. It is not crucial that the individual be a former alumni secretary, director of public relations, or director of development. It is important for the coordinating officer to have competencies in one or more of the areas to be coordinated and to have keen administrative ability.

In the final analysis, the extent of participation of the coordinator in academic planning and development will depend upon his intellectual inclinations. To be accepted as a leader or as a member of the team for academic planning, one must possess a personal and professional commitment to intellectual activities as being the central emphasis of an educational institution.

Questions for Discussion

1. In what ways are purposes related to public relations in higher education?
2. How does evaluation pertain to public relations?
3. Is it possible to place all public relations functions in a central office?
4. How does Schoenfeld rate and relate program and publicity in higher education?
5. How does a college determine its publics?
6. Why should planning and development functions be centralized under a vice-president?
7. How can the Van Hise experience at Wisconsin be applied to current problems?
8. What experiences and evidence can we advance that indicate the ability of citizens to participate intelligently in planning and development in higher education?

Bibliography

ASCH, SOLOMON E. *Groups, Leadership and Men,* ed. Harold Guetzkow. Pittsburgh: Carengie Press, 1951.

BERNAYS, EDWARD L. *The Engineering of Consent.* Norman: University of Oklahoma Press, 1955.

CENTER, ALLEN H. *Public Relations Ideas in Action.* New York: McGraw-Hill Book Co., Inc., 1957.

CRUTCHFIELD, RICHARD S. "Conformity and Character," *The American Psychologist,* (May, 1955), pp. 191-198.

DEWEY, JOHN. *The Public and Its Problems.* New York: Henry Holt & Co., 1927.

DODSON, J. MARVIN. *A Comparative Study and Analysis of Selected Procedures in Achieving Desirable School Legislation.* Unpublished Doctor's thesis, School of Education, Indiana University, Bloomington, 1961.

Educational Policies Commission. *Mass Communication and Education.* Washington, D. C., 1958.

EMCH, ARNOLD F. "The Organization and Management of Universities." An address delivered before the Association of Governing Boards of State Universities and Allied Institutions, 1949.

GALLUP, GEORGE H. *A Guide to Public Opinion Polls.* Princeton, N. J.: Princeton University Press, 1948.

HANSON, CARROLL. "The Strangers in Our Midst." A public address given at Indiana University, 1960.

HARLOW, REX F. *Social Science in Public Relations.* New York: Harper & Bros., 1957.

HARRAL, STEWART. *Tested Public Relations for Schools.* Norman: University of Oklahoma Press, 1952.

HILL, JOHN W. *Corporate Public Relations.* New York: Harper & Bros., 1958.

HOGARTH, CHARLES P. *The Crisis in Higher Education.* Washington, D. C.: Public Affairs Press, 1957.

HOPKINS, E. H. *The Advancement of Understanding and Support of Higher Education.* American College Public Relations Association, 1958.

KELLEY, STANLEY. *Professional Public Relations and Political Power.* Baltimore: Johns Hopkins Press, 1956.

The Pursuit of Excellence. Special Studies Project Report II, Rockefeller Brothers Fund, Garden City, New York: Doubleday & Co., Inc., 1958.

Research Division, National Education Association. *Teacher Supply and Demand.* 1962.

RUSSELL, JOHN DALE. *The Finance of Higher Education.* Chicago: The University of Chicago Press, 1954.

SCHOENFELD, CLARENCE A. *The University and Its Publics.* New York: Harper & Bros., 1954.

TEAD, ORDWAY. *The Climate of Learning.* New York: Harper & Bros., 1958.

VANCE, MAURICE M. *Charles Richard Van Hise.* Madison: The State Historical Society of Wisconsin, 1960.

VAN HISE, CHARLES R. "Inaugural Address." Jubilee of the University of Wisconsin, Madison, 1905.

WALLENFELDT, E. C. "A State University President and the Social Psychology of Meeting Legislative and Gubernatorial Opposition: A Case Study of the Manner in Which Charles Richard Van Hise Met Opposition in Wisconsin in 1915." Unpublished Doctor's thesis, School of Education, Indiana University, Bloomington, 1962.

WARNER, W. L., HAVIGHURST, ROBERT J., and LOEB, M. B. *Who Shall Be Educated? (The Challenge of Unequal Opportunities).* New York: Harper & Bros., 1944.

WEAVER, JOHN C. *Some Dilemmas in Graduate Education.* Lincoln: University of Nebraska Press, 1958.

Chapter

13

Eclipse of the Substance of
Higher Education

Most of the great debates in higher education in the decade of the sixties seem to involve the means of education. National leaders, from the late President Kennedy to college presidents, are dissipating their energies in attempting to arouse American citizens to the crisis in the support of higher education, even though the most enlightened leaders of this century have equated higher education not only with economic and social development but with national survival.

The great debate centers in the issues of keeping the doors of higher education open to increasing numbers of students and of ways and means to provide the financial resources necessary for minimum standards. These problems should not be the crucial issues of higher education in the United States. It is unthinkable that our greatest leaders must divert their time, intelligence, and energies to resolving questions of means, while politicians and technologists fix the goals of higher education and then appropriate ear-marked funds to carry them out.

Leaders in higher education and in government have defaulted in their responsibilities to American youth. Educational statesmen must lead faculties in developing the arts, sciences, and professions of men with vertical and horizontal dimensions commensurate with the problems and aspirations of free men approaching the twenty-first century. This is the challenge of leadership in higher education, and the challenge to political statesmen is to provide the means for implementing this dynamic educational idea.

Quantitative Dimensions of Education

Education, broadly conceived, includes all experiences, knowledge, attitudes, habits, skills, and appreciations which one gains through formal and informal interaction with the elements of his environment. It includes patterns of thought and action based upon knowing. Education is a continuous process of learning, being, and doing with increasing degrees of intellectual sophistication as a result of each new experience.

The formal aspect of education, made necessary because of the increasing gap between the young and the mature members of society, has been delegated by the citizenry to the schools and colleges. This is a small segment of the total education of the individual who lives a normal span of years and continues to learn. But the formal years of education are basic to effective living and continued learning in the complex society of this age.

These years of formal education are significant to the economic status of the individual and of society. It has been estimated that a college degree adds $100,000 to the income of an individual during the course of his career. With federal taxes at present levels, it is reasonable to assume that 20 per cent of the additional income, resulting from a bachelor's degree, will go to the government in the form of taxes. This should amount to $20,000 in added federal taxes alone for every bachelor's degree earned. If governments at all levels invested $5,000 in every earned bachelor's degree, the means of support for higher education would no longer be a problem; and government would receive a return of 300 per cent profit on the investment.

Economic returns, both to society and to the individual, do not approach in significance the social, political, and aesthetic returns. These are intangible dividends that cannot be measured so exactly as the economic results, but they are reflected in the quality of governments, in the tastes and aspirations of people, and in the sensitiveness and responsiveness of citizens living in an interdependent world.

Magnitude of Education Enterprises. The production and distribution of knowledge has become the greatest enterprise in America, both in terms of cost and in terms of long-range consequences. This has probably been true in all societies that have struggled to survive, but the world has now reached a point in space and time where the principal element of power is education.

America was able to transform industry and manpower from peace to war in record time during the two world wars of this century. Two oceans provided the necessary protection during the transition from peace to war. No such protection will exist at any time in the future, and no such transition from peace to war will be possible. Preparation for any eventuality means, above everything else, keeping our educational house in order. If research and education should lag ten years behind that of a potential competitor, transition from peace to war would be impossible, because the education of a superior researcher in the sciences or of qualified professors in the humanities and social sciences requires more years than were necessary to finish either of the great wars. The next war will not last so long. There will be no time for preparation, and there will be no victory except to keep the world at peace—an objective that is more likely to be achieved through world citizens sophisticated in the humanities and social sciences than through an exclusive national emphasis upon science and technology.

Formal education decreases with each passing year as a percentage of the total production and distribution of knowledge; but the decrease is quantitative not qualitative, for it is organized formal education that triggers the total production of knowledge. An automobile may have 400 horsepower; but, unless the starter functions, the 400 horsepower cannot function. The complex American economy, which involves $136 billion annually in the production and distribution of knowledge, is dependent upon formal education to trigger the national potential. Table 1 presents the major divisions of our economy through which knowledge is produced and disseminated.

TABLE 8

PRODUCTION OF KNOWLEDGE, 1958*	
Knowledge Production	Millions of Dollars
Education	$ 60,194
Research and Development	10,990
Media of Communication	38,369
Information Machines	8,922
Information Services	17,961
Total Knowledge Production	$136,436

*Source of data: Machlup, Fritz, *The Production and Distribution of Knowledge in the United States* (Princeton, New Jersey: Princeton University Press, 1962), pp. 354-357.

Machlup has interpreted the production of knowledge as "not only discovering, inventing, designing, and planning but also disseminating and communicating."[1] This comprehensive definition of knowledge production, including formal and informal methods of discovering, transmitting, and learning, becomes by far the major enterprise in the United States. As indicated in Table 8, the total cost for the production and distribution of knowledge in the United States was $136,436 billion in 1958.[2]

This analysis of the categories and cost of producing and disseminating knowledge very appropriately classifies formal education as only one aspect of the process. Producing, transmitting, and acquiring knowledge are functions that occupy a major place in American society. Education, in the institutional sense, is one limited aspect of the larger enterprise.

Table 9 indicates the distribution of research and development funds, by source, for 1953 to 1961. The greatest change in amount contributed during this period was the increased participation on the part of the federal government.

TABLE 9

SOURCES OF FUNDS USED FOR RESEARCH AND DEVELOPMENT, BY SECTOR, 1953-54—1960-61[a]* (Millions of dollars)					
Year	Total	Federal Government	Industry	Colleges and Universities[b]	Other Nonprofit Institutions[b]
1953-54	$ 5,150	$2,740	$2,240	$130	$ 40
1954-55	5,620	3,070	2,365	140	45
1955-56	6,390	3,670	2,510	155	55
1956-57	8,610	5,095	3,265	180	70
1957-58	10,030	6,380	3,390	190	70
1958-59	11,070	7,170	3,620	190	90
1959-60 (prelim.)	12,620	8,290	4,030	200	100
1960-61 (prelim.)	14,040	9,220	4,490	210	120

[a]Data are based on reports by the performers.

[b]State and local government funds spent for research and development by the colleges and universities and other nonprofit institutions are included with the respective sector's own funds.

Note: With the exception of data for 1953-54 and 1957-58, the years in which surveys covered all sectors, data on sectors as sources of funds are estimates.

*Source of data: National Science Foundation, Twelfth Annual Report, (March, 1962).

---

[1]Machlup, Fritz, *The Production and Distribution of Knowledge in the United States* (Princeton, New Jersey: Princeton University Press, 1962), p. 7.
[2]*Ibid.*, pp. 354-357.

In fiscal 1961, the federal government spent $964 million or 11 per cent of its total research and development funds through contracts with educational institutions. In fiscal 1962, the amount was approximately $1.2 billion and may reach $1.5 billion during fiscal 1963.

Both the extramural and intramural funds from Table 9 may be regarded as informal educational activities, because the universities contract to carry on research functions outside of their normal activities.

Federal funds are made available to universities, public and private, to accomplish a specific mission rather than to assist institutions of higher learning to achieve their own basic missions. Those institutions which have had the resources, over a period of many years, to attract and retain the most competent personnel, particularly in the areas of science and engineering, have received most of the funds. This approach tends to distort university programs, to create an imbalance in curricular emphasis, and to widen the gap between the support of large and small institutions.

Table 10 is a summary of expenditures for basic research for the period 1953 to 1961. The greatest increase was in federal intramural basic research, but funds for colleges and universities increased substantially over the eight-year period. It should be noted that this type of research is shifting from the almost exclusive prerogative of higher education to government and industry.

Over two-thirds of federal research funds going to higher education are allocated to twenty-five institutions; fifty institutions receive over 80 per cent of the funds; and one hundred institutions receive 95 per cent of the funds. These funds are made available for specific purposes and projects, the development of policy for which governing boards, college administrators, and faculties are almost completely ignored. Government officials play the dominant role.

In fiscal 1961, of the $969 million which the federal government spent for basic research, 41 per cent of the total was distributed to colleges and universities.

Table 11 shows that twenty-six institutions of higher learning received 28 per cent of the 1959-60 federal funds spent on project research in colleges and universities. The first twelve universities in terms of size of research grants were Michigan, M.I.T., Stanford, Harvard, Chicago, Berkeley, Texas, U.C.L.A., Cornell, Princeton, San Diego, and the California Institute of Technology. Their federal research funds ranged from approximately $5 million in one institution to $20 million at another. Moreover, of the $969 million in federal funds spent on basic

TABLE 10

SOURCES OF FUNDS USED FOR BASIC RESEARCH, BY SECTOR, 1953-54—1960-61[a]*
(Millions of dollars)

Year	Total	Federal Government	Industry	Colleges and Universities[b]	Other Nonprofit Institutions[b]
1953-54	$ 432	$195	$147	$ 62	$28
1954-55	485	n.a.	n.a.	n.a.	n.a.
1955-56	547	n.a.	n.a.	n.a.	n.a.
1956-57	694	n.a.	n.a.	n.a.	n.a.
1957-58	834	422	249	111	52
1958-59	1,016	565	275	118	58
1959-60 (prelim.)	1,150	646	293	140	71
1960-61 (prelim.)	1,302	745	313	161	83

[a]Data are based on reports by the performers.

[b]State and local government funds spent for basic research by the colleges and universities and other nonprofit institutions are included with the respective sector's own funds.

n.a.—Not available.

Note: With the exception of data for 1953-54 and 1957-58, the years in which surveys covered all sectors, data on sectors as sources of funds are estimates.

*Source of data: National Science Foundation, *op. cit.*, (March, 1962).

TABLE 11

FUNDS USED IN THE PERFORMANCE OF BASIC RESEARCH, APPLIED RESEARCH, AND DEVELOPMENT, 1959-60 (Preliminary)*
(Millions of dollars)

Sector	Amount			
	Total R & D	Research Basic	Applied Research	Development
Total	$12,620	$1,150	$2,850	$8,620
Federal Government[a]	1,830	220	460	1,150
Industry	9,550	345	1,955	7,250
Colleges and universities	1,000	500	330	170
Other nonprofit institutions	240	85	105	50

[a]Data on federal estimates of applied research and development were not obtained directly by survey but were derived from available related information.

*Source of data: National Science Foundation, *op. cit.*, (March, 1962).

research in 1961, 97 per cent was for physical and life sciences, 2 per cent for psychological sciences, and 1 per cent for the social sciences. No funds were allocated to research in the humanities.

Table 12 presents the problem of personnel in sharp focus. Of the 387,000 full-time scientists and engineers working in research and development in 1960, only 52,000 were in colleges and universities; but 41,800 were in the federal government, and 286,200 were in industry. These shifts of specialized talent from higher education to industry are making it increasingly difficult to staff the nation's colleges and universities with qualified personnel in technical departments. A continued shift in this direction could eliminate the source of specialized talent for the future, because the unique function of the professor in science and technology, as in other fields of higher learning, is to produce specialized talents. It is doubtful that any other agency will perform that function.

TABLE 12

SCIENTISTS AND ENGINEERS IN RESEARCH AND DEVELOPMENT, BY SECTOR, 1954, 1958, 1960[a]*

Sector	1954	1958	1960 (Prelim.)
	Full-time Equivalents		
	223,200	327,100	387,000
Federal Government[b]	29,500	40,200	41,800
Industry[c]	164,100	239,500	286,200
Colleges and universities[c]	25,200	42,000	52,000
Other nonprofit institutions[c]	4,400	5,400	7,000

[a]Data consist of number of full-time employees plus the full-time equivalent of part-time employees. (*See Technical Notes.*)
[b]Limited to civilian personnel.
[c]Includes professional research personnel employed at research centers administered by organizations under contract with federal agencies.
*Source of data: National Science Foundation, *op. cit.*, (March, 1962).

In Table 13, one can interpret the rapid growth in the cost of research and development as a percentage of the gross national product. The percentage is approximately three times the percentage going to higher education. The implications are clear. Traditional functions of higher education are being taken over by other sectors of American society. Directions are being determined by those who control funds, the principal power being with the federal government.

TABLE 13

R & D FUNDS IN RELATION TO THE GROSS NATIONAL PRODUCT, 1953-60*			
(Dollar amounts in millions, at current prices)			
Year[a]	Gross national product (GNP)	R & D funds (revised)	R & D funds as percentage of GNP
1953-1954	$365,385	$ 5,150	1.41
1954-1955	363,112	5,620	1.55
1955-1956	397,469	6,390	1.61
1956-1957	419,180	8,610	2.05
1957-1958	442,769	10,030	2.26
1958-1959	444,546	11,070	2.49
1959-1960	482,783	12,620	2.61
1960-1961	504,448	14,040	2.78

[a]The gross national product totals refer to the calendar years to the left.
*Source of data: National Science Foundation, *op. cit.,* (March, 1962). For GNP data, see U. S. Department of Commerce, Office of Business Economics, *Survey of Current Business,* (July, 1962).

Pious platitudes about our great humane emphasis as the national focus are as winnowed chaff beside the realism of the budget.. No responsible government official can escape the fact that the national budget represents the translation of American ideals into dollars and cents.

The federal government expects to obligate $14.7 billion for research and development during fiscal 1963. This will be an increase of 31 per cent over the $11.2 billion spent in fiscal 1962. It is anticipated that, of the total, $4.5 billion will be used for research, $8.5 billion for development, $1.6 billion for research and development of physical facilities, and $100 million for scientific and technical information.

Four of the twenty-seven reporting agencies account for 95 per cent of the total estimate for fiscal 1963. The Department of Defense reported $7.4 billion, up from $6.7 billion in 1962; the National Aeronautics and Space Administration expects to double its research and development funds from $1.4 billion in 1962 to $2.8 billion in 1963, indicating our determination to make a round trip to the moon. The Atomic Energy Commission and the Department of Health, Education and Welfare indicate very large gains in research and development plans for 1963.

It is anticipated that about 8 per cent of the research and development funds for fiscal 1963 will be expended through the following types of organization: industry, 65 per cent; educational institutions, 12 per cent;

and other non-profit organizations, 4 per cent. About 12 per cent of these federal extramural obligations is likely to go for federal contract research centers administered by industry, universities, or other non-profit organizations.

Special Functions of Foundations

There are over 12,000 private philanthropic foundations in the United States with assets of approximately $12 billion in 1961. In 1960, there were 272 foundations that spent $437.1 million, or 87 per cent of program expenditures of foundations for that year, in support of their various programs.[3] The distribution of these funds was as follows: education, $230.4 million; scientific research, $89.3 million; health and welfare, $74.2 million; humanities, $21.1 million; other, including religion, cultural relations, and peace programs, $22.1 million. The administration of these programs amounted to $36 million, 9.6 per cent of the total, bringing total expenditures to $473 million.

Foundations are interested in channeling private wealth to public purposes, and they are as varied in their ways of carrying out this concern as are the individuals who established them.[4] Perhaps there has been no improvement upon taxation as a method of channeling private funds to public purposes. This is a fundamental purpose of any good system of taxation.

Implications of Federal Monopoly of Revenue and Production of Knowledge

The total income of all colleges and universities in the United States in 1959-60 was $5,813 million, exclusive of funds for plant expansion. These funds came from the following sources; state and local governments, $1,541 million (27 per cent); federal government, $1,041 million (18 per cent); student fees, $1,162 million (20 per cent); private gifts and endowments, $590 million (10 per cent); sales and services, $379 million (7 per cent); auxiliary enterprise, $1,100 million (19 per cent). If one would have deducted auxiliary enterprises, which, for the most part, are self-supporting business operations, the budget would have been only $4,713 million. Moreover, the federal contribution of $1,041 million represents support only for federal programs and projects that bear very remote relationships to the central purposes of higher education.

---

[3] National Science Foundation, Reviews of Data on Research and Development, Washington, D. C., No. 35, (August, 1962).
[4] *Ibid.,* p. 2.

Resources for the production of knowledge are unlimited in the United States, provided that the types of knowledge to be produced, the research to be carried out, and the selection of individuals and institutions to be responsible are unconditional prerogatives of the federal government. Federal expenditures for research and development have reached $14 billion annually and will continue to increase as specialized knowledge and programs become even more important to the achievement of national goals.

Foundations and what they will support are variables in the national picture; and, although they have given consideration and funds for aspects of liberal education generally ignored by the federal government, contributions from foundations have been limited to a select few of America's liberal arts colleges.

This chapter was not designed to question the policy of the federal government in supporting whatever research and development programs are necessary for the defense of the United States and the free world. The purpose here was to indicate the subordinate role to which higher education has been reduced in the total enterprise of education. Even more disturbing is the fact that basic policies for higher education, both formal and informal, are being made according to sources of financial support.

Academic specialists, throughout most of our history, have represented the centrifugal force that has made it nearly impossible to achieve unity in educational institutions. This tendency toward disintegration is not unique to America. For example, no power from without eclipses the faculty of the individual colleges of Cambridge and Oxford.

The drive toward specialization at the expense of synthesis and integration in education is now being challenged, not by a better idea, but by control of the purse strings. Academic disintegration and diversity of programs according to sources and amounts of budgetary support must be challenged by a new force based upon educational leadership. Specialists in integration, in synthesis, and in leadership are needed to place the objectives of higher education in proper perspective and to use means or financial support to achieve objectives rather than to determine them.

Summary

Many of the greatest universities in the United States with long traditions of humanistic learning are degenerating into high level vocational schools under the block-busting weight of our federal bureaucracies. This is not in the long-range interest of America; for the most casual observations of higher education in underdeveloped countries of Latin America and Asia reveal the close relationship between the national control of education, including university education, and economic, political, and intellectual stagnation.

Freedom in American universities has caused scholars from almost every other country to make a beaten path to our institutions to find the secrets of our economic, social, and political strength. But America is faltering in maintaining that system. Some of our most famous universities are being purchased by the federal government. More than fifty important agencies in Washington have federal funds with which to persuade our greatest universities to place their major emphasis upon science and technology, to the neglect of the humanities and the social sciences. This is happening at a time when the people of the world are crying out for revival and application of great humanistic traditions.

Government is not the only threat to the integrity of United States universities. Foundations and their boards of directors are eclipsing the power of governing boards of many great universities, and still others are being taken over by professional fund raisers and public relations officers. These dangers to higher education are a consequence of the fact that there is no unified plan for keeping the doors of higher education open to American youth.

Questions for Discussion

1. What steps could be taken to shift the emphasis in higher education from advancement and support to substance?
2. In what specific ways is our emphasis in higher education a materialistic rather than a humanistic one?
3. How are programs in the social sciences and the humanities related to national security?
4. Is the allocation of federal funds enhancing diversity or is it encouraging conformity in higher education?
5. In what ways are the foundations a more effective means than taxation for channeling private wealth to public purposes?
6. How is the power of funds being used to change fundamental purposes of great universities?

Bibliography

ADAMS, HENRY. *The Education of Henry Adams.* New York: The Modern Library, 1931.

BARZUN, JACQUES. *The House of Intellect.* New York: Harper & Bros., 1959. 276 pp.

CHERRY, H. H. *Education: The Basis of Democracy*. Chicago, Illinois: D. C. Heath & Co., 1926.

FRANKEL, CHARLES. *Issues in University Education*. New York: Harper & Bros.

HENRY, DAVID. *What Priority for Education? The American People Must Soon Decide*. Urbana, Illinois: University of Illinois Press, 1961. 100 pp.

HOOK, SIDNEY. *Political Power and Personal Freedom*. New York: Criterion Books, Inc., 1959.

MACHLUP, FRITZ. *The Production and Distribution of Knowledge in the United States*. Princeton, New Jersey: Princeton University Press, 1962. 416 pp.

MILLETT, JOHN D., and HUTCHINS, ROBERT M. *What's A College For?* Washington, D. C.: Public Affairs Press, 1961. 47 pp.

NEWMAN, JOHN HENRY CARDINAL. *The Idea of a University*. London and New York: Longmans, Green & Co., 1888. Pp. 177-178.

SANFORD, NEVITT. *The American College*. New York: John Wiley & Sons, Inc., 1962.

WHITEHEAD, ALFRED NORTH. *The Aims of Education*. New York: The New American Library of World Literature Inc., 1958. 166 pp.

Chapter

Precedents for Separation of
Support and Control
of Higher Education

Higher education in most of the countries of the world is highly centralized. For example, San Marcos University in Lima, Peru, founded in 1551, has never been able to free itself from political influence even though the government support has been meager. When San Marcos celebrated its IV Centenario, a national senator was rector of the University. Its faculty was made up of business and professional people who worked for $25 per month. Not more than 5 per cent of the faculty served full time, and the administration was so inadequate that students were demanding membership on the University Council. In 1958, that membership was secured.

Chulalongkorn University in Bangkok, as late as 1956, had as its rector the deputy prime minister of Thailand. Its faculty was subjected to the same system of classification and pay scales as applied to the civil service personnel in the government, the latter positions, as in Latin America, being almost synonymous with charity.

In a study of German universities in 1962, Paul Davis found that professors enjoyed the highest possible status and freedom, even though most of their support came from the government. Indeed, the center of power in German universities is in the faculties. Davis has stated:[1]

From the beginning, universities in Germany occupied a unique position in the culture. The association of scholars and students enjoyed privileges and immunities from the Church and the State. It

[1]Paul Davis, "National Goals and Higher Education in West Germany and West Berlin," (Unpublished Doctor's thesis, School of Education, Indiana University, Bloomington, 1962), pp. 131-132.

323

was regarded as an international endeavor. Members of the institutions came from countries throughout Europe. . . .

Throughout the nineteenth century, the university in Germany provided the impetus for political and social action. . . .

Davis concluded that higher education in Germany was related to the national goal to guarantee civil freedom to the individual; the independence of the professor was the personification of this goal:

> The fountainhead of internal control [of each university of Germany] was the Senate, composed of all full professors and associate professors of the university. . . . The Senate performed the legislative, executive, and judicial functions of governance. [It also elected the rector.][2]

Similar research in France by Fred Bentley in 1962 revealed the high degree of autonomy enjoyed by French universities. Even though France has been regarded as having a highly centralized ministerial system of education, the universities enjoy a large measure of autonomy.

Bentley states that:[3]

> French higher education was conceived as a function of the State. Napoleon III thought that higher education could be dangerous unless it was a function of the State. Following that concept, he created the Imperial University in 1808 which molded the structure of higher education into a national pattern. Every faculty of the universities had exactly the same administrative structure, received almost total financial subsidy from the State, and operated on a standardized curriculum. This system existed and operated with few modifications in 1962.
>
> . . . In 1962 France was undergoing a period of transition within three broad divisions of its active population: agriculture, commerce, and industry. The universities and their related institutes found it their responsibility either to train the needed personnel in already existing curriculums or to expand the scope of their studies to meet this need. . . .
>
> Academic freedom had been protected even though the system of higher education was centralized. Prior to 1808, higher education in France had been subject to the throes of the controlling power whether it was the Church, monarchy, or municipality. In 1962 French higher education operated on the concept that it was necessary for the teaching personnel to have a status independent of the political powers which could impeach its liberty and freedom and, thus, the pursuit of knowledge. While the Minister of National Edu-

---

[2]*Ibid.*, p. 135.

[3]Freddie B. Bentley, "An Analysis of French Higher Education," (Unpublished Doctor's thesis, School of Education, Indiana University, Bloomington, 1962), pp. 186-188.

cation apparently had the final authority in all national educational matters, law and tradition had bound the Minister to accept and follow the recommendations of the Superior Council of National Education in national educational matters, such as recruitment of professors and curriculum formation and reform.

The State could control the direction of French higher education by controlling the financial allocations to the different faculties. However, the State could not control the manner in which the dean of the faculty proposed to disburse the budget after the allocation had been made.

Australia and New Zealand have ministries of education, but their universities and education in general are controlled locally. The same may be said for universities generally in Canada and in Great Britain. This chapter is concerned with consideration of reasons for the success of the system of central support and decentralized control in Great Britain.

University Grants System in Great Britain

In 1919, the British government initiated a unique plan for the support of the universities. That year marked the beginning of the University Grants Committee, which is a dependency of the British Treasury. U.G.C. is composed of sixteen members plus a full-time chairman, except when academic salaries are being considered; two additional laymen are then added to the Committee making a total of nineteen members. The chairman is the only member who works full time. Members of U.G.C. and the executive secretary are appointed by the Chancellor of the Exchequer with the approval of the Prime Minister. The executive secretary is a member of the civil service staff, a career government worker, but he is not an educator. In some respects his being a layman has added to his effectiveness in representing the universities before the government.

The paid staff of U.G.C. is small—a chairman, the executive secretary, an assistant secretary, and necessary clerical assistants. In 1961-62, the total secretariat included only forty people, and the budget for the London headquarters of this important staff came to only $168,000 per year. There seems to be a high premium in keeping the London staff as small as possible rather than making it as large as funds will allow.

U.G.C. has no official connection with the Ministry of Education, although a representative of the Ministry of Education attends all meetings of the Committee in order to provide desirable and necessary laison with the Ministry of Education. Technical colleges, teachers colleges, and other non-degree granting institutions present their budgetary requests to the Ministry of Education. These institutions enrolled approximately 150,000 students in 1961-62.

British citizens, students, and officials of non-degree-granting colleges are demanding greater status for these colleges. They may become degree-granting institutions as the demand for increased opportunities for higher education increases. There is some sentiment in favor of placing all colleges and universities under the Ministry of Education. Other leaders favor the creation of a separate Ministry for Higher Education.

The members of the U.G.C., other than the chairman and the executive secretary, are honorary workers. They are appointed by the Chancellor of the Exchequer for five-year terms and come from academic staffs of universities, from the professions and industry, or are directors of local education units. The object in making the selection is to have all important branches of knowledge and of British society represented. In 1962, the members were from the following positions: two local school administrators, four college administrators, seven professors, and six business and industrial leaders. Vice-Chancellors of the universities are not appointed to the Committee. They appear before the Committee to consider national policy for higher education.

Grants are made to the universities (twenty-three universities and two university colleges in 1961-62) on a quinquennial basis. The grant made to each university takes the form of a block grant to be used at the discretion of the university over the entire range of its activities. Since the second World War, there have been earmarked grants for medicine, dentistry, agriculture, veterinary sciences, and social studies; Oriental, African, and Slavonic studies; and science and technology. It is generally anticipated that earmarked grants, initiated by the government or by the universities, will shortly become a part of block grants on a recurring quinquennial basis.

The frame of reference of U.G.C. as announced by the Chancellor of the Exchequer in 1946 was to assist, in consultation with universities and other bodies concerned, in the preparation and execution of such plans for the development of universities as may from time to time be required in order to insure that they are fully adequate to national needs. The British government regards the universities as indispensable to the cultural, economic, and political life of the nation. This

policy demands coordinated planning, involving universities, government, and national needs unknown in British universities of the past.

Sir Cecil Syres, Executive Secretary to U.G.C., has stated the policy
clearly, noting that the government called upon the universities to meet
certain manpower requirements in science and technology, and that the
government provided the necessary financial resources for achieving
the objective. Responses of the universities to requests, adequately supported by the government, have been satisfactory in every way. The
cooperation has been unique.

Methods of Operation. U.G.C. has the policy of visiting each university beginning about the middle of the quinquennium. The objective is to have at least one-half of the committee visit each university.
It took 108 days to carry out this task in preparation for the 1962-67
quinquennial budget. These visits provide members with first-hand
information on which they can determine fiscal policy.

By the end of the fourth year of each quinquennium, all requests,
with supporting tables, statistics, and relevant data, are submitted to
U.G.C. by the various universities. These requests include new programs as well as recurring operations. Vice-Chancellors appear before
the committee to explain and justify their requests.

Requests are studied, evaluated, and consolidated by U.G.C. and
then submitted to the Chancellor of the Exchequer. The requests take
the form of a total grant for the universities. Generally, in March preceding the end of the quinquennium, which is July 31, the government
announces the grants for the five-year period beginning the first of
August. Announcement of the grants for the five-year period, 1962-67,
was made in March, 1962. Following this announcement, U.G.C. has
the responsibility of making an equitable distribution of the total funds
among the institutions involved.

The University Grants Committee serves in an intermediary position between the national government and the universities. The universities have no direct contact with the Treasury and are spared the
undesirable task of competing with one another and with other agencies
of government in a political arena.

Within the limitations imposed by the amount of grant to a university, there is internal freedom for the faculty and administration
to proceed with their own plans for the next quinquennium. The exception to this would be in the case of funds earmarked by the Treasury
or by the universities in their original requests; e.g., if a university

requests funds for a specific new function and receives the funds, it would be obligated to carry out that responsibility. Since the end of the second World War, there have been earmarked grants especially in sciences, technology, agriculture, and Oriental studies.

Following the completion of the quinquennial grants, the Secretariat is free to devote its time to various problems confronting higher education. For example, during the quinquennium ending July 31, 1962, U.G.C., in cooperation with the Vice-Chancellors, sponsored studies that eventuated in a recommendation to the government that six new universities be established during the next quinquennium. This reflects an intelligent response to the demand for expansion of higher education.

When U.G.C. was established in 1919, the budget for higher education was only a fraction of what it has been in recent years. As late as 1939, the year the second great war started, funds granted to the universities amounted to only $5,300,000 or 2,250,000 pounds. By 1961-62, grants amounted to $210,000,000 or 75,000,000 pounds, and provided about 70 per cent of the operating budgets and 95 per cent of the building programs of British universities. The enormous increase during the 1939-62 period was considerably out of proportion to the increase in student population, which grew from 50,000 in 1938-39 to approximately 111,000 in 1961-62. In twenty-two years, the enrollment increased by approximately 122 per cent, but the contribution of the British government increased by 3,862 per cent.

The total budget for higher education is not impressive compared with the cost of higher education in the United States, but the support of existing universities on the basis of cost per student for a university education does compare favorably with costs in the United States. For example, the United States and Great Britain spend less than 1 per cent and approximately .5 per cent respectively of their gross national products on higher education. In 1958-59, the percentage of United States students, eighteen to twenty-four years of age, in college was five times as high as in Great Britain.[4] On this basis, our percentage of GNP for higher education should have been 2.5 to compare favorably with Great Britain.

Great Britain has managed to keep the ratio of students to faculty in the universities at approximately 7 to 1. This compares favorably with the most adequately-supported universities in the United States, where the average is approximately 12 to 1.

---

[4]Selma J. Mushkin, *Economics of Higher Education* Department of Health, Education, and Welfare. (Washington, D. C.: Government Printing Office, 1962), p. 329.

Beginning in the fall of 1962, every university student in Great Britain received government support for his education. Even the son of a wealthy family received 50 pounds, after which the "means test" was applied. Capable students from very poor families received complete support for their university education. Britain has rejected the idea of loans instead of grants for needy students. One cannot help admiring this inclination to pay for higher education out of current income instead of passing the burden on to another generation, with interest and administrative costs added.

The purpose of this particular research involved attempting to find out why the British system has succeeded; e.g., how have officials in government and in education been able to keep the universities free as government support increased? There is no inclination here to defend the limitation which the British have placed upon opportunity for higher education. That is another matter, and one on which the British public is likely to demand dynamic changes very soon.

Rationale for the Success of the University Grants System

Officials in the British government, in the Ministry of Education, and in the universities have provided insight into the formal procedures by which U.G.C. operates and the reasons for the success which the scheme has enjoyed since it was first established. There seemed to be agreement among the various segments of the society concerning the desirability of supporting the universities from the British Treasury without interfering with their initiative to run their own affairs. Several specific characteristics of the British government, the universities, and the British people in general have contributed significantly to the success of the University Grants System.

The People Know One Another. Traditions within the government and within the universities have tended to work to the advantage of the University Grants System. Moreover, the fact that appointments to the Committee are made for a five-year term and that a majority of the members of the Committee come from the colleges and universities, has contributed to the development of a situation which operates as though it were a small village. Many of the leaders in government and in the universities were friends as undergraduate students. Although various members of the Grants Committee are known to their peers among university professors and administrators, there is no evidence that any member of the Committee uses his position to represent in a partisan way his own university. Each member represents all universities, as every member of a governing or coordinating body should.

Individuals within government, education, the Ministry of Education, and leaders in British society not only know one another but also share a common interest in maintaining their universities at a high standard. University and government officials have learned to trust one another. People in local governments trust the national government, and vice versa. People in the Ministry of Education speak highly of the members of the University Grants Committee and of the leaders in the universities. Officials of the universities and in the University Grants Committee have confidence in one another and in the government. There is no evidence of a sharp cleavage between local and national governments. Officials in the universities, in the Grants Committee, and in the Ministry regard their positions as a great public trust, designed to preserve freedom in the universities and to keep them cushioned against political influence.

The National Government Enjoys Prestige. It has never occurred to any Englishman that local government could be better than national government. Why should it be? Any student of public administration knows that no one level of government (local, state, or national) has a monopoly on virtue in any nation. This being the case, it has not occurred to university officials or to leaders in British society generally that universities are threatened by drawing most of their financial support from the British Treasury instead of from local units of government. National control could become more of an issue as the Treasury grants for higher education increase, but up to now, the universities have enjoyed maximum autonomy. This great precedent, the British government supporting enterprises that it does not control, is a mark of mature government concerned with preserving freedom. The source of support is not the issue. It is whether or not political leaders can resist the temptation to control everything that they support, albeit with the people's own money.

The Civil Service System. The tradition of the British in permitting employees to advance in terms of competencies and personal growth, rather than in terms of the size of bureaucracy which is developed and supervised, has set a precedent for the University Grants Committee voluntarily to limit the control which it exercises over the universities. The executive secretary and the chairman of the University Grants Committee regard themselves and their organization as an important service agency for the universities in securing government support, by representing the universities to the government, by serving as catalyst to bring about greater interaction between the universities and British society, and by serving as a buffer between the support and control of British universities.

The size of the Secretariat and the size of the budget for the University Grants Committee are clearly indicative of the absence of bureaucratic tendencies on the part of this organization. Indeed, one of the principal criticisms of those who would seriously change the University Grants Committee is that the central office in London is inadequately staffed and that perhaps there are not enough members on the Committee to cope with the increasing size and complexity of the program of higher education. The budget for the U.G.C.'s central office in London is one-twelfth of 1 per cent of the grants secured for the universities. This percentage is probably below the cost of raising funds, either from government or from private sources, in any college or university, public or private, in the United States or in any other country.

The Depreciation of Power. One of the most unique aspects of British Government and British universities is the fact that status is not synonymous with power. The British civil servant, who is inducted into the government at an early age on the basis of his ability to do a specific task and to grow in stature as a government servant, as well as the vice-chancellor, the dean, or the professor in a university, do not gain status in terms of the number of people whom they supervise. The drive, therefore, to build up large bureaucracies and to control large groups of people as a method of gaining status, so characteristic of other governments, has not become a characteristic of British government in general, or of the universities. The professor gets his status on the basis of competence in his field of specialization. Even if he becomes Master of a house at Cambridge, or if he becomes Vice-Chancellor of the university, these positions do not carry tremendous power. It is believed that the absence of power as an index of status in government and in the universities has been a psychological factor in limiting the authority of the government over the universities. When there is no tangible reward for the possession of power, it becomes less attractive to officials in government and in education.

Government Officials and the Universities. Most of the key officials of the British government are graduates of the universities. They do not hesitate to defend the integrity and the freedom of universities to pursue their objectives without interference from government officials. The Public Accounts Committee of Parliament has demanded the right to probe more deeply into the ways in which university funds are being used, particularly as university budgets increased after the war. It is generally known that the Chancellor of the Exchequer and other prominent members of the government, in such cases, come to the rescue of the universities and assist them in maintaining more fiscal independence than any other agency of the government. This is due in large measure to the fact that key government officials have attended the universities, have great confidence in the work of the universities, and believe that the intellectual and fiscal freedom of universities is associated with the welfare of the nation.

The Treasury has resisted the demands of the Public Accounts Committee for greater responsibility and authority over university funds by insisting that the relationship between the universities and the government is a very special one. The Treasury had never examined the universities' books and did not aim at detailed control. If the Comptroller were brought in, the Treasury would, before long, be compelled to expand their intervention in university matters in a way which would certainly be prejudicial to relationships between the universities and the U.G.C.

Determination to be Free. Inasmuch as the charters of the universities were granted by the British Crown, there is a degree of independence closely akin to the constitutional status of certain state universities in the United States. Of course, the universities are subject to visitation of the Crown, who has made investigations of the ancient universities and has taken specific steps to bring them more into line with the needs of modern society.

There exists among officials in government and in the universities, as well as in British society at large, a determination to maintain the freedom and integrity of British universities. This is one of the most dynamic forces in Western civilization. Freedom to pursue the truth, to do research, and freely to exchange ideas are characteristics of British universities which have been shared generously with scholars from all over the world, including those who have come from British colonies. Participation of colonial scholars in a free university society has contributed significantly to the disintegration of the British Empire and to the establishment of the British Commonwealth of Nations. The education of nationals from British colonies has been limited to a carefully selected few, but it has been thoroughly in keeping with traditions of liberal education.

Power is with the Faculties. The faculties of the universities elect the vice-chancellor for a period of two years. The center of power in the university lies with the faculties. If the power for directing the affairs of the university is with the faculties, it cannot be located in London or with any other level of government. It is not uncommon in many situations and many countries to proclaim the academic integrity, responsibility, and freedom of faculties, and then to proceed to have curricular developments of the most grave consequences handed down from departments of the central government, or from space agencies bent upon accelerating research in a certain direction, even though the long-range objectives of the university and of the nation may be seriously impaired by such expediency. In this case, the faculties do not control the university. The faculties do not control the most important aspect of the university, namely, the academic development, when it is possible for agencies outside the university community to dictate, either through government, philanthropic, or foundation support, the academic emphasis which the university pursues.

At both Cambridge and Oxford, government-inspired departments and curricular developments have been labeled, generally as "white elephants." Two important departments in both universities have had more faculty members than students because their origin was stimulated by generous funds from the Treasury, rather than upon the basis of educational needs and plans worked out by the faculties.

Major Problems Confronting U.G.C.

Two critical problems impinge upon the total scheme of higher education and, particularly, the academic traditions of the ancient universities: (1) The government definitely favors greater emphasis upon science and technology, and (2) there is divided responsibility, at the cabinet level, for higher education. For example, as of 1961-62, there were twenty-three universities and two university colleges operating under the University Grants System. These universities enrolled approximately 110,000 students. All other post-high school educational institutions, including the institutes of science and technology and teacher training colleges, were under the Ministry of Education. These institutions enrolled approximately 150,000 students. Their budgetary requests go to the Treasury by way of the Ministry of Education which enjoys full cabinet status.

The Minister of Education presents his over-all budget for education in England, including the colleges under his direction, to the Chancellor of the Exchequer. It is possible that colleges under his jurisdiction enjoy some advantages over the universities which are under the University Grants Committee. The institutions under the Ministry of Education seem to have received more favorable consideration for the quinquennium opening August 1, 1962, than did the universities. These institutions have been more responsive to government pressure in meeting the increasing demand for specialists in science and technology. In other words, the government has found that scientific and technical colleges, which by British custom are barred from giving the Baccalaureate Degree, are more susceptible to government policy than are the universities.

The Chancellor of the Exchequer, although generally responsible for approving grants for operating budgets for the various functions under different cabinet members, becomes the representative in the cabinet for securing adequate funds for the universities. If the Chancellor of the Exchequer is inclined to hold government expenditures to the minimum, he could be the principal conservative force responsible for the fact that universities are not so adequately supported as are non-degree institutions which are under the Ministry of Education.

This poses the principal dilemma in which the government as well as the universities now find themselves. There is an overwhelming determination on the part of university and government officials to maintain the ancient prerogatives of academic freedom and independence of the universities. On the other hand, there is definitely a compelling desire on the part of the government for accelerated training of personnel in science and technology. The quickest, if not the best, method for achieving the desired result is to support institutions that are, in the words of President Stoke, of Queens College, "an instrument of national policy."[5] This means giving more generous support to the technical and scientific institutions under the Ministry of Education.

Many people in Great Britain believe that the only way that universities can meet the increasing pressure for greater enrollments and new buildings, and at the same time maintain most of their time-honored freedoms, is either to bring the University Grants Committee up to date by increasing the number of its full-time workers and making it more representative of all the universities or to establish a Min-

---

[5]Harold W. Stoke, "National Necessity and Educational Policy," *Current Issues in Higher Education,* National Education Association, (1959), pp. 12-17.

istry for Higher Education. The latter scheme is the one followed in Moscow and undoubtedly will be challenged by many friends of the universities.

The report of the Robbins Committee, which is making an over-all study of British Higher Education, to be completed by 1963, is very likely to attempt to solve the dilemma and, at the same time, to preserve the autonomy of British universities.

Viewpoints of Organized Groups

Several organized groups in England have expressed the view that the universities should be placed under the Ministry of Education. This position has been advocated by the Trade Union Congress, which forms the base of support for the Labor Party. The London County Council, the Association of Municipal Corporations, the County Councils Association, the National Union of Students, and the Church of England have advocated coordination of all institutions of higher learning, either under a Board or Council for Higher Education or under the Ministry of Education.

The Conservative and Unionist Teachers Association (representative of the Conservative Party) believes that the present system has worked extremely well as far as universities are concerned and that it should not be altered in any way.

The Committee of Vice-Chancellors and Principals believes that any change in the structure and function of the Committee (U.G.C.) would be greatly deplored in university circles, though it is realized that, with more and larger universities and with the pattern of a new relationship with other bodies in the field of higher education emerging, some change in organization might be necessary.

The Association of University Teachers (corresponding to the AAUP) has suggested that the Committee (U.G.C.) be reinforced by adding several full-time members with special responsibilities; that U.G.C. be retained and strengthened; that there be a greater degree of coordination of various forms of higher education; but that such coordination should stop short of State control and direction.

Important political and education groups indicate that there is a need to revise any scheme as the size of the higher education enterprise increases. Failure to respond to increasing demands for education beyond high school and leading to a college degree, could result in loss of university freedom, a freedom which has been cherished by all groups.

Summary

Most Americans who have studied the University Grants System have concluded that, while it has been a successful scheme for supporting higher education in Great Britain, it would not work in America. There has been a tendency on the part of some Americans in higher education (as was the case with one of Lawrence College's professors who always concluded that anything that worked east of the Alleghenies would not work in the Middle West) to conclude that the fact that the system has worked so well in England is proof positive that it would not work in America. These conclusions are not without foundation, but the reasons for dismissing the scheme as impossible in America are generally without foundation. The difficulties in transplanting or in adapting this unique idea to higher education in America may be insurmountable.

One of the principal reasons that any centralized scheme for the support of higher education would meet with great difficulty, even if the political and academic climates were favorable to its success, is the sheer size of the United States in general, and of higher education in particular. One of the serious problems confronting the University Grants Committee in recent years has been the difficulty of having the various members visit the universities for the extended time necessary for intelligent appraisal of university budgetary requests. It is probably unreasonable to expect members of the committee to give up the necessary time for such visits without pay.

The reasons that have made the scheme work in Great Britain may not be valid in America. Everywhere that we went in Great Britain, whether to visit with officials in the Government or in the universities, or with members of the University Grants Committee, we received the same rationale for the success of the University Grants System. It seemed that there was actually a party line to which all individuals had subscribed. The rationale given, time after time, was that somehow officials in the government, in the universities, and on the University Grants Committee had learned to trust one another. Informal working relationships, without government manuals and written regulations or laws, have been established. These relationships were frequently referred to as being a part of the British tradition of building its constitution and many of its most important laws on unwritten customs. Custom is of the essence in this situation, and one of the great customs of Britain is to keep its universities free from politics and bureaucracies of government.

On this point Jacques Barzun has observed:[6]

> England is a business civilization, the first industrial power and once the world's greatest banker; yet despite its diminished financial strength its subsidy of learning is through a council of professionals not responsible to bureaucrats. . . . All students deemed of superior ability are put through the university at government expense. Scholarships are an honor and a full release from irrelevant drudgery.

In reality, the University Grants Committee and the Treasury have treated the problem of higher education as if England were as large as the United States. They have assumed that twenty-five universities cannot and should not be controlled from London; that support and control are not necessarily functions of the same public authority; that freedom and integrity in the universities must be protected against political whim; and that the ends of liberal education must not be distorted by permitting means to control the ends.

Questions for Discussion

1. How have the universities of Great Britain, France, and Germany avoided centralized governmental control of academic affairs?
2. In what ways have ministries of education been either a strength or a hindrance to the development of excellence in higher education?
3. Do most underdeveloped countries have centralized or decentralized systems of education? How is the system related to economic and social development?
4. How has the University Grants System of Great Britain avoided centralized control of higher education?
5. Is the principle of local institutional control over higher education stronger in the United States or in certain other countries?
6. Should the size of the United States be a reason for or against institutional freedom and integrity with respect to administering federal support for higher education?

Bibliography

ALEXANDER, W. P. *Education in England, The National System—How it Works.* London: Newnes Educational Publishing Co. Ltd., 1954. 147 pp.
ARMYTAGE, W. H. G. *Civic Universities, Aspects of a British Tradition.* London: Ernest Benn Ltd., 1955. 328 pp.

---

[6]Jacques Barzun, *The House of Intellect* (New York: Harper & Bros., 1959), p. 202.

BERDAHL, ROBERT O. *British Universities and the State.* Berkeley: University of California Press, 1959. 229 pp.

British Council. *Higher Education in the United Kingdom.* London: Longmans Green & Co., 1960. 221 pp.

Committee of Vice-Chancellors and Principals of the Universities of the United Kingdom. *Memorandum of Evidence to the Committee on Higher Education,* pamphlet. London: The Committee, 1961. 11 pp.

Communist Party. *The Development of Higher Education in Britain, Memorandum to the Committee on Higher Education,* pamphlet. London: The Party, 1961. 30 pp.

DODDS, HAROLD, AND OTHERS. *Government Assistance to Universities in Great Britain.* New York: Columbia University Press, 1952. 133 pp.

DUFF, SIR JAMES. *Universities in Britain.* London: Longmans, Green & Co., 1959. 40 pp.

FABIAN SOCIETY. *The Structure of Higher Education, Memorandum to the Committee on Higher Education,* pamphlet. London: The Society, 1961. 20 pp.

FOSTER, J. F. (ed.). *Commonwealth Universities Yearbook, 1962.* London: Association of Universities of the British Commonwealth, 1962. 1668 pp.

FURNEAUX, W. D. *The Chosen Few, An Examination of Some Aspects of University Selection in Britain.* London: Oxford University Press, 1961. 245 pp.

GIBSON, RAYMOND C. *Resources and Needs for Higher Education in Iowa . . . 1960-1970,* Iowa Legislative Research Bureau, State House, Des Moines, Iowa: 1961. 68 pp.

GIBSON, RAYMOND C., KELLER, ROBERT J., and PFNISTER, ALLAN O. *Expansion and Coordination of Higher Education in Missouri.* A Summary Report to the Governor's Council on Higher Education in Missouri. Columbia, Missouri: University of Missouri Press, 1962. 24 pp.

Headmasters' Conference. *Submission to the Committee on Higher Education.* The Conference, 1961. 404 pp.

KNELLER, GEORGE F. *Higher Learning in Great Britain.* Los Angeles: University of California Press, 1955. 301 pp.

University Grants Committee. *Halls of Residence.* London: Her Majesty's Stationery Office, 1961. 54 pp.

Methods Used by Universities of Contracting and of Recording and Controlling Expenditures. London: Her Majesty's Stationery Office, 1960. 28 pp.

Returns from Universities and University Colleges in Receipt of Treasury Grant, 1959-1960. London: Her Majesty's Stationery Office, 1961. 76 pp.

University Development, 1952-1957. London: Her Majesty's Stationery Office, 1961. 92 pp.

University Development. Interim Report on the Years 1957-1961. London: Her Majesty's Stationery Office, 1962. 28 pp.

WEIDNER, EDWARD W. *The World Role of Universities.* New York: McGraw-Hill Book Co. Inc., 1962. 366 pp.

Chapter

15

A Scheme for the Support
of Higher Education

Analysis of Competing Schemes

As has been pointed out in the previous chapter, the British Treasury grants nearly $2,000 annually toward the support of each student enrolled in British universities. In addition to these grants made to the universities, every student receives financial support from the Government. The governmental agency administering the total university grants requires a budget of only one-twelfth of 1 per cent of the total grant.

The normal overhead for raising private college funds in the United States is 15 per cent, and the overhead on education funds coming from the United States government is even higher.

If the annual cost of operating higher education in the United States reaches $10 billion by 1970, a 15 per cent overhead for bureaucratic expenses, probably a conservative figure if present trends continue, would total $1.5 billion. If this overhead could be used for direct operating costs by avoiding the governmental and private overhead costs, it would be sufficient to operate 100 private colleges enrolling 1,000 students each, at a cost of $1,500 per student. This is the challenge for leaders in higher education. It is a challenge that demands consideration in the development of any scheme for integrated support of higher education.

Separation of church and state is a convenient issue for playing upon the superstitions and ignorance of unsuspecting citizens who

339

otherwise would be willing to use public funds to support private colleges. Political duplicity masquerades under first one virtue and then another. In one part of the country, the virtue may be a combination of the poll tax, segregation of the races, and separation of church and state. If political duplicity and ignorance could be abolished for just one generation, the social, economic, and educational problems would be greatly alleviated.

Higher education of infinite variety is at stake, because the possibility of governmental direction and control is a reality in many of the greatest universities that receive major parts of their budgets from the federal government to support only those programs specified by the government.

Another value in our culture that is threatened is the principle of equality of educational opportunity. The accident of geographical location of a student or his economic position should not determine the availability of higher education. Those who believe that tuition should be raised to pay the total cost of higher education are recommending that higher education be selective in terms of an economic criterion; but America is safe from their error as long as the reasoned judgment of enlightened citizens is free to present the democratic alternative.

There is another element that would place a yoke of indebtedness around the neck of every college graduate; this would reduce the whole liberal education idea to stark vocationalism. We shall be unworthy of our heritage if we ever deny the capable student the right to a liberal education for its own sake. Lending money to young college students, particularly to women, as the sole means of keeping them in college would be placing the dollar sign on the last vestige of our cultural heritage.

Another plan for the support of higher education is that of continuing to send presidents and development officers forth with their begging bowls to persuade corporations and individuals to make voluntary contributions in sufficient amounts to pay the difference between tuition and actual costs. This system is doomed to failure also, because the individual of means and the corporation are free to give or not to give, and they are free to give to a select group of institutions and to ignore the others.

The support of higher education should not depend upon the generosity or whims of individuals. It should be compulsory and should bear upon each citizen according to his ability to pay. Moreover, it is imperative that the total cost come out of current national income. It should not be postponed to become a burden to later generations. It is good business for bonding companies and banks to lend money for the construction of buildings and for the payment of the cost of a college education, but this is a poor investment for the American people whose collective economic contribution is sufficient to pay the costs of education out of current income.

Consequences of Existing Federal Support for Higher Education

In a study by the Brookings Institution involving thirty-six universities and colleges, it was found that "one-half of the members of the liberal arts departments at twenty-four universities had submitted an application to a federal agency for a research grant or contract."[1] Many faculty members have submitted several project proposals to different agencies in the government. There is a critical shortage of qualified faculty members in areas on which federal grants are available. Should scarce academic personnel in disciplines critical to the nation's security spend a large proportion of their time securing and administering federal funds to support their valuable research?

Another limitation imposed by the federal government is illustrated by the student loan program of the National Defense Education Act because of the disclaimer affidavit in Title X, Sec. (f) which provides:

> No part of any funds appropriated or otherwise made available for expenditure under authority of this Act shall be used to make payments or loans to any individual unless such individual . . . has executed and filed with the Commissioner an affidavit that he does not believe in, and is not a member of and does not support any organization that believes in or teaches, the overthrow of the United States Government by force or violence or by any illegal or unconstitutional methods. . . .[2]

There have been many cases since the end of the second World War when the criterion of what constituted an organization interested in the overthrow of the United States government by force was left to the judgment or caprice of the Attorney General. This has resulted in such high-handed action as the recall of an innocent school teacher from the Point IV program in Latin America because of her membership in a local book club that she joined in order to secure a discount on purchases.

[1]Harold Orlans, *The Effects of Federal Programs on Higher Education; A Study of 36 Universities and Colleges* (Washington, D. C.: The Brookings Institution, 1962), p. 189.

[2]*Ibid.*, p. 285.

In another case, a responsible superintendent of schools was blocked from employment in the Foreign Operations Administration because a local banker objected to his progressive school consolidation program and was able to make a distorted picture stick with a not-so-insightful F.B.I. investigator. Under post-war hysteria, the traditional principle of being innocent until proven guilty gave way to the opposite principle of being guilty until proved innocent.

The government contract that encompasses a major block of the academic curricula in science and technology, in many instances, requires government scrutiny of admission policies and academic appointments. This leads to nationalism as the mark of a university, but universality was a more acceptable criterion, even among the earliest universities in Europe.

Present trends of government support for specialized functions in the universities will gradually reduce the freedom of both institutions and individuals associated with them. The scheme proposed in this chapter adheres to institutional freedom and integrity and suggests national support designed to preserve freedom rather than the present system which gnaws away the universality of higher learning.

A Few Hard Facts. There is an organizational and administrative vacuum in the support of higher education in the United States that borders on anarchy. It could become the graveyard of the American idea of infinite variety in advanced learning. There has been no clear vision or plan as to how to support higher education without compromising its integrity with respect both to content and to control.

The scheme presented here is predicated upon a few basic facts and principles:

1. It is important to preserve the private as well as the public sector of higher education.

2. Public support can be used to preserve or to destroy private colleges.

3. Massive federal support of private universities, particularly five or six of the best-known ones, is a fact that must be recognized. Moreover, we must realize that over 95 per cent of research grants are in the sciences and technology.

4. No clear voice speaks out for higher education in the United States. In fact, more than 100 national organizations with their hundreds of regional and state counterparts contribute more heat than light to national policy.

5. The federal government will continue to support higher education, but it must contribute part of the support for the total program rather than all of the support for parts of the program. The humanities and social sciences have been practically ignored in federal support at a time when they may be the key to survival.

6. Approximately 75 per cent of all accredited colleges and universities participate in at least one of the federal programs.

7. Every significant piece of federal legislation to support higher education, from the Land-grant Act of 1862 to the National Defense Education Act, has been a response to some catastrophe or emergency. Policy for N.D.E.A. was made in Moscow. It is high time that long-range policy for higher education be based upon a reasoned judgment instead of political considerations, national or international.

Higher education is linked with the social, economic, political, and military position of the United States as a world power. For this reason, the policy of governments at all levels has been to increase opportunities for higher education not only in proportion to an increasing population but, more significantly, in terms of increasing percentages of college-age students who pursue education beyond the high school.

The growing sophistication or tolerance among religious groups (apparently not so well known to the NEA and the 87th Congress) is certain to accelerate federal support to both public and private colleges. There is no other equitable solution to the burgeoning enrollments and rising costs.

Invoking the dichotomy between church and state is an antiquated gimmick. When religious freedom was a debatable condition in America, separation of church and state was a meaningful foundation upon which to build American society. But religious freedom is no longer debatable; it has been accepted by the leaders in every religious organization in America.

If religious freedom is a law of the land by voluntary associations and agreements, then the government of the United States, including the Supreme Court, should stop acting as if the country must be protected against religion.

Congress has been inclined to determine policy at the top and to make appropriations for higher education on the basis of that policy rather than upon the basis of intelligent consideration of needs expressed by governing boards, administrators, and faculties of the colleges and universities. This is a trend which should be reversed.

Each national crisis in higher education is approached without any long-range plan. The vacuum created by the lack of policy is an invitation for some national authority to solve the problem because of the availability of unlimited federal funds. Educational objectives, policy, programs, curricula, research activities, and determination of financial needs can and should originate with faculties, administrators, and governing boards when they are alert to the place of higher education in a dynamic society. Financing should be by state and national governments because this is the most equitable solution. The principle of local autonomy in the determination of educational policy has been well-established in America. We still entrust the determination of the most important policies affecting elementary and secondary schools to 37,000 local school boards, their administrators, and teachers.

The scheme that is now being followed is that of drawing most great professors and students in the sciences and technology to a few higher education combines which have become wards of the federal government. The principal role of these great centers of learning has been to set the tone for all higher education. They have been the private universities, made secure in their freedom by the respected Dartmouth College case. But what the Jeffersonian Republicans could not absorb through legislation or through the courts is rapidly capitulating to the power of the United States Treasury, and the whole scheme of political duplicity is clothed in the euphonious and distorted belief that the universities must remain free.

Princeton University gets about half of its annual budget from the federal government because Princeton does what the federal government prescribes. But Cambridge and Oxford get 75 per cent of their budgets from the British Treasury and do what their faculties and administrators believe they should do.

 It is not the purpose here to challenge the inevitability of earmarked federal grants to purchase the research deemed indispensable to the nation's defense. It is patently evident that these grants have been made without any differentiation between public and private universities. The concern here is for adequate support of a balanced program in higher education designed to improve our academic posture in the humanities and social sciences as well as in the biological and physical sciences and in the professional schools so necessary to the future of our society in education, medicine, and other social services. On the basis of recent, as well as historical, developments in the relationship of the federal government to higher education, there have emerged certain trends which must be reversed if private and public colleges and universities are to remain open and free.

The nature of education in a democratic society precludes the dictation of curricula and programs from the federal government. The absence of a nationwide plan of support emanating from the leaders in higher education is certain to result in increasing federal control of the colleges and universities of America. This will come about in consequence of the fact that the federal government must help to bear the cost of higher education; and the absence of a plan to keep control in the hands of governing boards, administrators, and faculties of the institutions could mean abdication to the federal government in this most important aspect of our national life.

A Plan for Integrated Support of Higher Education

Careful consideration of the plight of private as well as public institutions of higher learning in the United States, the increasing costs of physical plants, laboratory and library resources, administrative and academic personnel, and the rising costs to the student all mandate the reappraisal of the whole haphazard approach to the finance of higher education in the United States.

The overhead costs, administrative personnel, public relations and development offices, and other bureaucratic establishments in the colleges and universities in the United States are absolutely astounding in the proportion of the higher education budget which they consume, compared with the overhead cost of maintaining the University Grants Committee which secures 75 per cent of the budget of British universities. The overhead costs in both cases come from the gross national product.

The above conditions, together with America's desire to keep the control of education decentralized, form the backdrop and the rationale for the scheme herein proposed. Another aspect of the rationale is the fact that almost every state is concerned about the coordination of public higher education, and in some cases, of all higher education, in order to approach this increasingly complex problem with the maximum utilization of limited resources.

Scheme for Coordination. The scheme would include a Council on Higher Education in each of the fifty states. The number of members could vary from fifteen to twenty-five depending upon the size of the state, the number of educational institutions, and the total enrollment. Membership on the Council should be drawn from the academic disciplines and professions including the humanities, natural sciences, social sciences, medicine, engineering, education; and from representatives of the business, industrial, and agricultural society in which higher education operates. The academicians on the committee would be drawn from the colleges and universities of the state, representing the most distinguished professors and possibly certain deans of colleges, but excluding central administrators of the colleges and universities who would present budgetary requests to the Council.

University staff members should make up approximately 50 per cent of the membership of the Council. The reason for this is that the committee would be a coordinating agency, not a governing body. Governing boards of colleges and universities would continue their existing functions. The coordinating function requires the best judgment of professionals from the sciences, humanities, social sciences, professions, business, and industry. With the exception of a small research staff, located on the campus of one of the universities, the members should serve without pay, excepting the allowances necessary for the expense of attending meeetings.

Academic members of the Council in each state would be nominated by the college and university presidents operating as a group. Other members should be selected from among the leading citizens of the state. All appointments would be made by the governor, subject to the approval of the legislature. The governor would appoint two or three members each year, but no governor could appoint a majority of the Council during a four-year term. It would be desirable to have three members appointed every two years to serve ten-year terms.

Perhaps the division of the cost of higher education should be distributed somewhat equally among students, state governments, and the federal government. The average tuition would approach $500 annually by 1970, but the range in tuition might be from $200 to $1,000 depending on ability to pay; or this great range in ability to pay could be balanced by state scholarships on a sliding scale based upon the student's resources.

Such a distribution of the burden of higher education would mean approximately $3 billion from each level of government and $3 billion from the families whose 6,000,000 sons and daughters will be in college. It is doubtful that the tax support would be more than 1 per cent of the gross national product distributed equally between the state and federal governments.

Requests from all accredited institutions of higher learning, including community colleges, private colleges, state colleges, and universities, after careful consideration and approval by the governing board of each institution, would be submitted to this Council. The requests would indicate programs to be supported, the necessary costs, and sources of income, including tuition, fees, grants, and endowments, which would decrease the contribution from the state and federal governments. The chairman and executive secretary of the Council would be responsible for submitting a coordinated budget to the Bureau of the Budget and the legislature in each state. Certain designated presidents representing all the college presidents of the state would be called upon to appear before legislative committees in order to interpret statewide programs of higher education and to justify requests.

The portion of the total cost of higher education to be met by each state legislature would be in proportion to the gross income and college enrollment of that state compared with other states. State appropriations could be made on a biennial basis and would reflect short range needs and changes in educationai costs. Support would be provided for both public and private institutions.

The fifty executive secretaries of the Councils on Higher Education would form the National Grants Committee for Higher Education and would present a quinquennial request to the United States Bureau of the Budget to supplement institutional and state legislative funds for each state. The federal appropriation would be made on a five-year basis and would be in proportion to the college enrollment and the ability of states to pay for higher education. Federal government grants would go directly to the Council on Higher Education of each state for distribution to the institutions. Individual colleges and universities would have no direct contact with the federal government. The Grants Committee would perform the function of presenting the case for higher education to the federal government.

It would be necessary to maintain a small staff of research personnel in Washington which would serve as a secretariat for the fifty State Councils in the preparation of the quinquennial grants. The Washington staff would be a research and service agency, not a controlling or governing agency.

The Secretariat operating in each state would engage in institutional research involving costs, facilities, personnel, enrollment, program development and coordination. Each legislature should require a constant study of costs at different levels of higher education in order to approach the problem of appropriations objectively and without discrimination against any institutions.

If the United States government ever decides to establish an effective Federal Education Agency, it should perform the research function over each five-year period for the U. S .Grants Committee on Higher Education. Under no circumstances should any Washington agency have administrative responsibility for the distribution and control of federal funds for higher education. Failure of such an approach is guaranteed in advance.

Conclusions

The University Grants Committee has functioned effectively in Great Britain because the program has been as decentralized in administration and control as if England were as large as the United States. The United States government, in its administration of federal funds for higher education, has followed a centralized policy as if the whole nation were as small as the state of Rhode Island.

If the principle of decentralization is valid in a nation that is smaller geographically than one of fifty American states, then only administrative and educational ineptness could ever persuade the people of the United States to adopt any policy for higher education based upon centralization of control in Washington.

Under present conditions, we have nearly 2,000 institutions at the state level that deal directly with the federal government on research grants, loans, scholarships, and building programs. The number of separate applications would be greatly in excess of the number of institutions involved because schools, colleges, departments, and even individuals within an institution apply directly to various federal agencies for grants and research funds.

At the Washington level, the situation is equally confused because at least fifty major federal agencies, without any coordination, are involved as sources of funds available to colleges and universities. The expense, inefficiency, and waste of governmental and educational talent, operating through more than 2,000 project trails leading to Washington and more than fifty leading from Washington to the colleges, illustrate the ultimate in planned chaos.

This scheme proposed for the United States would change the 2,000 project trails leading to Washington to a maximum of fifty carefully marked channels, and these would narrow to one broad avenue to federal funds, the Bureau of the Budget. Moreover, there would be only one agency through which government funds would be distributed to higher education—the U. S. Grants Committee for Higher Education—which would coordinate requests from the fifty states and distribute grants to the fifty state councils on higher education.

Most Americans who have observed the University Grants system in Great Britain conclude that it would not work in the United States. Reasons stated are generally related to differences in the two countries on the basis of physical size, college enrollments, costs of higher education, and America's infinite variety in systems of education. In general, the arguments are no more convincing than if they were to state that representative government will not work in America because it works in England.

The typical British civil servant, such as the one who serves as executive secretary of the University Grants Committee, gets his status on the basis of years of service and level of competency rather than on the basis of the number of people whom he supervises.

The characteristics of British educators and government leaders as enumerated in Chapter 14 are the result of a greater maturity in the processes of democracy than we in the United States possess. The question as to whether or not a University Grants Committee could function in the United States hinges upon whether or not administrators, faculties, boards of control, and officials in state and national governments have, or can develop, the necessary intellectual and administrative sophistication to work together without power consciousness; can accept the theory that the survival of democratic processes hinges upon keeping the control of research, teaching, and learning within our universities even though support may come from the national government; and can accept the corollary principle that the development of an educational bureaucracy in Washington, to administer even 75 per cent of the budget for all higher education in America, because of the sheer magnitude of the problem, would be doomed to inevitable breakdown and failure to say nothing of the irreparable consequences of such a bureaucracy upon the fundamental programs of teaching, research, and learning.

Although the universities under the University Grants System enroll fewer students than do the colleges and universities in the State of Indiana, the British Government believes that it would be impossible from the standpoints of both efficiency and economy in administration and that it would be disastrous from the standpoint of integrity in research, teaching, and learning in the universities to attempt centralization of control in London.

If no such system, appropriately modified, will work in the United States, there are causes more basic than the differences in the size of the two countries, the differences in the number and size of the universities, the differences in the availability of higher education, and the differences in the size of the budgets for higher education.

In attempting to decide whether or not such a scheme could be applied to the United States, it is necessary that we examine ourselves on the fundamental reasons for the success of the University Grants System in Great Britain. The questions which follow imply decisions which must be made before it will be possible for the United States to have any coordination at the state and national levels in the support of higher education.

Questions for Discussion

1. Are we determined to keep our universities free?
2. Are we willing to give them status (albeit not Royal Charters) that will cushion them against politics and temporary emergencies?
3. Is it possible to upgrade officials in the United States government to the extent that they become intelligent advocates of freedom and integrity within the universities of America?
4. Can officials in government and in higher education learn to trust one another?
5. Is it possible for us to recognize the fact that no level of government has a monopoly on virtue; that no level of government can rise above the corporate intelligence of those who put the government in power; that federal government is a government of the people in the same sense as state government; and that the only leadership for higher education is within the institutions themselves rather than in government?
6. Is it possible to develop in the United States a system of university organization, administration, and control which rewards individuals upon the basis of their competencies in teaching, research, public service, and leadership rather than upon the basis of the power which they yield over a certain number of individuals?
7. Is it possible to by-pass the bureaucracies of Washington, D. C., and to go directly to the Treasury with requests for grants based upon careful research, to be carried on by civil servants and edu-

cators whose status does not depend upon the control of the expenditure of such funds and of personnel operating higher education?

8. Are we willing to place the control of our universities in the hands of boards of control, administrators, and faculties rather than to have them banded about in response to every national emergency?

Index